Your Guide to Toronto Neighbourhoods

David Dunkelman

Published by Maple Tree Publishing Inc.

NICE BACKYARD.

Too bad their neighbours have as much right to it as they do.

You may not be aware of rights of way, easements and access issues before closing the purchase of a new or resale home. For complete assurance when you buy, TitlePLUS® Title Insurance recommends using a professional Real Estate Lawyer for any real estate transaction.

TitlePLUS Title Insurance and your real estate lawyer. Together we make real estate real simple.

Visit titleplus.ca or call 1-800-410-1013 for more information.

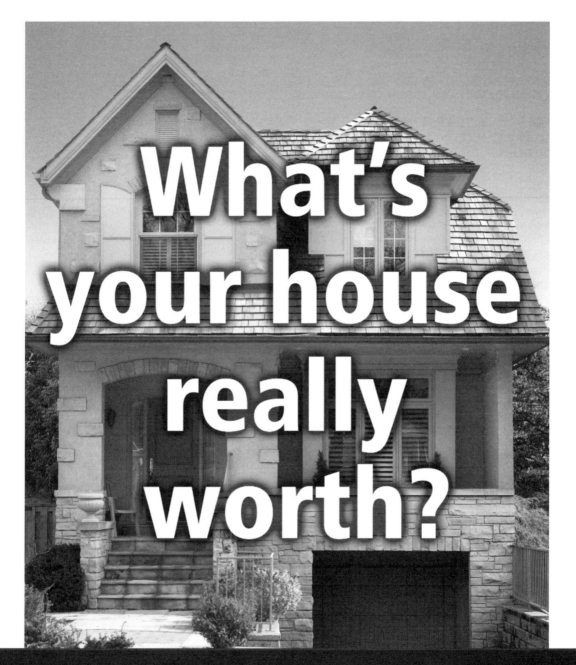

Published by Maple Tree Publishing Inc.
1370 Don Mills Road., Suite #300
Toronto, Ontario
M3B 3N7

National Library of Canada Cataloguing:

Dunkelman, David
Your Guide to Toronto Neighbourhoods

Annual.
1997-
ISSN 1484-7906
ISBN 0-9682667-1-1 (v.2)

1. Toronto (Ont)-Guidebooks. I. Title

FC3097.18.D85 1997-   917.13'541044   C98-300334-3

F1059.5.T683.D85 1997-

Printed and bound in Toronto, by Thistle Printing Limited.

Cover Design by William Atenn Chong

CONTENTS

This book is dedicated to the many hard-working individuals who give their time and expertise to neighbourhood residents' associations all across Toronto. It is these concerned citizens who help keep our neighbourhoods vibrant and strong.

ACKNOWLEDGEMENTS

I would like to thank the staff of the Archives of Ontario, the City of Toronto Archives, the City of Toronto Planning Department, the Metro Archives, the Toronto Land Registry Office, the University of Toronto Archives, the Metropolitan Toronto Reference Library (in particular their Baldwin Room), and all 95 branches of the Toronto Public Library for their help in guiding me to the research materials that contributed to the writing of *Your Guide To Toronto Neighbourhoods*.

The following individuals were particularly helpful in researching the material for this book. Thank you to Stephen Bell of the North York Archives; Madelaine Mcdowell, Chair of the Humber Heritage Committee; Barbara Myrvold of the Toronto Public Library; and Randall Reid of Montgomery Inn.

In publishing *Your Guide To Toronto Neighbourhoods* I feel fortunate to have had the privilege of working with the diverse and extraordinary talents of a number of people. First, I would like to thank Jane Davies and Stacie Scherer for overseeing the design and layout of this book. Also, I would like to thank Roark Andrade, Katherine S. Brown, Lisa Butler, Riccardo Cattapan, William Atenn Chong and Stephen Wilson, the artistic contributors who brought each neighbourhood to life with their outstanding pen and ink drawings. Thanks also to Stuart Kenn of KennKart Digital Mapping for providing the personalized maps that capture so well the geography and boundaries of each Toronto neighbourhood.

In addition, I would like to acknowledge the contributions of my editorial team. The editing of this book was expertly handled by the pens of Stacie Scherer, Sharon Loeb and Stephen Vuglac. Their talent and enthusiasm for this project was a great source of inspiration to me.

A special thank you to the sponsors of *Your Guide to Toronto Neighbourhoods* Vol. 4, including: the Toronto Real Estate Board; Jim Tourloukis, Advent Mortgages; Bussin and Bussin Barristers and Solicitors; National Home Inspection; Denise Wilson, RBC Royal Bank; Tippet-Richardson Limited; Title Plus; and Toronto Suites.

PREFACE

Toronto is a "city of neighbourhoods."

My research on Toronto neighbourhoods began with the arduous task of cross-referencing the abundant historical maps and books, geographical boundaries, political boundaries, city planning boundaries, real estate districts, business improvement areas and City of Toronto Residents and Ratepayers Association lists that I came upon.

Through this research, I discovered that Toronto has 161 distinct and identifiable residential neighbourhoods. In order to chronicle the character of each of these neighbourhoods, some of which I was learning about for the first time, it made sense to start with an examination of the history of each neighbourhood.

What I discovered is that the various neighbourhoods in Toronto have evolved in a myriad of different ways. Many began as small mill or farming hamlets, some were formed from old school or postal districts, while others began as villages or towns. Many neighbourhoods were developed as subdivisions for the upper or working classes. Some neighbourhoods were former resort towns, while others were created by city planners. One neighbourhood even originated as an artists colony.

As my research took me from the history of each neighbourhood into the present, I was able to distinguish one underlying theme. That common thread is that the residents of these neighbourhoods share a deep-rooted pride of ownership in their respective communities. It is this pride that has allowed Toronto neighbourhoods to endure the sweeping changes and growth in the overall city. Had it not been for the actions of determined residents groups some of these neighbourhoods would not be here today.

While each Toronto neighbourhood has forged its own distinct identity, collectively they have helped make Toronto one of the very best cities in the world in which to live. In a city of this size, it is nice to have so many neighbourhoods to call home.

INTRODUCTION

Welcome to Volume 4 of *Your Guide To Toronto Neighbourhoods*.

For your convenience, *Your Guide To Toronto Neighbourhoods* has been divided into six chapters that organize Toronto's neighbourhoods into the following sections: Old Toronto, East York, Etobicoke, North York, Scarborough and York. These designations represent the former boundaries of the five cities and one borough (East York) that amalgamated on January 1, 1998, to form the present-day City of Toronto.

Each of the neighbourhood write-ups include the following headings: History, Overview, Homes, Shopping, Recreation, Schools and Transportation. There is also an illustration of a typical home found in each neighbourhood and a personalized map that delineates the boundary of the neighbourhood.

If you are using this guide as a resource to buying a home please note that most of the schools listed in this guide have very definite enrolment boundaries. It is best to phone the school in which you are interested in enrolling your child to confirm that they accept children from the street you are considering buying a home on. Toronto District School Board catchment areas can be found on the website www.tdsb.on.ca.

As well, the commuting times provided for motorists in the transportation sections of this guide are approximate times only. Factors such as driving conditions and the time of day and week you are travelling will impact on your arrival times.

Finally, the price range of homes included for every neighbourhood is meant to give you a general overview of the real estate values in each neighbourhood. The price ranges of homes include houses but not condominiums, except for those neighbourhoods designated "condominium only." In most Toronto neighbourhoods where there are condominiums, the prices for condos will range from $200,000-$300,000 for a very small one-bedroom unit to $1,000,000 and more for a much larger penthouse unit. Please note: the price range of homes listed for each neighbourhood can fluctuate depending on market conditions, therefore it is wise to consult a real estate professional prior to making any home-buying decision.

Your Guide To Toronto Neighbourhoods is jam-packed with information, in an easy-to-follow format that is sure to make your travels through Toronto neighbourhoods both informative and enjoyable.

SCHOOL SYMBOLS

(P) Public School
(PH) Public High School
(C) Catholic School
(CH) Catholic High School
(PR) Private School
(PC) Private Catholic School
(PJ) Private Jewish School
(U) University

OLD TORONTO DOWNTOWN

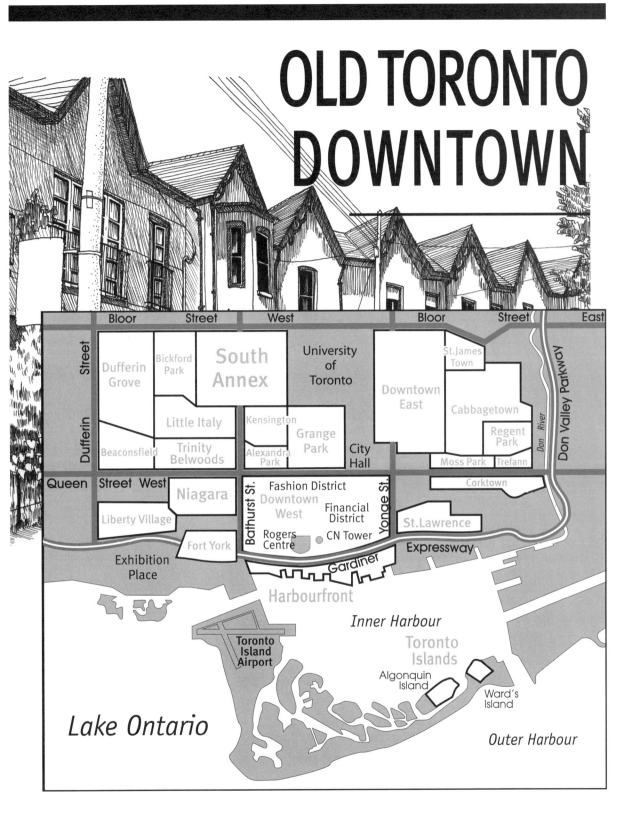

Bloor Street West | Bloor Street East

Street | Dufferin

Dufferin Grove · Bickford Park · **South Annex** · University of Toronto · Downtown East · St.James Town · Cabbagetown

Little Italy · Kensington · Grange Park · Regent Park

Beaconsfield · Trinity Belwoods · Alexandra Park · City Hall · Moss Park · Trefann

Queen Street West · Niagara · Bathurst St. · Fashion District · Downtown West · Financial District · Yonge St. · Corktown · St.Lawrence

Liberty Village · Rogers Centre · CN Tower · Expressway

Fort York · Gardiner

Exhibition Place · Harbourfront

Don River · Don Valley Parkway

Inner Harbour

Toronto Island Airport · Toronto Islands · Algonquin Island · Ward's Island

Lake Ontario · Outer Harbour

HISTORY:

Alexandra Park's history revolves around Sir Casimir Gzowski, a Polish engineer who immigrated to Toronto in 1841. Gzowski's distinguished career included the building of the Grand Trunk Railway from Toronto to Sarnia.

The Gzowski residence stood at the southeast corner of Bathurst and Dundas streets. This former Toronto landmark was known simply as "The Hall." In 1904, the City of Toronto purchased The Hall and its environs for use as a public park. This park was named Alexandra Park after Queen Alexandra.

The Alexandra Park neighbourhood has been the first home for many new Canadians. In the 1920s and 1930s large numbers of Polish and Ukrainian immigrants settled here. They were soon followed by immigrants from Germany, Italy, Greece, Portugal and Hungary.

In 1964 Toronto City council approved plans for the Alexandra Park Housing Cooperative. This led to the expropriation of 16 acres of private property and the subsequent demolition of many Alexandra Park houses. Today the Alexandra Park Housing Cooperative forms a vital part of this inner-city neighbourhood.

Map

Dundas Street West

Bathurst Street

Alexandra Park

Alexandra Park

Avenue

Spadina

Queen Street West

PRICE RANGE OF HOMES

$100,000 to $200,000	
$200,000 to $300,000	✓
$300,000 to $400,000	✓
$400,000 to $500,000	✓
$500,000 to $600,000	✓
$600,000 to $700,000	
$700,000 to $800,000	
$800,000 to $900,000	
$900,000 to $1,000,000	
$1,000,000 +	

OVERVIEW:
Alexandra Park has two distinct communities that are literally intertwined within the streets of this neighbourhood. The old section of Alexandra Park consists of privately owned residences, while the newer sections of the neighbourhood are part of the Alexandra Park Co-operative, which provides partially subsidized housing.

This mix of private and public housing in Alexandra Park seems to work, as both old and new complement each other in this small downtown Toronto neighbourhood.

HOMES:
The Victorian style homes in Alexandra Park date back to the 1880s and 1890s. There are also a few semi-detached homes and bungalows from the 1920s and 1930s.

Many townhouses in the neighbourhood were built in the 1960s, and are part of the Alexandra Park Housing Co-operative. Newer townhouses along Bathurst Street offer elegant urban residences.

SHOPPING:
Alexandra Park residents are within walking distance of Kensington Market, which is located west of Spadina Avenue and north of Dundas Street. Kensington is Toronto's largest outdoor food market. Another popular shopping destination for Alexandra Park residents is Toronto's downtown Chinatown district, centred at the intersection of Dundas Street West and Spadina Avenue. Chinatown features imported goods from the Far East, as well as fresh fruit and vegetable stands and a plethora of Chinese restaurants.

RECREATION:
Alexandra Park is the primary greenspace in this neighbourhood. It has an outdoor pool, a wading pool, an artificial ice rink and tennis courts. Next to the park is the Scadding Court Community Centre. Scadding Court's facilities include a gymnasium, an indoor pool, a weight room, and meeting rooms. Adjacent to the community centre is the Charles R. Sanderson Public Library, which offers programs for adults, children and preschoolers.

SCHOOLS:
(P) Alpha School Jr. and Sr., 20 Brant St., (416) 393-1880
(P) Ogden Jr., 33 Phoebe St., (416) 393-9110
(P) Ryerson Jr. and Sr., 96 Denison Ave., (416) 393-1340
(PH) West End Alternative, 70 D'arcy St., (416) 393-0660
(PH) Central Technical School, 725 Bathurst St., (416) 393-0060

TRANSPORTATION:
Regular streetcar service is available on all the major streets that border this neighbourhood. The streetcars link passengers to stations on Toronto's subway lines.

The Gardiner Expressway and Lake Shore Boulevard are just minutes away, providing motorists with quick access in and out of the city.

HISTORY:

Beaconsfield Village history begins with the Denison family, who were the major landholders in this district dating back to the early 1800s.

Captain John Denison was the owner of "Brookfield," built around 1815, at the northwest corner of Queen and Ossington. Henry Scadding recounts in his book *Toronto Of Old*, "Brookfield house was shaded by great willow trees and surrounded by flower gardens and lawns, no mean feat in an area of virgin forest."

The Denison heirs sold Brookfield in the 1850s. By the 1870s a network of streets had been laid out on the former Brookfield estate.

Beaconsfield Avenue became the signature street in the neighbourhood. It is named after former British Prime Minister Benjamin Disraeli, who was given the title of Lord Beaconsfield by Queen Victoria.

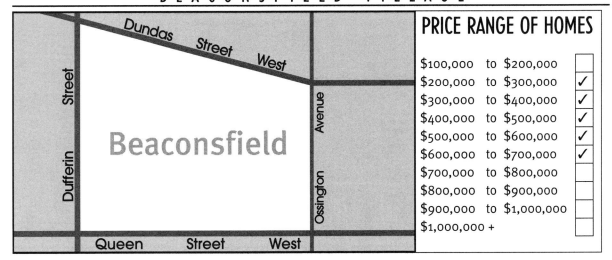

PRICE RANGE OF HOMES

$100,000 to $200,000	
$200,000 to $300,000	✓
$300,000 to $400,000	✓
$400,000 to $500,000	✓
$500,000 to $600,000	✓
$600,000 to $700,000	✓
$700,000 to $800,000	
$800,000 to $900,000	
$900,000 to $1,000,000	
$1,000,000 +	

OVERVIEW:

This downtown Toronto neighbourhood has a large Portuguese population that is centred around the Rua Acores shopping district on Dundas Street West.

Beaconsfield is popular with members of Toronto's arts community, who have gradually migrated westward along Queen Street to the affordable houses and studios found in this neighbourhood.

HOMES:

Beaconsfield Village homes were mostly built in the 1880s and 1890s. Beaconsfield Street is the signature street in the neighbourhood. This street has been designated by the Toronto Historical Board for its magnificent collection of Victorian houses.

The majority of homes in this neighbourhood are Victorian row and semi-detached houses. Many of these houses have been extensively renovated and converted into two- and three-family dwellings.

SHOPPING:

The colourful Rua Acores shopping district on Dundas Street West is brimming with Portuguese restaurants, fresh fruit and vegetable markets, mouth watering bakeries and an assortment of gift shops.

Queen Street West is an eclectic mix of small clothing boutiques and interesting one-of-a-kind arts and crafts stores mixed in with the usual convenience-type stores. Art galleries and cafés abound in this vibrant and eclectic neighbourhood.

RECREATION:

The McCormick Recreation Centre at 66 Sheridan Avenue and the Trinity Community Recreation Centre at 155 Crawford Street both have an indoor pool, a gymnasium, a weight room and a games room. McCormick also has an indoor arena that offers a variety of skating programs. The McCormick playground features a tot park and a wading pool.

Beaconsfield is only a few minutes from Toronto's Harbourfront district, which includes Ontario Place, Exhibition Place, Rogers Centre, the Harbourfront Recreation Centre and the Toronto Islands.

SCHOOLS:

(P) Alexander Muir/Gladstone Jr. & Sr., 108 Gladstone Ave., (416) 393-9140

(PH) Central Technical School, 725 Bathurst St., (416) 393-0060

(C) St. Anthony, 645 Gladstone Ave., (416) 393-5210

TRANSPORTATION:

The Dufferin and Ossington streetcars connect passengers to their respective stations on the Bloor-Danforth subway line, while the Queen and Dundas streetcars connect passengers to the Yonge-University-Spadina subway line.

Motorists can be downtown in minutes and are approximately five minutes from the Gardiner Expressway.

HISTORY: The Bickford Park neighbourhood is named after Colonel E. Oscar Bickford, a former Toronto businessman and politician.

Bickford, a wealthy landowner, owned what is now the Bickford Ravine Park. His widow Emily A. Bickford sold this property to the City of Toronto in 1908 for $44,250.

In 1913, the Elizabethan Recreation Centre was built at the north end of Bickford Park. This playground was named after the "Lizzies," a collection of local sports teams that achieved nationwide fame at all levels of amateur sport, particularly in baseball and basketball. The Centre's name was changed in 1990 to The Bob Abate Community Recreation Centre in honour of the Lizzies popular long-time coach.

Almost 90 years after its inception, the Bickford Park playground still represents a field of dreams for this quiet west-end neighbourhood.

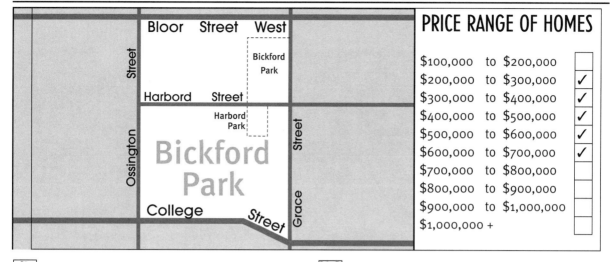

PRICE RANGE OF HOMES

$100,000	to $200,000	
$200,000	to $300,000	✓
$300,000	to $400,000	✓
$400,000	to $500,000	✓
$500,000	to $600,000	✓
$600,000	to $700,000	✓
$700,000	to $800,000	
$800,000	to $900,000	
$900,000	to $1,000,000	
$1,000,000 +		

OVERVIEW:

The Bickford Park neighbourhood revolves around the Bob Abate Centre and the Bickford Park playground. These local landmarks are the social and recreational hubs of this family-oriented community.

Originally settled by Jewish, Italian and Portuguese immigrants, Bickford Park is still home to people from a wide range of cultural backgrounds. Affordable houses, excellent shopping and convenient access to public transit are hallmarks of this neighbourhood.

HOMES:

Bickford Park's Victorian homes were built between 1880 and 1930. There is a good mix of two- and three-storey semi-detached and detached homes.

Bickford Park's streetscape features pretty front gardens and mature trees. The flow of traffic in front of the houses is light, as all the streets are one way traffic only and garages are situated off rear laneways at the back of the properties.

SHOPPING:

The Bloorcourt Village shopping district along Bloor Street has a large variety of stores and restaurants. Every June, the Village hosts festival days where strolling musicians, bands, clowns and magicians perform to the delight of shoppers.

College Street is home to the Little Italy shopping district which is famous for its Italian restaurants, cafés and pizza parlours.

Harbord Street is an intimate shopping district with a variety of specialty shops, neighbourhood restaurants and the Harbord Bakery — a Toronto landmark.

RECREATION:

The social and recreational hub of this neighbourhood is the Bob Abate Recreation Centre on Montrose Avenue. This centre has a small gymnasium, an arts and crafts room and community meeting rooms. Located next door to the Bob Abate Centre is The Bickford Centre, which has a pool and a large gymnasium.

Bickford Park playground, located just south of the community centre, has two baseball diamonds that service an active baseball program including rookie ball and T-ball leagues for boys and girls that live in the neighbourhood.

Across the street from Bickford Park is the smaller Harbord Park, which features children's playgrounds and a wading pool.

SCHOOLS:

(P)   Montrose Jr., 301 Montrose Ave, (416) 393-9770
(P)   Delta Sr., 301 Montrose Ave, (416) 393-9770
(PH) Central High School of Commerce, 570 Shaw St., (416) 393-0030
(PH) Harbord Collegiate Institute, 286 Harbord St., (416) 393-1560
(PH) St. David, 486 Shaw St., (416) 393-5238

TRANSPORTATION:

This neighbourhood has regular bus or streetcar service on Harbord Street, College Street and Ossington Avenue. Local subway stations at Ossington and at Christie Street, provide Bickford Park residents with direct access to the Bloor-Danforth subway line.

Motorists can be downtown in minutes and are approximately 15 minutes from the Gardiner Expressway and Lake Shore Boulevard.

HISTORY: Cabbagetown's history began in the 1840s when thousands
of Irish immigrants settled here after fleeing the potato famine in their
homeland. These first Cabbagetown residents were very poor. To put food
on the table they grew cabbages on their front lawns, which is how this
district came to be known as Cabbagetown.

Cabbagetown's working class community was particularly hard hit by the
Depression of the 1930s. Historian Hugh Garner, the author of *Cabbagetown*,
chronicles how the Depression turned Cabbagetown into "the worst Anglo
Saxon slum in North America." The worst slums were concentrated south of
Gerrard Street. These homes were razed in the 1950s and replaced by the
Regent Park housing development.

Cabbagetown was revitalized in the 1970s and 1980s by new home
buyers, who restored much of this neighbourhood's fine collection of
Victorian homes. Cabbagetown is now considered one of Toronto's most
gentrified neighbourhoods.

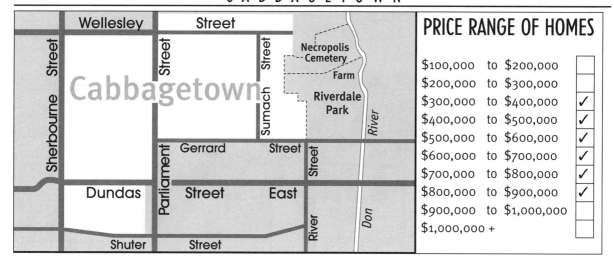

PRICE RANGE OF HOMES

$100,000	to	$200,000	
$200,000	to	$300,000	
$300,000	to	$400,000	✓
$400,000	to	$500,000	✓
$500,000	to	$600,000	✓
$600,000	to	$700,000	✓
$700,000	to	$800,000	✓
$800,000	to	$900,000	✓
$900,000	to	$1,000,000	
$1,000,000 +			

OVERVIEW:
Cabbagetown is one of Toronto's most popular neighbourhoods. Its residents come from a wide variety of backgrounds, however they all share a strong sense of community spirit and pride in their neighbourhood.

This community spirit is put on display every September during the Cabbagetown Fall Festival, which runs for an entire weekend and features a mini-marathon, historical walking tours, a parade and a community-wide yard sale.

HOMES:
The Cabbagetown neighbourhood was once described by *The New York Times* as "containing the largest collection of Victorian homes in North America."

Cabbagetown's houses were built between 1860 and 1895. Most of these houses have been lovingly restored under the watchful eye of the Cabbagetown Preservation Association. The Association, which comprises local residents, plays a vital role in ensuring that all Cabbagetown renovations and new developments are in keeping with this historical neighbourhood.

SHOPPING:
The Old Cabbagetown shopping district on Parliament Street features many one-of-a-kind shops and a vast array of restaurants. The Carlton Street shopping district is similar in tone to Parliament Street, but on a much smaller scale.

Cabbagetown also has small retail pockets on Gerrard Street, Sherbourne Street and Wellesley Avenue.

RECREATION:
Cabbagetown's recreational centre is Riverdale Park. This park is the home of Riverdale Farm. Riverdale Farm is modelled after a late 19th-century Victorian farm and includes horses, cows, pigs, sheep, goats, chickens, geese and ducks. Riverdale Farm is open seven days a week and admission is free.

Riverdale Park also contains sports fields and some of the best tobogganing hills in Toronto. The Lower Don Recreation Trail can be accessed from this park.

The Cabbagetown Community Arts Centre on Parliament Street has music, drama and dance programs for children. The Cabbagetown Youth Centre on Lancaster Avenue offers sports, as well as arts and crafts programs.

The Cabbagetown Public Library is located at the corner of Gerrard and Parliament streets.

SCHOOLS:
(P)   Lord Dufferin Jr. & Sr., 303 Berkeley Street, (416) 393-1760
(P)   Sprucecourt Jr., 70 Spruce Street., (416) 393-1552
(P)   Winchester Jr. & Sr., 15 Prospect St., (416) 393-1520
(PH)   Rosedale Heights Secondary School, 711 Bloor St.E., (416) 393-1580
(PH)   Jarvis Collegiate Institute, 495 Jarvis St., (416) 393-0140
(C)   St. Martin Annex, 55 Salisbury Ave., (416) 393-5222
(C)   Our Lady of Lourdes, 444 Sherbourne St., (416) 393-5221

TRANSPORTATION:
The Sherbourne bus and Parliament bus connect passengers to stations on the Bloor-Danforth subway line. The Wellesley and Carlton street buses connect commuters to the Yonge-University-Spadina subway line.

For motorists, the Don Valley Parkway is approximately five minutes away, and Toronto's downtown business and entertainment districts are less than 10 minutes from Cabbagetown.

HISTORY:

Corktown was originally settled by working class immigrants in the early 1800s. Many of these families came from the County of Cork in Ireland, which explains how this neighbourhood became known as Corktown.

Most Corktown residents found employment at one of the local breweries or brickyards. These families were very poor and could not afford the lofty pew rents at nearby St. James Cathedral. This led to the building of their own "Little Trinity Church" in 1843. Little Trinity Church is still standing today, at 417 King Street East.

The Trinity Schoolhouse on Trinity Street, just south of Little Trinity Church, was built in 1848. This was Toronto's first "free school." Its benefactor was Enoch Turner, a prominent Corktown brewer, and one of Toronto's great philanthropists.

A century and a half later children and adults are still being educated in the Trinity Schoolhouse, which is now run as a museum designed to replicate a mid-19th-century classroom.

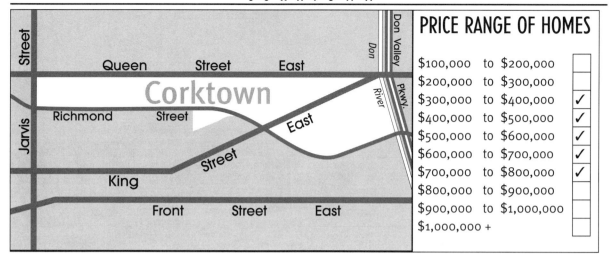

PRICE RANGE OF HOMES		
$100,000	to	$200,000	
$200,000	to	$300,000	
$300,000	to	$400,000	✓
$400,000	to	$500,000	✓
$500,000	to	$600,000	✓
$600,000	to	$700,000	✓
$700,000	to	$800,000	✓
$800,000	to	$900,000	
$900,000	to	$1,000,000	
$1,000,000 +		

OVERVIEW:
Corktown is one of Toronto's most up-and-coming neighbourhoods. It has recently become popular with young professionals, who find this location extremely convenient to Toronto's downtown business and entertainment districts.

New and more relaxed zoning bylaws in the Corktown district have resulted in the speedy conversion of many commercial buildings into live-in work studios, condominium lofts and professional offices, all of which has helped to revitalize the entire neighbourhood.

HOMES:
Corktown contains some of the oldest Victorian row-houses in Toronto. Some of these houses date back to the 1850s and 1860s. These former workers' cottages can be found on the quaint narrow laneways that are discreetly tucked away off Corktown's main streets.

Corktown has also recently experienced a number of retrofit projects on its commercial and industrial buildings, which have been revitalized by new zoning by-laws. As a result many former commercial buildings in this neighbourhood have been transformed into funky live-work lofts and studio space. New condominiums and townhouses round out the housing stock in this neighbourhood.

SHOPPING:
The intersection of Queen and Parliament streets is the hub of the Corktown neighbourhood in terms of shops and restaurants. These tend to be smaller, family-run retail stores and diners. There is still a grittiness to the area that one would expect to find in a downtown neighbourhood with working-class roots. However, this has not deterred families and professionals from enjoying this shopping district, which appears headed towards gentrification.

Corktown residents enjoy the luxury of being located within walking distance of the St. Lawrence Market — Toronto's premiere food market.

The Distillery District, east of Parliament Street on Mill Street, features numerous artists' studios, restaurants and pubs that complement the magnificent Victorian architecture that has been so well preserved and restored on this site.

RECREATION:
In the summer, the Distillery District hosts a diverse lineup of events, from music and arts festivals to a flea market, a farmers' market and a circus festival.

The John Innes Community Recreation Centre on Sherbourne Street has an indoor swimming pool, a gymnasium, a running track, a weight room, a cardio training room, a games room, a woodworking shop and a craft room. Next door to the community centre is the Moss Park indoor hockey arena.

The Sackville playground located along King Street East has a tot park, a basketball court and a wading pool. The St. Lawrence Community Centre on The Esplanade includes squash courts, a swimming pool, a gymnasium, a piano room, a weight room and a games room.

SCHOOLS:
(C)   St. Paul, 80 Sackville St., (416)393-5204
(PH) Inglebrook Alternative School, 14 Sackville St., (416) 393-0560
(PH) Jarvis Collegiate Institute., 495 Jarvis St., (416) 393-0140

TRANSPORTATION:
The Queen and King streetcars connect to stations on the Yonge-University-Spadina subway line, while the Parliament bus connects passengers to the Castle Frank station on the Bloor-Danforth subway line.

Motorists are only a few minutes from the Adelaide Street on-ramp to the Don Valley Parkway, and an equally short distance to the Gardiner Expressway and Lake Shore Boulevard.

HISTORY: The Downtown was originally settled by some of early

Toronto's most prominent families. The street names in this neighbourhood are clues to its rich history.

For instance, Jarvis Street is named after the family of William Jarvis, the former provincial secretary of Upper Canada. Homewood Avenue is named after the estate of George Allan, a former mayor of Toronto. McGill Street is named after Captain John McGill, and Sherbourne Street commemorates the ancestral home of the Ridout family who came to Canada from Sherbourne, Dorsetshire, England.

When the aforementioned families subdivided their large estates in the mid-1800s, the current neighbourhood was born. The mansions on Jarvis and Sherbourne streets set the tone for the Downtown, which, up until the early 1900s, was considered Toronto's most fashionable suburb.

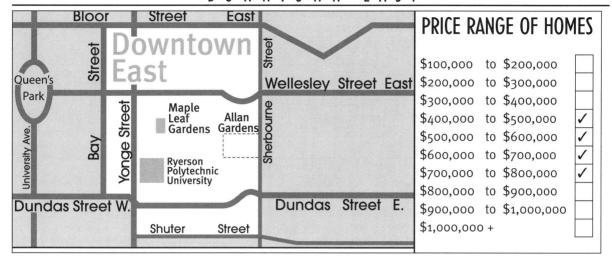

PRICE RANGE OF HOMES

$100,000	to	$200,000	
$200,000	to	$300,000	
$300,000	to	$400,000	
$400,000	to	$500,000	✓
$500,000	to	$600,000	✓
$600,000	to	$700,000	✓
$700,000	to	$800,000	✓
$800,000	to	$900,000	
$900,000	to	$1,000,000	
$1,000,000 +			

OVERVIEW:
Downtown Toronto residents come from a myriad of different backgrounds, and span the entire spectrum of the socio-economic scale.

There is a large number of rental accommodations in this neighbourhood. This reflects the mobility of the population, which comprises mostly singles and couples.

Toronto's Gay Village is centred at Church and Wellesley streets.

HOMES:
Downtown's Victorian houses were built in the mid-to late 1800s. Most of these houses have been converted to commercial uses or into multi-family homes. The Downtown East also contains a number of newer heritage-style townhouses that complement the older homes in the neighbourhood.

The Downtown is where you will find Toronto's most diverse selection of apartment buildings. There are art-deco designed, walk-up apartment buildings from the 1920s; high-rise apartment buildings from the 1950s; and newer luxury condominium apartment buildings. The Met Condominium on Carlton Street is the first Toronto condo to include a pet spa.

SHOPPING:
Downtown residents have a wide variety of shopping opportunities available to them. This mix includes high-end fashion stores on Bloor Street, trendy shops and restaurants on Church Street, and day-to-day retail shopping on Wellesley, Gerrard, Sherbourne and Charles streets.

The major shopping centre in this part of the city is the Eaton Centre, which is Toronto's largest indoor shopping mall, with over 300 stores.

RECREATION:
Allan Gardens is the largest public park in the Downtown core. This park is the home of the Allan Gardens Conservatory, a botanical garden with six greenhouses that feature unusual and exotic plants from around the world. Allan Gardens' calender of events includes spring, Easter, and fall flower shows, as well as a Victorian Christmas show.

The John Innes Community Centre located at 150 Sherbourne Street has an indoor swimming pool, a gymnasium, a running track, a weight room, a cardio training room, a games room, a woodworking shop and a craft room. Adjacent to the community centre is the Moss Park Arena which includes pleasure and power skating programs as well as hockey leagues and a summer hockey camp.

SCHOOLS:
(P) Church Street Jr., 83 Alexander St., (416) 393-1250
(P) Lord Dufferin Jr. & Sr., 303 Berkeley St., (416) 393-1760
(PH) Jarvis Collegiate Institute, 495 Jarvis St., (416) 393-0140
(C) Our Lady of Lourdes, 444 Sherbourne St., (416) 393-5221
(PR) YMCA Academy, 42 Charles St. East, 5th Floor, (416) 928-0124

TRANSPORTATION:
Bus services on Wellesley and Carlton streets connect to the Sherbourne station on the Yonge-University-Spadina subway line. The Sherbourne Street bus connects to the Sherbourne station on the Bloor-Danforth subway line. There is also an express bus that runs on Jarvis Street during rush hour only.

Motorists are approximately 10 minutes from Lake Shore Boulevard and the Gardiner Expressway.

HISTORY:

Downtown West was originally part of the vast military garrison lands that were established to protect the Town of York – the forerunner to Toronto – against attack from the United States. Following the war of 1812 peaceful relations were established with our neighbour to the south and the garrison lands were sold to the railway, which became a vital cog in the booming industry then taking place along Toronto's harbourfront.

By the 1960s much of Toronto's port-based industry had moved north of the city, thus rail service dwindled to a trickle. The railway lands — a site bound by the Rogers Centre to the east, Bathurst Street to the west, Front Street to the north, and Lakeshore Boulevard to the south — then lay dormant and derelict for over 30 years while the City of Toronto debated what to do with them. In 1998 city council finally approved the sale of the railway lands, which are currently being redeveloped into a $2 billion condominium development known as CityPlace.

Another re-birth in the Downtown West is the King/Spadina/Bathurst district, which was at the heart of Canada's garment industry until the early 1990s. Now many of these shop worn buildings are finding new life as trendy loft condominium projects and funky office space for the media services, high-tech communications and graphic industries.

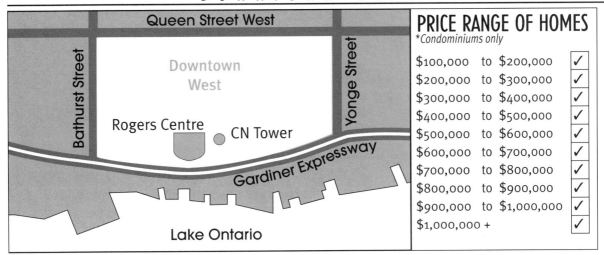

PRICE RANGE OF HOMES
*Condominiums only

$100,000	to	$200,000	✓
$200,000	to	$300,000	✓
$300,000	to	$400,000	✓
$400,000	to	$500,000	✓
$500,000	to	$600,000	✓
$600,000	to	$700,000	✓
$700,000	to	$800,000	✓
$800,000	to	$900,000	✓
$900,000	to	$1,000,000	✓
$1,000,000 +			✓

OVERVIEW:

Downtown West is Toronto's most lively neighbourhood. This neighbourhood's vitality is due to the fact that Toronto's Entertainment, Fashion, and Financial districts are all located here.

Until recently there were limited residential options in Downtown West. However, in the past few years the rezoning of King-Spadina commercial buildings into residential lofts, the downtown condominium and townhome building boom, and the massive redevelopment currently underway at the former railway lands have now made it possible for many more people to live, work and play in this urban neighbourhood.

HOMES:

New condominium projects have recently been built or are underway on Richmond, Queen and Wellington streets and in the King-Spadina area. Many of these projects are mid-rise loft-style buildings. The glitzier high-rise buildings feature sleek designs with brick, glass and metal facades. By far the largest development in the area is taking place on the former railway lands next to the Rogers Centre. This new community is called CityPlace. Over the next several years 21 condominium buildings will stand on the area bounded by Rogers Centre to the east, Bathurst Street to the west, Front Street to the north, and Lake Shore Boulevard to the south. When complete, CityPlace — a technologically advanced fibre-optic community — will consist of approximately 7,000 condominium units that will bring around 12,000 new residents to this neighbourhood.

Hertitage home fans should check out the Second Empire and Victorian-style houses on Draper Street and the Clarence Terrace townhomes on Clarence Square.

SHOPPING:

The trendy Queen West shopping district, the old world Kensington Market north of Dundas Street and west of Spadina Avenue, Chinatown right on Spadina Avenue, and the Fashion District, located between Bathurst Street and Spadina Avenue from Front Street north to Queen Street, provide a plethora of shopping opportunities for Downtown West residents.

Toronto's underground PATH walkway contains many hidden shopping treasures. The PATH can be accessed from many buildings in the Financial District, east of University Avenue including: First Canadian Place at 50 King Street West, the Toronto Dominion Centre at 55 King Street West, the Design Exchange at 234 Bay Street,

Commerce Court at 234 Bay Street, the Royal Bank Plaza at 200 Bay Street, and BCE Place at 181 Bay Street. The PATH, which winds its way underground along almost 100 buildings, is 10 kilometres long and is lined with retail shops, services and restaurants.

RECREATION:

The Entertainment District, centred along Wellington Street from Spadina Avenue east to Yonge Street, is home to the Royal Alexandra and Princess of Wales theatres. Both host world-class musicals such as the *The Lion King* and *Mama Mia*. Just to the east of these theatres is Roy Thompson Hall, home of the Toronto Symphony Orchestra. The world famous Second City comedy club is located on Blue Jays Way, across the street from Wayne Gretzky's restaurant. Festival Hall on John Street is anchored by the giant Famous Players Paramount multi-screen theatre complex which features digital sound, stadium seating and a licensed lounge.

Sports fans are within walking distance of the Air Canada Centre, home of the Toronto Maple Leafs and the Toronto Raptors, and the Rogers Centre, home to the Toronto Blue Jays and Toronto Argonaut professional sports teams. Before or after a game fans can select from a vast array of trendy bars and restaurants that proliferate throughout Downtown West.

SCHOOLS:

(P)   The Waterfront School Jr. & Sr., 635 queens Quay West, (416) 393-0684
(P)   Alpha School Jr. and Sr., 20 Brand St., (416) 393-1880
(P)   Downtown Alternative, jk-3, 20 Brant St., (416) 393-1882
(PH) Oasis Alternative School, 707 Dundas St., (416) 393-9830
(PH) Central Technical School, 725 Bathurst Street., (416) 393-0060

TRANSPORTATION:

Streetcar lines on King and Queen streets and Spadina Avenue connect to the Yonge-University-Spadina subway line. The Bathurst Street bus links up with the Bloor-Danforth subway line. Motorists are just a few minutes from Lake Shore Boulevard and the Gardiner Expressway which link up with all the major highways that service the greater Toronto area.

HISTORY: The Dufferin Grove district was first settled by the Denison family, who emigrated to Canada from England in 1792. The Denisons were active participants in Toronto's early military and political affairs. Their country villas were Toronto landmarks, with titles such as "Dover Court," "Rush Holme" and "Heydon Villa."

In 1834, with the city encroaching at their doorstep, the Denisons decided to clear the dense forest covering their property and began cultivating this land. The fertile soil in the area yielded abundant crops and brought the Denisons great wealth. However, by the 1880s, the value of the Denison estates lay in housing development, not agriculture. Thus rows of crops were gradually replaced by rows of houses and the current neighbourhood was developed.

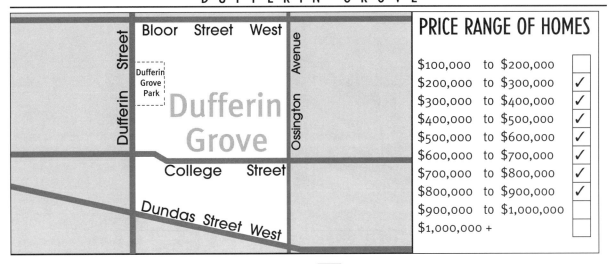

PRICE RANGE OF HOMES

$100,000	to	$200,000	
$200,000	to	$300,000	✓
$300,000	to	$400,000	✓
$400,000	to	$500,000	✓
$500,000	to	$600,000	✓
$600,000	to	$700,000	✓
$700,000	to	$800,000	✓
$800,000	to	$900,000	✓
$900,000	to	$1,000,000	
$1,000,000 +			

OVERVIEW:
The Dufferin Grove neighbourhood is home to families from many different cultural backgrounds. The whole neighbourhood has recently been revitalized by improvements to Dufferin Grove Park.

Dufferin Grove Park is truly one of the great experiments in community planning that Toronto has seen in recent times. This park is basically a community centre without any walls! It is so popular that local residents affectionately refer to it as their "Big Backyard."

HOMES:
The majority of Dufferin Grove houses were built between 1890 and 1930. Dufferin Grove's semi-detached and detached houses are larger than those found in most downtown Toronto neighbourhoods. The architectural style of the homes in Dufferin Grove range from early and late Victorian to Edwardian and English Cottage designs.

SHOPPING:
The Dufferin Mall is anchored by national department stores and includes over 100 retail outlets, plus medical and dental offices. The mall also has a "family place" play area for toddlers, and a youth learning centre that includes reading programs, arts and crafts, and storytelling.

Street shopping for everyday household needs is plentiful on Dundas, College and Bloor streets, where you will find an eclectic mix of grocers, bankers, diners, fashion stores and art galleries.

RECREATION:
Dufferin Grove Park is the most innovative community park in the city. It includes a community bake oven, a music circle, a campfire, a community flower and vegetable garden, live theatre, a summer music festival, arts and crafts classes, and a naturalization project. It also has traditional recreational facilities, including tennis courts, a basketball court, a wading pool, an artificial ice rink and a playing field.

The West-End YMCA at 931 College Street has a gymnasium, a swimming pool and community programs. The Bloor/Gladstone Public Library also offers community-based programs.

SCHOOLS:
(P) Alexander Muir/Gladstone Jr. & Sr., 108 Gladstone Ave., (416) 393-9140
(P) Dewson St, Jr., 65 Concord Ave., (416) 393-9120
(P) Kent Sr., 980 Dufferin St., (416) 393-0400
(P) Ossington/Old Orchard Jr., 380 Ossington Ave., (416) 393-0710
(C) St. Luke, 319 Ossington Ave., (416) 393-5347

TRANSPORTATION:
The Dufferin bus connects passengers to the Dufferin subway station on the Bloor-Danforth subway line, while the Dovercourt and Ossington buses connect passengers to the Ossington subway station, also on the Bloor-Danforth subway line. The College and Dundas streetcars connect passengers to stations on the Yonge-University-Spadina subway line.

Motorists can be downtown in five to 10 minutes and the Gardiner Expressway is approximately 15 minutes away.

ROARK ANDRADE

HISTORY: This neighbourhood is the namesake of Historic Fort York, which has stood at the foot of Toronto near the shoreline of Lake Ontario since 1793. During the Battle of York in 1811, Fort York was destroyed by the Americans but was rebuilt in 1814.

In the 1850s the railway began operating just north of Fort York, bringing a plethora of industry to the area. Fort York would carry on in relative obscurity from the citizens of Toronto, however, it continued to be used as a military establishment right up until 1934 when it opened as a historic museum.

Fort York was under siege once again in 1943, this time by short-sighted city planners who unceremoniously proposed demolishing it to make way for the Gardiner Expressway. Fortunately, community groups came to the defence of the fort, and the expressway was ultimately re-routed to the south.

In a twist of fate, it is the Gardiner Expressway that now faces an uncertain future — many would like to see it demolished as part of the plan to revitalize Toronto's waterfront — while Historic Fort York is now a protected national historic site.

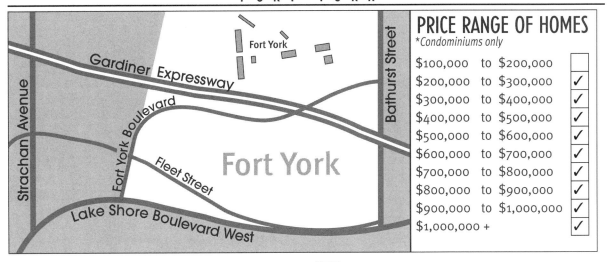

PRICE RANGE OF HOMES
Condominiums only

$100,000	to $200,000	
$200,000	to $300,000	✓
$300,000	to $400,000	✓
$400,000	to $500,000	✓
$500,000	to $600,000	✓
$600,000	to $700,000	✓
$700,000	to $800,000	✓
$800,000	to $900,000	✓
$900,000	to $1,000,000	✓
$1,000,000 +		✓

OVERVIEW:
Fort York is Toronto's newest neighbourhood. This newly minted high-density neighbourhood is just now welcoming its first residents. When completed 10 to 15 years from now, Fort York is expected to have approximately 6,000 condominium homes.

HOMES:
Fort York will contain a mix of high-rise towers and mid- and low-rise buildings. These slick glass and concrete edifices will include selling features such as floor-to-ceiling windows, and balconies. Unit owners on higher floors will enjoy spectacular city views to the north and lakeshore views to the south.

SHOPPING:
Residents of this neighbourhood can shop for household goods along Queens Quay and King Street.

RECREATION:
Fort York neighbourhood residents are within walking distance of the theatres and Entertainment District along King Street, and the parks and trails along the waterfront. Coronation Park is directly across the street, next to Ontario Place and the Canadian National Exhibition grounds.

SCHOOLS:
(P) Ogden Jr., 33 Phoebe St., 416-393-9110
(P) Niagara Street Jr., 222 Niagara St., 416-393-1371
(P) Ryerson Commercial School, 96 Denison Ave., 416-393-1340
(PH) Parkdale Collegiate Institute, 209 Jameson Ave., 416-393-9000
(PH) Central Technical School, 725 Bathurst St., 416-393-0060
(PH) West Toronto Collegiate Institute, 330 Lansdowne Ave., 416-393-1500

TRANSPORTATION:
Fort York residents can easily walk or cycle downtown. They also enjoy convenient access to public transit, with bus and streetcars being easily accessible.

Lake Shore Boulevard and the Gardiner Expressway provide motorists with easy access to Toronto's network of commuter highways.

HISTORY:
Grange Park was Toronto's first elite neighbourhood. It is named after Grange House, built in 1817 by D'Arcy Boulton Jr., a member of one of early Toronto's wealthiest and most prominent families.

Grange House, now part of the Art Gallery of Ontario, and the mansions on Beverley Street are the sole reminders of this neighbourhood's period of affluence. In the late 1800s Grange Park's upper class gentry headed for the newer, more fashionable suburbs in Parkdale, Rosedale and the Annex.

By the early 1900s, Grange Park's large estates had been transformed into rows of modest workers' houses that became home to many new Canadians.

Jewish immigrants were followed by Eastern Europeans and, more recently, Chinese immigrants, who migrated to Grange Park after Toronto's first Chinatown at Dundas and Elizabeth Street was razed in the 1960s to make room for the new city hall.

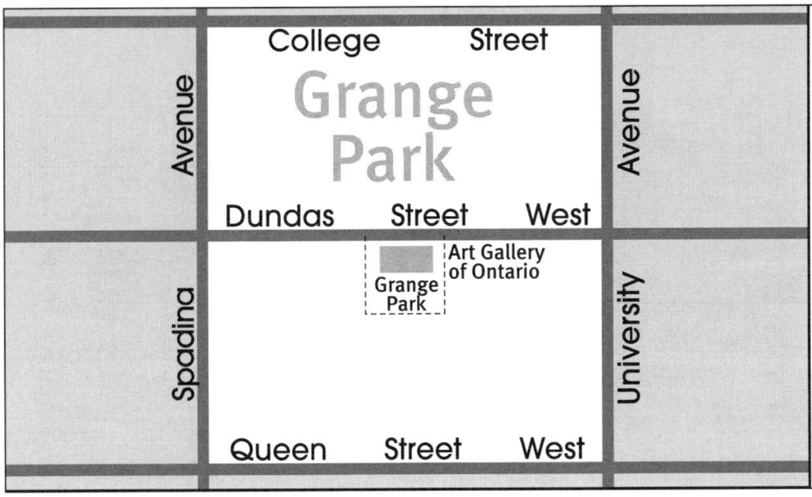

PRICE RANGE OF HOMES	
$100,000 to $200,000	
$200,000 to $300,000	
$300,000 to $400,000	✓
$400,000 to $500,000	✓
$500,000 to $600,000	✓
$600,000 to $700,000	✓
$700,000 to $800,000	✓
$800,000 to $900,000	✓
$900,000 to $1,000,000	✓
$1,000,000 +	✓

Map: College Street, Grange Park, Dundas Street West, Queen Street West, Spadina Avenue, University Avenue, Avenue, Art Gallery of Ontario, Grange Park.

OVERVIEW:

The Grange Park neighbourhood has become synonymous with Toronto's Chinatown district. Grange Park's street signs, telephone booths, and even the local police station, all have signage in Chinese as well as English.

Grange Park is also home to a large number of artists. The Art Gallery of Ontario, Ontario Crafts Council and Ontario College of Art are all located in Grange Park.

HOMES:

Grange Park's narrow, tree-lined streets are lined with ornate Victorian row houses, built between 1870 and the 1890s. These houses feature all the Victorian trimmings.

Condominium buyers should check out Village-by-the-Grange. Built in 1980, this is one of Toronto's first mixed-use developments. It features condominiums, retail stores and offices, all in the same complex. New street-level townhomes have recently been added to this development, now commonly referred to as Grangetown.

South of Village by the Grange is the Beaver Hall Artist's Co-op. Beaver Hall has 24 apartments and a large communal studio space. It was designed to provide local artists with affordable "live and work" space.

SHOPPING:

The Chinatown shopping district, at Spadina Road and Dundas Street, is a festival of fruit and vegetable markets, fish markets, exotic crafts and herbal remedy stores.

Queen Street West has a distinct arts flavour with many bookstores, galleries, fashion boutiques, and trendy restaurants along this route. The tiny Baldwin Village shopping district, on Baldwin Street between McCaul and Beverley streets, is one of Toronto's prettiest places to shop. This street is filled with cosy little cafés and restaurants that will delight any palate.

RECREATION:

The Grange City Park is one of Toronto's most dignified public promenades. Its paved walkways provide passageways to the Art Gallery Of Ontario, Grange House, St. George's Church, Ontario College of Art and the Harrison Baths and Swimming Pool. A children's play area is located next to the Harrison Community Centre.

University Settlement, at 23 Grange Road, has a large community centre with recreational facilities as well as social-service programs.

SCHOOLS:

(P)   Ogden Jr., 33 Phoebe St., (416) 393-9110
(P)   Ryerson Jr. & Sr., 96 Denison Ave., (416) 393-1340
(P)   Oasis Alternative School, 707 Dundas St., (416) 393-9830
(P)   West End Alternative Secondary, 70 Darcy St., (416) 393-0060
(U)   Ontario College of Art and Design, 100 McCaul St., (416) 977-6000

TRANSPORTATION:

The Queen and Dundas streetcars connect with subway stations on the Yonge-University-Spadina subway line, while the Spadina streetcar links passengers to the Bloor-Danforth subway.

Motorists are already downtown, but can link up with the major highways leading out of the city, via either Lake Shore Boulevard or the Gardiner Expressway.

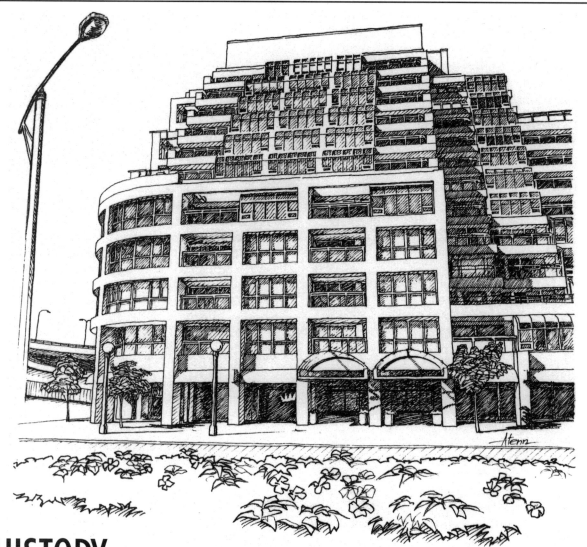

HISTORY: Toronto's Harbourfront district was created from landfill in
the early 1800s. The land south of Front Street was previously under water.
Harbourfront quickly developed into a tangled web of industry that included
shipping facilities, warehouses, railway tracks, grain silos and factories, all
dotting the shoreline. Unfortunately, these physical barriers cut Harbourfront
off from the rest of Toronto.

It wasn't until 1972, with the creation of the federally sponsored
Harbourfront Corporation, that Toronto citizens began to reclaim their waterfront. Harbourfront has been undergoing a renaissance ever since.

A shining example of Harbourfront's transformation is the Queens Quay
Terminal. This building was one of the largest warehouses in North America
when it opened in 1927. The Terminal was remodelled in 1980, and today
includes a successful mix of high-end residential, commercial and retail
space, all under one roof.

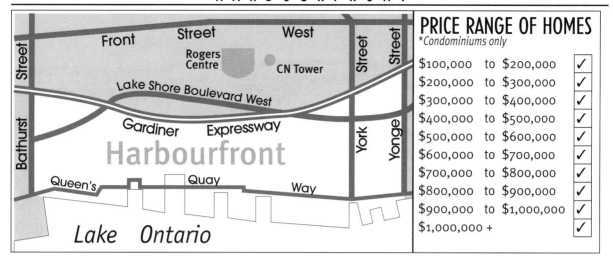

PRICE RANGE OF HOMES
Condominiums only

$100,000	to $200,000	✓
$200,000	to $300,000	✓
$300,000	to $400,000	✓
$400,000	to $500,000	✓
$500,000	to $600,000	✓
$600,000	to $700,000	✓
$700,000	to $800,000	✓
$800,000	to $900,000	✓
$900,000	to $1,000,000	✓
$1,000,000 +		✓

OVERVIEW:
The Harbourfront neigh-bourhood incorporates a unique blend of residential, cultural, recreational, and commercial uses, all within the same community. Harbourfront also serves as Toronto's playground by the lake. It is enjoyed by all Toronto residents, as well as being a popular destination point for tourists.

HOMES:
Harbourfront has the highest concentration of luxury condominium apartment buildings in the City of Toronto. Harbourfront condominiums were first built in the 1980s. The newer, more upscale buildings, featuring balconies and a lake view, were built in the late 1990s right up until the present.

Harbourfront also has a handful of Marinas that provide seasonal moorings on a rental basis for local and out of town boaters. Many of these hearty souls make Harbourfront their summer home.

SHOPPING:
Harbourfront's main shopping district is located along Queens Quay West. The shopping here is mixed, being geared towards both the local residents and tourists. Queens Quay West is anchored by the Queens Quay Terminal, located at the foot of York Street. The terminal is open seven days a week, and features two floors of shops, galleries and restaurants.

The Harbourfront is conveniently located within walking distance of the St. Lawrence Market, Toronto's oldest and largest food market. The St. Lawrence Market offers a cornucopia of culinary delights, including farm fresh eggs, exotic herbs, organic chicken, and an assortment of fruits, vegetables, cheeses, deli meats and seafood. A recent addition to Toronto's Harbourfront is the giant Loblaws food and retail centre located on Queens Quay at the foot of Jarvis Street. In addition to groceries and a pharmacy, this three-storey complex features a variety of retailers, a popular restaurant, and a community meeting place where workshops, cooking classes and public meetings are held.

RECREATION:
Harbourfront has more recreational opportunities than any other Toronto neighbourhood. The Air Canada Centre, Rogers Centre and the C.N. Tower, are all located within this neighbourhood. The Canadian National Exhibition, the Marine Museum, and Historic Fort York are all just minutes from Harbourfront, while the Toronto Islands are 10 minutes away by ferry boat.

The social, cultural, and recreational hub of the neighbourhood is the Harbourfront Centre, located at the York Quay at 235 Queens Quay West. This popular lakeside venue hosts close to 4,000 events per year, ranging from craft workshops and sailing lessons to jazz festivals and food fairs.

SCHOOLS:
(P)   The Waterfront School Jr. & Sr., 635 Queens Quay West, (416) 393-0684
(PH) Jarvis Collegiate Institute, 495 Jarvis St., (416) 393-0140
(PH) Central Technical School, 725 Bathurst St., (416) 393-0060

TRANSPORTATION:
Queens Quay West has both express and regular streetcar service, with connections to Union Station. From Union Station you can ride Toronto Transit or Go Transit lines to just about anywhere in Metropolitan Toronto.

Motorists also have easy access in and out of the city via the Gardiner Expressway and Lake Shore Boulevard. An added bonus of living at the foot of the city is that commuters are generally going against the prevailing rush-hour traffic.

HISTORY: Kensington was originally part of a 100-acre park lot granted to Captain John Denison in 1815. By the 1870s, this district had developed into a middle class Anglo-Saxon neighbourhood with distinctive British street names such as Kensington Avenue, Fitzroy Terrace, Oxford Street and Wales Avenue.

The Kensington neighbourhood began to change in the 1920s, when Jewish immigrants from Eastern Europe started to settle here. Excluded from the Toronto business community, Kensington's Jewish families opened stalls in front of their houses and sold goods to each other. This Jewish market was the start of an old world marketplace in the heart of the Kensington neighbourhood.

Since the 1940s Kensington has attracted immigrants from all parts of the world, and it is now one of Toronto's most culturally diverse neighbourhoods.

Former Toronto Mayor Mel Lastman was born and raised in Kensington along with his childhood friend, the late Al Waxman, who starred as the King of Kensington, a popular CBC television series that ran from 1975 to 1980.

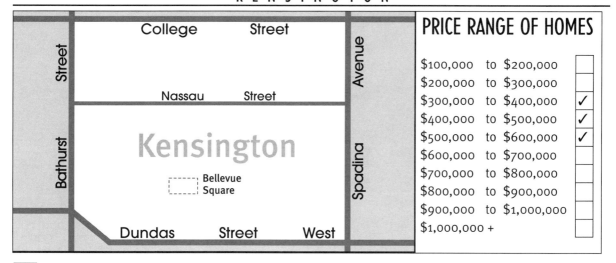

PRICE RANGE OF HOMES

$100,000 to $200,000	
$200,000 to $300,000	
$300,000 to $400,000	✓
$400,000 to $500,000	✓
$500,000 to $600,000	✓
$600,000 to $700,000	
$700,000 to $800,000	
$800,000 to $900,000	
$900,000 to $1,000,000	
$1,000,000 +	

OVERVIEW:
The Kensington neighbourhood is defined by its popular outdoor market, which has become a hot spot for tourists and a popular Toronto shopping destination. The international flavour of Kensington Market reflects the diverse cultural mix of this vibrant and colourful Toronto neighbourhood.

HOMES:
Kensington's Victorian rowhouses are small to moderate in size and feature many decorative accents. These houses were built between the 1870s and 1890s.

The houses in the heart of the Kensington Market have market stalls on their front lawns. Many of these houses are oriented to the rear of the property where tiny laneways offer privacy from the hustle and bustle of the marketplace.

The Kensington neighbourhood has recently been revitalized by a handful of new housing projects. These new developments include the Victorian-inspired townhomes on Oxford Street and the Kensington Market Lofts, a unique condominium project situated in three former George Brown College buildings on Baldwin and Nassau streets.

SHOPPING:
The Kensington Market is Toronto's only year-round outdoor market. It is a place of organized confusion, where merchants sell their goods right out on the sidewalks, and restaurant radios trumpet the words and music of a far-off land. If you have never experienced the sights and sounds of this old world market, it is certainly worth a visit.

The shopping on the periphery of the Kensington neighbourhood includes Chinatown on Spadina Avenue, Portugal Village on Dundas Street West, and the trendy shops and restaurants along Queen Street West.

RECREATION:
The local park and meeting place for Kensington residents is Bellevue Square, which is located right in the centre of the neighbourhood. This park has a tot's playground and a wading pool.

Cecil Community Centre, at Spadina and College, features a large Hall that is used for theatre productions, sports, games, parties and weddings.

The Shaw College Public Library serves as a community meeting place and offers reading material in a number of languages that reflect the cultural diversity of Kensington residents.

SCHOOLS:
(P) Ryerson Jr. & Sr., 96 Denison Ave, (416) 393-1340
(PH) Oasis Alternative Secondary, 707 Dundas St, (416) 393-9836
(PH) West End Alternative Secondary, 70 D'Arcy St, (416) 393-0660

TRANSPORTATION:
Streetcar service on Bathurst Street connects passengers to the Bloor-Danforth subway line. The Spadina, Dundas, and Queen streetcars travel to the Spadina station on the Yonge-University-Spadina subway line.

Motorists are already downtown and are just minutes from the Gardiner Expressway and Lake Shore Boulevard.

ROARK ANDRADE

HISTORY: In the late 1700s and early 1800s the area now known as
Liberty Village was part of the Garrison Common — a military fortification for
the Town of York (which would later become Toronto). Historic Fort York,
located at 100 Garrison Road, served as the base for the Canadian militia in
the Battle of York against the Americans in 1813.

The arrival of the railway to this area in the 1850s attracted industry,
which in turn led to the building of warehouses and factories. Many of these
are now enjoying a new purpose in Liberty Village as funky lofts, hip
live/work spaces and studio offices.

The name Liberty Village is said to be a reference to the Central Prison
and the Mercer Reformatory for Women that were situated here in the late
1800s and early 1900s. Story has it that Liberty Street — the neighbourhood's main east-west thoroughfare — is so named because it was the first
ground prisoners set foot on upon their release.

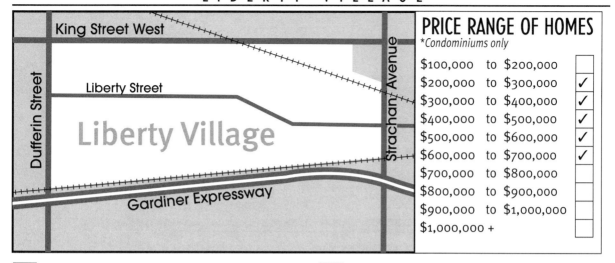

PRICE RANGE OF HOMES
*Condominiums only

$100,000	to	$200,000	
$200,000	to	$300,000	✓
$300,000	to	$400,000	✓
$400,000	to	$500,000	✓
$500,000	to	$600,000	✓
$600,000	to	$700,000	✓
$700,000	to	$800,000	
$800,000	to	$900,000	
$900,000	to	$1,000,000	
$1,000,000 +			

OVERVIEW:
Liberty Village is a 43-acre master-planned community, combining residential, commercial and retail uses. This neighbourhood is attracting young professionals in media, high-tech and design businesses who live and work in the urban core.

There is a gritty, urban feel and a unique vibrancy to Liberty Village, which emanates from the red brick Victorian industrial architecture that dominates the streetscape. The tall chimney smoke stacks that project from some of these old buildings serve as neighbourhood landmarks.

HOMES:
Nodules of new townhouses can be found throughout Liberty Village and along King Street West. Hard lofts in restored industrial buildings feature soaring ceilings, huge windows and exposed brick. New concrete and glass condo towers provide an ultra-modern contrast to the older buildings in the area.

SHOPPING:
Liberty Village has gained a reputation as a destination spot for those seeking unique furniture and design stores, as well as art galleries, hip coffee shops and urban fusion restaurants.

The Dominion supermarket anchors a shopping strip that includes a video store, a pet-supply store, a dry cleaner and a bank.

RECREATION:
Liberty Village residents can take advantage of the nearby waterfront trail that is used by walkers, joggers, cyclists and in-line skaters.

This neighbourhood is just minutes away from Toronto's Entertainment District and world-class sporting venues such as Air Canada Centre and Rogers Centre.

SCHOOLS:
(P) Givins/Shaw, 49 Givins St., 416-393-1240
(P) Alexander Muir/Gladstone Jr. & Sr., 108 Gladstone Ave., 416-393-9140
(PH) Parkdale Collegiate Institute, 209 Jameson Ave., 416-393-9000
(PH) Central Technical School, 725 Bathurst St., 416-393-0060
(PH) West Toronto Collegiate Institute, 330 Lansdowne Ave., 416-393-1500

TRANSPORTATION:
Streetcar lines on Queen and King streets provide quick and easy access to the downtown financial and entertainment districts. Go Transit's Exhibition Station is within walking distance of this neighbourhood.

Motorists can scoot downtown in minutes or quickly access the Gardiner Expressway and Lake Shore Boulevard, which provide access to a network of highways leading out of the downtown core.

HISTORY: It was during the 1920s that College Street's "Little Italy" became recognized as the residential and commercial centre of Toronto's Italian community.

However, by the 1960s many of Little Italy's residents began to move north to the the Corso Italia district on St. Clair Avenue West.

The Italian families that moved out of Little Italy were replaced by Portuguese, Chinese, Vietnamese and Spanish families. This mix of cultures gives Little Italy the international flavour that it enjoys today.

In 1985 the local business association on College Street officially adopted the Little Italy name, in recognition of the role this neighbourhood played as the starting point for Italians in Toronto.

PRICE RANGE OF HOMES

$100,000 to $200,000		
$200,000 to $300,000		
$300,000 to $400,000	✓
$400,000 to $500,000	✓
$500,000 to $600,000	✓
$600,000 to $700,000	✓
$700,000 to $800,000	
$800,000 to $900,000	
$900,000 to $1,000,000	
$1,000,000 +	

OVERVIEW:
Little Italy is not an exclusively Italian neighbourhood, as its name might suggest. While there is still a strong Italian community in this neighbourhood, there is also a large Portuguese population, centred around the First Portuguese Canadian Cultural Centre on College Street and the Portugal Village shopping district on Dundas Street West.

Today, Little Italy's Italian and Portuguese residents are welcoming new neighbours from around the world to what is now considered one of Toronto's most multi-cultural neighbourhoods.

HOMES:
The majority of Little Italy's rowhouses and attached Victorian homes were built between 1880 and 1910. These houses are set on narrow, tree-lined streets with parking facilities located at the back of the property, off of rear laneways. New townhome and loft condominium developments have attracted many new residents to this vibrant downtown neighbourhood.

SHOPPING:
The Little Italy shopping district on College Street, between Shaw Street and Euclid Avenue, features authentic Italian restaurants and European fashions.

The Portugal Village shopping district on Dundas Street includes fresh fruit and vegetable markets, mouth-watering bakeries, as well as seafood restaurants and cafés that feature an authentic Portuguese cuisine.

RECREATION:
The West End YMCA at 931 College Street includes a gymnasium, a swimming pool, and community meeting rooms.

The First Portuguese Canadian Cultural Centre at 722 College Street, has recently undergone a major renovation/expansion. The centre's facilities include lecture halls, a games room, a bar, meeting rooms and a restaurant. Evening programs range from performances of Fado music to dances.

The College/Shaw Public Library serves as a community meeting place and offers reading material in a number of languages that reflect the general population of the area.

SCHOOLS:
(P)   Charles G. Fraser Jr., 79 Manning Ave., (416) 393-1830
(P)   Givins/Shaw Jr. & Sr., 180 Shaw St., (416) 393-1240
(PH) Central High School of Commerce, 570 Shaw St., (416) 393-0030
(PH) Harbord Collegiate Institute, 28 Harbord St., (416) 393-1650
(C)   St. David, 486 Shaw St., (416) 393-5238
(C)   St. Lucy, 60 Clinton St., (416) 393-5304

TRANSPORTATION:
Little Italy is well served by regular bus routes on Ossington Avenue, and streetcar service on College Street, Dundas Street, and Bathurst Street.

Motorists are within 10 minutes of the Gardiner Expressway and Lake Shore Boulevard.

HISTORY:

The Moss Park neighbourhood was originally part of a 100-acre park lot owned by William Allan, one of early Toronto's wealthiest citizens. In 1830, Allan built a huge mansion on his estate and named it Moss Park. The mansion stood where the city park of the same name is today.

When Allan passed away in 1853, he left his Moss Park estate to his son George, who would later become the Mayor of Toronto. George Allan immediately subdivided his father's estate and this area soon became known for its Victorian homes.

Today, little is left of the original Moss Park neighbourhood. Its houses were demolished in 1962 in order to make room for the Moss Park Apartment Buildings, which make up the current Moss Park neighbourhood.

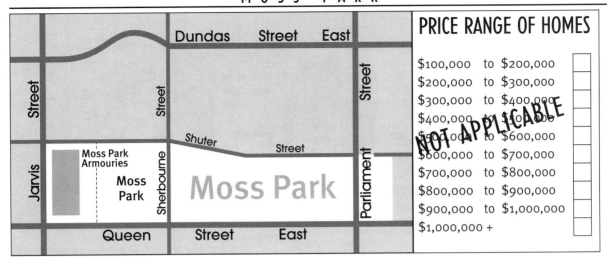

PRICE RANGE OF HOMES

$100,000 to $200,000	
$200,000 to $300,000	
$300,000 to $400,000	
$400,000 to $500,000	
$500,000 to $600,000	
$600,000 to $700,000	
$700,000 to $800,000	
$800,000 to $900,000	
$900,000 to $1,000,000	
$1,000,000 +	

NOT APPLICABLE

OVERVIEW:

Moss Park is one of Toronto's largest public housing projects. It is situated in Toronto's gritty downtown core. The Salvation Army Hostel is located across the street from Moss Park at the corner of Sherbourne and Queen streets.

The Moss Park neighbourhood is anchored on the west side by a large public park, which also happens to be the home of the Moss Park Armoury, a training centre for the Canadian Armed Forces.

HOMES:

Moss Park has three double-wing high-rise apartment buildings and one single-tower apartment building. All the apartment buildings are well-set back from the street. They are surrounded by both greenspace and an internal network of roadways that discourage outside traffic from entering the neighbourhood.

SHOPPING:

There is local shopping on both Sherbourne and Parliament streets. Queen Street East is an eclectic mix of local stores and design and decorating stores that draw shoppers from Toronto's more affluent neighbourhoods.

RECREATION:

The Moss Park apartment buildings contain their own recreation centre, as well as an outdoor basketball court and a children's playground.

Moss Park, situated to the west of the neighbourhood apartment buildings, is one of Toronto's larger parks. It includes a sports field, a baseball diamond and two tennis courts. Moss Park is located right next to the John Innes Community Recreation Centre. This modern recreational facility features an indoor swimming pool, a gymnasium, a running track, a weight room, a cardio training room, a games room, a woodworking shop and a craft room. Next door to the community centre is the Moss Park Arena.

SCHOOLS:

(P) Nelson Mandela Park Jr. & Sr., 440 Shuter St., (416) 393-1620
(P) Regent Park/Duke of York Jr., 20 Regent St., (416) 393-1730
(PH) Jarvis Collegiate Institute, 495 Jarvis St., (416) 393-0140
(PH) Inglenook Alternative School, 19 Sackville St., (416) 393-0560
(C) St. Paul, 80 Sackville St., (416) 393-5204

TRANSPORTATION:

There are a number of public transportation routes within the Moss Park neighbourhood, including the Queen streetcar, and bus service on Sherbourne Street and Parliament Street. These surface routes connect to stations on the Bloor-Danforth and Yonge-University-Spadina subway lines.

HISTORY:
The Niagara neighbourhood has a rich history that dates back to 1793, when it was part of a military garrison for the fledgling Town of York. Historic Fort York is still standing on Garrison Road, between Bathurst Street and Strachan Avenue.

Street names in the Niagara neighbourhood are reminders of its military past. For example, Stanley Street is named after the former Stanley Barracks now located on the Exhibition grounds, Niagara Street is named after the former military capital of Upper Canada, and Tecumseh Street is named for the great warrior chief of the Shawnee, who fought for Canada in the war of 1812.

The second chapter in this neighbourhood's history began in the 1850s, when Niagara emerged as a prominent industrial centre. Niagara's factories and mills created a demand for workers' housing which ultimately led to the residential development of the Niagara neighbourhood in the mid- to late 1800s.

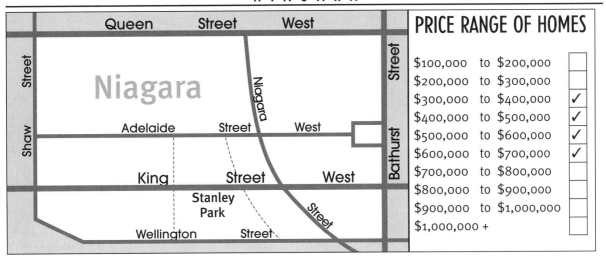

PRICE RANGE OF HOMES	
$100,000 to $200,000	
$200,000 to $300,000	
$300,000 to $400,000	✓
$400,000 to $500,000	✓
$500,000 to $600,000	✓
$600,000 to $700,000	✓
$700,000 to $800,000	
$800,000 to $900,000	
$900,000 to $1,000,000	
$1,000,000 +	

OVERVIEW:

The physical and social centre of Niagara is Stanley Park, a multi-recreational facility that is well used by area residents. Niagara offers residents convenient access to Toronto's Financial and Entertainment districts. It is also very handy to the Rogers Centre, Exhibition Place, Harbourfront and the Toronto Islands. Many Niagara residents are young urban professionals employed in the high-tech, media and arts companies that have converged on this part of the city.

HOMES:

Niagara's historic Second Empire row-houses and cosy one storey 'Ontario Cottages' were built in the 1870s and 1880s.

The Niagara neighbourhood also contains pockets of newer townhouse and urban loft developments that reflect the renewed demand for housing in this historic Toronto neighbourhood.

SHOPPING:

Queen Street West provides Niagara residents with an eclectic mix of antique shops, art galleries, bookstores, fashion stores, natural food markets and restaurants.

King Street also has stores and restaurants that serve the day-to-day needs of Niagara residents.

RECREATION:

Niagara is a close-knit neighbourhood with its own small community centre located on the Stanley Park grounds. This centre is used for local residents' meetings, community-based programming and social functions.

Stanley Park is a favourite neighbourhood meeting place. It contains two baseball diamonds, two tennis courts, a soccer field, a small outdoor pool and a children's playground.

Historic Fort York, located on Garrison Road, was the scene of the bloody Battle of York during the War of 1812. Today this important Toronto landmark serves as a museum where knowledgeable historical interpreters wearing period costumes conduct tours and demonstrate historical activities. Historic Fort York also contains a variety of exhibits and displays.

SCHOOLS:

(P)   Niagara Jr. School, 222 Niagara St, (416) 393-1371
(P)   Alpha School Jr. & Sr., 20 Brant St, (416) 393-1880
(P)   Downtown Alternative, JK-Grade 3, 20 Brant St, (416) 393-1882
(PH) Central High School of Commerce, 570 Shaw St, (416) 393-0030
(PH) Oasis Alternative School, 707 Dundas St, (416) 393-9830
(C)   St. Mary, 20 Portugal Square, (416) 393-5205
(C)   Senhor Santo Christo, 30 Humber St, (416) 393-5367

TRANSPORTATION:

Regular streetcar service runs on Queen Street, King Street, and Bathurst Street.

Motorists are just minutes from the Gardiner Expressway and Lake Shore Boulevard.

HISTORY:
Regent Park rose from the rubble of what was once the south part of the Cabbagetown neighbourhood. During the 1930s, South Cabbagetown was one of Toronto's worst slums and as such was targeted by Toronto city planners for a grand urban renewal scheme called Regent Park.

Built in 1949, Regent Park holds the distinction of being Canada's first public housing project. Regent Park was expanded in the 1950s to include the area south of Gerrard Street, which came to be known as Regent Park South.

A promising new chapter in the history of Regent Park is now being written; a $1 billion redevelopment of this neighbourhood is being carried out in phases, and will take a minimum of 12 years to complete.

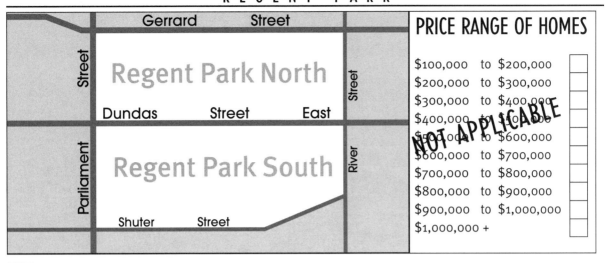

PRICE RANGE OF HOMES	
$100,000 to $200,000	
$200,000 to $300,000	
$300,000 to $400,000	
$400,000 to $500,000	
$500,000 to $600,000	
$600,000 to $700,000	
$700,000 to $800,000	
$800,000 to $900,000	
$900,000 to $1,000,000	
$1,000,000 +	

NOT APPLICABLE

OVERVIEW:
Regent Park is Toronto's oldest and largest public housing project. It is home to more than 10,000 people and is managed by the Metro Toronto Housing Authority.

Regent Park residents come from a wide variety of cultural backgrounds including many new Canadians from Africa, Asia, and Latin America. There are more than 60 different first languages spoken here, making Regent Park one of Toronto's most culturally diverse neighbourhoods.

HOMES:
The revitalization of Regent Park's housing stock will include both high- and low-rise apartment buildings. Many of these will be subsidized apartments, however, there will also be some privately owned units. At least on of the high-rise buildings is slated as a seniors' residence.

SHOPPING:
A limited amount of shops and services are located along Gerrard, River, and Parliament Streets. There is also a community health centre and a handful of local convenience type stores, located in the middle of Regent Park on Belshaw Place.

RECREATION:
The Regent Park Community Centre at 203 Sackville Green has a gymnasium, a games room, an arts and crafts room, and a weight room. The community centre also has a highly acclaimed media program.

The Regent Park Recreation Centre at 415 Gerrard Street East includes a small gymnasium, a meeting room, and an outdoor pool.

There are two outdoor artificial ice rinks in Regent Park. The Regent North rink is located north of Dundas Street East, west of River Street. The Regent South rink is located at Shuter and Sumach streets. These two single-surface rinks have allotted times for pleasure skating, permit hockey and shinny hockey, as well as learn-to-skate and hockey-school programs.

Regent Park also has a baseball diamond, a swimming pool, and many small parks, some of which contain children's playgrounds and wading pools.

The Parliament Street Public Library on Gerrard Street East offers a variety of programs for children and adults.

SCHOOLS:
(P)   Nelson Mandela Park Jr. & Sr., 440 Shuter St., (416) 393-1620

(P)   Regent Park/Duke of York Jr., 20 Regent St., (416) 393-1730

TRANSPORTATION:
The Gerrard bus and the Dundas streetcar connect passengers to the Yonge-University-Spadina subway line. The Parliament streetcar connects to Castle Frank station on the Bloor-Danforth subway line.

The Gardiner Expressway, Lake Shore Boulevard and the Don Valley Expressway are just minutes away.

HISTORY:
St. James Town began in the 1870s as a desirable upper-middle-class neighbourhood. It was filled with picturesque Victorian houses and remained popular with Toronto home buyers until well into the 1900s.

A turning point for the St. James Town neighbourhood occurred in 1953 when the City of Toronto announced major zoning amendments for the downtown core. The new zoning significantly increased building coverage in St. James Town, making it an instant target for private developers.

By the end of the 1950s, a consortium of developers had bought up and demolished St. James Town's entire housing stock in order to build Toronto's first high-rise residential apartment towers.

The St. James Town apartments were originally planned and designed as a neighbourhood for upwardly mobile singles and professionals. However, almost from the start St. James Town has been populated by low- to moderate-income families.

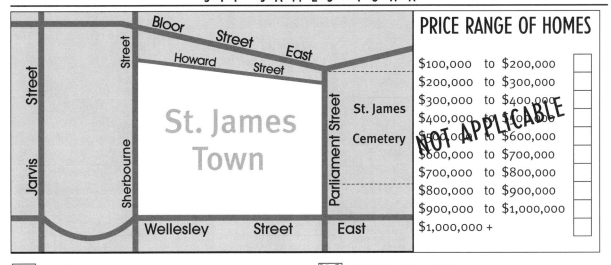

PRICE RANGE OF HOMES

$100,000 to $200,000	
$200,000 to $300,000	
$300,000 to $400,000	
$400,000 to $500,000	
$500,000 to $600,000	NOT APPLICABLE
$600,000 to $700,000	
$700,000 to $800,000	
$800,000 to $900,000	
$900,000 to $1,000,000	
$1,000,000 +	

OVERVIEW:
Over 100 languages are spoken by the residents of St. James Town, which contains 18 high-rise apartment buildings, almost 7,000 units and over 18,000 residents in an area of 32.1 acres. These demographics combine to make St. James Town the most densely populated census tract in Canada.

The architecturally dramatic Wellesley Community Centre at 495 Sherbourne Street is a much welcome addition to St. James Town. This new centre includes a library, athletic facilities and a children's early learning centre, which offers hope for a better future for the many new Canadians that populate this inner-city neighbourhood.

HOMES:
St. James Town apartment buildings contain rental units ranging in size from bachelor to three-bedroom apartments.

St. James Town includes 14 privately owned buildings. Many of these buildings are named after large Canadian cities. These buildings offer typical marketplace rents.

The other four apartment buildings in St. James Town are owned by the Toronto Community Housing Authority. These buildings offer rents geared towards income.

SHOPPING:
A limited amount of day-to-day convenience-type shopping exists in the interior of the St. James Town neighbourhood. Grocery stores, drug stores, dry cleaners, clothing stores, banks and restaurants are located on the main streets that border this neighbourhood including Wellesley Street, Sherbourne Street, and Parliament Street.

RECREATION:
There are swimming pools and children's playgrounds sprinkled throughout the St. James Town neighbourhood.

The Rose Avenue Community Centre located in the Rose Avenue Public School is open to the public both during the evening and on weekends. Their facilities include a gymnasium, a games room and meeting rooms.

St. James Town is conveniently located near many city parks, including Wellesley Park, Riverdale Park West, Winchester Park and Allan Gardens.

The Parliament Street branch of the Toronto Public Library is located nearby at the southwest corner of Parliament and Gerrard streets.

SCHOOLS:
(P)   Rose Ave., Jr., 675 Ontario St., (416) 393-1260
(PH) Jarvis Collegiate Institute,, 495 Jarvis St., (416) 393-0140
(PH) Rosedale Heights Secondary School, 711 Bloor St., East, (416) 393-1580
(C)   Our Lady of Lourdes, 444 Sherbourne St., (416) 393-5221

TRANSPORTATION:
There is bus service on all of the major streets that border St. James Town. The Sherbourne subway station on the Bloor-Danforth line is a short walk from this neighbourhood.

Motorists are only a few minutes away from the Don Valley Parkway on-ramps on Bloor Street.

HISTORY: The land on which the St. Lawrence neighbourhood is built
was originally part of the shoreline of Lake Ontario. Immediately to the north
of here, above Front Street, was the Town of York, the forerunner to the City
of Toronto.

The site of the present-day St. Lawrence neighbourhood was created from
landfill in the early 1800s. It was originally intended to serve as a public
promenade with a grand esplanade along the waterfront. However, the city
turned the land over to the railways, which in turn attracted industry to the
St. Lawrence area.

By the early 1900s, St. Lawrence had become one of Toronto's most
prominent industrial centres. It remained a vital industrial area until the late
1940s, when Toronto's industrial base began moving to the suburbs.
Consequently, St. Lawrence went into a period of decline lasting until the
1970s, when Toronto politicians made the decision to create the present-day
St. Lawrence neighbourhood.

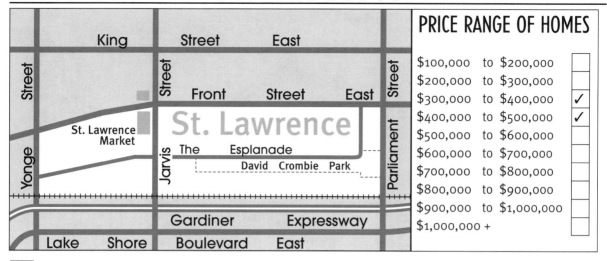

PRICE RANGE OF HOMES

$100,000 to $200,000		
$200,000 to $300,000		
$300,000 to $400,000	✓	
$400,000 to $500,000	✓	
$500,000 to $600,000		
$600,000 to $700,000		
$700,000 to $800,000		
$800,000 to $900,000		
$900,000 to $1,000,000		
$1,000,000 +		

OVERVIEW:

Planned and developed by the City of Toronto in the 1970s as a mixed-use housing development, the St.Lawrence neighbourhood has been critically acclaimed as a major success story in urban planning. It has become a model for the design and planning of new neighbourhoods across North America.

HOMES:

The co-op and condominium apartment buildings and townhouses south of The Esplanade in the St. Lawrence neighbourhood were designed by some of Toronto's most accomplished architects.

The historic section of this neighbourhood along Front Street is designated by yellow and white street signs reminding us that this area was the centre of the former Town of York, the forerunner to the city of Toronto. This location has been revitalized. Noteworthy are the St. Lawrence Lofts located at 78-85 Front Street East. These lofts are being built in three converted pre-confederation warehouses that date back to the 1850s and 1860s.

SHOPPING:

The Esplanade, which runs through the middle of the St. Lawrence neighbourhood, contains retail stores and services that meet the day-to-day needs of the St. Lawrence residents. The Esplanade's restaurants, bars and specialty stores appeal to tourists as well as Torontonians visiting from other neighbourhoods.

St. Lawrence residents have the luxury of being able to walk to the historic St. Lawrence Market, where they can purchase everything from fresh seafood to farm fresh eggs and organic chicken. The South Market is open all week long while the north building, also known as the "farmers market," is open only on Thursdays and Saturdays.

RECREATION:

David Crombie Park is a multi-faceted linear park that runs through the centre of the St. Lawrence neighbourhood, along The Esplanade. This park includes pretty strolling and sitting gardens, a waterfall, a handball court and a basketball court.

The St. Lawrence Community Recreation Centre is located on The Esplanade. This modern facility includes squash courts, a swimming pool, a gymnasium, a piano room, a weight room and a games room.

SCHOOLS:

(P) Market Lane Jr. & Sr., 85 Lower Jarvis St., (416) 393-1300

(C) St. Michael School, 50 George St., (416) 393-5387

(PH) Jarvis Collegiate Institute, 495 Jarvis St., (416) 393-0140

(PH) School, 19 Sackville St., (416) 393-0560

TRANSPORTATION:

Union Station is within walking distance of the St. Lawrence neighbourhood. TTC, Go Transit and Via Rail services operate out of Union station.

The Gardiner Expressway, Lake Shore Boulevard and Don Valley Expressway are all conveniently accessed within minutes of the St. Lawrence neighbourhood.

HISTORY: The South Annex neighbourhood was subdivided in the early 1850s, on land formerly owned by the Jarvis, Crookshank and Denison families, all of whom played a prominent role in the history of Toronto.

Advertisements promoting Villa and Town lots for sale in the South Annex highlighted "the close proximity to the locality of the new Parliament Buildings." The South Annex was also popularly described as being "situated in the most healthy and pleasant part of the City upon a considerable elevation above the Lake."

The establishment of the University of Toronto just east of here in the late 1850s provided the impetus for the building of homes in the South Annex, which took place largely between the 1870s and early 1900s.

	Bloor	Street	West		PRICE RANGE OF HOMES	

Map of South Annex showing streets: Grace Street, Palmerston Boulevard, Bathurst Street, Bloor Street West, College Street, Spadina Avenue, University of Toronto.

PRICE RANGE OF HOMES

$100,000 to $200,000	
$200,000 to $300,000	
$300,000 to $400,000	✓
$400,000 to $500,000	✓
$500,000 to $600,000	✓
$600,000 to $700,000	✓
$700,000 to $800,000	✓
$800,000 to $900,000	✓
$900,000 to $1,000,000	✓
$1,000,000 +	✓

OVERVIEW:

The South Annex is a vibrant and colourful downtown Toronto neighbourhood. Much of the South Annex's vitality comes from being located right next door to the University of Toronto.

Naturally, many University students, faculty, and alumni rent or own houses in the South Annex. The university population mixes well with the young urban professionals who have been buying and fixing up South Annex houses, giving these old houses new life, and in the process, revitalizing this historic Toronto neighbourhood.

HOMES:

The signature street in the South Annex is Palmerston Boulevard. Stone and iron gateposts, one on College Street and one on Bloor Street, set the tone for this distinctive boulevard which also features decorative cast iron street lamps, ancient trees and grandiose homes.

Overall, the houses in the South Annex come in a variety of shapes and sizes. Each house is whimsically decorated with Victorian accents that all blend together to form one of the most pleasing streetscapes of any Toronto neighbourhood. Most South Annex homes are built circa 1870s to 1910.

SHOPPING:

Bloor Street, west of Spadina, is a mini-university village lined with pubs, music shops, bookstores and restaurants. Cyclists and in-line skaters compete with cars and pedestrians in this high-energy shopping district.

The Mirvish Village shopping district on Markham Street south of Bloor Street is a dignified city block, filled with craft stores, bookstores, antique shops, galleries and specialty boutiques.

Harbord Street provides South Annex residents with one of the more sophisticated and intimate shopping districts in the city. In addition to many fine restaurants, Harbord Street also includes a number of excellent craft stores, bookstores and galleries.

RECREATION:

Fitness enthusiasts can get a good workout at the University of Toronto Athletic Centre. This facility has an Olympic-size pool, squash, tennis and badminton courts, weight machines, aerobics, a gymnasium and a 200-metre indoor track.

The Hart House University of Toronto athletic centre, located at 7 Hart House Circle on the U of T campus, has a vast array of facilities including an indoor swimming pool, squash courts, indoor running track and free weights, in addition to a variety of fitness programs.

Queen's Park is the site of Ontario's Legislative Buildings. It's the focal point of many civic events and parades. Queen's Park is also a quiet place, an oasis in the City, where one can sit on a park bench under a tall shade tree, and paint the landscape.

SCHOOLS:

(P)   Clinton St. Jr., 460 Manning Ave., (416) 393-9155
(P)   Montrose Jr., 301 Montrose Ave., (416) 393-9770
(P)   Delta Sr., 301 Montrose Ave., (416) 393-9730
(PH) Collegiate Institute, 286 Harbord St., (416) 393-1650
(PH) Central Technical School, 725 Bathurst St, (416) 393-0060
(PRI) University of Toronto Schools, 371 Bloor St. West, (416) 978-3212
(U)   University of Toronto, St. George Campus, (416) 978-2011
(S)   Loretto College Secondary School, 391 Brunswick Ave., (416) 393-5511 or South Campus, 783 Bathurst St., (416) 393-5543
(S)   St. David, 486 Shaw St., (416) 393-5238

TRANSPORTATION:

The South Annex is well served by public transit. College and Bathurst Streets have regular streetcar service, while Harbord Street has a regular bus route. The Bathurst and Spadina subway stations at Bloor Street link up with Toronto's rapid transit lines.

The major highways north and south of the city are a 20- to 30- minute drive from the South Annex.

HISTORY:
The Toronto Islands were created in 1858 after a tremendous storm separated Toronto's eastern peninsula from the city's mainland. Once the Islands had been formed they immediately became a popular Toronto summer playground containing hotels, amusement parks, and summer cottages.

A housing crisis during the Second World War led to the winterization of Islands cottages and marked the beginning of year-round occupancy here. However, in 1953 Metro Toronto Council mandated that all the Islands houses be demolished so that the Toronto Islands could be used exclusively as parkland.

Residents of Toronto Islands fought a long and hard battle with the City of Toronto to save their community from the wrecking ball. However, when the dust settled the houses on Hanlan's Point and Centre Island were lost, while the houses on Ward's Island and Algonquin Island were saved.

The status of the Toronto Islands neighbourhood remained clouded until 1994, when the province signed a 99-year lease deal with Toronto Islands residents, finally securing the future of the "Islanders" and their neighbourhood.

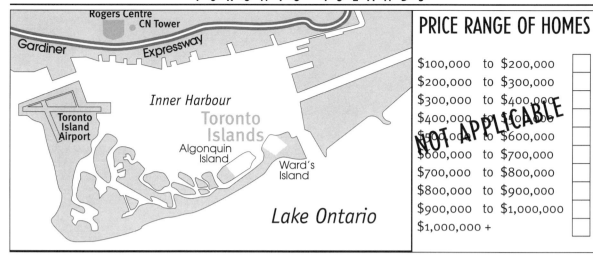

PRICE RANGE OF HOMES

$100,000	to	$200,000
$200,000	to	$300,000
$300,000	to	$400,000
$400,000	to	$500,000
$500,000	to	$600,000
$600,000	to	$700,000
$700,000	to	$800,000
$800,000	to	$900,000
$900,000	to	$1,000,000
$1,000,000 +		

NOT APPLICABLE

OVERVIEW:

The Toronto Islands communities are located on Ward's and Algonquin islands. There are a total of 262 houses and approximately 700 residents on these two Islands.

Islands residents own their own houses but lease their property from the provincial government. At the present time there is a purchasers' waiting-list of more than 500 people who hope to one day assume a lease on the Islands.

Toronto Islands is the only Toronto neighbourhood that does not allow cars. Walking and cycling are the standard modes of transportation here.

HOMES:

The Toronto Island Residential Community Trust manages the buying and selling of homes on the Islands. Islanders are permitted to hand down both houses and leases to their heirs but no profit is allowed on the sale of Island houses or on the transfer of leases.

The Islands' house values are calculated based on the cost to build less depreciation. The land leases fluctuate slightly over time but are currently at $45,000 for Ward's Island and $57,000 for Algonquin Island. Algonquin's leases are higher because the lots are bigger.

Toronto Islands' craftsman-style houses have mostly wood exteriors, which blend in well with the rustic setting of this neighbourhood. Each Island home is decorated with a variety of whimsical accents that add to the overall charm of these picture postcard houses. For more information on how to go about acquiring a home on the Toronto Islands go to the website www.torontoisland.org.

SHOPPING:

Islands residents do most of their shopping on the mainland. However, a grocery store delivers food once a week and the milkman delivers twice a week.

RECREATION:

Ward's Island has tennis courts, lawn bowling, a baseball diamond, a children's playground, a soccer field and one of the nicer beaches in Toronto. Ward's Island also has a clubhouse and snack bar. The clubhouse on Algonquin Island is winterized, and is used for a variety of community events. Islands residents enjoy spending a great deal of time on their gardens, which are among the prettiest in Toronto.

The Toronto Islands are an excellent place to go cycling, jogging and canoeing. During the winter there is cross-country skiing and skating on Lake Ontario.

SCHOOLS:

(P) Island Public Jr. & Sr. School, Hanlan's Point, (416) 393-1910

(PR) Waterfront Montessori Childrens Centre, 18 Wyandot Ave., (416) 203-1017

TRANSPORTATION:

The Toronto Island Ferries run seven days a week and operate all year round, shuffling Islands residents to and from the mainland. The ferry ride from the mainland to the Ward's Island dock takes approximately 10 minutes.

HISTORY:
Trefann Court began as a working-class neighbourhood in the mid-1800s. Its future was threatened in 1966, when Toronto city planners recommended that Trefann Court's deteriorated housing stock be demolished and the entire neighbourhood be rebuilt from scratch.

The city's plans were vigorously opposed by Trefann Court residents who were led by a young lawyer named John Sewell – who later became Mayor of Toronto. In response to Toronto city planners, Trefann Court residents created their own blueprint to save their neighbourhood. The residents' plan advocated restoring the existing housing stock wherever possible, and replacing dilapidated houses with new houses that would be in keeping with the neighbourhood. This plan was adopted by city council in 1972.

The battle over Trefann Court was historically significant in that it brought forth new urban planning ideas that advocated greater community involvement, less government interference and an enlightened interest in rehabilitating and preserving Toronto's historic neighbourhoods.

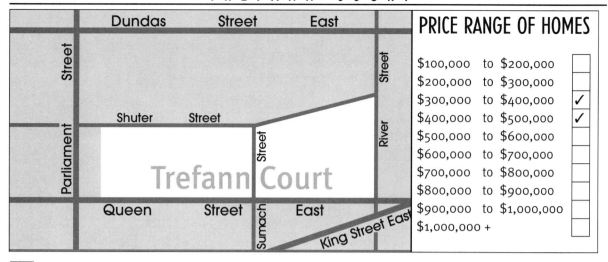

PRICE RANGE OF HOMES

$100,000 to $200,000	
$200,000 to $300,000	
$300,000 to $400,000	✓
$400,000 to $500,000	✓
$500,000 to $600,000	
$600,000 to $700,000	
$700,000 to $800,000	
$800,000 to $900,000	
$900,000 to $1,000,000	
$1,000,000 +	

OVERVIEW:

Trefann Court is a quiet little pocket of homes located in the downtown section of Toronto. This affordable Toronto neighbourhood includes a mix of both public and private housing.

Trefann Court is conveniently located near Toronto's waterfront, as well as the city's financial and entertainment districts.

HOMES:

Trefann Court's housing stock consists of Victorian houses from the late 1800s, as well as newer two- and three-storey townhouses. The newer homes blend in well with the older Victorian houses in this neighbourhood.

Some of Trefann Court's commercial buildings have recently been converted to live/work lofts. These new home projects have enhanced the residential tone of the Trefann Court neighbourhood.

SHOPPING:

Everyday shopping needs are addressed both on Queen Street West and on Parliament Street.

Trefann Court residents enjoy the luxury of being able to walk to the St. Lawrence Market, where they can choose from a vast array of meats, seafood, cheeses, fruits and vegetables.

RECREATION:

Trefann Court cycling enthusiasts are just minutes away from the Lower Don Bikeway, an off-street bike path network that provides links with the Rosedale Valley bikepath and the Martin Goodman Trail located along Toronto's waterfront. These trails are also popular with in-line skaters and joggers

The Regent South artificial ice rink at Shuter and Sumach streets operates from November through to the end of February, and offers skating lessons, shinny hockey, permit hockey and pleasure skating.

The Sumach and Shuter Parkette off Queen Street includes a children's playground and a wading pool.

SCHOOLS:

(P)   Lord Dufferin Jr. & Sr., 303 Berkeley St., (416) 393-1760

(P)   Park Jr. & Sr., 440 Shuter St., (416) 393-1620

(P)   Regent Park/Duke of York Jr., 20 Regent St., (416) 393-1730

(PH) Inglenook Alternative School, 19 Sackville St., (416) 393-0560

(PH) Jarvis Collegiate Institute, 495 Jarvis St., (416) 393-0140

(C)   St. Michael, 50 George St., (416) 393-5387

(C)   St. Paul, 80 Sackville St., (416) 393-5204

TRANSPORTATION:

The Sherbourne Street bus and Parliament Street streetcar connect to subway stations on the Bloor-Danforth subway line. The Queen Street streetcar connects to the Queen station on the Yonge-University-Spadina subway line.

For motorists travelling in and out of the city, the Don Valley Parkway and Lake Shore Boulevard are only a few minutes away.

HISTORY:
In the early 1800s, Trinity-Bellwoods was part of a tract of land belonging to Captain Samuel Smith. Smith named his 100-acre park lot "Gore Vale." Gore was in honour of Lieutenant-Governor Francis Gore, and Vale denoted the ravine that is now Trinity-Bellwoods Park.

The lower half of Gore Vale became the grounds of Trinity College, after which this neighbourhood is named. Trinity College was built in 1852 on the site where Trinity-Bellwoods Park is now situated. The entrance gates to Trinity College are still standing at the foot of Queen Street and Strachan Avenue, and serve as a lonely reminder of this once-proud institution.

The present day neighbourhood began to take shape in the 1880s. By the early 1900s, the Trinity Bellwoods neighbourhood was completely developed.

Ed. Note: The Farr house at 905 Queen West, facing Trinity Bellwoods Park, is the oldest standing house in this neighbourhood. This stately Georgian style house was built in 1847 by prominent brewer James Farr, and now provides the backdrop for the Trinity Park Lofts.

PRICE RANGE OF HOMES		
$100,000	to	$200,000	
$200,000	to	$300,000	✓
$300,000	to	$400,000	✓
$400,000	to	$500,000	✓
$500,000	to	$600,000	✓
$600,000	to	$700,000	✓
$700,000	to	$800,000	
$800,000	to	$900,000	
$900,000	to	$1,000,000	
$1,000,000 +		

OVERVIEW:
The focal point of this inner-city neighbourhood is the very picturesque Trinity-Bellwoods Park, which spans the entire length of the neighbourhood. This park features a paved walking path that is highlighted by distinguished cast iron lamp poles and a lush greenery.

In addition to Trinity-Bellwoods Park, this neighbourhood also features affordable Victorian houses, excellent shopping districts, and convenient access to major transportation routes for motorists and pedestrians.

HOMES:
Trinity-Bellwoods houses were built largely between 1880 and 1905. They are small to medium in size, and are typical of the Victorian period of architecture found in Toronto's downtown neighbourhoods.

Many of the houses in this neighbourhood either front or back onto Trinity-Bellwoods Park. Some of Trinity-Bellwoods' larger houses are located on Shaw Street, a pretty tree-lined boulevard that is twice as wide as the other streets in this neighbourhood.

Trinity-Bellwoods also contains a handful of interesting lofts that offer an alternative to those seeking a relatively maintenance-free lifestyle, with all of the modern amenities.

SHOPPING:
The Portugal Village shopping district on Dundas Street between Grace and Markham streets, caters to the large Portuguese community in the Trinity-Bellwoods neighbourhood.

Queen Street is known for its arts flavour and culinary delights. This part of Queen Street includes galleries, antique shops, bookstores, vegetarian restaurants, natural food markets, fashion and accessory stores and a variety of cafés and restaurants.

RECREATION:
Trinity-Bellwoods Park is located in the centre of this neighbourhood. The park's facilities include a children's playground, a wading pool, sports fields, a baseball diamond and four tennis courts. There is also an artificial ice rink that is used for pleasure skating, permit hockey, shinny hockey, women's and girls' ice hockey and a hockey school.

The Trinity Community Recreation Centre at 155 Crawford Street, has an indoor pool, a gymnasium, a track and a weight room.

SCHOOLS:
(P) Charles G. Fraser Jr., 79 Manning Ave., (416) 393-1830
(P) Grace Street Jr., 65 Grace St., (416) 393-1820
(P) Givens/Shaw Jr. & Sr., 180 Shaw St., (416) 393-1240
(PH) Central High School of Commerce, 570 Shaw St., (416) 393-0030
(PH) Harbord Collegiate Institute, 286 Harbord St., (416) 393-1650
(C) Senator Santo Christo, 30 Humbert St., (416) 393-5367

TRANSPORTATION:
Streetcar service on both Bathurst Street and Ossington Avenue provides regular service to the Bloor-Danforth subway.

For motorists travelling in and out of the city there is convenient access to both Lake Shore Boulevard and the Gardiner Expressway, which are each approximately a five-minute drive from this neighbourhood.

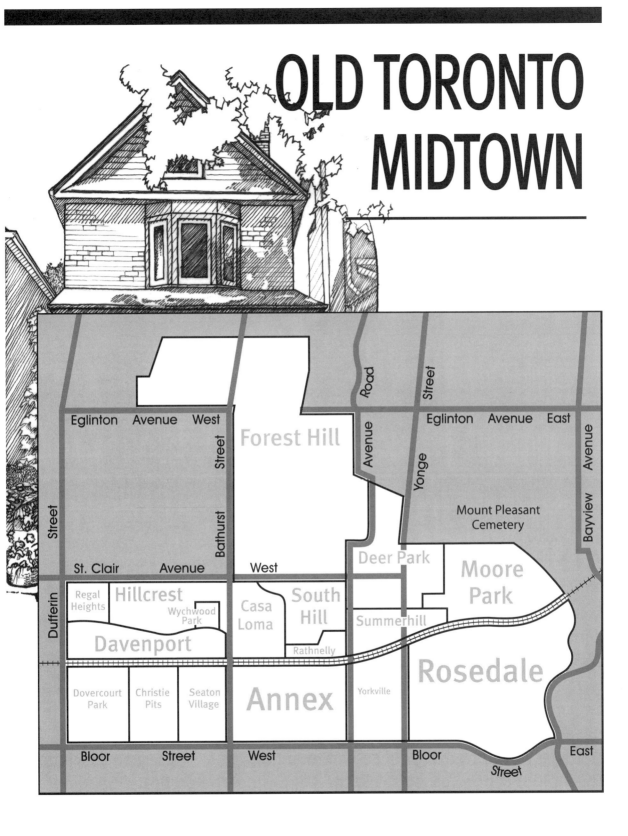

OLD TORONTO MIDTOWN

Eglinton Avenue West

Road

Street

Eglinton Avenue East

Forest Hill

Avenue

Street

Yonge

Bayview Avenue

Bathurst

Mount Pleasant
Cemetery

St. Clair Avenue West

Deer Park

Moore
Park

Street

Dufferin

Regal
Heights

Hillcrest

Casa
Loma

South
Hill

Summerhill

Wychwood
Park

Davenport

Rathnelly

Rosedale

Dovercourt
Park

Christie
Pits

Seaton
Village

Annex

Yorkville

Bloor Street West

Bloor Street

East

HISTORY: The Annex was subdivided in the 1870s and 1880s. It immediately became one of Toronto's elite neighbourhoods. The Annex's first residents included the likes of Timothy Eaton, the patriarch of Eaton's department store, and George Gooderham, president of the Gooderham and Worts Distillery.

The Annex's golden era lasted until the 1920s, when the upper classes began to migrate northward to newer, more fashionable suburbs in Forest Hill and Lawrence Park.

Those who stayed behind helped form the Annex Residents Association. This powerful lobby group saved the Annex from the proposed Spadina Expressway that would have divided the Annex in half, had it been built.

The Annex has endured and is now over 100 years old. It remains one of Toronto's premier neighbourhoods.

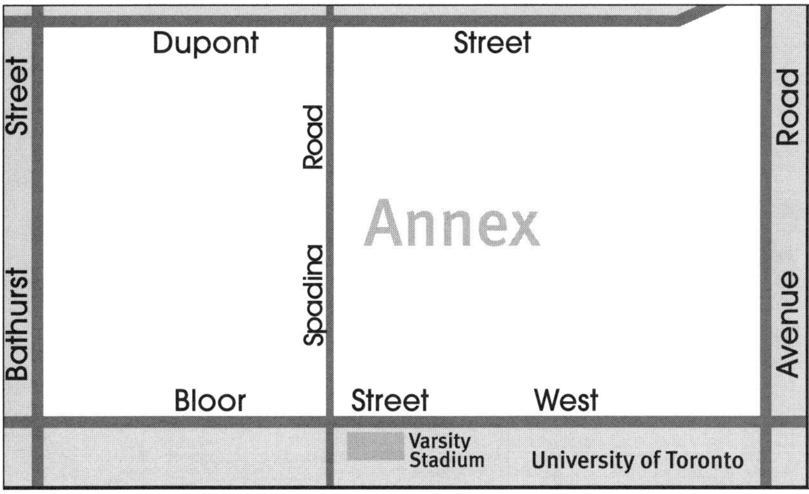

PRICE RANGE OF HOMES	
$100,000 to $200,000	
$200,000 to $300,000	
$300,000 to $400,000	✓
$400,000 to $500,000	✓
$500,000 to $600,000	✓
$600,000 to $700,000	✓
$700,000 to $800,000	✓
$800,000 to $900,000	✓
$900,000 to $1,000,000	✓
$1,000,000 +	✓

Map labels: Bathurst Street, Dupont Street, Spadina Road, Annex, Bloor Street West, Avenue Road, Varsity Stadium, University of Toronto

OVERVIEW:
The Annex is Toronto's most heterogenous community. Its residents include successful business people, prominent artists, University of Toronto students and faculty, and people from all walks of life.

This is a vibrant neighbourhood that draws its energy from the University of Toronto, as well as from the bars, restaurants and nightclubs that crowd together along Bloor Street. Many of the rooming houses and multi-unit homes in the Annex have recently been converted back to single-family houses, reflecting the return to prominence of this historic Toronto neighbourhood.

HOMES:
The Annex houses, built between 1880 and 1910, are fine examples of Victorian, Queen Anne and Richardsonian Romanesque architectural styles. Plum- and pink-coloured Credit River sandstone, rich red brick, and terra cotta clay tiles make up the exterior facades of many of these homes. The architectural detail is among the finest in the city, ranging from pyramidal roofs and turrets to recessed grand archways and wooden spindled porches.

A second wave of Annex homes dates from 1910 to 1930. These homes are less elaborate than their predecessors, but are nonetheless fine examples of English-Cottage-, Edwardian-, Georgian- and Tudor-style architecture.

SHOPPING:
The Annex's main shopping district is on Bloor Street. This stretch of stores includes a hodgepodge of clothing boutiques, bookstores, food markets, travel agencies, restaurants and outdoor cafés.

The Mirvish Village shopping district on Markham Street, south of Bloor Street, is a quaint collection of bookstores, art galleries, antique stores, and one-of-a-kind specialty stores.

RECREATION:
The Annex really comes alive at night when people from all over the city converge upon its restaurants, bars and nightclubs.

Fitness enthusiasts can get in shape at either the University of Toronto's Athletic Centre, or the recently renovated Miles Nadal Jewish Community Centre at Bloor and Spadina.

The Native Canadian Centre of Toronto is located in the Annex at 16 Spadina Road. This centre offers a variety of programs and services for Toronto's Native community as well as the general public.

The Spadina Road Public Library at 10 Spadina Road offers a wide variety of programming for neighbourhood residents.

SCHOOLS:
(P)   Huron Jr., 541 Huron St., (416) 393-1570
(P)   Jesse Ketchum Jr. & Sr., 61 Davenport Rd., (416) 393-1530
(P)   Palmerston Jr., 734 Palmerston Ave., (416) 393-9305
(P)   Central Technical School, 725 Bathurst St., (416) 393-0060
(C)   Loretto College, 391 Brunswick Ave., (416) 393-5511 or South Campus, 783 Bathurst St., (416) 393-5543
(PRI) University of Toronto School, 371 Bloor West., (416) 978-3212
(PRI) Royal St. Georges College, 120 Howland Ave., (416) 533-9481
(U)   University of Toronto, St. George Campus, (416) 978-2011

TRANSPORTATION:
The Annex is well served by public transit. There are subway stations both at Spadina and at Bathurst on the Bloor-Danforth line, and at Dupont Street on the Yonge-University-Spadina line.

Motorists are within minutes of Toronto's business and entertainment districts and are approximately 25 minutes from the commuter highways.

HISTORY:

The sightlines and majestic beauty of the Avenue Road hill have, over the years, inspired many of Toronto's wealthiest citizens to build their homes here.

The one home that stands out above all the others is Casa Loma, a real-life medieval castle. Casa Loma was built in 1911 by Sir William Henry Mill Pellatt, a prominent financier, industrialist and military man.

It took 300 men nearly three years to build Casa Loma, at a cost of $3.5 million, which was an unprecedented amount of money to pay for a home at that time. Sir Henry enjoyed his dream home for less than 10 years before mounting debts forced him to turn Casa Loma over to the City of Toronto.

In the 1920s, shortly after Sir Henry's departure from Casa Loma, the extensive grounds and greenhouses to the north of the castle were subdivided, and the current neighbourhood began.

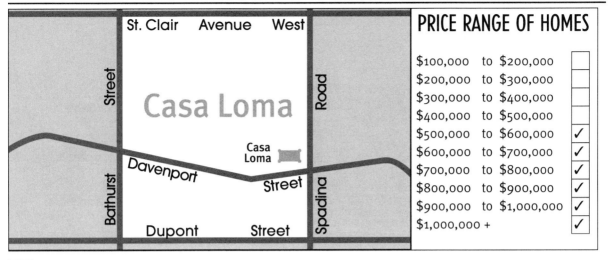

PRICE RANGE OF HOMES	
$100,000 to $200,000	
$200,000 to $300,000	
$300,000 to $400,000	
$400,000 to $500,000	
$500,000 to $600,000	✓
$600,000 to $700,000	✓
$700,000 to $800,000	✓
$800,000 to $900,000	✓
$900,000 to $1,000,000	✓
$1,000,000 +	✓

OVERVIEW:
The striking silhouette of Casa Loma provides a romantic backdrop to this posh Toronto neighbourhood.

Nestled on the brow of the Avenue Road hill, and surrounded by ravines and parkland, this residential enclave looks and feels more like an enchanted forest filled with storybook homes, than the big-city neighbourhood it really is.

HOMES:
Casa Loma's large Tudor-, Georgian-, Edwardian-, and English-cottage-style homes were built mostly between 1905 and 1940. The houses on the south side of Lyndhurst Court enjoy a spectacular view of Toronto's skyline and Lake Ontario. Many homes in this neighbourhood back onto the Nordheimer ravine, a virtual forest of mature oak and maple trees.

In addition to single-family houses, the Casa Loma neighbourhood contains a mix of duplex and triplex houses, luxury townhouses, condominiums and co-ownership apartment buildings.

SHOPPING:
The closest shopping for Casa Loma residents is the Bathurst and St. Clair shopping district. These are mostly convenience-type stores that cater to everyday household needs.

Gourmet food shops, high-end boutiques and all kinds of professional services are available on Spadina Road north of St. Clair, in the heart of Forest Hill Village.

RECREATION:
Sir Winston Churchill Park is located at the southeast corner of Spadina Road and St. Clair Avenue. This park has 10 floodlit tennis courts, a children's playground and a popular makeshift running path that skirts the perimeter of the park.

Wrapped around Sir Winston Churchill Park is the Nordheimer Ravine. This quiet oasis features a rustic wood path with many excellent picnic spots, and a large variety of trees, plants and wildlife

Wells Hill Park contains a children's playground and a wading pool. Across the street from this park is the Wells Hill Lawn Bowling Club and the Wychwood Public Library.

The local community centre operates out of Hillcrest School and includes an indoor pool and a gymnasium.

SCHOOLS:
(P) Hillcrest Jr. School, 44 Hilton Ave., (416) 393-9700
(PH) Oakwood Collegiate Institute, 991 St. Clair Ave. West, (416) 393-1780
(PH) Forest Hill Collegiate Institute, 730 Eglinton Ave. West (416) 393-1860
(PR) Bishop Strachan School, 298 Lonsdale Rd., (416) 484-4325
(PR) Upper Canada College, 200-220 Lonsdale Rd., (416) 484-4325
(PC) St. Michaels College, 1515 Bathurst St., (416) 653-3180

TRANSPORTATION:
The Casa Loma neighbourhood is well-served by public transit. There is regular bus service on Bathurst Street and streetcar service on St. Clair Avenue West. The St. Clair West subway station is a short walk from the homes in this neighbourhood.

For motorists, the main arterial roadways are Bathurst Street and St. Clair Avenue.

HISTORY: The Christie Pits neighbourhood is named after the former

Christie Sand Pits, which were a local landmark in this area until the early 1900s. Christie Street is named after William Mellis Christie, who co-founded the Christie & Brown Cookie Company in downtown Toronto in 1861.

The Christie Sand Pits were rich in sand, gravel and clay deposits – remnants of the last ice age. These deposits were excavated in the late 1800s and early 1900s and used in the construction of many of Toronto's early roadways and public buildings.

By 1909, the Christie Sand Pits were depleted and the city turned the former quarry into Willowvale Park. However, the Christie Pits name has endured and is used in reference to the park and the surrounding neighbourhood to this day.

Ed. note: On August 16, 1933, Christie Pits was the site of the worst race riot in the history of Toronto. Fighting spilled out into the streets of the neighbourhood when supporters of an east-end baseball team waved swastikas and hurled racial slurs at the supporters of a predominantly Jewish local team, during a championship game at the storied baseball diamond in Christie Pits Park.

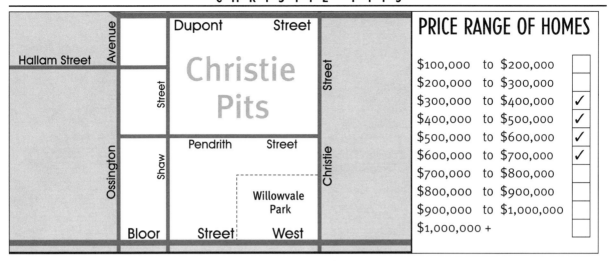

PRICE RANGE OF HOMES	
$100,000 to $200,000	
$200,000 to $300,000	
$300,000 to $400,000	✓
$400,000 to $500,000	✓
$500,000 to $600,000	✓
$600,000 to $700,000	✓
$700,000 to $800,000	
$800,000 to $900,000	
$900,000 to $1,000,000	
$1,000,000 +	

OVERVIEW:
Christie Pits is one of Toronto's most vibrant multicultural neighbourhoods. It has historically been a transitional home for immigrants upon their arrival to Toronto. However, as Christie Pits continues to mature and prosper, more people are choosing to stay here rather than move to the suburbs. This stability bodes well for the future of the Christie Pits neighbourhood.

HOMES:
Christie Pits has traditionally been a working class neighbourhood. Its houses are modest in size, and the lots are typically narrow. There is a good mix of detached and semi-detached houses, built between 1906 and the 1930s.

The streetscapes in the neighbourhood are pretty and uncluttered, thanks to rear laneways that provide off-street parking for Christie Pits homeowners.

SHOPPING:
The Christie Pits neighbourhood is served by the Bloorcourt Village Shopping District. There is a huge variety of shops and services to choose from along this route. Every June, the Bloorcourt merchants host festival days with strolling musicians, bands, clowns, and magicians performing for the many shoppers in the area.

Christie Pits residents enjoy the convenience of being located near two shopping malls: the Dufferin Mall, at Bloor and Dufferin streets, and the Galleria Mall, located at Dupont and Dufferin streets.

RECREATION:
Willowvale Park — also known as Christie Pits — is a multi-use recreational facility that includes one of Toronto's prettiest baseball diamonds. This park serves as the home field for the Toronto Maple Leafs Inter-County Baseball team. Additional facilities at Willowvale Park include the Alex Duke Memorial Pool and water slide, basketball courts, and a large children's playground. Winter activities in the park include skating, hockey and tobogganing.

SCHOOLS:
(P) Essex Jr. & Sr. School, 50 Essex St., (416) 393-0717
(P) Hawthorne Two, 50 Essex St., (416) 393-0727
(PH) Bloor Collegiate Institute, 1141 Bloor St. West, (416) 393-1420
(C) St. Raymond, 270 Barton Ave., (416) 393-5293
(C) St. Anthony, 645 Gladstone Ave., (416) 393-5210

TRANSPORTATION:
The Christie Street bus connects passengers to the St. Clair West station on the Yonge-University-Spadina subway line, and Christie station on the Bloor-Danforth line. There is also bus service on Ossington Avenue, with a connection at Ossington station.

Bloor Street provides an excellent starting point for motorists commuting within the city.

HISTORY: Davenport's history can be traced back thousands of years, to the days when Davenport Road was used as an ancient footpath by the First Nations people seeking an overland route between the Humber and Don Rivers.

Davenport Road continued to be an important passageway, for French Fur traders in the 1600s, and for the first European settlers who arrived in this area in the 1790s. One of these early settlers was Ensign John McGill, the original owner of Davenport House, after whom this neighbourhood is named.

Davenport was primarily a farming community until 1861, when the Northern Railway opened a line just south of here. The Railway attracted industry to this area, and a small village named Davenport emerged.

Davenport amalgamated with the Village of West Toronto Junction in 1889. Then in 1909, Davenport was annexed by the City of Toronto. Residential development of this neighbourhood began shortly thereafter.

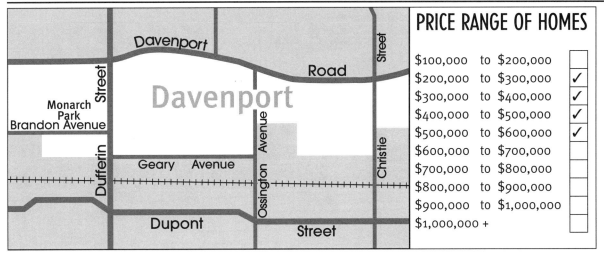

PRICE RANGE OF HOMES		
$100,000	to $200,000	
$200,000	to $300,000	✓
$300,000	to $400,000	✓
$400,000	to $500,000	✓
$500,000	to $600,000	✓
$600,000	to $700,000	
$700,000	to $800,000	
$800,000	to $900,000	
$900,000	to $1,000,000	
$1,000,000 +		

OVERVIEW:

Davenport is a quiet, centrally located neighbourhood that features modest single-family houses, convenient public transit and a close proximity to downtown Toronto.

The four blocks from Christie Street to Shaw Street, immediately south of Davenport Road, are part of the Frankel Lambert housing co-operative, which contains private homes as well as Cityhome rental units and senior citizen accommodations.

HOMES:

Davenport's rows of attached late-Victorian-style houses were built between 1900 and 1929. Some of these houses have been replaced with newer semi-detached homes.

The Frankel Lambert townhouses, built in the early 1980s, include brick and wood exteriors, front porches and private backyards. Some low- and medium-rise apartment buildings for seniors are located along Christie Street and Shaw Street.

SHOPPING:

The south side of Davenport Road contains a small selection of convenience-type stores that are within walking distance of this neighbourhood.

The shops spread out along Dupont Street include the Galleria Mall, a major grocery store, a hardware centre and a variety of restaurants.

RECREATION:

Davenport residents are located near the Wallace Emerson Community Centre at 1260 Dufferin Street. This multi-purpose facility includes an indoor pool, a gymnasium, and four floodlit tennis courts that double as an artificial ice rink in the wintertime.

Hillcrest Park, at the northwest corner of Davenport Road and Christie Street, offers a spectacular view of the city skyline and Lake Ontario. This picturesque park has four tennis courts, a wading pool and a children's playground.

Melita Park has a playground and a wading pool, while the South Park has swings, a playwall and bocce courts.

The Davenport Branch of the Toronto Public Library has programs for children and preschoolers.

SCHOOLS:

(P) McMurrich Jr. School, 115 Winona Dr., (416) 393-1770
(P) Winona Drive Sr. School, 101 Winona Dr., (416) 393-1680
(PH) Oakwood Collegiate Institute, 991 St. Clair Ave. West, (416) 393-1780
(C) St. Bruno, 402 Melita Cres., (416) 393-5376

TRANSPORTATION:

The Davenport neighbourhood is criss-crossed by a network of bus lines that run on Dufferin, Dovercourt, Ossington, Bathurst, Dupont and Davenport. These bus routes connect passengers to either the St. Clair West or Dupont subway stations.

Motorists are 10 to 15 minutes from downtown and approximately 20 minutes from Toronto's major expressways.

HISTORY: Deer Park used to be referred to by the First Nations people

as "Mushquoteh," which means a meadow or opening in the wood where deer come to feed. In 1837, the Heath family purchased 40 acres of land in Mushquoteh. Appropriately, they named their estate Deer Park.

By the 1850s the Deer Park area had grown to include a handful of country villas, a general store, a school, a cemetery, a race track, and a hotel that was located at the intersection of Yonge and St. Clair. Patrons at the Deer Park Hotel used to delight in feeding the deer that roamed on the hotel grounds.

The deer were long gone by the time Deer Park was annexed to the City of Toronto in 1908. Deer Park filled in very quickly after annexation. By the 1930s the Deer Park neighbourhood was established as one of Toronto's finest residential districts.

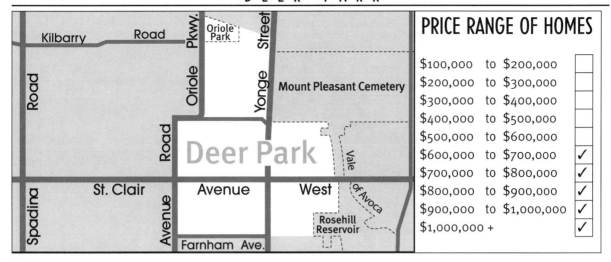

PRICE RANGE OF HOMES

$100,000 to $200,000	
$200,000 to $300,000	
$300,000 to $400,000	
$400,000 to $500,000	
$500,000 to $600,000	
$600,000 to $700,000	✓
$700,000 to $800,000	✓
$800,000 to $900,000	✓
$900,000 to $1,000,000	✓
$1,000,000 +	✓

OVERVIEW:
Deer Park is different from many upscale Toronto neighbourhoods in that its homes are not isolated on the periphery of the neighbourhood. The residential streets spill out onto either Yonge Street or St. Clair Avenue, right into the heart of one of Toronto's busiest shopping, entertainment and business districts.

Deer Park's commercial centre is juxtaposed with lush green parkland, majestic trees and the Vale of Avoca Ravine, which provide a green backdrop to the neighbourhood.

HOMES:
Deer Park has a wonderful mix of detached and semi-detached houses that encompass a variety of architectural styles. Most of the original Deer Park houses were built between 1875 and 1920. Deer Park also contains a large number of newer townhouses that blend in well with the older homes in the neighbourhood.

Deer Park has one of the largest selections of luxury condominium apartment buildings in Toronto. Most of these apartments have balconies with picturesque views of the park, the ravine or the city.

SHOPPING:
The Yonge and St. Clair shopping district is known for its many fine restaurants. The high profile retailers in this area attract shoppers from all over the city.

Most of the local staple and grocery stores are located inside the St. Clair Centre and The Towne Mall or at the Delisle Court.

RECREATION:
The Rosehill Reservoir Park, on Pleasant Boulevard, is one of Toronto's prettiest parks. Wrapped around the park is a surfaced path that's ideal for walking, jogging and cycling. The top tier of the park has a large children's playground and a wading pool. This part of the park is also decorated with a water fountain, a reflecting pool, and a waterfall.

Next to the Rosehill Reservoir Park is the David Balfour Park which includes a hiking trail through the wilderness of the Vale of Avoca Ravine.

Oriole Park is located at the northern tip of Deer Park. It has a playground, a wading pool, two tennis courts and access to the "Belt Line," a seven-kilometre path that follows the route of Toronto's old Belt Line Railway.

SCHOOLS:
(P)   Deer Park Jr. & Sr., 23 Ferndale Ave., (416 393-1550
(P)   Brown Jr., 454 Avenue Rd., (416) 393-1560
(PH)   North Toronto C.I., 70 Roehampton Ave., (416) 393-9180
(PH)   Northern Secondary, 851 Mt. Pleasant Rd., (416) 393-0270
(PR)   Bishop Strachan School, 298 Lonsdale Rd., (416) 483-4325
(PR)   Upper Canada College, 200-220 Lonsdale Rd., (416) 488-1125
(PR)   The York School, 1320 Yonge St., (416) 926-1325

TRANSPORTATION:
The St. Clair subway station is within walking distance of every home in Deer Park.

Motorists are approximately 10 minutes from downtown, and 20 minutes from Toronto's expressways and highways.

HISTORY: The Dovercourt Park neighbourhood began as the Village of Dovercourt back in the 1870s. Dovercourt's first residents were poor immigrants that came to Canada from England.

By 1884, there were a few dozen houses scattered throughout Dovercourt. These first houses were one- and two-bedroom tar and paper shacks, which would eventually earn Dovercourt the unflattering nickname "Shantytown."

Better days were just around the corner however; the City of Toronto annexed the Village of Dovercourt in 1910. Annexation brought proper city services to Dovercourt which in turn helped to stimulate the growth of this neighbourhood. Dovercourt Park was fully developed by 1923.

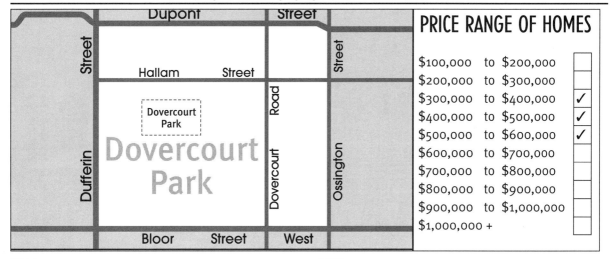

PRICE RANGE OF HOMES

$100,000	to	$200,000	
$200,000	to	$300,000	
$300,000	to	$400,000	✓
$400,000	to	$500,000	✓
$500,000	to	$600,000	✓
$600,000	to	$700,000	
$700,000	to	$800,000	
$800,000	to	$900,000	
$900,000	to	$1,000,000	
$1,000,000 +			

OVERVIEW:

The Dovercourt Park neighbourhood is conveniently located close to the centre of the city of Toronto. Its residents are mostly low- to moderate-income families from many different cultural backgrounds.

A focal point in this neighbourhood is the Dovercourt Boys and Girls Club. Their clubhouse, located at Dovercourt Park, is open year round and offers a myriad of social and recreational programs for neighbourhood children.

HOMES:

Dovercourt Park houses were built between 1900 and 1923. These houses are moderate in size, and generally well maintained. As this is a first-time-buyers area, many of the houses have been converted into two- and three-family homes in order to help offset the cost of home ownership.

Parking is limited in this neighbourhood with less than half the residential blocks being served by laneways. However, there is permit street parking available to Dovercourt residents for a nominal annual fee.

SHOPPING:

The Bloorcourt Village shopping district on Bloor Street West extends from Montrose Avenue over to Dufferin Street. Here you will find a wide variety of shops and services.

The local shopping centre is the Galleria Mall, located at the southwest corner of Dufferin and Dupont. The Galleria Mall has 45 stores, including a major department store and a good selection of smaller independent stores.

RECREATION:

The main recreational facility in this neighbourhood is Dovercourt Park. This park is six acres in size and features a children's playground, a wading pool, two tennis courts, a baseball diamond, sports fields and natural ice rinks in the winter.

Dovercourt Park is also the home of the Dovercourt Boys and Girls Club for children ages seven through 17. This club is open year round and includes a small gymnasium, a pool, a games room, an arts and crafts room, and two computer rooms.

The Bloor Gladstone branch of the Toronto Public Library offers programs for both children and adults.

SCHOOLS:

(P)   Dovercourt Jr., 228 Bartlett Ave., (416) 393-9220
(P)   Pauline Jr., 100 Pauline Ave., (416) 393-9360
(P)   Kent Sr., 980 Dufferin St., (416) 393-0400
(PH) Bloor Collegiate Institute, 1141 Bloor St. West, (416) 393-1420
(C)   St. Anthony, 645 Gladstone Ave., (416) 393-5210
(C)   St. Raymond, 270 Barton Ave., (416) 393-5293

TRANSPORTATION:

Most Dovercourt Park houses are within walking distance of either the Ossington or Dufferin subway stations on the Bloor-Danforth subway line.

Dovercourt Park's main arterial roadways are Bloor and Dufferin Streets which provide motorists with excellent access routes to all parts of the city.

HISTORY:

Forest Hill was incorporated as a village in 1923. It was named after the summer residence of John Wickson, built in 1860 at the junction of Eglinton Avenue and Old Forest Hill Road. The hill is still there, but the forest is long gone, having been replaced by apartment buildings.

Prior to its incorporation, Forest Hill had been known as "Spadina Heights." Spadina is a derivative of the First Nations word "Ishapadenah," which means a hill or sudden rise in land. The boundaries of the present-day neighbourhood are shaped from the old Spadina Heights school district.

Lower Forest Hill, south of Eglinton, was completely developed by the 1930s. Upper Forest Hill was slower to develop due to the fact it had previously been occupied by the old Belt Line railway, and then by industry.

In 1967, Forest Hill Village joined Swansea Village as one of the last two independent villages to be annexed by the City of Toronto.

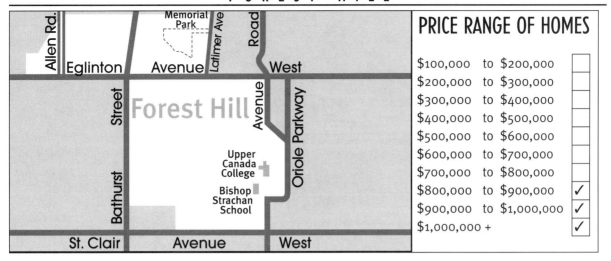

PRICE RANGE OF HOMES

$100,000	to	$200,000	
$200,000	to	$300,000	
$300,000	to	$400,000	
$400,000	to	$500,000	
$500,000	to	$600,000	
$600,000	to	$700,000	
$700,000	to	$800,000	
$800,000	to	$900,000	✓
$900,000	to	$1,000,000	✓
$1,000,000 +			✓

OVERVIEW:

The Forest Hill neighbourhood is one of Toronto's most prestigious districts. The mansions in Lower Forest Hill are rivaled only by those found in Rosedale. Forest Hill's schools are among the best in the country. They include two of Canada's most revered private schools: Upper Canada College for boys, and Bishop Strachan School for girls.

Forest Hill is one of Toronto's prettier districts. Its topography is very diverse with gently sloping hills, winding roads and numerous little parkettes, all adding charm to the neighbourhood.

HOMES:

Forest Hill's old building codes and bylaws, dating back to the 1920s and 1930s, required that all Forest Hill houses be designed by an architect, and that a tree be planted at the front of each property. This foresight by Village planners has left a legacy of beauty in the brick and stone mansions, and majestic trees that grace the streets of Lower Forest Hill.

The Upper Village houses were built mostly in the 1940s and 1950s. These houses are more modest than their Lower Village counterparts, however the lot sizes are comparable between the two districts.

Forest Hill contains a fair number of luxury condominium apartment buildings, located west of Spadina on Lonsdale Road and on Heath Street West. There are also a handful of quaint co-ownership apartment buildings located on Eglinton Avenue West that offer surprisingly affordable units and an entry into this exclusive neighbourhood.

SHOPPING:

The Forest Hill Village shopping district is centred around the intersection of Spadina Road and Lonsdale Road. The ambience of this private enclave of stores is that of a small town rather than a big city. The Village's boutiques and shops cater to the specific needs of Forest Hill's affluent residents.

The Eglinton West Village shopping district has a large variety of stores to suit every taste and budget. This street also contains many fine restaurants and food stores.

RECREATION:

The Belt Line fitness and nature trail follows the route of the former Belt Line railway, which was Toronto's first commuter train. This 14.5-kilometre track passes through Forest Hill on its way down to the Don Valley. The Belt Line path is enjoyed by both nature and fitness enthusiasts.

Forest Hill's Public Library has a myriad of programs for adults, children and preschoolers.

SCHOOLS:

(P) Forest Hill Jr. & Sr., 78 Dunloe Rd., (416) 393-9335
(P) Alternative Primary Jr., 1100 Spadina Rd., (416) 393-9199
(P) North Preparatory Jr., 1100 Spadina Rd., (416) 393-9230
(P) West Preparatory Jr., 70 Ridge Hill Dr., (416) 393-1633
(C) Holy Rosary, 308 Tweedmuir Ave., (416)393-5225
(PH) Forest Hill Collegiate Institute, 730 Eglinton Ave. W., (416) 393-1860
(PR) Bishop Strachan School, 298 Lonsdale Rd., (416) 483-4325
(PR) Upper Canada College, Upper School, 200 Lonsdale Rd., (416) 488-1125 & Upper Canada College, Prep School, 220 Lonsdale Rd., (416) 488-1125
(PC) St. Michaels College, 1515 Bathurst St., (416) 653-3180

TRANSPORTATION:

Forest Hill is conveniently located within walking distance of numerous bus routes that connect passengers to Toronto's rapid transit subway lines

The Allen Expressway serves as a conduit for motorists commuting into and out of the city.

HISTORY:
Hillcrest was first settled in the 1840's by Robert John Turner, a reformer from England. The Turner house, named "Bracondale," stood where Hillcrest Park is today.

By 1884, a small village grew up on the edge of the Turner estate, at the intersection of Christie and Davenport. This settlement became known as Bracondale Village. The Village consisted mostly of farmers and a few stores. Its first postmaster was Frank Turner, the son of Robert Turner.

In 1909, Bracondale Village was annexed by the City of Toronto. Shortly thereafter, Frank Turner's heirs subdivided the Bracondale estate and turned it into an exclusive subdivision named Bracondale Hill Park.

The Turner family retained ownership of the Bracondale house until 1937, when it was sold to the city and demolished in order to make room for Hillcrest Park.

Ed. note: Hillcrest residents have shown great pride in their Community History Project, which has raised funds to preserve and restore The Tollkeeper's Cottage in Davenport Park, at the northwest corner of Davenport and Bathurst. This cottage-style dwelling, circa 1835, is the earliest known toll-keepers' cottage in Canada. To learn more about this exciting historical initiative please visit the website www.tollkeeperscottage.ca.

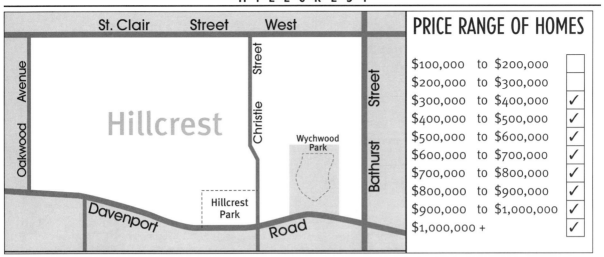

PRICE RANGE OF HOMES

$100,000 to $200,000	
$200,000 to $300,000	
$300,000 to $400,000	✓
$400,000 to $500,000	✓
$500,000 to $600,000	✓
$600,000 to $700,000	✓
$700,000 to $800,000	✓
$800,000 to $900,000	✓
$900,000 to $1,000,000	✓
$1,000,000 +	✓

OVERVIEW:
Hillcrest is a mature, established neighbourhood with quiet tree-lined streets and whimsical-looking houses that make you feel as if you are far away from the bright lights of the big city.

The distinguishing feature of Hillcrest is its location perched on the ridge of the Davenport escarpment. The rich topography of this area has resulted in some of the prettier streets in Toronto.

HOMES:
The houses at the north end of Hillcrest were built in the late 1800s and early 1900s. These houses are loaded with turn-of-the-century charm and character, and are a wonderful mix of shapes and sizes.

There is also a pocket of larger, detached homes, built between 1910 and 1930, near Hillcrest Park. Some of these dignified residences were built with stone from the original Union Station, which was torn down after the First World War.

SHOPPING:
The Hillcrest shopping district is located on St. Clair Avenue West. These stores are mostly independent retailers that cater to the day-to-day needs of the local community. There is also an eclectic mix of culturally diverse restaurants along this route.

The small convenience-type stores on Davenport Road and Vaughan Road also serve the Hillcrest community. These are mostly independent owner-operated stores that provide personalized and friendly service to the neighbourhood residents.

RECREATION:
In yet another example of great community planning and pride, Hillcrest residents have been donating their time, money and resources to the development of the Wychwood Barns Art Park, which will see the conversion of the historic Toronto Transit Commission repair barns on Christie Street south of St. Clair. This multifaceted community meeting place will include studio space and live/work space for artists, festivals, a greenhouse and a community bake-oven. The park's greenspace will include a natural ice rink, playing fields, a stage, chess tables, beach volleyball, a water play area and children's swings and climbers. This massive community park is scheduled for completion in late 2007.

The Hillcrest Community Centre is located in the Hillcrest Public School on Bathurst Street. This facility includes an indoor pool and a gymnasium. Just north of the Hillcrest Community Centre is the Wychwood Public Library, which offers year-round programs for the neighbourhood children.

Hillcrest Park, perched atop the Davenport escarpment at the south perimeter of this neighbourhood, offers a spectacular view of the city skyline and Lake Ontario. This park has a wading pool, a children's playground and four tennis courts.

SCHOOLS:
(P)   McMurrich Jr., 115 Winona Dr., (416) 393-1770
(P)   Winona Drive. Sr., 101 Winona Dr., (416) 393-1680
(P)   Hillcrest Jr., 44 Hilton Ave., (416) 393-9770
(PH) Oakwood Collegiate Institute, 991 St. Clair Ave. West, (416) 393-1780
(C)   St. Alphonsus, 60 Atlas Ave., (416) 393-5326
(C)   St. Clare, 124 Northcliffe Blvd, (416) 393-5214

TRANSPORTATION:
Hillcrest is well served by public transit. The streetcar runs along St. Clair Avenue West, while regular bus service runs along Oakwood Avenue and Bathurst Street. Davenport Road also has a limited bus service.

Motorists are just minutes from downtown. It is approximately a 15-minute drive from this neighbourhood to the Allen Expressway, which connects commuters to Toronto's major highways.

HISTORY:

Moore Park was subdivided in 1889 as an exclusive Toronto suburb for the very wealthy. The developer was a gentleman by the name of John Thomas Moore who resided in a house named Avoca Villa, which was situated on the southeast corner of Inglewood Drive and Rose Park Drive. Avoca Villa was described as a stone house with beautiful gardens.

Moore felt certain he could attract many homebuyers to his new subdivision on the outskirts of the city if he could only provide commuter service to Toronto. Sensing an opportunity he spearheaded the building of the Belt Line Railway, which would become Toronto's first commuter train. Moore personally oversaw the construction of the Belt Line's showpiece station, which was situated in the Moore Park ravine. This whimsical train station had four distinctive turrets and was built in the Shingle style of architecture that was fashionable in the United States at the time.

In the early 1890s a poor economy and competition from the Toronto Street Railway led to the demise of the Belt Line Railway, only a few short years after it had begun. The Belt Line train tracks were eventually removed and the Moore Park train station demolished.

John Thomas Moore did not live to see his dream for Moore Park become a reality, however as Moore predicted, Toronto homebuyers have indeed come to cherish this sylvan setting. By the 1930s Moore Park was completely developed and has since earned a reputation as one of Toronto's finest neighbourhoods.

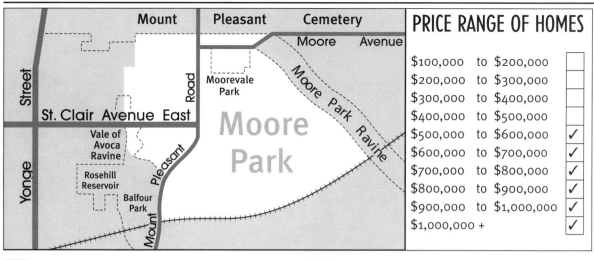

PRICE RANGE OF HOMES

$100,000	to	$200,000	
$200,000	to	$300,000	
$300,000	to	$400,000	
$400,000	to	$500,000	
$500,000	to	$600,000	✓
$600,000	to	$700,000	✓
$700,000	to	$800,000	✓
$800,000	to	$900,000	✓
$900,000	to	$1,000,000	✓
$1,000,000 +			✓

OVERVIEW:
Moore Park is surrounded on all sides by natural barriers. To the north is the Mount Pleasant Cemetery, to the south is the Park Drive Ravine and the railway tracks, to the east is the Moore Park Ravine and to the west is the Vale of Avoca Ravine.

With so much nature at its doorstep, it is not surprising that Moore Park is one of Toronto's most sought-after neighbourhoods.

HOMES:
Moore Park includes primarily English-Cottage-, Georgian-, and Tudor-style houses built between 1908 and 1930. Moore Park lots are generally quite large, and many of the houses back on to one of the ravines that skirt this neighbourhood.

Moore Park also contains many newer town-houses as well as a fair number of duplex and multiplex homes. For such a high-end neighbour-hood it is somewhat surprising that many of the houses have shared, rather than private, driveways. However, the streets are so quiet and uncluttered that parking is not a problem.

SHOPPING:
Moore Park residents do most of their shopping at either the Yonge and St. Clair or the Mount Pleasant and Davisville shopping districts. Both these areas are well known for their gourmet food shops and fine dining.

Moore Park residents who live in the more secluded southeast pocket of the neighbourhood can walk across a railway overpass to the small collection of neighbourhood stores on Summerhill Avenue.

RECREATION:
Nature and fitness enthusiasts will enjoy the Moore Park Ravine foot path, an eight-kilometre trail that passes through the Rosedale Ravine, the Mt. Pleasant cemetery and the old Don Valley brickworks.

Moorevale Park, one block east of Mount Pleasant Road, has five tennis courts, a baseball diamond and a wading pool.

For moviegoers Moore Park is close to a number of theatres on Yonge Street, Eglinton Avenue and Mount Pleasant Road.

SCHOOLS:
(P)   Deer Park Jr. & Sr., 23 Ferndale Ave., (416) 393-1550
(P)   Whitney Jr, 119 Rosedale Heights Dr., (416) 393-9380
(C)   Our Lady of Perpetual Help, 1-1/2 Garfield Ave., (416) 393-5239
(PH) North Toronto Collegiate Institute, 70 Roehampton Ave., (416) 393-9180
(PH) Northern Secondary, 851 Mount Pleasant Rd., (416) 393-0270

TRANSPORTATION:
Moore Park has bus service on St. Clair Avenue, Mount Pleasant Road and Moore Avenue. The Yonge and St. Clair subway station is within walking distance of many Moore Park houses.

Motorists have quick access via Moore Avenue to both the Bayview Extension and the Don Valley Parkway.

HISTORY:

Rathnelly's history revolves around the former Rathnelly house built in 1830 by Senator William McMaster. McMaster's home was named after his birth place in Rathnelly, Ireland. The McMaster estate remained intact until the 1880s, when it was sold to developers. The present day neighbourhood began shortly thereafter.

The Rathnelly neighbourhood made headlines in 1967, while celebrating Canada's 100th birthday. During the celebrations Rathnelly residents playfully declared themselves as an independent republic of Canada. To mark their independence, the "Republic of Rathnelly" elected a queen, organized a parade, formed an "air farce" of 1,000 helium balloons, and issued Republic of Rathnelly passports to everyone in the neighbourhood.

Forty years later the "Republic of Rathnelly" is still going strong.

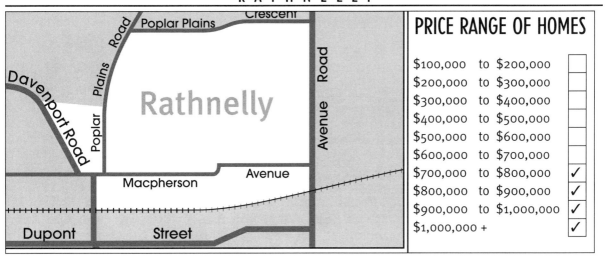

PRICE RANGE OF HOMES

$100,000 to $200,000		
$200,000 to $300,000		
$300,000 to $400,000		
$400,000 to $500,000		
$500,000 to $600,000		
$600,000 to $700,000		
$700,000 to $800,000	✓
$800,000 to $900,000	✓
$900,000 to $1,000,000	✓
$1,000,000 +	✓

OVERVIEW:

Rathnelly is a picturesque little enclave of homes, situated at the bottom of the Avenue Road Hill. It is home to a large number of artists, academics, writers and media people.

Rathnelly residents organize a one-of-a-kind street festival, held either every year or "when the mood strikes." The highlight of the festival is a much-anticipated pancake breakfast that Rathnelly residents literally flip over.

HOMES:

Rathnelly's impressive Victorian homes are shaded by a canopy of silver maple trees. These solid brick detached and semi-detached houses were built between 1880 and 1910.

SHOPPING:

Rathnelly residents are within walking distance of a small pocket of exclusive shops and restaurants, clustered around the southwest corner of Davenport and Avenue roads.

South of Davenport Road east of Avenue Road is the Bloor-Yorkville shopping district. This prestigious shopping mecca features an impressive array of international retailers, antique shops, art galleries, and a myriad of coffee shops, cafés and restaurants.

RECREATION:

The Brown Community Centre and School on Avenue Road, south of St. Clair Avenue, features an indoor pool, a gymnasium, a baseball diamond and two tennis courts.

Access to the Nordheimer Ravine and Nature Trail is available off Boulton Drive. This ravine trail cuts through Sir Winston Churchill Park, which has 10 floodlit tennis courts, a wading pool and a children's playground.

SCHOOLS:

(P)   Brown Jr., 454 Avenue Rd., (416) 393-1560
(P)   Cottingham Jr., 85 Birch Ave., (416) 393-1895
(P)   Jesse Ketchum Jr. & Sr., 61 Davenport Rd., (416) 393-1530
(PH) Forest Hill Collegiate Institute, 730 Eglinton Ave. W., (416) 393-1860
(PH) North Toronto Collegiate Institute, 70 Roehampton Ave., (416) 393-9180
(PC) De La Salle College, 131 Farnham Ave., (416) 969-8771

TRANSPORTATION:

The Avenue Road bus has rush-hour service to and from downtown. The Davenport Road bus connects passengers to the Bay Street station on the Bloor-Danforth subway line. The St. Clair streetcar takes passengers to the St. Clair subway station on the Yonge-University-Spadina subway line.

Motorists are minutes from Toronto's business and entertainment districts. It is approximately 20 minutes south to Lake Shore Boulevard, and the same distance north to Highway 401.

HISTORY:
Regal Heights was settled in 1818, by an Irishman from Tipperary County by the name of Bartholomew Bull. Bull was responsible for building Davenport Road, which was originally known as Bull's Road.

Bull's second house, built in 1830, was called Springmount. This was the first brick building in York Township, and as such was considered quite a novelty in its early years. Springmount was descriptively named after a water course that once meandered down the Davenport escarpment in front of the Bulls' homestead.

Springmount remained in the possession of the Bull family until the estate was sold to developers in 1910. The Springmount name has been perpetuated in Springmount Avenue, which is one of the signature streets in the Regal Heights neighbourhood.

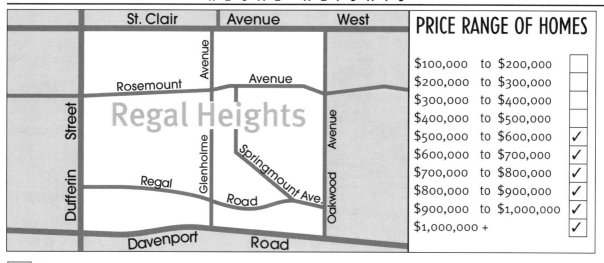

PRICE RANGE OF HOMES

$100,000	to $200,000	
$200,000	to $300,000	
$300,000	to $400,000	
$400,000	to $500,000	
$500,000	to $600,000	✓
$600,000	to $700,000	✓
$700,000	to $800,000	✓
$800,000	to $900,000	✓
$900,000	to $1,000,000	✓
$1,000,000 +		✓

OVERVIEW:

The Regal Heights neighbourhood is situated on the western crest of the Davenport escarpment. This neighbourhood has many distinguishing characteristics including very large turn-of-the-century houses, winding tree-lined streets, and an elevation atop the Davenport escarpment that offers many home owners unparalleled views of the Toronto skyline.

HOMES:

Regal Heights's detached and semi-detached three-storey houses were built between 1912 and 1923. These homes feature many traditional charms including oak trim, beamed ceilings, stained and leaded glass windows, hardwood floors, and fireplaces.

Some of the larger Regal Heights homes have been converted into multiplex dwellings.

SHOPPING:

Regal Heights is located at the edge of the "Corso Italia" shopping district along St. Clair Avenue West. This area has a lively Italian atmosphere that features some of the city's best Italian restaurants and cafés. Corso Italia is also known for its fashion and accessory stores.

RECREATION:

Hillcrest Park, located at the northwest corner of Davenport Road and Christie Street, features four floodlit tennis courts, a children's playground and a wading pool. This park also has a spectacular view of the Toronto skyline and Lake Ontario.

Earlscourt Park and Recreation Centre, located at St. Clair Avenue West and Caledonia Park Road, is one of Toronto's largest multi-use recreational facilities. This recreation centre includes a large gymnasium, an outdoor pool, soccer fields, tennis courts and an artificial ice-skating rink.

The Dufferin/St. Clair Public Library contains the largest collection of Italian books in the city's public library system. It also offers a variety of programming for children and preschoolers.

SCHOOLS:

(P) Regal Rd., Jr., 95 Regal Rd, (416) 393-1390
(P) Winona Dr. Sr., 101 Winona Dr., (416) 393-1680
(PH) Oakwood Collegiate Institute, 991 St. Clair Ave. W., (416) 393-1780
(C) Richard W. Scott, 151 Rosemount Ave., (416) 393-5317
(C) St. Mary of the Angels, 1477 Dufferin St., (416) 393-5228

TRANSPORTATION:

The Regal Heights neighbourhood is well served by public transit. The St. Clair streetcar is within walking distance of every home, and additional bus service is available on Oakwood Avenue, Dupont Street, and Bathurst Street.

Motorists are approximately 10 minutes from downtown Toronto and from the Allen Expressway, which links commuters to Toronto's major highways.

HISTORY: Rosedale began when Sherrif William Botsford Jarvis and

his wife Mary settled on a homestead here in the 1820s. It was Mary Jarvis who came up with the Rosedale name, as a tribute to the profusion of wild roses that graced the hillsides of the Jarvis estate.

Mary's frequent walks and horseback rides through Rosedale blazed a trail for the meandering and winding streets that are today a Rosedale trademark. The Jarvis family sold the Rosedale homestead in 1864, which led to the subdivision and development of South Rosedale.

North Rosedale's development began in 1909 when a bridge was built over the Park Drive ravine. Prior to its residential development North Rosedale had been the original home of St. Andrews College and the Rosedale Golf Club. It was also the site of the former lacrosse grounds, where the Canadian Football League's first Grey Cup game was played.

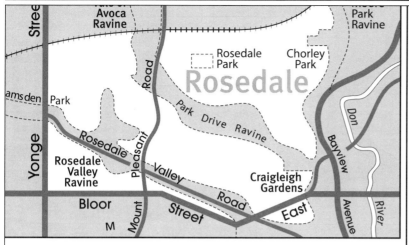

PRICE RANGE OF HOMES	
$100,000 to $200,000	
$200,000 to $300,000	
$300,000 to $400,000	
$400,000 to $500,000	
$500,000 to $600,000	
$600,000 to $700,000	
$700,000 to $800,000	
$800,000 to $900,000	✓
$900,000 to $1,000,000	✓
$1,000,000 +	✓

OVERVIEW:
For over 100 years, Rosedale has held the distinction of being Toronto's most fashionable address. Many of Toronto's wealthiest and most prominent citizens reside in the Rosedale neighbourhood.

Rosedale is unique in that it is surrounded by beautiful ravines and parkland that make you feel as if you are far away from the city, when in reality Rosedale is just a few minutes from Toronto's major business, entertainment, and shopping districts.

HOMES:
Rosedale's Victorian-, Georgian-, Tudor-, and Edwardian-style mansions were built between 1860 and 1930. Many Rosedale homes are listed on the Toronto Historical Board's Inventory of Heritage Properties.

South Rosedale also contains a number of condominium, co-operative and co-ownership apartment buildings. These apartments are surprisingly affordable and provide a good entry into the neighbourhood.

SHOPPING:
Rosedale residents living west of Mount Pleasant Road are within walking distance of the upscale shops and restaurants located on Yonge Street, in the Summerhill area.

North Rosedale residents, east of Mt. Pleasant, can obtain all of their household needs within a small commercial block on Summerhill Avenue, at the very north end of Rosedale.

RECREATION:
Rosedale is traversed by a network of ancient ravines, including the Vale of Avoca, Moore Park, Park Drive and Rosedale Valley ravines. The beautiful trails in these ravines are enjoyed by nature and fitness enthusiasts alike. Access points to Rosedale's ravine trails are located at designated spots throughout the neighbourhood.

Rosedale Park, located off Schofield Avenue, has eight tennis courts, a sports field, an artificial ice rink and a wading pool. Ramsden Park, off Yonge Street, features four tennis courts, an artificial ice rink and a wading pool.

Mooredale House, at 146 Crescent Road, is a community centre run by the Rosedale and Moore Park resident associations. There is a small annual fee to join Mooredale, which offers sports, fitness, arts, and music programs for adults and children.

SCHOOLS:
(P) Rosedale Jr., 22 South Dr., (416) 393-1330
(P) Whitney Jr., 119 Rosedale Heights Dr., (416) 393-9380
(P) Jesse Ketchum Jr. & Sr., 61 Davenport Rd., (416) 393-5130
(PH) Rosedale Heights Secondary School, 711 Bloor St. E., (416) 393-1580
(PH) Jarvis C. I., 495 Jarvis St., (416) 393-0150
(PR) Branksome Hall, 10 Elm Ave., (416) 920-9741
(PR) Bishop Strachan School, 298 Lonsdale Rd., (416) 483-4325
(PR) Upper Canada College, 200-220 Lonsdale Rd., (416) 488-1125
(PR) The York School, 1320 Yonge St., (416) 483-0541

TRANSPORTATION:
Rosedale buses run on South Drive, Crescent and Glen roads, as well as Summerhill, Maclennan, Highland and Elm avenues. These buses connect with the Rosedale station on the Yonge-University-Spadina subway line or the Sherbourne station on the Bloor-Danforth subway line.

Motorists are just minutes away from the Don Valley Parkway which links commuters to Toronto's major highways.

HISTORY:
Seaton Village was originally settled by Colonel David Shank and Captain Samuel Smith. Both men were loyalists who served under John Graves Simcoe in the Queens Rangers. In the early 1800s the Shank and Smith farm lots were acquired by George Crookshank.

The Crookshank estate began at the foot of Bathurst Street where it overlooked the lake. A laneway from the Crookshank house ran north to his country farm, where Seaton Village is today. The Crookshank laneway is now part of Bathurst Street.

Seaton Village is named after Lord Seaton, a former Lieutenant Governor of Canada. The Village was laid out on the old Crookshank farm in the 1850s. However, residential development of the present-day neighbourhood did not commence until around 1888, when Seaton Village was annexed by the City of Toronto.

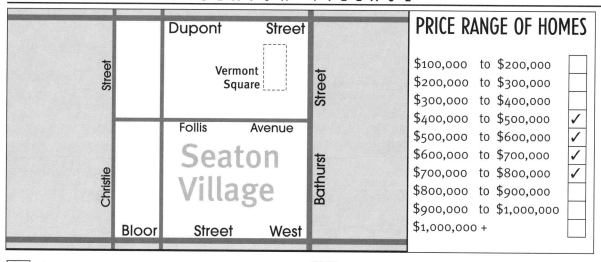

PRICE RANGE OF HOMES	
$100,000 to $200,000	
$200,000 to $300,000	
$300,000 to $400,000	
$400,000 to $500,000	✓
$500,000 to $600,000	✓
$600,000 to $700,000	✓
$700,000 to $800,000	✓
$800,000 to $900,000	
$900,000 to $1,000,000	
$1,000,000 +	

OVERVIEW:
Seaton Village is a centrally located family-oriented neighbourhood. Remarkably, this neighbourhood has managed to maintain the feel of a small town village, even though it is situated in a busy part of the city.

The focal point of this neighbourhood is Vermont Square. This city park is the home of the St. Alban's Boys and Girls Club, a community agency that offers children and families a variety of social and recreational programs.

HOMES:
Seaton Village's housing stock consists mostly of semi-detached Victorian-style houses, built in the 1890s and early 1900s. These whimsical houses are shaded by a canopy of storybook silver maple trees that are even older than the neighbourhood itself.

The streets are generally devoid of cars as most houses have parking off laneways at the rear of the properties.

SHOPPING:
Bloor Street from Bathurst Street west to Christie Street is the home of Toronto's Koreatown retail corridor. This vibrant shopping area is highlighted by a number of Korean restaurants, Karaoke bars, and Korean food and gift shops. The Bloor Street shopping area east of Bathurst Street is brimming with trendy restaurants, cafés and nightclubs that attract students from the nearby University of Toronto, as well as a diverse mix of people from all over the city.

The Bathurst Street shopping area has more of a quieter, residential tone than Bloor Street. It includes small cafés, and professional offices and stores that are geared towards the local homeowners. The Dupont and Christie intersection is anchored by a large national grocery store chain that has just recently moved into the neighbourhood.

RECREATION:
Vermont Square is located right in the centre of the Seaton Village neighbourhood. This lush city park is lined with trees, and includes a children's playground and a wading pool. This park is also home to the St. Albans Boys and Girls Club which has a myriad of programs for families and children including preschool programs, a summer camp, a games room, a computer room, a weight room, a gymnasium and much more.

Christie Pits Park, located at the corner of Bloor and Christie Streets, is one of Toronto's busiest parks. Its facilities include baseball diamonds, an artificial ice rink, a children's playground, an outdoor pool and a wading pool.

SCHOOLS:
(P) Palmerston Jr. School, 734 Palmerston Ave., (416) 393-9305
(P) Delta Sr. School, 301 Montrose Ave., (416) 393-9730
(PH) Bloor Collegiate Institute, 1141 Bloor St. W., (416) 393-1420
(PH) Subway Academy Two, 304 Brunswick Ave., (416) 393-1445
(C) Loretto College, 391 Brunswick Ave., (416) 393-5511

TRANSPORTATION:
Seaton Village is well served by public transit. Most homes are within walking distance of the Bathurst or Christie subway stations on the Bloor-Danforth subway line, or the Dupont station on the Yonge-University-Spadina subway line. There is also bus service on Christie and Dupont Streets and streetcar service on Bathurst Street.

HISTORY: The South Hill neighbourhood is defined by the Avenue Road Hill. This historic land formation was the former shoreline of ancient Lake Iroquois whose chilly waters receded into present day Lake Ontario some 12,000 years ago, at the end of the last ice age.

The escarpment that Lake Iroquois left behind was covered by a dense forest interrupted only by the ponds, creeks and waterfalls that graced the Avenue Road Hill up until the early 1900s.

South Hill's natural beauty made it an instant favourite with wealthy Toronto landowners. In the mid- to late 1800s, South Hill was dotted with mansions that were unsurpassed in variety and scope anywhere else in Toronto. Oaklands, the gingerbread mansion overlooking Avenue Road, Spadina House at 285 Spadina Road, and Casa Loma, the 98-room dream home of Sir Henry William Pellatt, still endure from this bygone era.

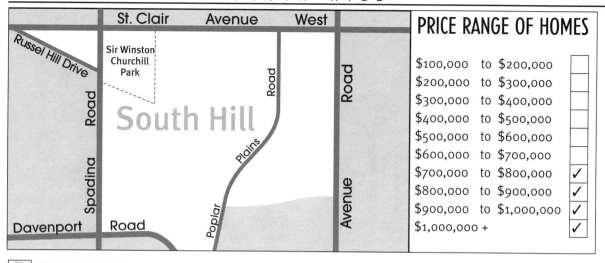

PRICE RANGE OF HOMES

$100,000 to $200,000	
$200,000 to $300,000	
$300,000 to $400,000	
$400,000 to $500,000	
$500,000 to $600,000	
$600,000 to $700,000	
$700,000 to $800,000	✓
$800,000 to $900,000	✓
$900,000 to $1,000,000	✓
$1,000,000 +	✓

OVERVIEW:

South Hill may not have the same name recognition as Rosedale or Forest Hill, but it is every bit as glamorous and exclusive as these other elite Toronto neighbourhoods.

South Hill is centrally located near Toronto's business and entertainment districts, and is also conveniently located near many of Toronto's highly regarded public, private and Catholic schools.

HOMES:

South Hill contains some of the largest houses in Toronto. Many of the homes on the crest of the Avenue Road hill command spectacular views of downtown Toronto, and even offer a distant glimpse of Lake Ontario.

The first generation of South Hill homes were built between 1890 and 1920. South Hill also contains a number of townhouses that have been built within the last 20 years.

In addition to houses South Hill also possesses luxury rental apartment buildings on both sides of Avenue Road, on the crest of the hill, overlooking the city to the south.

SHOPPING:

Like many of Toronto's high end neighbourhoods, shopping is kept very much on the periphery of this neighbourhood. However, South Hill residents are only minutes by car or public transit from the upscale shopping districts in Forest Hill Village, Yonge and St. Clair, and Yorkville.

RECREATION:

South Hill is bordered on the west side by the Nordheimer ravine, a popular destination point for fitness and nature enthusiasts.

The ravine is located next to Sir Winston Churchill Park which has 10 tennis courts, a children's playground, a wading pool and a jogging path.

Brown School and Community Centre has an indoor pool and a gymnasium. There are two tennis courts behind the community centre.

SCHOOLS:

(P) Brown Jr., 454 Avenue Rd., (416) 393-1560
(P) Forest Hill Jr. & Sr., 78 Dunloe Rd., (416) 393-9335
(PH) Forest Hill Collegiate Institute, 730 Eglinton Ave. W., (416) 393-1860
(PH) North Toronto Collegiate Institute, 70 Roehampton Ave., 393-9180
(PR) Upper Canada College, Upper School: 200 Lonsdale Rd., (416) 488-1125; Prep School: 220 Lonsdale Rd, (416) 488-1125
(PR) Bishop Strachan School, 298 Lonsdale Rd, (416) 483-4325
(PR) The Mabin School, 50 Poplar Plains Road, (416) 964-9594
(PC) De La Salle College, 131 Farnham, Ave., (416) 969-8771

TRANSPORTATION:

The South Hill neighbourhood is well served by public transportation. The Avenue Road bus connects passengers to the Museum subway station on the Bloor-Danforth subway line and the St. Clair streetcar connects passengers to stations on the Yonge-University-Spadina subway line.

South Hill motorists enjoy convenient access to major roadways including Yonge Street, Avenue Road and Bathurst Street. These roads provide commuters with quick and easy access both into and out of the city.

HISTORY:
The Summerhill neighbourhood is named after Summer Hill House, a magnificent Regency cottage built in 1842 by transportation baron Charles Thompson. Summer Hill stood on the crest of the hill where the houses on Summerhill Gardens are located today.

Thompson's 200-acre Summer Hill estate stretched from the present-day Yonge Street to Mt. Pleasant Road. On this site Thompson established the Summer Hill Spring Park and Pleasure Grounds. This amusement park featured rides, games, swimming and a popular dance pavilion that was located inside the Summer Hill house. Thompson's heirs subdivided Summer Hill in the 1860s.

From the 1880s onward Summerhill's development revolved around the railway. The first residents of this neighbourhood worked at the North Toronto Railway station which was established on Yonge Street near Summerhill in the 1880s. This station is distinguished by its grand clock tower and now serves as the posh neighbourhood liquor store.

In 1916 the Canadian Pacific Railway made Summerhill its main station in Toronto, bringing industry and prosperity to the area. However, the boom times were short lived. In 1927 downtown Union Station would replace Summerhill as the railway's hub station. Summerhill would return to prominence once again — thanks to a railway — when the Toronto Transit Commission opened the Summerhill subway station in 1965.

Ed. Note: The former Summer Hill Coach House, circa 1865, is still standing today, at the rear of 36 Summerhill Gardens. This house, with its distinctive slate roof, can be seen from the south end of the Rosehill Reservoir.

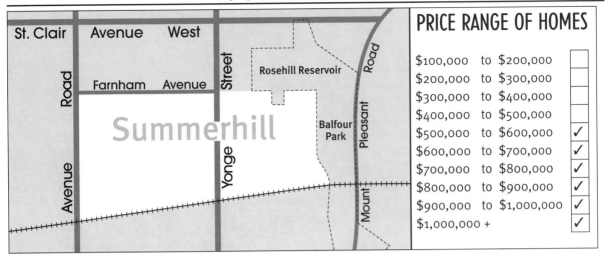

PRICE RANGE OF HOMES

$100,000 to $200,000	
$200,000 to $300,000	
$300,000 to $400,000	
$400,000 to $500,000	
$500,000 to $600,000	✓
$600,000 to $700,000	✓
$700,000 to $800,000	✓
$800,000 to $900,000	✓
$900,000 to $1,000,000	✓
$1,000,000 +	✓

OVERVIEW:

Summerhill's turn-of-the-century houses, winding tree-lined streets, and abundance of parkland have made it one of Toronto's most preferred neighbourhoods. It is conveniently located along the Yonge Street corridor, providing Summerhill residents with easy access to Toronto's downtown business and entertainment districts.

HOMES:

Summerhill's original housing stock consists of semi-detached and detached Victorian houses, and detached Edwardian-style houses, built between 1880 and 1915. Many of these houses do not include driveways, however permit street parking is available from the city for a nominal annual fee.

Summerhill's newer housing stock includes a large number of modern townhouses and luxury condominium apartment buildings that offer all the conveniences of a mid-town lifestyle.

SHOPPING:

Summerhill residents are within walking distance of the many fine shops and restaurants centred around Yonge Street and Summerhill Avenue.

The Bloor-Yorkville and Yonge and St. Clair shopping districts are also easily accessed from the Summerhill neighbourhood.

RECREATION:

The Rosehill Reservoir Park is located east of Yonge Street, with access from Summerhill Gardens. The lower portion of this park features a foot path that is used by walkers, joggers, and cyclists. The northeast corner of this path leads to the David A. Balfour Park, a nature trail that winds through the Vale of Avoca Ravine.

The upper portion of the Rosehill Reservoir Park includes a children's playground, a wading pool, a waterfall and reflecting pools.

Lionel Conacher Park, situated off Birch Avenue, is a memorial to Lionel Conacher who was Canada's athlete of the first half of the 20th century. Conacher, who grew up in the Summerhill neighbourhood, played on two Toronto Maple Leaf Stanley Cup teams. He also competed at the highest level in a dozen other sports and served in the Ontario Legislature, as well as the House of Commons.

SCHOOLS:

(P)   Cottingham Jr., 85 Birch Ave., (416) 393-1895
(P)   Deer Park Jr. & Sr., 23 Ferndale Ave., (416) 393-1550
(PH) North Toronto Collegiate Institute, 70 Roehampton Ave., (416) 393-9180
(PH) Jarvis Collegiate Institute, 495 Jarvis St., (416) 393-0140
(PR) Branksome Hall, 10 Elm Ave., (416) 920-9741
(PR) Bishop Strachan School, 298 Lonsdale Rd., (416) 4834325
(PR) Upper Canada College, 200 Lonsdale Rd., (416) 488-1125
(PR) The York School, 1320 Yonge St., (416) 926-1325
(PC) De La Salle College, 131 Farnham Ave., (416) 969-8771

TRANSPORTATION:

The Summerhill subway station on the Yonge-University-Spadina subway line is within walking distance of every home in this neighbourhood.

Located along the Yonge Street corridor, Summerhill provides motorists with easy access to the downtown core and to major highways.

HISTORY:

Yorkville was subdivided in the 1830s, by a prominent brewer named Joseph Bloor and Sheriff William Botsford Jarvis, who also founded the Rosedale neighbourhood.

Yorkville was named after the Town of York, the forerunner to the City of Toronto. Yorkville was incorporated as a Village in 1853. The initials and trades of Yorkville's first council members are displayed on the Village coat of arms which is proudly displayed above the front door of the historic Yorkville Fire Hall, located at 34 Yorkville Avenue.

In 1883, Yorkville had the distinction of being the first village annexed by the City of Toronto. Despite being part of a big city, Yorkville has always maintained its own identity. It had gained notoriety first as a hippie haven in the 1960s, and then became known as a shopping mecca in the 1980s and 1990s.

Yorkville now has international appeal, with world-class hotels and the most expensive condominium apartment buildings per square footage in Toronto.

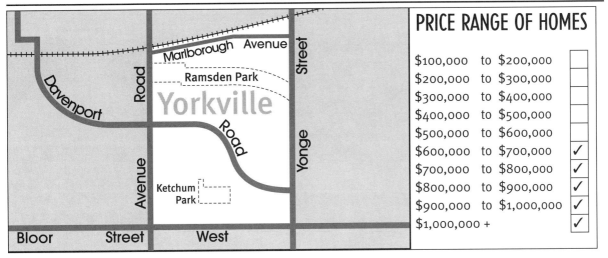

PRICE RANGE OF HOMES

$100,000 to $200,000	
$200,000 to $300,000	
$300,000 to $400,000	
$400,000 to $500,000	
$500,000 to $600,000	
$600,000 to $700,000	✓
$700,000 to $800,000	✓
$800,000 to $900,000	✓
$900,000 to $1,000,000	✓
$1,000,000 +	✓

OVERVIEW:

Yorkville is one of Toronto's most dynamic neighbourhoods. It is an eclectic mix of luxury condominium apartment buildings, commercial office towers, four star hotels, theatres, gourmet restaurants, a prestigious shopping district and picture-postcard Victorian homes.

The commercial heart of Yorkville is located on both Yorkville Avenue and on Cumberland Street. The transition to Yorkville's quiet residential pocket is gradual, as Victorian houses shift from retail to residential uses in a seamless pattern that is uniquely Yorkville.

HOMES:

Yorkville's gentrified Victorian houses were built mainly between 1870 and 1895. These historical homes exhibit many decorative features including ornamental brick patterns, gingerbread gables, cast iron fences, and richly landscaped gardens. Many of Yorkville's houses are listed on the Toronto Historical Board's Inventory of Heritage Properties.

The Yorkville landscape has changed dramatically in the last few years with the addition of a number of new luxury condominium apartment buildings. Yorkvillle condominiums have the highest square footage values in the city of Toronto. These high-end buildings cater to the foot-loose and fancy-free lifestyles of the residents of this upscale neighbourhood

SHOPPING:

Bloor-Yorkville is generally acclaimed as Canada's pre-eminent shopping district. Its many specialty stores, fashion boutiques, jewellery stores, antique shops and art galleries are a destination point for tourists, as well as Torontonians from all over the city.

Yorkville's shops and restaurants are located in pretty Victorian houses on Yorkville Avenue, Hazelton Avenue, Cumberland Street and Scollard Street.

The Hazelton Lanes shopping centre at 55 Avenue Road features over 100 exclusive shops and restaurants. It is anchored by Whole Foods, which offers a vast culinary array of take-out foods as well as nutritional items,

organic foods and traditional grocery items. Pusateri's, on Bay Street at Yorkville Avenue, is famous for its prepared foods, meat and fish counter, and a tantalizing array of desserts and chocolates.

RECREATION:

Ramsden Park is located at the north end of Yorkville, off Yonge Street. This large city park includes four tennis courts, an artificial ice rink, a children's playground and a wading pool.

The Yorkville Public Library, at 22 Yorkville Avenue, is an intimate library geared towards the local community. It includes programs for both children and adults. The Metropolitan Toronto Reference Library at 789 Yonge Street is Canada's largest and most extensive reference library.

The George R. Gardiner Museum of Ceramic Art and the recently-renovated Royal Ontario Museum are all within walking distance of this neighbourhood.

The Manulife Centre situated at the southeast corner of Bay and Bloor features 12 new state-of-the-art movie theatres.

SCHOOLS:

(P)   Jesse Ketchum Jr. & Sr., 61 Davenport Rd.,
      (416) 393-1530
(P)   Jarvis Collegiate Institute, 495 Jarvis St.,
      (416) 393-0140
(PR) University of Toronto Schools, 371 Bloor St., W.,
      (416) 978-2011

TRANSPORTATION:

Yorkville is ideally located within walking distance of the Bloor/Yonge subway station on the Yonge-University-Spadina subway line and the Bay station on the Bloor-Danforth subway line.

For those commuting by car, the Don Valley Parkway is approximately five minutes from Yorkville.

HISTORY:
Wychwood Park was founded by Marmaduke Matthews, a landscape painter who purchased land here in the 1870s with the hope of establishing an artist colony at Wychwood Park. Matthews named Wychwood Park after Wychwood Forest, located near his childhood home in Oxfordshire, England.

In 1874, Matthews built the first house in the community, at 6 Wychwood Park. The second Wychwood Park house, at 22 Wychwood Park, was built in 1877 by Matthews' friend Alexander Jardine.

Matthews and Jardine jointly bought the land that abutted their estates, and in 1891 registered a plan of subdivision for what is now the Wychwood Park neighbourhood.

Wychwood Park is historically significant for the architecture of its homes, and for being one of Toronto's earliest planned communities. The Wychwood Park neighbourhood was designated as an Ontario Heritage Conservation district in 1985.

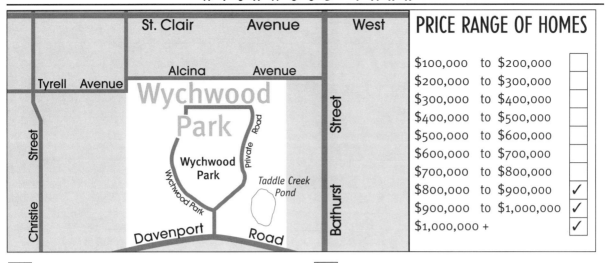

PRICE RANGE OF HOMES

$100,000 to $200,000		
$200,000 to $300,000		
$300,000 to $400,000		
$400,000 to $500,000		
$500,000 to $600,000		
$600,000 to $700,000		
$700,000 to $800,000		
$800,000 to $900,000	✓
$900,000 to $1,000,000	✓
$1,000,000 +	✓

OVERVIEW:

Wychwood Park is an exclusive enclave of 60 homes tucked away in a private ravine setting atop the rolling wooded hills of the Davenport Ridge.

This community is unique in that it has its own executive council that overseas the private roads and parkland within the Wychwood Park neighbourhood. The price for this privacy is a special park tax paid by every Wychwood Park home owner. This tax varies depending on the size of each property.

HOMES:

All of Wychwood Park's houses are listed on the Toronto Historical Board's Inventory of Heritage Properties. A handful of the first Wychwood Park houses were built in the late 1800s. However, most of the houses in Wychwood Park were built in stages between 1906 and 1935. A few houses were also built in the early 1950s.

Many of the older Wychwood Park houses were designed by Eden Smith, an architect who specialized in the English Arts-and-Crafts-house style. The influence of Smith's traditional English house forms is evident throughout Wychwood Park.

SHOPPING:

Wychwood Park residents enjoy convenient access to a large number of shops and restaurants along St. Clair Avenue West. There is also a limited amount of convenience-type shopping on Vaughan and Davenport roads, and on Bathurst Street. Loblaws grocery stores are located nearby on Dupont Street and on St. Clair Avenue.

RECREATION:

Nestled in a thickly wooded valley at the south end of Wychwood Park is the Taddle Creek pond. This pond is home to goldfish, mallard ducks and the occasional blue heron. In the wintertime the pond is used as a skating rink. Near the pond is the Wychwood Park tennis court which is situated in an enchanted forest setting.

The Wychwood Public Library and the Hillcrest Community Centre are both located on Bathurst Street, within a short walk of the Wychwood Park neighbourhood.

SCHOOLS:

(P) McMurrich Jr., 115 Winona Dr., (416) 393-1770
(P) Hillcrest Jr., 44 Hilton Ave., (416) 393-9770
(P) Winona Drive Sr., 101 Winona Dr., (416) 393-1680
(PH) Oakwood Collegiate Institute, 991 St. Clair Ave. W., (416) 393-1780

TRANSPORTATION:

Both the bus service on Davenport Road and the streetcar on St. Clair Avenue connect passengers to the Dupont station on the Yonge-University-Spadina subway line. The Bathurst bus connects passengers to the Bathurst station on the Bloor-Danforth subway line.

Motorists are approximately 10 minutes from downtown and about the same distance north to the Allen Expressway off Eglinton Avenue.

OLD TORONTO NORTH

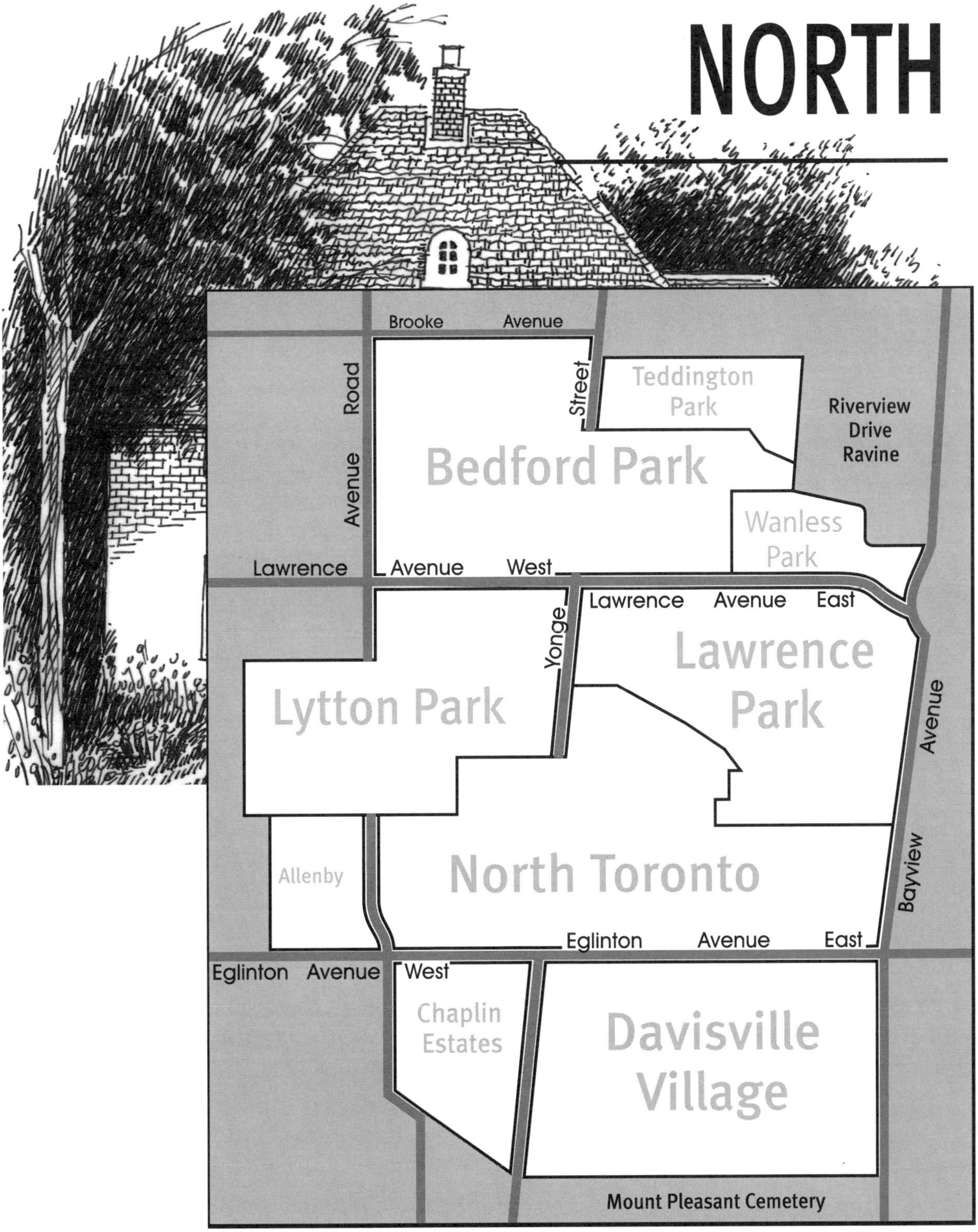

Brooke Avenue

Road

Avenue

Street

Teddington Park

Riverview Drive Ravine

Bedford Park

Lawrence Avenue West

Wanless Park

Lawrence Avenue East

Yonge

Lytton Park

Lawrence Park

Avenue

Allenby

North Toronto

Bayview

Eglinton Avenue East

Eglinton Avenue West

Chaplin Estates

Davisville Village

Mount Pleasant Cemetery

HISTORY:
Allenby was first settled in the 1400s by the Huron Tribe, which had a village here until sometime in the early 1700s.

This village is described in Lyman B. Jackes's *Tales of North Toronto* as "a well organized and extensive community that had its centre in an artesian spring of pure water. The spring flowed where the modern water tower rears its head on Roselawn Avenue, just to the west of Avenue Road. The great tribal huts were on the site of the present day Allenby Public School."

Jackes goes on to say that the Allenby school hill is not natural but was man-made, the result of the Huron's practice of burrowing food stocks underground.

The present-day neighbourhood was developed when Allenby Public School opened in 1927. The school was named after Lord Allenby, a British hero of the First World War.

Ed. Note: The water tower Jackes refers to is situated on Roselawn Avenue and is now a police communications tower.

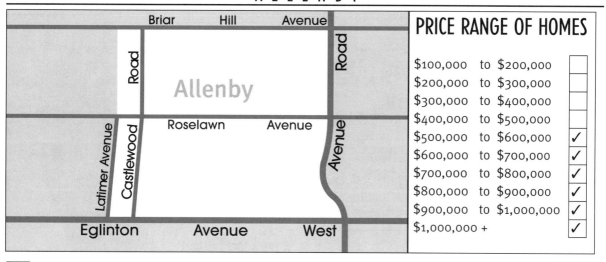

PRICE RANGE OF HOMES

$100,000 to $200,000	
$200,000 to $300,000	
$300,000 to $400,000	
$400,000 to $500,000	
$500,000 to $600,000	✓
$600,000 to $700,000	✓
$700,000 to $800,000	✓
$800,000 to $900,000	✓
$900,000 to $1,000,000	✓
$1,000,000 +	✓

OVERVIEW:
Allenby is very popular with families that have young children. This neighbourhood's biggest drawing card is the Allenby Public School, which has an excellent reputation built around its French immersion program for students in grades 1 through 6.

HOMES:
Allenby's Tudor-style houses were built in the 1930s and 1940s. They include a mix of detached two-storey homes and bungalows. Overall, Allenby's lot sizes are above average, with 25- to 35-foot frontages being typical. All Allenby houses have either a mutual or private driveway.

Much of Allenby's housing stock has undergone extensive renovations by new owners who have been careful to preserve the original wood detail and decorative accents found in many of the houses in this neighbourhood.

The Hunt Club Residences at Avenue Road and Roselawn Avenue are a nice addition to the neighbourhood. This collection of luxury townhomes and condominiums is designed around the former Toronto Hunt Club clubhouse, which has been a landmark on Avenue Road since the early 1900s.

SHOPPING:
Allenby residents are well served by the shops and restaurants along Eglinton Avenue West. In particular there are a large number of shops and professional services geared towards families with young children. There are also many fine clothing stores, food shops and restaurants in this shopping district.

RECREATION:
The ultra-modern North Toronto Memorial Community Recreation Centre, on Eglinton Avenue West, has an indoor and outdoor pool, a gymnasium, a walking track, aerobic and weight rooms, and two artificial ice rinks that are used as tennis courts in the summertime. The centre is located next to Eglinton Park, which has a baseball diamond, sports field and a wading pool.

Allenby residents are also close to the Belt Line Trail, a popular seven-kilometre leisure and exercise path that winds through the central part of the city. There is local access to the Belt Line south of Eglinton off Chaplin Avenue, and at Oriole Parkway.

SCHOOLS:
(P)   Allenby Jr., 391 St.Clements Ave., (416) 393-9115
(P)   Glenview Sr., 401 Rosewell Ave., (416) 393-9390
(PH) Forest Hill Collegiate Institute, 730 Eglinton Ave. West, (416) 393-1860
(PH) North Toronto Collegiate Institute, 70 Roehampton Ave., (416) 393-9180
(PR) Havergal College, 1451 Avenue Road, (416) 483-3519
(PR) St Clement's School, 21 St.Clements Ave., (416) 483-4835
(CH) Marshall McLuhan Catholic School, 1107 Avenue Rd., (416) 393-5561

TRANSPORTATION:
Regular bus service on Eglinton Avenue and on Avenue Road connect passengers to the Eglinton station on the Yonge-University-Spadina subway line.

Motorists are 10 to 15 minutes from the Allen Expressway and approximately 15 minutes to the Avenue Road on-ramp to Highway 401. Toronto's downtown business and entertainment districts are within a 20-minute drive of this neighbourhood.

HISTORY: Bedford Park began as a farming hamlet centred around the crossroads of Yonge Street and Lawrence Avenue. This village was a popular stopover for farmers travelling to and from the markets in Toronto. It is likely that Bedford Park is named after the Bedford Park Hotel, which opened in 1873 at the southwest corner of Yonge Street and Fairlawn Avenue.

The residential development of Bedford Park was linked to the Metropolitan Street Railway which began service to this area in 1890. That same year Bedford Park amalgamated with the former Town of North Toronto, which was then annexed by the city of Toronto in 1912. To this day Bedford Park is commonly referred to as North Toronto.

Ed. Note: The former Bedford Park General Store and Post Office building is still standing at the southwest corner of Yonge Street and Bedford Park Avenue.

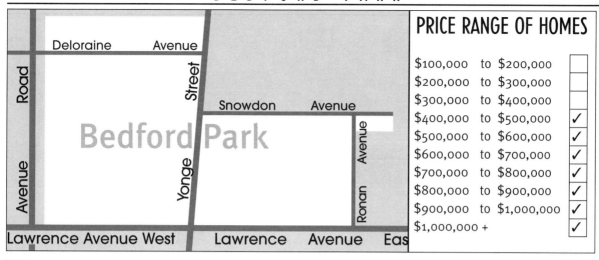

PRICE RANGE OF HOMES

$100,000 to $200,000	
$200,000 to $300,000	
$300,000 to $400,000	
$400,000 to $500,000	✓
$500,000 to $600,000	✓
$600,000 to $700,000	✓
$700,000 to $800,000	✓
$800,000 to $900,000	✓
$900,000 to $1,000,000	✓
$1,000,000 +	✓

OVERVIEW:

The Bedford Park neighbourhood is geared toward families with young children. It has an excellent selection of public, private and separate schools, many parkettes and playgrounds, a community centre, a library, and convenient access to Toronto's transit system.

HOMES:

Bedford Park has a good mix of detached and semi-detached homes. The original housing stock was built between 1890 and 1940. However, many of the bungalows in the neighbourhood have recently been torn down and replaced with custom-designed houses. New condominium apartment buildings have recently been built on both sides of Yonge Street, just a few blocks north of Lawrence Avenue.

SHOPPING:

Yonge Lawrence Village is a family-oriented shopping district with a good cross-section of stores. It also features a good selection of coffee shops, bakeries and restaurants.

The Avenue Road shopping district, north of Lawrence, has a diverse mix of shops and restaurants including national chain stores, home decorating stores, fast food restaurants, gift stores and gourmet food shops.

RECREATION:

Wanless Park is the largest park in the neighbourhood. It has five floodlit tennis courts, a basketball court, a baseball diamond, a tots playground and a wading pool. Wanless Park is close to the Bedford Park Community Centre. Located at the Bedford Park Public School, this Community Centre includes a gymnasium and an indoor pool.

The Woburn parkette, west of Yonge street, is a popular destination point for neighbourhood parents with toddlers and preschoolers. It features a new tots playground and a wading pool. A few blocks north of the Woburn parkette is the Fairlawn Neighbourhood Centre, which operates out of the Fairlawn Heights United Church. This centre includes seasonal programming for residents of all ages.

The George Locke Public Library at the southeast corner of Yonge and Lawrence, offers year round programs for adults, children and preschoolers.

SCHOOLS:

(P)   Bedford Park Jr., 81 Ranleigh Ave., (416) 393-9424
(P)   John Wanless Jr., 250 Brookdale Ave., (416) 393-9350
(P)   Glenview Sr., 401 Rosewell Ave., (416) 393-9390
(PH) Lawrence Park Collegiate Institute, 125 Chatsworth Dr.,
      (416) 393-9500
(C)   Blessed Sacrament, 24 Bedford Park Ave.,
      (416) 393-5226
(PR) Havergal College, 1451 Avenue Rd., (416) 483-3519
(PR) Toronto French School, 296 Lawrence Ave. East,
      (416) 484-6533

TRANSPORTATION:

The Lawrence subway station off Yonge Street is within reasonable walking distance of all the homes in this neighbourhood. There is also regular bus service on Yonge Street, as well as limited service on both Avenue Road and Mount Pleasant Road.

Motorists are 20 minutes from downtown and approximately five minutes from the Yonge Street on-ramp to Highway 401.

HISTORY: The Chaplin Estates neighbourhood began with a plan of subdivision registered by William John Chaplin and his son James D. Chaplin in 1913. The Chaplin family had been landowners in this area dating back to 1860, when this district was known simply as "Eglinton."

Chaplin Estates was marketed as a high-class residential district. The developers included a long list of building restrictions and zoning bylaws in the sale of each property. There were no semi-detached houses allowed, and stucco exteriors were not to cover more than half the house.

The marketing of the subdivision was handled by the Chaplin Realty Company. Prices ranged from $500 to $9,000 per lot. Most of the lots were sold between 1921 and 1925.

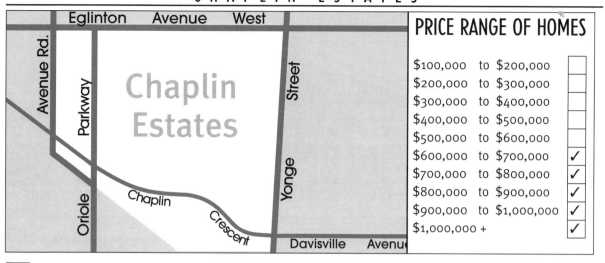

PRICE RANGE OF HOMES

$100,000 to $200,000		
$200,000 to $300,000		
$300,000 to $400,000		
$400,000 to $500,000		
$500,000 to $600,000		
$600,000 to $700,000	✓
$700,000 to $800,000	✓
$800,000 to $900,000	✓
$900,000 to $1,000,000	✓
$1,000,000 +	✓

OVERVIEW:

This distinguished neighbourhood has always been one of Toronto's most exclusive addresses. Chaplin Estates homeowners enjoy convenient access to excellent public and private schools, shopping, parks and recreation, and transit service.

HOMES:

Chaplin Estates' two- and three-storey detached houses are situated on premium lots with private driveways.

The houses in this neighbourhood were built in the 1920s and 1930s, and include many fine examples of Tudor-, Georgian-, and English-cottage-style architecture.

SHOPPING:

Chaplin Estates residents are within walking distance of "The Eglinton Way" shopping district along Eglinton Avenue West. This ritzy shopping area includes high-end fashion boutiques, gourmet food shops, professional offices, restaurants, and the Eglinton movie theatre.

The Yonge street shopping district is also within walking distance of Chaplin Estates. This highly visible shopping area includes many one-of-a-kind stores, and trendy restaurants that draw customers from all over the city.

RECREATION:

The ultra-modern North Toronto Community Centre has an indoor and outdoor pool, water slides, a gymnasium, a walking track and exercise rooms.

Eglinton Park is adjacent to the community centre. Its facilities include: a baseball diamond, tennis courts, a wading pool and an artificial ice hockey rink.

The historic Belt Line Trail walking and cycling path is easily accessed from Oriole Park, at the south end of the neighbourhood.

The Northern District branch of the Toronto Public Library is located on Orchard View Boulevard. This branch offers programs for seniors, adults and children.

SCHOOLS:

(P)   Oriole Park Jr., 80 Braemar Ave., (416) 393-5215
(PH) North Toronto Collegiate Institute, 730 Eglinton Ave. West, (416) 393-1860
(PR) Bishop Strachan School, 298 Lonsdale Road, (416) 483-4325
(PR) St. Clement's School, 21 St. Clement's Ave., (416) 484-4835
(PR) Upper Canada College, Upper School, 200 Lonsdale Rd., (416) 488-1125
(PR) Upper Canada College Prep School, 220 Lonsdale Rd., (416) 488-1125

TRANSPORTATION:

Chaplin Estates residents can walk to the bus stops on Yonge Street, Eglinton Avenue, Oriole Parkway and Chaplin Crescent. The Davisville and the Eglinton subway stations are also within walking distance of this neighbourhood.

The main east-west arterial roadway is Eglinton Avenue. Residents are approximately 15 minutes from the Allen Expressway and the Don Valley Parkway.

Motorists can be downtown in 15 minutes via Yonge Street or Avenue Road.

HISTORY:
Davisville Village is named after John Davis, who immigrated to Canada from Staffordshire, England in 1840. John Davis served as Davisville's first postmaster and helped found the Davisville Public School. He also operated the Davis Pottery, which became the Village's largest employer.

The south part of Davisville was subdivided in the 1860s on land owned mostly by the Davis family. The north part of the village belonged to the church. This tract of land, known as the Davisville Glebe, remained undeveloped until 1911, when it was sold to the Dovercourt Land and Building Company — the same company that oversaw the development of the Lawrence Park neighbourhood.

Ed. Note: The former Davisville Post Office was run by John Davis' grandson, Jack. This two-storey building is still standing on the northeast corner of Yonge Street and Davisville Avenue.

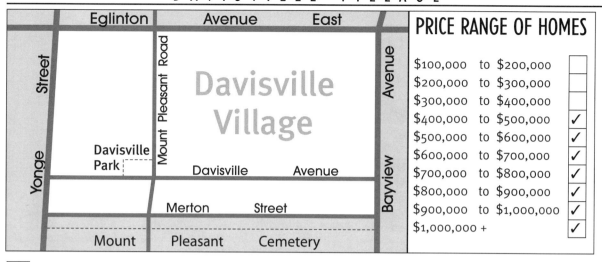

PRICE RANGE OF HOMES	
$100,000 to $200,000	
$200,000 to $300,000	
$300,000 to $400,000	
$400,000 to $500,000	✓
$500,000 to $600,000	✓
$600,000 to $700,000	✓
$700,000 to $800,000	✓
$800,000 to $900,000	✓
$900,000 to $1,000,000	✓
$1,000,000 +	✓

OVERVIEW:

This centrally located neighbourhood has always been popular with singles, young couples and families. The Davisville neighbourhood is known for its excellent recreational facilities, outstanding shopping districts and active nightlife, which includes bars, restaurants and movie theatres.

HOMES:

The majority of Davisville houses were built in the 1920s and 1930s. The houses west of Mount Pleasant Road are mostly large two- and three-storey English-cottage- and Edwardian-style homes. There are also a number of duplexes and walk-up apartment buildings in this area.

The houses east of Mount Pleasant Road are made up primarily of smaller detached houses, semi-detached houses and bungalows. This part of the neighbourhood also contains a handful of historical homes from the late 1800s, and a growing number of new, custom-built homes.

Davisville Village also contains a number of newer condominium apartment buildings located mostly on Merton and Balliol streets and along Eglinton Avenue. The many high-rise apartment buildings on Davisville Avenue are popular with renters.

SHOPPING:

Davisville's main shopping district is on Mount Pleasant Road. This stretch of stores is highlighted by a large group of antique and collectable shops that attract people from all over the city. Home decorating stores, children's clothing and toy stores, and an excellent selection of restaurants all add to the ambience of this street.

Davisville residents also shop on Yonge Street and Bayview Avenue. These two streets contain a plethora of gift shops, clothing and accessory stores, bakeries, cafés and coffee shops.

RECREATION:

Davisville Park is the social and recreational centre of this neighbourhood. During the day, it is a beehive of activity with preschoolers enjoying the Davisville Park playground and wading pool.

Davisville Park's six tennis courts are used by the Davisville Tennis Club on evenings and weekends. This club has an active house league and tournament schedule. Adjacent to the tennis courts is the Davisville Park baseball diamond, which is extensively used by children and adult baseball leagues.

Davisville also has an active nightlife with many pubs, restaurants and movie theatres.

SCHOOLS:

(P)   Davisville Jr. School, 43 Millwood Rd., (416) 393-0570
(P)   Metro Toronto School for the Deaf, 43 Millwood Rd., (416) 393-0630
(P)   Eglinton Jr. School, 223 Eglinton Ave. East, (416) 393-9315
(P)   Hodgson Sr. School, 282 Davisville Ave, (416) 393-0390
(P)   Maurice Cody Jr. & Sr., 364 Belsize Dr., (416) 393-9240
(P)   Spectrum Sr. Alternative School, 223 Eglinton Ave. East, (416) 393-9311
(PH) North Toronto Collegiate Institute, 70 Roehampton Ave., (416) 393-9180
(PH) Northern Secondary School, 851 Mt. Pleasant Rd., (416) 393-0270
(PR) Greenwood College School, 443 Mt. Pleasant Rd., (416) 482-9811

TRANSPORTATION:

There is local bus service on Mount Pleasant Road, Yonge Street, Davisville Avenue and Eglinton Avenue. These bus routes connect passengers to the Yonge-University-Spadina subway line. The Davisville and the Eglinton subway stations at Yonge Street are within a reasonable walking distance of this neighbourhood.

This area offers motorists quick access to downtown Toronto via either Mount Pleasant Road or Yonge Street. Toronto's highways and expressways are located within a 20-minute drive of Davisville Village.

HISTORY: The Lawrence Park subdivision was assembled in 1907 by the Dovercourt Land Building and Saving Company. The Dovercourt Land Company acquired the north parcel of Lawrence Park from John Lawrence, after whom this neighbourhood is named.

Wilfred Servington Dinnick was the president of the Dovercourt Land Company. It was under Dinnick's direction that Lawrence Park was developed as a suburb for the "well to do."

The first advertisement for Lawrence Park trumpeted it as an "aristocratic neighbourhood," "400 feet above Lake Ontario," and "far from the lake winds in winter."

Despite all its fanfare, Lawrence Park's development was sporadic. The building of houses was interrupted by two world wars, a recession, and the Depression. It wasn't until the 1950s that this neighbourhood was completely developed.

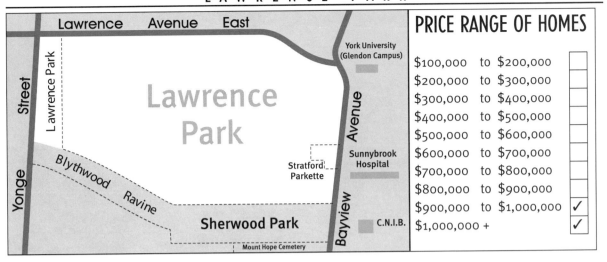

PRICE RANGE OF HOMES	
$100,000 to $200,000	
$200,000 to $300,000	
$300,000 to $400,000	
$400,000 to $500,000	
$500,000 to $600,000	
$600,000 to $700,000	
$700,000 to $800,000	
$800,000 to $900,000	
$900,000 to $1,000,000	✓
$1,000,000 +	✓

OVERVIEW:

Lawrence Park is one of Toronto's most exclusive residential neighbourhoods. It is located in a very peaceful and tranquil setting that includes gently rolling hills, winding roads and a lush topography.

Lawrence Park's shops, schools and recreational facilities are located on its periphery, which keeps traffic on the residential streets to a minimum.

HOMES:

Lawrence Park's whimsical houses include a variety of architectural styles including English Cottage, Tudor Revival and Georgian and Colonial designs. Lawrence Park houses were built between 1910 and the late 1940s.

Lawrence Park is a good place to find a house that blends the old with the new. Renovations in this neighbourhood have been sensitive to preserving the old-world charm of these houses, including leaded glass windows, wood trims around door and window frames, decorative fireplace mantels and rich hardwood floors.

SHOPPING:

The high-profile shops and restaurants in the Yonge and Lawrence area are well patronized by Lawrence Park residents. This shopping district includes fashion stores, children's stores, sporting goods stores, gift shops, bakeries and gourmet coffee shops.

RECREATION:

Most of this neighbourhood's recreational facilities centre around Lawrence Park, east of Yonge Street and south of Lawrence. This park has three clay-surface tennis courts, a lawn bowling club, and the Alexander Muir Memorial Gardens, an award winning multi-level strolling garden. This park also provides access to the Lawrence Park Ravine footpath, which is popular with fitness and nature enthusiasts.

The George Locke Public Library at the northwest corner of Lawrence Park offers a variety of programs for adults, children and preschoolers.

SCHOOLS:

(P) Blythwood Jr, 2 Strathgowan Cres., (416) 393-9105
(P) Sunny View Jr.& Sr., 450 Blythwood Rd., (416) 393-9275
(PH) Lawrence Park Collegiate Institute, 125 Chatsworth Dr., (416) 393-9500
(PH) North Toronto Collegiate Institute,, 70 Roehampton Ave., (416) 393-9180
(PH) Northern Secondary, 851 Mt. Pleasant Rd., (416) 393-0270
(PR) St. Clements School, 21 St. Clements Ave., (416) 483-4835
(PR) Havergal College, 1451 Avenue Rd., (416) 483-3519
(PR) The Toronto French School, 296 Lawrence Ave. E., (416) 484-6533

TRANSPORTATION:

Most Lawrence Park residents are within walking distance of bus routes that run along Yonge Street, Mount Pleasant Road, Bayview Avenue and Lawrence Avenue. The Lawrence subway station, located at the intersection of Yonge and Lawrence, is part of the Yonge-University-Spadina subway line.

The Yonge Street on-ramp to Highway 401 is a five- to 10-minute drive from Lawrence Park.

HISTORY:

Lytton Park owes its development to the Metropolitan Street Railway, whose single horse-car line began service to this area in 1886. Prior to the advent of the railway, Lytton Park was a rural outpost with limited access to the City of Toronto.

The Metropolitan Company recognized the impact on land values that their railway service would bring to this district. Thus in 1888, the Railway purchased the 200-acre Beatty farm, near their station at Yonge and Glengrove.

In 1888, the former Beatty farm became the Glen Grove Park subdivision, and the residential development of Lytton Park was underway.

Lytton Park's major period of growth began in 1912, when it became part of the City of Toronto. It was during the next 15 years that most of Lytton Park's houses, schools, churches and parks were built.

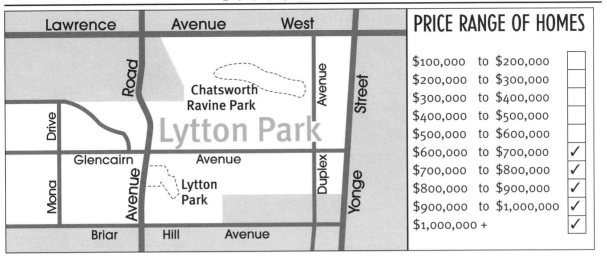

PRICE RANGE OF HOMES	
$100,000 to $200,000	
$200,000 to $300,000	
$300,000 to $400,000	
$400,000 to $500,000	
$500,000 to $600,000	
$600,000 to $700,000	✓
$700,000 to $800,000	✓
$800,000 to $900,000	✓
$900,000 to $1,000,000	✓
$1,000,000 +	✓

OVERVIEW:

Lytton Park is one of Toronto's most exclusive neighbourhoods. It is home to doctors, lawyers, stockbrokers and corporate executives who value Lytton Park's quiet charm, and its convenient access to transportation corridors leading in and out of the city.

Lytton Park's biggest asset is its highly regarded public schools, including the junior, senior and high schools (listed below) that are smartly located right next door to each other. These schools are within walking distance of every home in the neighbourhood. Havergal College, a highly regarded girls' private school, and two Catholic schools, Blessed Sacrament and Marshall McLuhan, provide Lytton Park families with a myriad of outstanding school options.

HOMES:

Lytton Park's Tudor-revival, Georgian-revival, and Colonial-style houses were built primarily between 1890 and 1945. All of the houses are detached, and are situated on large lots with lush gardens.

The interior of a typical Lytton Park house includes traditional accents such as hardwood floors, leaded glass windows and a wood-burning fireplace.

SHOPPING:

Lytton Park is well served by a myriad of upscale shopping districts located along Yonge Street, Avenue Road and Eglinton Avenue West. These shopping districts are all within walking distance.

The Yonge and Eglinton Centre is anchored by Toys "R" Us, HMV, and a SilverCity movie theatre. Movie goers can enjoy a pre- or post-movie meal at the Pickle Barrel restaurant located right next to the movie theatre.

RECREATION:

Lytton Park, from which this neighbourhood takes its name, is nestled in a deep valley and is hidden by trees from the roaring traffic of Avenue Road above. This serene park includes three public tennis courts, and is also home to the North Toronto Lawn Bowling Club. Across from Lytton Park is the Herbert Begg Memorial Garden. This picturesque strolling garden was donated to the city by Herbert Begg's daughters, as a memorial to their father.

Otter Creek Park, on Cheritan Avenue between Chatsworth Drive and Rosewell Avenue, contains four tennis courts that are retrofitted for use as an artificial ice rink in the wintertime. This park also provides access to the Chatsworth Ravine. A nature trail passes through the Chatsworth Ravine on its way through Lawrence Park and the Blythwood Ravine on its way to Sherwood Park.

SCHOOLS:

(P)   John Ross Robertson Jr, 130 Glencairn Ave. West, (416) 393-9400
(P)   Glenview Sr, 401 Rosewell Ave., (416) 393-9350
(PH) Lawrence Park Collegiate Institute, 125 Chatsworth Dr., (416) 393-9500
(PR) Havergal College, 1451 Avenue Rd, (416) 483-3519
(C)   Blessed Sacrament, 24 Bedford Park Ave., (416) 393-5226
(CH) Marshall McLuhan Catholic Secondary, 1107 Avenue Rd., (416) 393-5561

TRANSPORTATION:

Both the Eglinton and the Lawrence subway stations on Yonge Street are within walking distance of many Lytton Park houses. Yonge Street and Avenue Road both have bus routes that connect to the Yonge subway line.

Motorists can be downtown in 15 minutes. For commuters heading out of the city by car, the Yonge Street and Avenue Road on-ramps to Highway 401 are approximately five minutes from Lytton Park.

HISTORY: The town of North Toronto was incorporated in 1890. It was formed as the result of an amalgamation between Davisville Village, Eglinton Village and Bedford Park Village.

At the time of its incorporation, North Toronto was primarily an agricultural farming community. However, large parcels of land in North Toronto were already subdivided and were being held by speculators.

The actual building of houses in this area began in the 1890s, when the Metropolitan Street Railway made North Toronto the northernmost stop on its 5¢ line from downtown Toronto.

By the early 1900s, North Toronto had emerged as one of Toronto's most popular commuter suburbs. However, frustrated by the poor level of municipal services being offered by the town, North Toronto residents voted in favour of annexation to the City of Toronto on December 15, 1912. North Toronto filled in quickly after annexation and was completely developed by the 1940s.

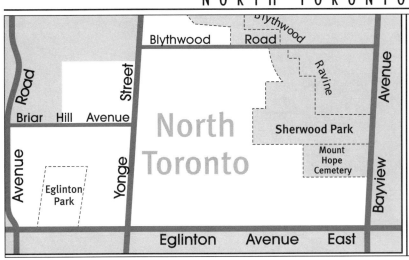

PRICE RANGE OF HOMES

$100,000 to $200,000		
$200,000 to $300,000		
$300,000 to $400,000		
$400,000 to $500,000	✓
$500,000 to $600,000	✓
$600,000 to $700,000	✓
$700,000 to $800,000	✓
$800,000 to $900,000	✓
$900,000 to $1,000,000	✓
$1,000,000 +	✓

OVERVIEW:

When the expanded mega-city of Toronto was formed in 1998 the North Toronto neighbourhood went from being located at the north end of the old city to occupying a central location within the new city boundaries. Despite these changes North Toronto's identity as a neighbourhood endures.

North Toronto is especially popular with families raising school-age children. It has everything families are looking for in a neighbourhood including good-sized houses, an excellent selection of public, private and separate schools, convenient access to Toronto's transit system, and a multitude of parks and recreational facilities.

HOMES:

North Toronto's housing stock includes bungalows, as well as semi-detached and fully detached houses, built mostly between 1910 and 1940. North Toronto houses are well maintained and a pride of ownership is painted on the face of every home.

North Toronto also contains a large number of low- and high-rise apartment buildings centred around the Yonge and Eglinton area. These apartment buildings range from luxury condominiums to affordable co-ops and a wide range of rental opportunities. The recent conversion of St. George church on Sheldrake Boulevard into stylish condominium suites has been popular with homebuyers.

SHOPPING:

North Toronto residents patronize the local shops and restaurants on Yonge Street, between Eglinton and Lawrence avenues. The mix of stores on Yonge Street is very diverse, ranging from mom and pop owner-operated stores, to international chain stores that have added a certain luster to the entire area. Indoor shopping is available nearby at the Yonge and Eglinton Centre, which has recently undergone a major renovation and expansion.

The Yonge and Eglinton corridor has been coined "Young and Eligible" due to the many bars, restaurants, nightclubs and movie theatres that proliferate at this intersection.

RECREATION:

The ultra-modern North Toronto Community Centre is located on Eglinton Avenue, just east of Avenue Road. This centre includes a gymnasium, squash courts, a walking track and a water slide. Adjacent to the community centre is Eglinton Park, which has sports fields, a baseball diamond, a wading pool, a children's playground and tennis courts that become an artificial ice rink in the wintertime.

Sherwood Park, located east of Mount Pleasant Road, has a wonderful walking path highlighted by some of the oldest and largest trees in the city. This park contains a picturesque children's playground and a wading pool.

The Northern District Public Library, on Orchard View Boulevard, offers programs for both children and adults.

SCHOOLS:

(P) Blythwood Jr., 2 Strathgowan Cres., (416) 393-9105
(P) Eglinton Jr., 223 Eglinton Ave. E, (416) 393-9315
(P) John Fisher Jr., 40 Erskine Ave., (416) 393-9325
(P) Spectrum Sr., 223 Eglinton Ave. E., (416) 393-9311
(P) Sunnyview Jr. & Sr., 450 Blythwood Rd., (416) 393-9275
(PH) North Toronto Collegiate Institute, 70 Roehampton Ave., (416) 393-9180
(PH) Northern Secondary, 851 Mount Pleasant Rd., (416) 393-0270
(C) St. Monica, 14 Broadway Ave., (416) 393-4224
(PR) St. Clement's School, 21 St. Clements Ave., (416) 483-4835

TRANSPORTATION:

North Toronto has bus routes on Eglinton Avenue, Mount Pleasant Road, Yonge Street and Avenue Road. All of these surface routes connect to Eglinton station on the Yonge-University-Spadina subway line.

Motorists can be downtown in 10 minutes. Highway 401 and the Allen Expressway are both approximately 10 minutes from North Toronto.

HISTORY: Teddington Park formed the northern boundary of the City
of Toronto in 1912. That same year, separate plans of subdivision were registered by two prominent Toronto businessman: Nicholas Garland and Robert
Dack. These plans led to the eventual building of homes in Teddington Park.

Teddington Park's development as a high-end residential district was
inspired by the Rosedale Golf Club, which had moved from Rosedale to the
Teddington Park area in 1909.

Teddington Park's older houses on Riverview Drive were originally given
descriptive names such as "Donnybrook," "Silverwood" and "Treetops."
These names were in leu of municipal addresses, which were not issued
until some time after the houses were built. Some of these houses still display their historical names.

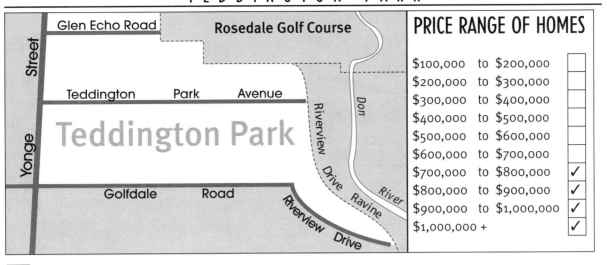

PRICE RANGE OF HOMES	
$100,000 to $200,000	
$200,000 to $300,000	
$300,000 to $400,000	
$400,000 to $500,000	
$500,000 to $600,000	
$600,000 to $700,000	
$700,000 to $800,000	✓
$800,000 to $900,000	✓
$900,000 to $1,000,000	✓
$1,000,000 +	✓

OVERVIEW:

The Teddington Park neighbourhood is one of the smallest and most exclusive districts in Toronto. Over the years many important and influential Torontonians have called this neighbourhood their home.

Teddington Park is conveniently located along the Yonge Street corridor. However, it is remarkably quiet, thanks to its natural boundaries which include the Rosedale Golf Club and the Riverview Drive Ravine.

HOMES:

Teddington Park's houses were built between 1910 and 1935. The signature street in the neighbourhood is Teddington Park Avenue, a wide, tree-lined boulevard that contains large Tudor- and Georgian-style houses.

Riverview Drive is a winding, countrified road, lined by majestic maple trees. The properties on Riverview Drive are especially large as many of these homes back onto the Riverview Drive Ravine.

SHOPPING:

Local convenience shopping on Yonge Street is within walking distance of many Teddington Park homes. Included in the mix are a large national grocery store, a hardware store, dry cleaners, a toy shop, fashion stores, restaurants and coffee shops.

RECREATION:

The Bedford Park Community Centre, on Ranleigh Avenue, includes an indoor gymnasium and a swimming pool. Wanless Park has five tennis courts, a basketball court, a wading pool, a children's playground and a baseball diamond.

Golf enthusiasts have the option of a private membership at the Rosedale Golf Club, or paying public fees at the nearby Don Valley Golf Course, off Yonge Street just north of York Mills.

The George Locke Public Library at Yonge and Lawrence offers neighbourhood residents a wide range of programming for children and adults.

SCHOOLS:

(P)   Bedford Park Jr., 81 Ranleigh Ave., (416) 393-9424
(PH) Lawrence Park Collegiate Institute, 125 Chatsworth Dr., (416) 393-9500
(PR) Havergal College, 1451 Avenue Rd., (416) 483-3519
(PR) Crescent School, 2365 Bayview Ave., (416) 449-2556
(PR) Toronto French School, 296 Lawrence Ave., E., (416) 484-6533
(C)   Blessed Sacrament, 24 Bedford Park Ave., (416) 393-5226
(C)   Loretto Abbey, 101 Mason Blvd., (416) 393-5510

TRANSPORTATION:

Bus lines on Yonge Street and Mount Pleasant Road connect passengers to the Lawrence station on the Yonge-University-Spadina subway line.

Motorists can travel directly downtown by way of either Yonge Street or Mount Pleasant Road. For commuters travelling out of the city by car, the Yonge Street on-ramp to Highway 401 is just minutes away.

HISTORY:
In 1912, Toronto Suburbs Ltd., guided by George Kappele and D.F. Crowagen, registered a plan of subdivision for the old Waverley farm at Mount Pleasant Road and Lawrence Avenue. The developers named this new subdivision Waverley Park.

Like other Toronto neighbourhoods from this era, the actual building of homes in Waverley Park was stalled initially by the First World War and then by the Depression.

In 1931 the City of Toronto expropriated the properties in the centre of Waverley Park for the creation of a public park. The Park was named Wanless Park, and eventually the entire neighbourhood adopted this name.

Wanless Park, Wanless Road, Wanless Avenue, and Wanless Crescent are all named after John Wanless, a former Toronto alderman and educator.

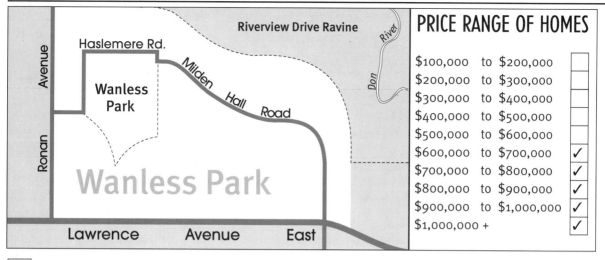

PRICE RANGE OF HOMES

$100,000 to $200,000	
$200,000 to $300,000	
$300,000 to $400,000	
$400,000 to $500,000	
$500,000 to $600,000	
$600,000 to $700,000	✓
$700,000 to $800,000	✓
$800,000 to $900,000	✓
$900,000 to $1,000,000	✓
$1,000,000 +	✓

OVERVIEW:
Wanless Park is a very popular neighbourhood among families with young children. The main attraction is Wanless Park, an island of green space right in the centre of the neighbourhood.

Wanless Park residents enjoy the convenience of being able to walk to all the local amenities including the Bedford Park Public School and Community Centre, the George Locke Public Library, Yonge Street shopping and the Lawrence subway station.

HOMES:
Wanless Park's solid brick detached houses were built mostly in the 1930s and 1940s. Most of the houses are two storey, however there is a sprinkling of bungalows in this neighbourhood; many of these are being torn down and replaced with new, custom-designed homes.

Overall, the property sizes in Wanless Park are excellent, with most homes having at least a 30-foot frontage and either a mutual or private driveway. The majority of Wanless Park houses either face the park or back onto the Riverview Drive ravine.

SHOPPING:
Wanless Park residents can walk to the Yonge Lawrence Village shopping district that includes hundreds of stores, restaurants, and professional and medical offices along Yonge Street from Lawrence to Yonge Boulevard. Many of these stores are geared towards families with young children, reflecting the demographics of the surrounding neighbourhood.

RECREATION:
Wanless Park is the social and recreational hub of this neighbourhood. Its facilities include five floodlit tennis courts, a baseball diamond, a basketball court, a wading pool and a children's playground.

Indoor recreational facilities are available at the Bedford Park Community Centre, located on Ranleigh Avenue, inside the Bedford Park Public School. This recreation centre has a gymnasium and an indoor pool.

The George Locke Public Library at Yonge and Lawrence has a variety of programs for preschoolers, children and adults.

SCHOOLS:
(P)   Bedford Park Jr., 81 Ranleigh Ave., (416) 393-9424
(P)   Glenview Sr., 401 Rosewell Ave., (416) 393-9390
(PH) Lawrence Park Collegiate Institute, 125 Chatsworth Dr., (416) 393-2500
(PH) Northern Secondary School, 851 Mt. Pleasant Rd., (416) 393-0270
(PH) York Mills Collegiate Institute, 490 York Mills Rd., (416) 395-3340
(PR) Toronto French School, 296 Lawrence Ave. East, (416) 484-6533
(C)   Blessed Sacrament, 24 Bedford Park Ave., (416) 393-5226

TRANSPORTATION:
The Lawrence subway station on Yonge Street is within walking distance of this neighbourhood. This station is part of the Yonge-University-Spadina subway line. Bus routes on Mount Pleasant Road and on Lawrence Avenue also make connections to the Yonge subway line.

It is approximately 20 minutes by car to downtown Toronto. The Yonge Street on-ramp to Highway 401 is approximately five minutes from Wanless Park.

OLD TORONTO EAST

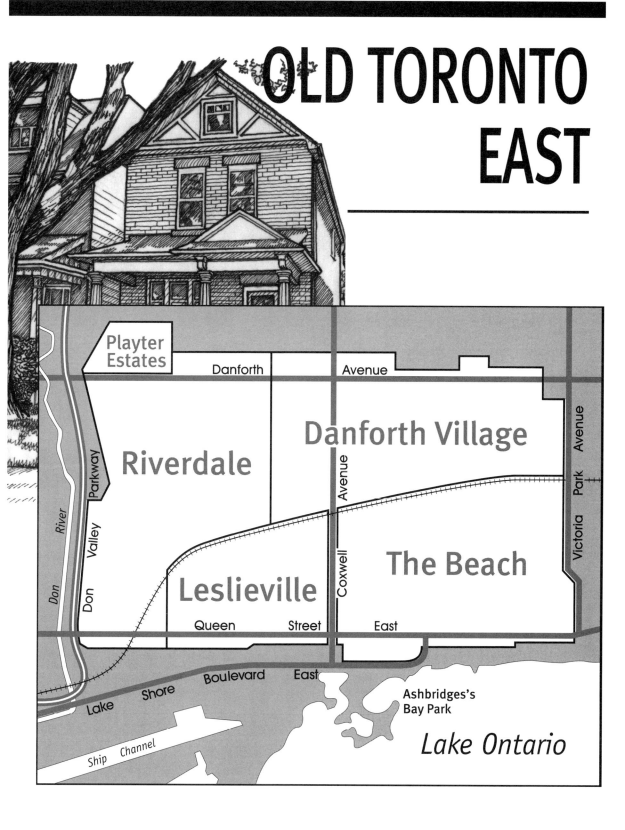

Playter Estates

Danforth Avenue

Danforth Village

Riverdale

Don River

Don Valley Parkway

Avenue

Victoria Park Avenue

Coxwell Avenue

The Beach

Leslieville

Queen Street East

Lake Shore Boulevard East

Ship Channel

Ashbridges's Bay Park

Lake Ontario

HISTORY: Danforth Village, north of the Danforth, was land origi-
nally held by the Church of England. Local street names like Glebemount and
Glebeholme are reminders that this was once church land.

The land south of the Danforth was not held by the church. This land was
originally owned by families engaged in either farming or in the brick-making
business.

Danforth Avenue, this neighbourhood's main thoroughfare, is named
after Asa Danforth, an American contractor who built Kingston Road in 1799;
ironically, he had nothing to do with the building of Danforth Avenue.

After being annexed to the City of Toronto in 1908 Danforth Village began
to be subdivided. The two most significant events in the growth of this
neighbourhood were the completion of the Prince Edward Viaduct in 1918
and the opening of the Bloor-Danforth subway in 1966.

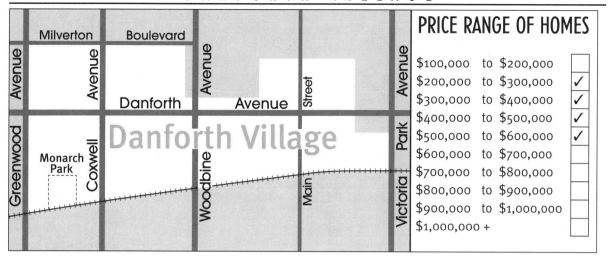

PRICE RANGE OF HOMES	
$100,000 to $200,000	
$200,000 to $300,000	✓
$300,000 to $400,000	✓
$400,000 to $500,000	✓
$500,000 to $600,000	✓
$600,000 to $700,000	
$700,000 to $800,000	
$800,000 to $900,000	
$900,000 to $1,000,000	
$1,000,000 +	

OVERVIEW:

The relative affordability of the houses in Danforth Village, together with the convenience of the Bloor-Danforth subway line, make this neighbourhood an excellent choice for first-time home buyers.

There are now a significant number of young professionals and families moving into this neighbourhood, which is helping to revitalize the whole area.

HOMES:

North of Danforth Avenue the streets are lined with semi-detached houses that feature distinctive front porches. South of Danforth Avenue the homes are more varied, ranging in size and style from Victorian semis to bungalows and newer townhouses.

The typical Danforth Village home was built in the 1920s or 1930s. The renovation boom has taken hold in this neighbourhood, with many of the wartime bungalows being fitted for second-storey additions, while others are being torn down and replaced with new home.

SHOPPING:

Danforth Avenue offers local residents a full range of shops and services. The Danforth is well known for it's authentic Greek restaurants and fresh fruit and vegetable markets.

Danforth Avenue is also known for its many bargain and discount stores. Shoppers World, an outdoor mall at the corner of Victoria Park and the Danforth is one of Toronto's largest discount malls.

RECREATION:

Monarch Park, located south of the Danforth between Coxwell and Greenwood features a variety of recreational facilities including an artificial ice rink, a wading pool and a swimming pool. The East Toronto Athletic Field located at Gerrard and Main streets encompasses a number of sports fields. The Ted Reeve Indoor Hockey Arena is situated adjacent to the sports fields.

The Earl Beattie Community Centre on Woodington Avenue, just north of Danforth Avenue, has an indoor swimming pool and a gymnasium.

The Danforth/Coxwell Public Library offers programs for toddlers and preschoolers.

SCHOOLS:

- (P)   Earl Haig Jr., 15 Earl Haig Ave., (416) 393-1640
- (P)   Earl Beatty Jr. and Sr., 55 Woodington Ave., (416) 393-9070
- (P)   Gledhill Jr., 2 Gledhill Ave., (416) 393-1745
- (PH) Monarch Park Collegiate., 1 Hanson St., (416) 393-0190
- (PH) Malvern Collegiate Institute, 55 Malvern Ave., (416) 393-1480
- (C)   St. Patrick, 45-49 Felstead Ave., (416) 393-5546
- (C)   Georges Etienne Cartier, 250 Gainsborough Rd., (416) 393-5314

TRANSPORTATION:

Danforth Village is well served by public transit. The Bloor-Danforth subway has stations at Greenwood, Coxwell, Woodbine, Main and Victoria Park. There is also a Go Train station at Danforth and Main. Regular bus or streetcar service runs on Greenwood, Coxwell, Gerrard and Woodbine.

Danforth Avenue provides motorists with easy access to the downtown while commuters are 10 to 15 minutes from the Don Valley Parkway and Lake Shore Boulevard.

HISTORY:

Leslieville began as a small village back in the 1850s. The village grew up around the Toronto Nurseries owned by George Leslie and sons, after whom this neighbourhood is named.

Most of Leslieville's residents were either market gardeners or were employed at one of several brick-making companies that used to operate in the area.

One of the first buildings in the village was the Leslieville Public School, built in 1863. Leslieville's first principal was Alexander Muir, the composer of *The Maple Leaf Forever*, which served as Canada's unofficial national anthem until 1967, when *O Canada* took over.

Muir's poetic verse was inspired when a brilliant autumn maple leaf fell from a Leslieville tree onto his jacket. That maple tree is still standing today and has become Leslieville's most famous landmark. It is designated by an historic plaque at the intersection of Laing Street and Memory Lane.

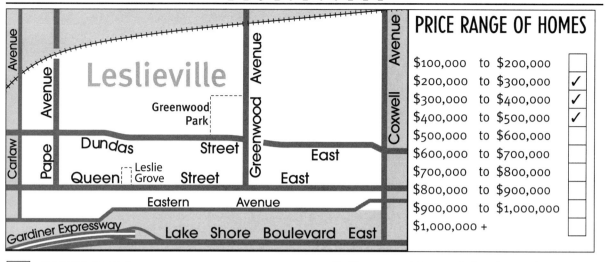

PRICE RANGE OF HOMES	
$100,000 to $200,000	
$200,000 to $300,000	✓
$300,000 to $400,000	✓
$400,000 to $500,000	✓
$500,000 to $600,000	
$600,000 to $700,000	
$700,000 to $800,000	
$800,000 to $900,000	
$900,000 to $1,000,000	
$1,000,000 +	

OVERVIEW:
The green and white Leslieville street signs that run along Queen Street were installed in 1987. These historic markers are symbolic of a renewed interest and pride in Leslieville among the residents of this up-and-coming east-end neighbourhood.

While Leslieville has retained its small village character, with its cozy houses, quaint stores and tree-lined streets, it has also been revitalized by the "Hollywood North" studio district along Eastern Avenue, where former industrial buildings and warehouses have been converted into lofts, film studios and production houses. It is not surprising then that Leslieville has become popular with young professionals looking for good value in a neighbourhood close to the downtown core.

HOMES:
Leslieville's older houses along Queen Street and south to Eastern Avenue were built in the late 1800s. They include Ontario Cottages, Second Empire row houses and Victorian houses.

Leslieville's second generation of houses, north of Queen Street, were built in the early 1900s. This district includes modest detached and semi-detached houses, as well as a large number of bungalows that are among the tiniest houses in Toronto.

Leslieville's newest housing stock includes a variety of condominium-loft ownership opportunities. Many of these have been built in former industrial buildings that have a beautiful aesthetic, lending an urban charm to the neighbourhood.

SHOPPING:
Leslieville's main shopping district runs along historic Queen Street. Here you will find one-of-a-kind antiques shops, art galleries, design shops and bakeries, as well as trendy cafés and restaurants.

The area on Gerrard Street East between Greenwood Avenue and Coxwell Avenue is known as the "India Bazaar." commercial centre of Toronto's East Indian community. The

smell of incense and the sound of music provide an exotic backdrop to the shops on this street.

The clothing stores sell imported silk fabrics, and the restaurant vendors barbecue spicy corn on the cob out on the sidewalk.

RECREATION:
Greenwood Park has three baseball diamonds, an artificial ice rink, a pool and a playground. The Jonathan Ashbridge Park on the south side of Queen Street features two tennis courts, a children's playground and a wading pool.

The S.H. Armstrong Community Recreation Centre on Woodfield Road has a gymnasium, an indoor pool, a fitness room, a craft room and meeting rooms.

The Gerrard/Ashdale Public Library has a wide variety of programs for children, adults and seniors.

SCHOOLS:
(P) Bruce Jr., 51 Larchmount Ave., (416) 393-0670
(P) Roden Jr., 151 Hiawatha Rd., (416) 393-9555
(P) Leslieville Jr., 254 Leslie St., (416) 393-9480
(P) Duke of Connaught Jr. and Sr., 70 Woodfield Rd., (416) 393 - 9455
(PH) Riverdale Collegiate Institute, 1094 Gerrard St., East., (416) 393-9820
(C) St. Joseph, 176 Leslie St., (416) 393-5209
(C) St. William, 343 Jones Ave., (416) 393-5303

TRANSPORTATION:
Leslieville is well served by the public transit system which operates bus or streetcar routes on Carlaw, Jones, Greenwood, Coxwell and Eastern avenues, as well as Queen and Gerrard streets. Most of these bus routes link up with stations on the Bloor-Danforth subway line.

Motorists can be downtown in minutes. Lake Shore Boulevard, the Gardiner Expressway and the Don Valley Parkway are also close by.

HISTORY: Playter Estates is named after the Playter family, who held the original land grants on both sides of the Don River near Bloor Street. Captain George Playter, the patriarch of the family, was an United Empire Loyalist who emigrated to Canada from Pennsylvania in the 1790s.

George's son, James Playter, owned the land where Playter Estates is today. It was James's eldest brother John who farmed and settled on this land. James's grandson, John Lea Playter, built the landmark Playter Homestead at 28 Playter Crescent in the mid 1870s. This grand historical home was owned by descendents of the Playter family right up until 2006.

The Playter house would set the residential tone for this neighbourhood, which began to be developed in 1912. Following completion of the Bloor Viaduct in 1918 the neighbourhood filled in rapidly. Playter Estates remained one of Toronto's best-kept secrets until only recently; it has now become one of Toronto's most desirable residential districts.

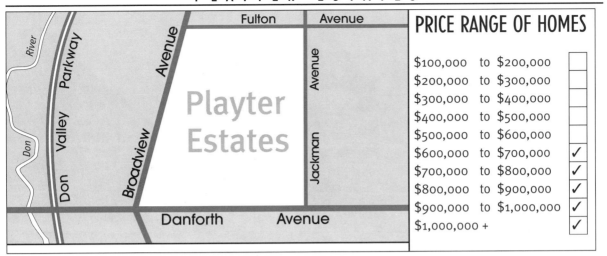

$100,000	to	$200,000	
$200,000	to	$300,000	
$300,000	to	$400,000	
$400,000	to	$500,000	
$500,000	to	$600,000	
$600,000	to	$700,000	✓
$700,000	to	$800,000	✓
$800,000	to	$900,000	✓
$900,000	to	$1,000,000	✓
$1,000,000 +			✓

OVERVIEW:

Playter Estates is an exclusive enclave of homes located just east of the Don Valley. This neighbourhood has many desirable features including beautiful vintage homes, a first class shopping district on Danforth Avenue, and convenient access to Toronto's transit system.

HOMES:

Playter Estates comprises large detached and semi-detached Edwardian- and Victorian-style homes, built mostly between 1912 and 1930.

The size and style of these homes is fairly uniform. However, each house has its own decorative accents ranging from slate roofs and fish scale shingles to stone gates and whimsical front porches.

SHOPPING:

An appealing aspect of living in Playter Estates is its easy access to the excellent shopping on Danforth Avenue. Here you will find everything from fashion boutiques and wine-making shops to gourmet coffee shops and the best selection of Greek restaurants in the city.

The Carrot Common, on the Danforth at Jackman Avenue, features many stores with a nature or health theme. Carrot Common's anchor store is the Big Carrot, a natural food market that attracts shoppers from all over the city.

RECREATION:

Riverdale Park East, located south of the Danforth, is one of Toronto's largest parks. This park's recreation facilities include seven tennis courts, an artificial ice rink, sports fields, a swimming pool and a walking/running track.

Riverdale Park also provides access to the Don Valley Ravine. This ravine includes a bicycle trail that runs south through the city along the west side of the Don River, where it connects to the Martin Goodman Trail along the waterfront.

Pape/Danforth is the closest public library. It offers a variety of children's programs.

SCHOOLS:

(P)   Jackman Avenue Jr., 79 Jackman Ave., (416) 393-9710
(P)   Earl Grey Sr., 100 Strathcona Ave., (416) 393-9545
(PH) Rosedale Heights Secondary School, 711 Bloor St. East., (416) 393-1580
(PH) Riverdale Collegiate Institute, 1094 Gerrard St. East., (416) 393-9820
(C)   Holy Name, 690 Carlaw Ave., (416) 393-5215

TRANSPORTATION:

The Bloor-Danforth subway stations at Broadview and at Chester are each a short walk from the Playter Estates homes.

Motorists travelling in and out of the city can gain immediate access to the Don Valley Parkway on-ramps, located just west of Broadview Avenue.

HISTORY: Riverdale was a small rural community until the Grand
Trunk Railway began steaming through here in the 1850s. The railway
brought industry and employment opportunities to Riverdale. It also attracted a pool of labourers who built the first homes in Riverdale, south of the
railway tracks.

Riverdale remained largely undeveloped north of Queen Street until 1884,
when it was annexed by the City of Toronto. At that time Riverdale was called
Riverside. The name was probably changed to Riverdale as a reference to the
city park of the same name that has long been a landmark in this area.

Riverdale's development was accelerated in 1918 with the building of
Toronto's largest bridge, the Prince Edward Viaduct. The Viaduct provided
Riverdale with an important link to the City of Toronto west of the Don River,
and marked a coming of age for this popular Toronto neighbourhood.

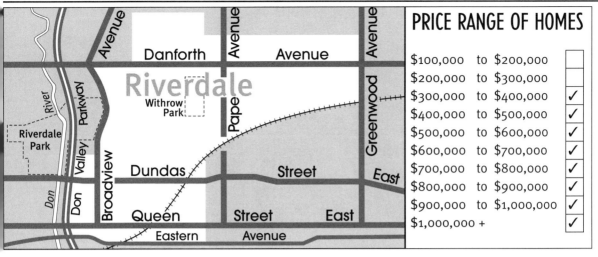

PRICE RANGE OF HOMES

$100,000	to	$200,000	
$200,000	to	$300,000	
$300,000	to	$400,000	✓
$400,000	to	$500,000	✓
$500,000	to	$600,000	✓
$600,000	to	$700,000	✓
$700,000	to	$800,000	✓
$800,000	to	$900,000	✓
$900,000	to	$1,000,000	✓
$1,000,000 +			✓

OVERVIEW:
Riverdale is the gateway to Toronto's east-end neighbourhoods. It is a large and diverse community that is especially well known for its colourful shopping districts and quaint Victorian homes.

North Riverdale, from Gerrard Street to Danforth Avenue, is very popular with young affluent professionals and families. South Riverdale, which has been dubbed "Studio City," is a popular home for music, art and film professionals. South Riverdale, which is home to over 50 film-related companies and approximately 70 per cent of Ontario's studio space, is now one of the top five filming locations in Ontario.

HOMES:
Riverdale's two- and three-storey Victorian houses were built largely between 1880 and 1924. These homes are shaded by some of the tallest maple trees in the city. Many Riverdale homes have parking off a rear laneway.

The houses in South Riverdale are smaller, older and less expensive on average than those in North Riverdale. There are also a number of new townhouse and condominium loft-style developments that have recently introduced to this neighbourhood.

SHOPPING:
Riverdale's best known shopping district is along Danforth Avenue, east of Broadview. The Danforth is the heart of Toronto's Greek community. It features many first-class Greek restaurants and a dazzling array of stores. If you enjoy great food be sure not to miss the "Taste of the Danforth" held annually in August.

Riverdale also has a Chinatown shopping district centred around Gerrard and Broadview. This stretch of stores is known for its bakeries, grocery stands and restaurants.

Another shopping destination point for Riverdale residents is Queen Broadview Village. This historic shopping district includes some interesting antique and collectible stores.

Gerrard Square, located at the corner of Pape Avenue and Gerrard Street, is a large indoor shopping mall with over 70 stores.

RECREATION:
Riverdale has a myriad of parks and parkettes situated throughout the neighbourhood. The three largest parks are Riverdale Park East, Withrow Park and Jimmie Simpson Park. Each of these Parks contain tennis courts, a wading pool, a hockey rink and a baseball diamond. Riverdale Park also has an outdoor pool and a running track.

The Jimmy Simpson Recreation Centre has an indoor swimming pool, a games room and a gymnasium. The Pape Recreational Centre has a gymnasium, an indoor pool, a weight room and meeting rooms. Riverdale has four public libraries that offer a myriad of programs for children, adults and seniors.

SCHOOLS:
(P) Earl Grey Sr., 100 Strathcona Ave., (416) 393-9545
(P) Frankland Jr., 816 Logan Ave., (416) 393-9720
(P) Blake Street Jr., 21 Boultbee Ave., (416) 393-9415
(P) Pape Avenue Jr., 404 Pape Ave., (416) 393-9470
(P) Quest Alternative Sr., 25 Bain Ave., (416) 393-9430
(P) Withrow Avenue Jr., 25 Bain Ave., (416) 393-9440
(P) Morse Jr., 180 Carlaw Ave., (416) 393-9494
(P) Queen Alexandria Sr., 181 Broadview Ave., (416) 393-9535
(P) Dundas Jr., 935 Dundas Street East (416) 393-9565
(P) First Nations, 935 Dundas street East., (416) 393-0555
(PH) Rosedale Heights Secondary School., 711 Bloor Street East, (416) 393-1580
(PH) Eastdale Collegiate Institute., 701 Gerrard Street East., (416)393-9630
(PH) Riverdale Collegiate Institute., 1094 Gerrard Street East (416) 393-9820
(C) Holy Name, 690 Carlaw Ave., (416) 393-5215

TRANSPORTATION:
Riverdale is an ideal location for commuters. The Don Valley Expressway, Lake Shore Boulevard, and the Gardiner Expressway are all quickly accessed from this neighbourhood.

Riverdale also has excellent access to public transit. There is regular bus service or streetcar service on Broadview, Carlaw, Jones and Greenwood avenues, as well as Queen and Gerrard streets. The Bloor-Danforth subway has five stations serving Riverdale, including Broadview, Chester, Pape, Donlands and Greenwood.

HISTORY:
The Beach was first settled by the Ashbridge family, who came to Canada from Philadelphia in 1793. Ashbridge's Bay Park is named after these pioneers.

The Ashbridges and a handful of other families farmed this district until the latter part of the 1800s, when many of The Beach properties were subdivided. At that time, large parcels of land were set aside for local parks.

Woodbine, Kew Gardens, Scarboro, Balmy Beach and Victoria Park collectively became Toronto's playgrounds by the lake. These amusement parks also attracted many summer cottagers to the area.

By the 1920s, the City of Toronto was expanding eastward and The Beach was subdivided for year-round residential development. Over the years The Beach has emerged as one of Toronto's most popular neighbourhoods.

PRICE RANGE OF HOMES

$100,000 to $200,000	
$200,000 to $300,000	✓
$300,000 to $400,000	✓
$400,000 to $500,000	✓
$500,000 to $600,000	✓
$600,000 to $700,000	✓
$700,000 to $800,000	✓
$800,000 to $900,000	✓
$900,000 to $1,000,000	✓
$1,000,000 +	✓

OVERVIEW:

The Beach looks and feels more like a lakeside resort town than a big-city neighbourhood. In the summertime, thousands of Torontonians and tourists flock to The Beach to walk on The Boardwalk, exercise along the Martin Goodman Trail, relax by the water, or shop and dine at the colourful stores and restaurants along Queen Street.

The social centre of The Beach neighbourhood is Kew Gardens, which hosts many annual events including a Christmas Tree and Menorah lighting festival, a Jazz festival and an Arts and Crafts show.

Ed. Note: A long-standing debate has ensued over the proper name for this neighbourhood. Some refer to it as "The Beach," others as "The Beaches." To be politically correct use "The Beach," otherwise both are acceptable.

HOMES:

The Beach has the greatest variety of architectural house styles of any Toronto neighbourhood. The charm of these homes is accentuated by the tree-lined streets that wind their way down to the lake.

Many of the original frame Beach cottages, built in the latter half of the 1800s and the early 1900s, have been modernized and are still standing today. However, the majority of The Beach homes were built during the 1920s and 1930s.

The former Greenwood racetrack site located at the foot of Woodbine Avenue is now the site of a large new home development known as "The Beach." This large collection of heritage-inspired custom-built homes include detached and semi-detached houses, as well as townhomes and a handful of low-rise condominium apartment buildings.

SHOPPING:

Queen Street is the most commercial of The Beach shopping districts. Many of these stores and restaurants have a beach motif that caters to the tourist trade.

The shops on Kingston Road also have a beach flavour, however they attract a more local clientele than the stores on Queen Street.

RECREATION:

The Beach's most famous landmark is The Boardwalk. The Boardwalk is skirted by the Martin Goodman Trail which spans the city's waterfront from The Beach to the Humber River.

Ashbridge's Bay Park is a good spot for family picnics and windsurfing. Its also a popular spot for beach volleyball. Glen Stewart Park off Queen Street has a picturesque ravine and nature trail. Donald Summerville Pool at the foot of Woodbine Avenue overlooks the lake and includes an Olympic-sized pool, a diving pool and a children's pool.

Kew Gardens has one of Toronto's most active tennis programs with 10 flood lit courts. This park also has a baseball diamond, an artificial ice rink, a children's playground, a wading pool and a concert bandstand. The Beach branch of the Toronto Public Library is right next to Kew Gardens, off Queen Street.

SCHOOLS:

(P)   Adam Beck Jr., 400 Scarborough Rd., (416) 393-1682
(P)   Balmy Beach Jr., 14 Pine Ave., (416) 393-1565
(P)   Beaches Alternative, JK-Gr.4, 50 Swanwick Ave.,
       (416) 393-1451
(P)   Glen Ames Sr., 18 Williamson Rd., (416) 393-1800
(P)   Kew Beach Jr., 101 Kippendavie Ave., (416) 393-1810
(P)   Kimberley Jr., 50 Swanwick Ave., (416) 393-1450
(P)   Norway Jr., 55 Corley Ave., (416) 393-1700
(P)   Williamson Rd, Jr., 24 Williamson Rd., (416) 393-1740
(PH) Malvern Collegiate Institute, 55 Malvern Ave.,
       (416) 393-1480
(C)   St.Dennis, 67 Balsam Ave., (416) 393-5310
(C)   St. John, 780 Kingston Rd., (416) 393-5220
(CH) Notre Dame, 12 Malvern Ave., (416) 393-5501

TRANSPORTATION:

There are bus or streetcar routes along Queen Street, Kingston Road, Gerrard Street, Victoria Park Avenue, Main Street and Woodbine Avenue. All these surface routes connect to Toronto's rapid transit lines and subway stations.

Motorists have the convenience of being located close to the Don Valley Expressway, the Gardiner Expressway and Lake Shore Boulevard.

OLD TORONTO WEST

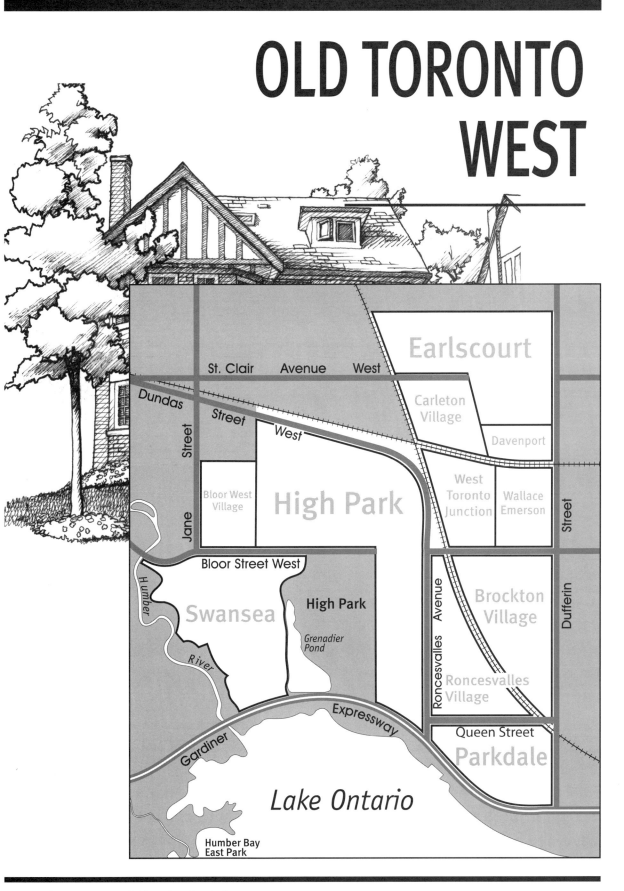

Earlscourt

St. Clair Avenue West

Dundas Street West

Carleton Village

Davenport

Bloor West Village

High Park

West Toronto Junction

Wallace Emerson

Jane Street

Bloor Street West

Swansea

High Park

Grenadier Pond

Humber River

Roncesvalles Avenue

Brockton Village

Dufferin Street

Roncesvalles Village

Gardiner Expressway

Queen Street

Parkdale

Lake Ontario

Humber Bay East Park

HISTORY:
In the 1850s the area now known as Bloor West Village was the property of Lieutenant Colonel William Smith Durie, the first commanding officer of the Queens Own Rifles. The street that ran through his estate is now known as Durie Street.

The present-day neighbourhood began to be developed in 1909 when this district became part of the City of Toronto. Soon after amalgamation with Toronto, Bloor West's roads were paved and city services were made available.

Bloor West's first residents were immigrants of Eastern European background. These are the residents who helped found the Bloor West Village Business Improvement Area, the first of its kind in Canada. Bloor West Village's European-style bakeries, cafés, delis and cheese shops have have been attracting shoppers from all over the city for many years, and have helped make this one of Toronto's premier neighbourhoods.

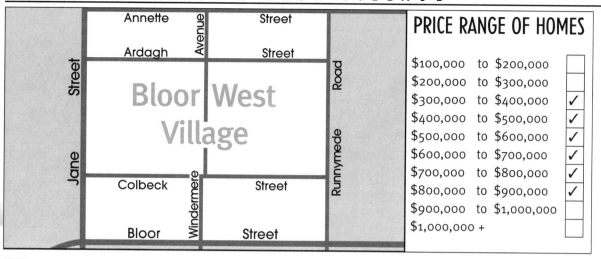

PRICE RANGE OF HOMES	
$100,000 to $200,000	
$200,000 to $300,000	
$300,000 to $400,000	✓
$400,000 to $500,000	✓
$500,000 to $600,000	✓
$600,000 to $700,000	✓
$700,000 to $800,000	✓
$800,000 to $900,000	✓
$900,000 to $1,000,000	
$1,000,000 +	

OVERVIEW:

Bloor West Village is a popular neighbourhood for families. It has many excellent schools and is within walking distance of High Park, Toronto's biggest and best known park.

Bloor West Village has one the best neighbourhood shopping districts in the city. The mix of brand-name retail franchises alongside locally owned specialty stores and neighbourhood pubs and restaurants offers residents big-city convenience with a small-town appeal.

HOMES:

Bloor West Village homes are all fairly similar in size and style, having been built in a relatively short period of time between 1912 and 1923.

Bloor West Village houses feature deep front porches that are well shaded by the majestic oak and maple trees that line the streets of this neighbourhood.

The majority of houses feature decorative oak accents, hardwood floors and fireplaces.

SHOPPING:

The Bloor West Village shopping district is as much about eating as it is about shopping. It's a virtual smorgasbord of bakeries, delicatessens, fruit and vegetable markets, coffee shops, cafés and restaurants.

The Baby Point Village shopping district, on Annette Street just east of Jane Street, includes a floral design store, a home decorating store, a neighbourhood pub and other neighbourhood retailers.

RECREATION:

High Park, a 399-acre parkland, is within walking distance of Bloor West Village. This Toronto landmark contains picnic areas, flower gardens, animal paddocks, a restaurant, an outdoor amphitheatre, sports facilities, a trackless train, an adventure playground and a large pond.

Annette Recreation Centre is attached to the Annette Street public school. This centre has an indoor pool, a small gymnasium and a baseball diamond. A little bit east of the Annette Centre is the Annette Street Public Library, which offers programs for adults, children and preschoolers.

Bloor West Village also has one movie theatre — the Humber — which is conveniently located on Bloor Street, just west of Jane Street. The former Runneymede Theatre on Bloor Street is now a Chapters bookstore.

SCHOOLS:

(P) Annette Jr. & Sr., 265 Annette Street., (416) 393-9040
(PH) Humberside Collegiate Institute, 280 Quebec Ave.,
     (416) 393-0000
(PH) Western Technical Commercial School,
     125 Evelyn Cres., (416) 393-0500
(C) St. Cecilia, 355 Annette St., (416) 393-5218
(C) St. Pius X, 71 Jane St., (416) 393-5237

TRANSPORTATION:

The Jane and Runnymede subway stations are part of the Bloor-Danforth subway line. They are both within walking distance of the homes in Bloor West Village.

The Annette Street bus connects passengers to the Dupont subway station on the Yonge-University-Spadina subway line. There are additional bus routes on Jane Street and Runnymede Road.

Motorists are approximately 10 minutes from the Gardiner Expressway and Lake Shore Boulevard. These routes both provide quick access into and out of the city.

HISTORY:

The Village of Brockton was likely named after Captain James Brock, who held a large parcel of land in this area in the early 1800s. Captain Brock was a cousin of Sir Issac Brock, a Canadian war hero who fought in the War of 1812.

Brockton was initially settled in the 1840s by Irish immigrants. These first settlers found employment in Brockton's two rope factories. They also cultivated their land and tended to their livestock as a source of income.

In 1881 Brockton was incorporated as a village. However, only three years after its incorporation Brockton had accumulated a large debt. Brockton's financial troubles led the residents of the village to vote in favour of amalgamation with the City of Toronto. This merger became official on March 25, 1884.

Ed. Note: The Village of Brockton Town Hall, built in 1882, is still standing on the southwest corner of Dundas Street and Brock Avenue. This historic building is now being used as a retail store.

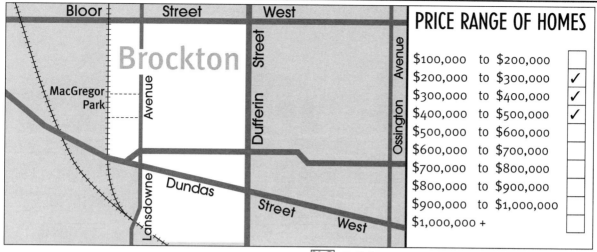

PRICE RANGE OF HOMES	
$100,000 to $200,000	
$200,000 to $300,000	✓
$300,000 to $400,000	✓
$400,000 to $500,000	✓
$500,000 to $600,000	
$600,000 to $700,000	
$700,000 to $800,000	
$800,000 to $900,000	
$900,000 to $1,000,000	
$1,000,000 +	

OVERVIEW:

Brockton Village is a quiet, unassuming neighbourhood in west downtown Toronto. Historical street signs along Dundas Street mark the entrance way to the commercial centre of the neighbourhood.

Industry was a big part of Brockton Village until the 1980s, when numerous plant closings left this area in despair. However, a recent housing boom throughout the city has spilled over into Brockton and is helping to revitalize this traditionally blue-collar neighbourhood.

HOMES:

The majority of Brockton Village houses were built between 1880 and 1920. There are many types of homes here, but the most common is the Victorian semi-detached, or row house.

The streetscape is very European. Many of the older brick houses have been brightly painted and feature a front porch with pillars, wrought iron railings and beautifully maintained gardens.

The houses are fairly narrow, and so are the lots. Parking is accessed from laneways at the rear of the properties.

New townhouses, condominiums and lofts have recently been built in this neighbourhood, providing an affordable mix of new housing options.

SHOPPING:

Brockton Village's main shopping districts are on Dundas Street West and on College Street. These two shopping areas contain mostly Portuguese food shops and restaurants, which cater to the large Portuguese community in this neighbourhood.

The Bloordale Village shopping district along Bloor Street has a wide range of shops and restaurants. The merchants here frequently sponsor special events for the local community.

The Dufferin Mall, south of Bloor Street, includes large chain department stores and over 100 retail outlets.

RECREATION:

The McCormick Recreation Centre has a gymnasium, an exercise room, a games room and an indoor pool. The playground adjacent to the centre has a wading pool and a baseball diamond.

Dufferin Grove Park has a myriad of sports facilities including tennis courts, a basketball court, a playing field and an artificial ice rink. This park also offers some wonderful arts and crafts and nature programs.

SCHOOLS:

(P) Alexander Muir/Gladstone Jr. and Sr., 108 Gladstone Ave., (416) 393-9140
(P) Brock Jr., 93 Margueretta St., (416) 393-9245
(P) Shirley St., Jr., 38 Shirley St., (416) 393-9270
(P) Kent Sr., 980 Dufferin St., (416) 393-0400
(PH) Bloor Collegiate Institute, 1141 Bloor St.West, (416) 393-1420
(PH) Brockton High School, 90 Croatia Street., (416) 393-0430
(PH) West Toronto Collegiate, 330 Lansdowne Ave., (416) 393-1500
(C) St. Helen, 1196 College St., (416) 393-5208
(C) St. Veronica, 30 Bank St., (416) 393-5280
(C) Bishop Marrocco/Thomas Merton Secondary School, 1515 Bloor St. West, (416) 393-5545
(C) St. Mary Secondary School, 66 Dufferin Park Ave., (416) 393-5528

TRANSPORTATION:

Regular bus service on Lansdowne Avenue and Dufferin Street connect passengers to stations on the Bloor-Danforth subway line. The streetcar lines on Dundas Street and College Avenue connect commuters to Toronto's downtown business and commercial districts.

Motorists are approximately 15 minutes from the Gardiner Expressway and Lake Shore Boulevard, via Dufferin Street.

HISTORY:
Carleton Village is named after Guy Carleton, who served as the first Governor of Canada in 1768.

The spelling of the Carleton Village name, with or without an "e," has been contentious since the areas inception in the 1850s. Even today, the historical street markers in the Village spell Carleton without an "e," while the local public school spells Carleton with an "e" in its name.

By the 1860s, despite its spelling controversy, Carleton Village had emerged as a prosperous railway and industrial centre.

Carleton Village amalgamated with the Town of West Toronto in 1889. Then, in 1909, this district was annexed by the City of Toronto.

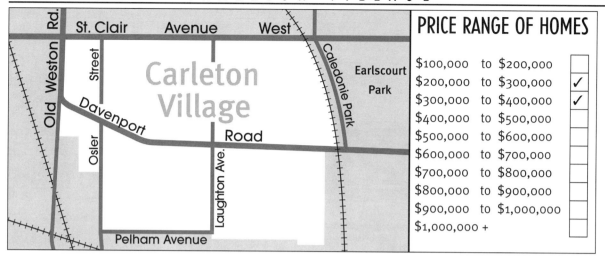

PRICE RANGE OF HOMES

$100,000 to $200,000		
$200,000 to $300,000	✓	
$300,000 to $400,000	✓	
$400,000 to $500,000		
$500,000 to $600,000		
$600,000 to $700,000		
$700,000 to $800,000		
$800,000 to $900,000		
$900,000 to $1,000,000		
$1,000,000 +		

OVERVIEW:

Carleton Village has always been a working-class neighbourhood. Today, it is populated mostly by Portuguese, Italian, and Asian families.

Carleton Village was designated as an historical district by the City of Toronto in 1989. This recognition has helped raise the profile of this quiet, west-end neighbourhood.

HOMES:

Some of the old labourers' cottages on Old Weston Road date back to the 1850s and 1860s. However, the majority of Carleton Village homes were built between the 1880s and 1920s.

Carleton's housing stock is a mix of detached, semi-detached, and attached Victorian-style homes. The front facades of some of these houses have been refaced with new brick, creating a modern look that is in sharp contrast to the older houses in the neighbourhood.

SHOPPING:

Some national retail stores have recently moved into the area around the intersection of Keele and St. Clair. Their close proximity to Carleton Village is an added convenience for shoppers in this neighbourhood.

The local shopping district on St. Clair Avenue is called St. Clair Gardens. It features a large variety of shops and services. There are many cosy cafés and restaurants along this route.

Davenport Road contains a limited number of convenience-type shops for residents located at the south end of the neighbourhood.

RECREATION:

Earlscourt Park and the adjacent recreation centre attract residents from the entire St. Clair West district. Their facilities include: an indoor/outdoor pool, a gymnasium, an artificial ice rink, tennis courts, a seniors lounge and day care.

Wadsworth Park is smaller and less busy. It's perfect for young children as it contains both a playground and a wading pool.

The St. Clair/Silverthorn branch of the Toronto Public Library has programs for children and preschoolers.

SCHOOLS:

(P)   Carleton Jr. & Sr. School, 2054 Davenport Road, (416) 393-1600
(P)   The City School, 315 Osler St., (416) 393-1470
(PH) Oakwood Collegiate Institute, 991 St. Clair Ave. West, (416) 393-1780
(C)   Pope Paul, 270 Laughton Ave., (416) 393-5374
(CH) Brother Edmund Rice Secondary School, 55 Pelham Ave., (416) 393-5523

TRANSPORTATION:

The St. Clair streetcar and the Davenport bus connect commuters to stations on the Yonge-University-Spadina subway line.

Carleton Village's main arterial roadways include St. Clair Avenue and Davenport Road. These roads provide motorists with easy access to all parts of the city.

HISTORY:
The Earlscourt neighbourhood was settled in 1906 by labourers from the British Isles. In addition to their work at the local factories, Earlscourt families would toil day and night building meagre tar and paper shacks as temporary homes until they could save enough money to build a proper brick house.

The spiritual leader of the Earlscourt community during these difficult times was the Reverend Peter Bryce. Each night, Bryce would trek through Earlscourt's muddy streets, aided only by a lantern and a pair of high boots. His visits were said to have offered hope and inspiration to many families.

The quality of life in Earlscourt began to improve once it was annexed by the City of Toronto in 1910.

Ed. Note: During the First World War, Earlscourt's enlistment rate per capita was among the highest in the British Empire. This wave of patriotism prompted the Prince of Wales (later Edward VIII) to visit the veterans' section of Prospect Cemetery in 1919. The Prince of Wales planted a silver maple tree there; it's still standing and its seeds have propagated a great number of Prospect Cemetery's majestic maples.

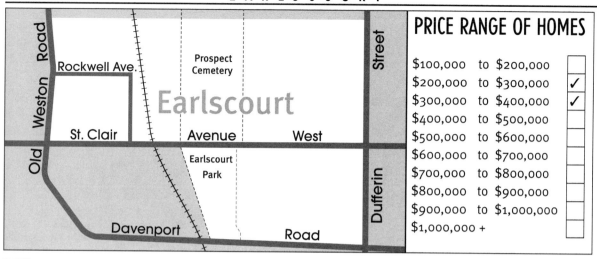

PRICE RANGE OF HOMES

$100,000 to $200,000	
$200,000 to $300,000	✓
$300,000 to $400,000	✓
$400,000 to $500,000	
$500,000 to $600,000	
$600,000 to $700,000	
$700,000 to $800,000	
$800,000 to $900,000	
$900,000 to $1,000,000	
$1,000,000 +	

OVERVIEW:

Since the 1960s the Earlscourt neighbourhood has been recognized as the business and cultural centre of Toronto's Italian community. However, in recent years the ethnic mix in this neighbourhood has begun to change as Canadians of West Indian, Portuguese, Greek, Latin American and East Indian descent have begun moving into the area. Earlscourt is also being rediscovered by Anglo-Canadians from other parts of Toronto.

HOMES:

Earlscourt's solid brick homes were built mostly between 1910 and 1950. There is a good mix of detached and semi-detached houses, as well as bungalows.

Most of the houses contain a "cantina" — the Italian equivalent of a cold cellar. You will be hard pressed to find a backyard with a lawn; instead, these areas are reserved for fruit and vegetable gardens.

SHOPPING:

The Corso Italia Shopping district along St. Clair Avenue West has a lively Italian atmosphere that emanates from its open-air cafés and bistros. Corso Italia has been dubbed "Hollywood North" because of the many major motion pictures that have been filmed on location here.

RECREATION:

Earlscourt Park, located along St. Clair Avenue West, is one of Toronto's busiest parks. This 36-acre park includes four tennis courts, soccer fields, a baseball diamond and an outdoor ice rink. The Joseph J. Piccininni Community Centre is located right next to Earlscourt Park. This modern facility boasts an indoor soccer field and probably the only indoor bocce courts in Canada. It also has a 25-metre swimming pool, a gymnasium and a seniors' lounge.

The Dufferin/St. Clair Library, or "biblioteca," contains the largest collection of Italian books in the city's public library system. The St. Clair-Silverthorn Library reflects the area's diverse population by offering books in many languages, including Italian, Greek and Punjabi.

SCHOOLS:

(P)   General Mercer Jr., 30 Turnberry Ave., (416) 393-1414
(PH) Oakwood Collegiate Institute, 991 St. Clair Ave. W., (416) 393-1780
(C)   Pope Paul, 270 Laughton Ave., (416) 393-5374
(C)   Richard W. Scott, 151 Rosemount Ave., (416) 393-5317
(CH) Brother Edmund Rice Secondary, 55 Pelham Ave., (416) 393-5523

TRANSPORTATION:

The St. Clair West streetcar takes passengers through a scenic route to the St. Clair station on the Yonge-University-Spadina subway line. At the south end of Earlscourt there is a limited bus service on Davenport Road.

Motorists are within 15 minutes of downtown Toronto and are approximately 10 minutes from the Allen Expressway, which provides commuters with access to Toronto's major highways.

HISTORY: The High Park neighbourhood contains a wealth of history. The area
north of Bloor Street was formerly part of the Town of West Toronto Junction, which was
annexed by the City of Toronto in 1909. The historical house at 191 High Park Avenue was
built in 1888 for D.W. Clendenan, the first mayor of West Toronto Junction. The affluence
of this former town is recalled in the grand estates that line High Park Avenue.

The High Park property south of Bloor Street was purchased in 1836 by John Howard,
Toronto's first surveyor. Howard named his estate High Park because of its magnificent
view of Lake Ontario. In 1873 Howard deeded his beloved High Park estate to the City of
Toronto. John Howard's former residence – Colborne Lodge – is still situated on its original site in High Park, where it is now a museum.

Howard also owned the land abutting the east side of the park, where he intended to
create a residential neighbourhood. Unfortunately, Howard would not live to see the
development of this area. That did not take place until the early 1900s, when the streetcar began service to High Park, which led to the building of most of the homes adjacent
to High Park.

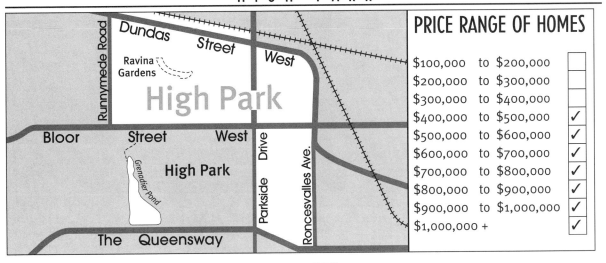

PRICE RANGE OF HOMES	
$100,000 to $200,000	
$200,000 to $300,000	
$300,000 to $400,000	
$400,000 to $500,000	✓
$500,000 to $600,000	✓
$600,000 to $700,000	✓
$700,000 to $800,000	✓
$800,000 to $900,000	✓
$900,000 to $1,000,000	✓
$1,000,000 +	✓

OVERVIEW:

The High Park neighbourhood is home to a wide range of people. Its highly regarded schools, including Humberside Collegiate, attract many families with school-age children to this neighbourhood. High Park contains numerous rental opportunities that are popular with singles and couples. There are also a handful of seniors' accommodations within this neighbourhood.

The topography of the High Park neighbourhood features gently rolling hills, winding streets and towering oak trees that enchant and delight all those who live here. The beauty of this neighbourhood emanates from High Park, which is one of Toronto's largest and most popular parks.

HOMES:

High Park's winding, tree-lined streets are lined with impressive Victorian-, Edwardian-, and Tudor-style homes. These captivating houses were built largely during the late 1800s and early 1900s. Several of these houses have been divided into multiple-family dwellings.

New upscale condominium and loft developments have recently sprung up in this neighbourhood, providing home-buyers with a myriad of options. The High Park neighbourhood also features a selection of older condominium apartment buildings along Quebec Avenue, north of Bloor Street. These apartments are in the entry-level price range. They include balconies, some of which feature south views that overlook High Park and Lake Ontario.

SHOPPING:

High Park is conveniently located within walking distance of Bloor West Village, one of Toronto's most popular shopping districts. The "Village" is known across the city for its European bakeries, delicatessens, specialty food shops, cafés and restaurants. The Roncesvalles Village shopping district along Roncesvalles Avenue is known for its european delis, bakeries and fruit and vegetable markets. This village atmosphere is enhanced by neighbourhood coffee shops and a wide selection of restaurants. The Junction Gardens shopping district along Dundas Street West has recently been revitalized. This shopping strip has gone back to its roots as an important railway centre, by incorporating a railway lantern into the heritage street signs along Dundas Street.

RECREATION:

High Park encompasses 399 acres of public parkland. This city park includes a fishing pond, an outdoor theatre, animal paddocks, picnic grounds, playgrounds, a restaurant, an historic museum, flower gardens, an adventure playground and a trackless train.

The sports facilities of this park include tennis, baseball, soccer, lawn bowling, swimming, and skating, as well as walking, jogging and cycling paths found throughout the park.

You can read all about the rich history of High Park at the Runnymede Public Library on Bloor Street or the High Park Public Library on Roncesvalles. Both libraries offer a myriad of programs for neighbourhood residents.

SCHOOLS:

(P)   High Park Alternative Jr., 265 Annette St., (416) 393-9040
(P)   Keele St. Jr., 99 Mountview Ave., (416) 393-9035
(P)   Mountview Alternative Jr., 99 Mountview Ave., (416) 393-9037
(P)   Runnymede Jr. & Sr., 357 Runnymede Rd., (416) 393-9055
(P)   Annette Jr.& Sr., 265 Annette St., (416) 393-9040
(PH) Humberside Collegiate Institute, 280 Quebec Ave., (416) 393-0000
(PH) Western Technical Commercial School, 125 Evelyn Cres., (416) 393-0500
(C)   St. Cecelia, 355 Annette St., (416) 393-5218
(PR) Montessori High Park School, 35 High Park Gdns., (416) 763-6097
(PR) Montessori Humberside School, 411 Clendenan Ave., (416) 762-8888

TRANSPORTATION:

The Bloor-Danforth subway line has three stations serving the High Park neighbourhood, including the Runnymede, High Park, and Keele stations.

Motorists are approximately five minutes from the Queensway, which connects commuters to Lake Shore Boulevard and the Gardiner Expressway.

HISTORY:
Parkdale's history began in the late 1800s when it was an elite residential suburb that rivaled Rosedale as Toronto's most desirable address.

Parkdale's popularity led to its incorporation as a village in 1878. Then, in 1889 and after many heated public debates, Parkdale's citizens voted in favour of amalgamation with the City of Toronto.

Parkdale became Toronto's playground by the lake in 1922, when the Sunnyside Amusement Park and Bathing Pavilion opened for business on Parkdale's beaches. Sunnyside was the place to be and be seen for a generation of Torontonians.

In 1956, Sunnyside was shut down by the city in order to make room for the Gardiner Expressway and a revamped Lake Shore Boulevard. Unfortunately, these new expressways cut Parkdale off from the lake and its glorious past. Parkdale then went into a period of decline that it is still recovering from today.

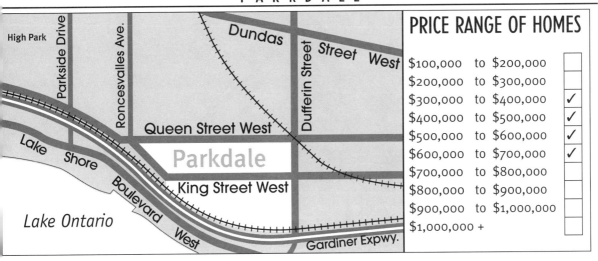

PRICE RANGE OF HOMES

$100,000	to $200,000	
$200,000	to $300,000	
$300,000	to $400,000	✓
$400,000	to $500,000	✓
$500,000	to $600,000	✓
$600,000	to $700,000	✓
$700,000	to $800,000	
$800,000	to $900,000	
$900,000	to $1,000,000	
$1,000,000 +		

OVERVIEW:

Parkdale still has many big-city social problems to contend with. However, these concerns are being addressed by a local residents' group known as the Parkdale Community Watch. The Parkdale Community Watch recently received an award as the best neighbourhood watch group. This award was presented by the International Society of Crime Prevention.

The Parkdale neighbourhood possesses many positive attributes. It has some of Toronto's most vibrant shopping districts, wonderful tree-lined streets, affordable Victorian homes, and impressive mansions that remind onlookers that Parkdale was once Toronto's wealthiest district. Parkdale is also within walking distance of Toronto's waterfront parks.

HOMES:

South Parkdale's grandiose mansions were built between 1875 and 1895. Some of these houses have been converted into bacherlorettes or rooming houses. However, the current by-laws advocate restoring these houses to single-family use.

SHOPPING:

The main commercial shopping area in Parkdale has historically been on Queen Street. This vibrant shopping district seems to be in a state of perpetual activity; it includes an eclectic mix of shops and restaurants.

The Roncesvalles Village shopping district, north of Queen Street, is the cultural centre of Toronto's Polish community. There are many outstanding food markets, delis and restaurants along this route.

RECREATION:

Parkdale is conveniently located within walking distance of High Park and the recreational paths and parks along Toronto's waterfront.

Parkdale has four community centres that serve the residents of this neighbourhood. They include Holy Family Community Centre on Close Avenue, Masryk-Cowan Community Recreation Centre on Cowan Avenue, McCormick Recreation Centre on Sheridan Avenue, and the Parkdale Community Centre on West Lodge Avenue.

The Parkdale Public Library on Queen Street and the High Park Public Library on Roncesvalles both provide programming for Parkdale residents.

SCHOOLS:

(P) Fern Avenue Jr. & Sr., 128 Fern Ave., (416) 393-9130
(P) Gordon Avenue Jr., 225 Garden Ave., (416) 393-9165
(P) Howard Jr., 30 Marmaduke Street., (416) 393-9255
(P) Parkdale Jr. & Sr., 46 West Lodge Ave., (416) 393-1280
(P) Queen Victoria Jr., 100 Close Ave., (416) 393-9200
(PH) Bloor Collegiate Institute, 1141 Bloor St. W., (416) 393-1420
(PH) Parkdale Collegiate, 209 Jameson Ave., (416) 393-9000
(C) Holy Family, 141 Close Avenue, (416) 393-5212
(C) St. Veronica 30 Bank St., (416) 393-5280

TRANSPORTATION:

Streetcar service on Queen Street, King Street, Dundas Street, Roncessvales Avenue and Macdonell Avenue connect passengers to the downtown, or to subway stations on the Bloor-Danforth subway line.

Motorists are just minutes from downtown. There is direct access to both the Gardiner Expressway and Lake Shore Boulevard at the south end of Parkdale.

ROARK ANDRADE

HISTORY:
Roncesvalles was originally settled by Colonel Walter O'Hara in 1850. O'Hara was a soldier in the British army prior to immigrating to Canada. O'Hara was wounded and captured by the French in the Roncesvalles Gorge in northern Spain; hence the name Roncesvalles. O'Hara, who was originally from Ireland, named the streets here; O'Hara, Geoffrey, Constence, Marion and Sorauren are named after his family members, and Fermanaugh is the province in Northern Ireland where the O'Hara clan originated.

The development of the present-day neighbourhood was spurred on by the street-car, which came to this area in the early 1900s. Roncesvalles was a family-oriented neighbourhood right from the start. Nearby industries offered employment to the many British immigrants that settled here. The landmark St. Vincent de Paul Roman Catholic Church on Roncesvalles was the spiritual centre of these first residents.

Following the Second World War an influx of Eastern Europeans, predominantly Poles, settled in Roncesvalles. They built their own church: St. Casimir's. Sir Casimir Gzowski, a Polish patriot, settled in Toronto in the early 1850s and was instrumental in the building of Toronto's roads and railways.

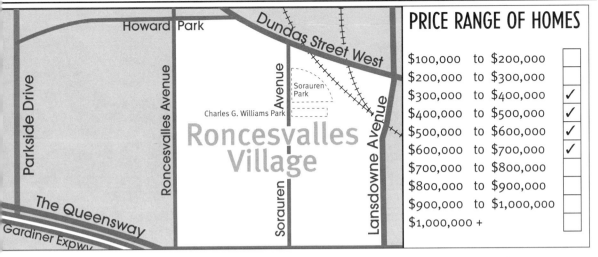

PRICE RANGE OF HOMES

$100,000	to	$200,000	
$200,000	to	$300,000	
$300,000	to	$400,000	✓
$400,000	to	$500,000	✓
$500,000	to	$600,000	✓
$600,000	to	$700,000	✓
$700,000	to	$800,000	
$800,000	to	$900,000	
$900,000	to	$1,000,000	
$1,000,000 +			

OVERVIEW:

Roncesvalles is known for its European ambience and small-town feel. This neighbourhood is popular with young families who appreciate the convenience of the location just west of downtown. The close proximity to High Park, easy access to public transit, and the Roncesvalles shops and restaurants are also popular drawing cards.

The Roncesvalles Polish Festival, which takes place annually in September, attracts thousands of visitors. Roncesvalles Avenue is closed off for this festival that includes Polish dancers, children's games and rides, polka bands and lots of food and refreshments.

Roncesvalles Avenue is said to be a favourite among streetcar enthusiasts, who relish the fact that the stops are distanced far enough apart for the streetcar to build up some speed, and who appreciate the picturesque and lively atmosphere along the route.

HOMES:

Roncesvalles's housing stock consists primarily of Victorian and Edwardian detached, semi-detached and attached homes. These include two-storey, two-and-a-half-storey and three-storey homes. These brick homes have many whimsical features including Victorian gables, columned front porches and nice interior wood trim. Parking ranges from permit street parking to rear laneway parking that may include a garage.

Roncesvalles has a nice selection of loft conversions, which have recently taken place in former commercial and industrial buildings in pockets of this neighbourhood.

SHOPPING:

The Roncesvalles Village shopping district along Roncesvalles Avenue has a small-town, village feel. Most of the shops and restaurants are independently owned, family-run businesses. However, there are a growing number of chain stores along this route as well.

Sometimes referred to as "Little Poland," Roncesvalles Avenue is the perfect place to indulge in traditional Polish culinary delights such as perogies, borscht, schnitzel, sausage, sauerkraut and paczki — a round, sugar-coated and fruit-filled doughnut.

In addition to Polish fare, Roncesvalles Avenue patrons can also enjoy traditional Canadian fare, as well as Greek, Asian, Indian and Thai cuisine.

RECREATION:

High Park is a short walk west of this neighbourhood. Visitors to this park can engage in a myriad of sport opportunities, from tennis to fishing in Grenadier Pond. There is also a popular children's playground and a zoo. Walkers, joggers and nature enthusiasts will enjoy the many trails that traverse this park.

Local parks include Sorauren Park, at the northeast corner of Sorauren and Wabash, and the Charles G. Williams Park at the southeast corner of Sorauren and Wabash. The Keele Community Centre on Glenlake Avenue has an indoor pool. High Park Library on Roncesvalles Avenue offers programs for children and adults.

SCHOOLS:

(P)   Fern Avenue Jr. & Sr., 128 Fern Ave., (416) 393-9130
(P)   Gordon Avenue Jr., 225 Garden Ave., (416) 393-9165
(P)   Howard Jr., 30 Marmaduke Street., (416) 393-9255
(P)   Parkdale Jr. & Sr., 46 West Lodge Ave., (416) 393-1280
(PH) Parkdale Collegiate, 209 Jameson Ave., (416) 393-9000
(PH) West Toronto Secondary School, 330 Lansdowne Ave., (416)393-1500
(C)   St. Vincent de Paul Separate School, 116 Fermanaugh Ave., (416) 393-5227
(CH) Bishop Marrocco/Thomas Merton, 1515 Bloor St. West, (416) 393-5545

TRANSPORTATION:

Streetcar service is available on Queen Street, Dundas Street and Roncesvalles Avenue, with stops at numerous subway stations along the Yonge-University-Spadina and Bloor-Danforth lines. The Lansdowne bus stops at the Lansdowne subway station on the Bloor-Danforth line.

Go Transit has a station at the Crossways, on the northeast corner of Bloor Street West and Dundas Street West. Commuters can access Union Station from this line. Motorists are approximately a 15-minute drive from the downtown core.

HISTORY:

Swansea was incorporated as a village in 1926. The Swansea Village corporate seal reveals a great deal about the colourful history of this neighbourhood.

Included on the Swansea seal is explorer Etienne Brûlé, who in 1615 became the first European to set foot on what is now Swansea. Also shown is a First Nations member. This is symbolic in that it recognizes that First Nations members were the first people to inhabit Swansea, hundreds of years ago.

The hills in the Swansea Village seal represent Swansea's rolling countryside, which is similar to the topography found in Swansea, Wales, after which this neighbourhood is named. The water in the Swansea seal refers to Swansea's natural boundaries, which include Lake Ontario, the Humber River and Grenadier Pond.

In 1967 Swansea Village joined Forest Hill Village as one of the last two independent villages to be annexed by the City of Toronto.

Ed. note: Legendary Canadian writer Lucy Maud Montgomery, author of Anne of Green Gables, *penned her last two novels at Journey's End, her final home, which is situated on scenic Riverside Drive in Swansea.*

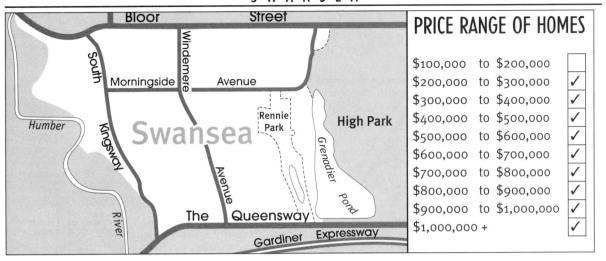

PRICE RANGE OF HOMES

$100,000	to	$200,000	
$200,000	to	$300,000	✓
$300,000	to	$400,000	✓
$400,000	to	$500,000	✓
$500,000	to	$600,000	✓
$600,000	to	$700,000	✓
$700,000	to	$800,000	✓
$800,000	to	$900,000	✓
$900,000	to	$1,000,000	✓
$1,000,000 +			✓

OVERVIEW:
Swansea Village is the only Toronto neighbourhood that has its own community-run Town Hall. Swansea is also the only Toronto neighbourhood to have a lake, a river and a pond as its natural boundaries. Swansea's hilly terrain, winding roads and many mature trees accentuate the storybook houses that line the residential streets of this neighbourhood.

HOMES:
Swansea's high-end homes are located either at the western edge of High Park overlooking Grenadier Pond, or at the Brule Gardens enclave found in the northwest pocket of Swansea. Some of these Tudor-style mansions sell for more than $1 million.

Swansea also contains a large number of semi-detached houses and bungalows, located mostly in the centre of the neighbourhood. The typical Swansea house was built between 1905 and 1935.

At the south end of Swansea, down Windermere Avenue, is a cluster of rental apartment buildings. This pocket includes some of the original Swansea workers cottages, built in the 1880s.

New to the neighbourhood is the "Windermere by the Lake" development at the foot of Windermere Avenue, south of the Queensway. This residential development includes 120 traditional townhomes and three condominium towers.

SHOPPING:
The most convenient shopping district for Swansea residents is the Bloor West Village shopping district on Bloor Street West. Bloor West Village features Toronto's best selection of European bakeries and delis.

RECREATION:
The Swansea Town Hall and Community Centre includes a small gymnasium, and a selection of meeting rooms available for a variety of functions. Swansea Town Hall is also the home of the Swansea Memorial Public Library, the smallest branch of the Toronto Public Library system. This branch specializes in material for children and seniors and provides complete interlibrary loan services.

Rennie Park, located on the east side of Rennie Terrace south of Morningside Avenue, has four tennis courts, an artificial ice rink and a wading pool. High Park, which can be accessed from Bloor Street, features a full day's worth of recreational activities including fishing, theatre performances, train rides, an animal zoo, historical exhibits, a restaurant and a myriad of fitness opportunities.

SCHOOLS:
(P) Swansea Jr. & Sr., 207 Windermere Ave., (416) 393-9080
(PH) Humberside Collegiate Institute, 280 Quebec Ave., (416) 393-0000
(PH) Western Technical Commercial School, 125 Evelyn Cres., (416) 393-0500
(C) St. Pius X, 71 Jane St., (416) 393-5237

TRANSPORTATION:
Swansea is served by a bus route on Windermere and Morningside avenues. The Runnymede and Jane subway stations on the Bloor-Danforth subway line are within walking distance of many of the houses in this neighbourhood.

Motorists enjoy the convenience of being located only minutes away from the Gardiner Expressway and Lake Shore Boulevard.

HISTORY: The Wallace Emerson neighbourhood owes its development to the Canadian Pacific and Canadian National railway lines, which began freight services to this area in the late 1800s. The railways attracted industries to the Wallace Emerson area which in turn led to the residential development of what historically has been a working class neighbourhood.

Wallace Emerson did not become a clearly defined neighbourhood until 1970. In fact, city planners identified it only for the sake of convenience, making reference to the two major cross-streets – Wallace and Emerson – that intersect the middle of this Toronto neighbourhood.

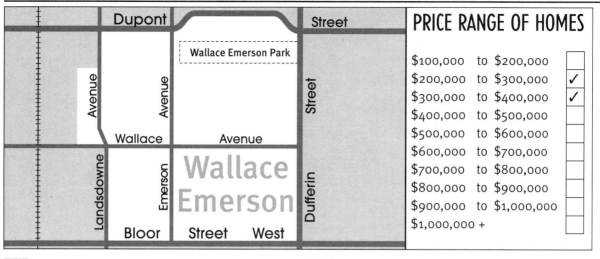

PRICE RANGE OF HOMES	
$100,000 to $200,000	
$200,000 to $300,000	✓
$300,000 to $400,000	✓
$400,000 to $500,000	
$500,000 to $600,000	
$600,000 to $700,000	
$700,000 to $800,000	
$800,000 to $900,000	
$900,000 to $1,000,000	
$1,000,000 +	

OVERVIEW:
Wallace Emerson is a mixed-use residential and industrial area. This is a neighbourhood in transition, as former industrial land continues to be converted to non-industrial use. Ultimately, these changes are strengthening the residential character and the desirability of the Wallace Emerson neighbourhood.

HOMES:
The modest-sized brick houses in this neighbourhood were built in the late 1800s and early 1900s. They include a mix of detached and semi-detached houses. Wallace Emerson's narrow streets and narrow lots are supported by an extensive network of laneways that provide additional parking options for area residents.

SHOPPING:
The Dufferin Mall at Bloor and Dufferin streets and the Galleria Shopping Centre at the southeast corner of Dufferin and Dupont streets both include department stores, small retail shops and medical and dental offices. Together these two shopping centres provide a strong shopping base for Wallace Emerson residents.

Street shopping is also available at the intersections of Wallace and Lansdowne avenues, and at the recently revitalized Dufferin and Dupont area. There are also a fair number of variety stores that are conveniently dispersed throughout this neighbourhood.

RECREATION:
The Wallace Emerson Community Centre is located off Dufferin Street, south of Dupont Street. This modern facility includes an indoor swimming pool, a gymnasium, a games room, a large children's playground and an active seniors' lounge.

Wallace Emerson Park located next to the community centre features four floodlit tennis courts, and a twin-surface artificial ice rink that offers pleasure skating, permit hockey, shinny hockey, learn-to-skate programs, an ice hockey house league, and parent and children skating programs.

The Bloor/Gladstone Public Library, on Bloor Street east of Dufferin Street, offers programs for adults and children.

SCHOOLS:
(P) Pauline Jr., 100 Pauline Ave., (416) 393-9360
(P) Kent Sr., 980 Dufferin St., (416) 393-0400
(P) Bloor Collegiate Institute, 1141 Bloor St. West, (416) 393-1420
(PH) Brockton High School, 90 Croatia St., (416) 393-0430
(C) St. Anthony, 645 Gladstone Ave., (416) 393-5210
(C) St. Sebastian, 717 Brock Ave., (416) 393-5354

TRANSPORTATION:
The Wallace Emerson neighbourhood is very well served by public transit, with every home in the neighbourhood being located within a few minutes' walk of a public transit line. The Bloor-Danforth subway has stations at Dufferin and at Lansdowne. There are also bus routes along Dufferin and Dupont streets, as well as Lansdowne Avenue.

HISTORY:

The history of "The Junction" dates back to the 1880s when the Grand Trunk, Toronto Grey and Bruce and Northern railway lines began service to this area. The railways attracted industry to West Toronto Junction which in turn attracted the labourers who were the first residents of this neighbourhood.

The Heintzman and Company piano factory, Canada Cycle and Motor Works, Comfort Soapworks, the Union Stock Yards and the Queen City Flour Mills were some of the most prominent industries to operate here. However, by the 1960s the commercial railway lines bypassed West Toronto Junction and this led to a decline in the local industry and jobs.

Now West Toronto Junction is being revitalized as abandoned warehouses and factory buildings are being converted to urban lofts, or simply torn down and replaced with new townhomes. Once again this neighbourhood seems poised to become an integral part of the west Toronto landscape.

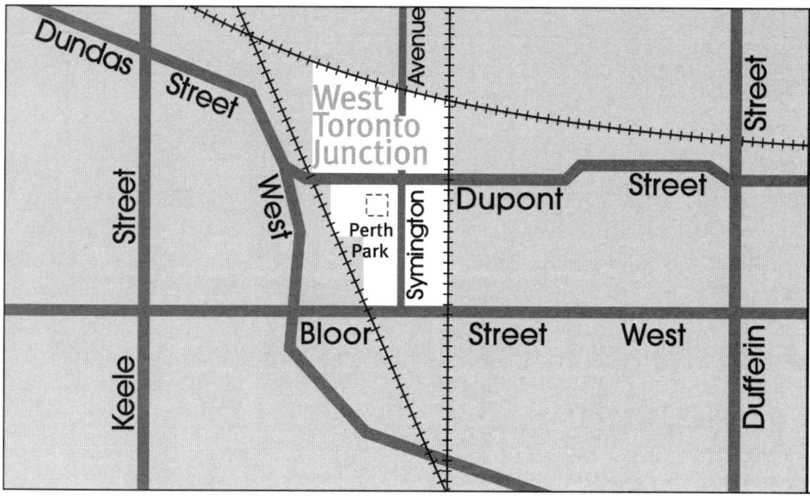

PRICE RANGE OF HOMES

$100,000 to $200,000		
$200,000 to $300,000		✓
$300,000 to $400,000		✓
$400,000 to $500,000		✓
$500,000 to $600,000		
$600,000 to $700,000		
$700,000 to $800,000		
$800,000 to $900,000		
$900,000 to $1,000,000		
$1,000,000 +		

OVERVIEW:

West Toronto Junction is currently undergoing a major revitalization that has seen much of its former industrial core replaced by residential lofts and townhomes. This neighbourhood has attracted the attention of developers, due to its close proximity to High Park and the revitalized Junction Gardens shopping district on Dundas Street West, as well as its easy access to the Bloor subway line. The City of Toronto has also shown an interest in jump-starting this vital west-end neighbourhood; it purchased land alongside an old CN rail right-of-way to create a bicycle path, which suits the preferred mode of transportation for many residents in this neighbourhood.

HOMES:

West Toronto Junction's narrow tree-lined streets are framed by two- and three-storey Victorian-style houses, built mostly in the 1910s and 1920s. The brick exterior on many of these houses has been colourfully painted, giving these older homes a bit of a facelift.

West Toronto Junction is currently undergoing a building boom of new townhome and condominium loft developments. As far as new homes go, this is one of Toronto's most affordable neighbourhoods.

SHOPPING:

The Galleria Shopping Centre, at the corner of Dupont and Dufferin streets, and the Crossways, at the corner of Dundas and Bloor, provide convenient, indoor shopping combined with professional services.

Across the tracks on historic Dundas Street West is the "Junction Gardens" shopping district, which contains a huge variety of shops and restaurants. Local street shopping is also available on Dupont Street, Bloor Street, and the north part of Symington Avenue. Big-box retailers are situated at the St. Clair Avenue and Keele Street intersection.

RECREATION:

Residents of this neighbourhood are less than one mile from High Park, which contains a myriad of recreational opportunities. There are also four local parks located within this neighbourhood. Their facilities include playgrounds, wading pools and artificial ice rinks.

The local YMCA, at Perth and Annette, offers a wide variety of programs for children and seniors. The Perth Dupont Public Library has programs for preschoolers and children.

SCHOOLS:

(P)   Indian Rd. Crescent Jr., 285 Indian Rd. Cres., (416) 393-9025
(P)   Perth Ave. Jr., 14 Ruskin Ave., (416) 393-1410
(PH) Brockton High School, 90 Croatia St., (416) 393-0430
(PH) The City School, 315 Osler St., (416) 393-1470
(C)   St. Josephat, 160 Franklin Ave., (416) 393-5291
(C)   St. Luig, 2 Ruskin Ave., (416) 393-5370
(C)   St. Rita, 178 Edwin Ave., (416) 393-5216

TRANSPORTATION:

The West Toronto Junction has bus service on Dupont, Dundas and Keele streets as well as on Symington and Lansdowne avenues. The Dupont and Dundas buses connect passengers to the Yonge-University-Spadina subway line, while the Keele, Lansdowne, and Symington buses connect with stations on the Bloor-Danforth subway line.

Motorists can be downtown in approximately 10 minutes by way of either Bloor Street or Dundas Street.

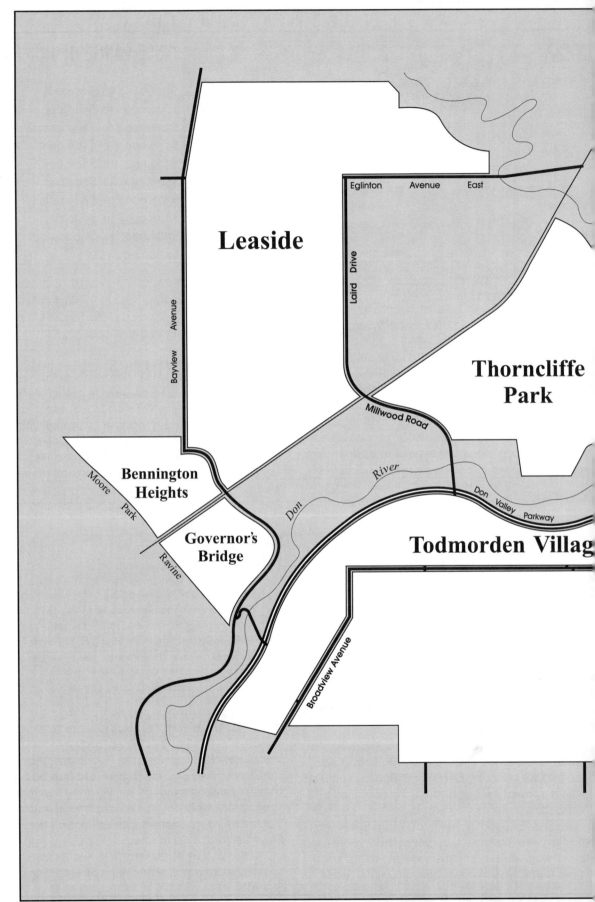

Leaside

Eglinton   Avenue   East

Laird   Drive

Bayview   Avenue

Thorncliffe
Park

Millwood Road

Bennington
Heights

Moore   Park

River

Don

Don   Valley   Parkway

Governor's
Bridge

Ravine

Todmorden Villag

Broadview Avenue

East York

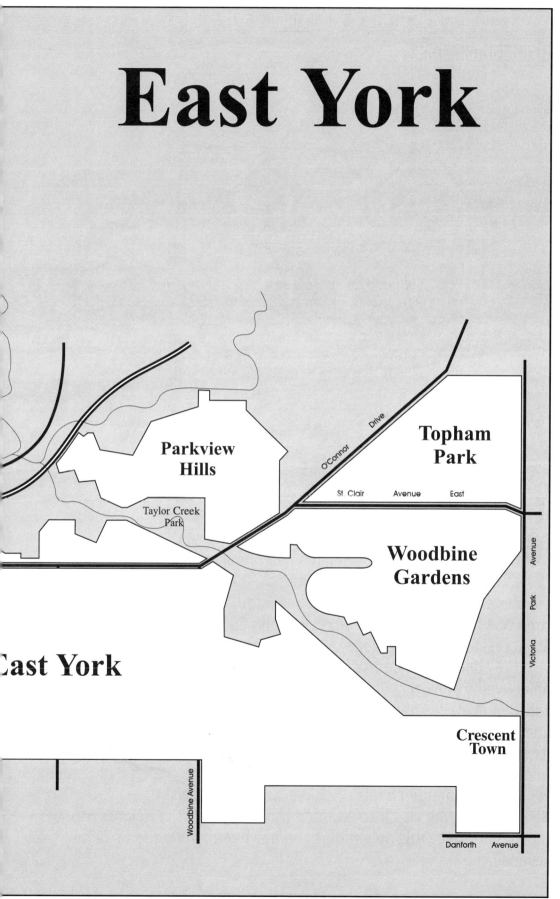

Parkview
Hills

O'Connor Drive

Topham
Park

St. Clair   Avenue   East

Taylor Creek
Park

Woodbine
Gardens

Victoria   Park   Avenue

East York

Crescent
Town

Woodbine Avenue

Danforth   Avenue

HISTORY: The Bennington Heights neighbourhood is situated on a flat plain of land, on the crest of an escarpment that, thousands of years ago, had been part of the shoreline of ancient Lake Iroquois — the forerunner to Lake Ontario.

This area was first settled in the 1870s by John Cudmore and Daniel Ryan, who operated successful market gardens on their respective properties. The Cudmore farm was subdivided for residential development in 1889 and later re-subdivided in 1912. Daniel Ryan's property, which was located just north of the Cudmore farm was subdivided in stages between 1891 and 1946.

The first resident of the present-day neighbourhood was Thomas Weatherhead, a solicitor for the East York School Board. In 1925, when Weatherhead purchased 30 Rosemount Avenue, he had the Rosemount street name changed to Bennington, which was his wife's maiden name.

The Bennington name was also adopted by the Bennington Heights School when it opened in 1950. This neighbourhood has been referred to as Bennington Heights ever since.

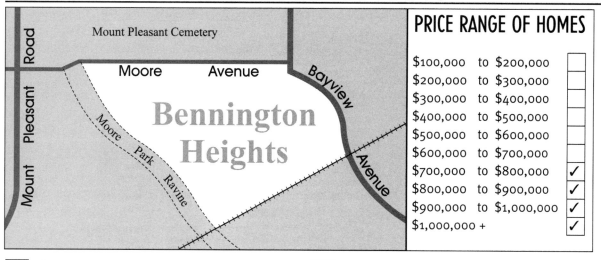

PRICE RANGE OF HOMES

$100,000 to $200,000	
$200,000 to $300,000	
$300,000 to $400,000	
$400,000 to $500,000	
$500,000 to $600,000	
$600,000 to $700,000	
$700,000 to $800,000	✓
$800,000 to $900,000	✓
$900,000 to $1,000,000	✓
$1,000,000 +	✓

OVERVIEW:

Bennington Heights is one of Toronto's most exclusive and expensive neighbourhoods. Over the years it has been the home of many prominent Torontonians, including author Margaret Atwood, whose highly acclaimed novel *Cat's Eye* is loosely based on her childhood growing up in Bennington Heights.

Bennington Heights is bounded on two sides by the bluffs of the Don River Valley ravine and on the north by Mount Pleasant Cemetery. These natural barriers help preserve the peaceful tranquility of this neighbourhood.

HOMES:

Bennington Heights English Manor stone houses were built in the 1920s and 1930s. The cottage-style two-storey homes and bungalows were built in the late 1940s and early 1950s.

Bennington Heights's winding roads, culs-de-sac and ravine properties all add to the charm of owning a home in this neighbourhood. With so much nature at your doorstep don't be surprised if you spot a fox gingerly taking an afternoon stroll through Bennington Heights — as I had the pleasure of witnessing while touring this neighbourhood.

SHOPPING:

Bennington Heights residents can shop for all of their household needs at the mall located on the southeast corner of Bayview and Moore avenues. This mall features a popular grocery store, a large pharmacy and a bank. Further north on Bayview Avenue is the Leaside shopping district, which contains an excellent selection of specialty stores, food shops and restaurants.

RECREATION:

Bennington Park, located off of Bayview Heights Drive, has a nice view of the Don River Valley. This park is the home of the Bennington Heights Tennis Club, which has two tennis courts. Next to the park is the Bennington Heights School. The school's recreational facilities include a soccer field, two baseball diamonds and a large children's playground. Evergreen Gardens Park, off Moore Avenue, also has a children's playground.

Nature lovers and fitness enthusiasts can access the Moore Park Ravine walking trail from Moore Avenue east of Hudson Drive or from the Bayview Avenue extension. The Moore Park trail is a remnant of the former Belt Line Railway, a commuter train that serviced Toronto in the early 1890s.

SCHOOLS:

(P) Bennington Heights School, 76 Bennington Heights Dr., (416) 396-2310
(P) Bessborough Drive School, 211 Bessborough Dr., (416) 396-2315
(PH) Leaside High School, 200 Hanna Rd., (416) 396-2380
(C) St. Anselm, 770 Millwood Rd., (416) 393-5243
(C) Our Lady of Perpetual Help, 1-1/2 Garfield Ave., (416) 393-5239
(PR) Junior Academy, 235 McRae Dr., (416) 425-4567
(PR) Crescent School, 2365 Bayview Ave., (416) 449-2556

TRANSPORTATION:

The Moore Avenue bus connects passengers to the St. Clair station on the Yonge-University-Spadina subway line.

Motorists can hop on the Bayview Extension, which will usher them downtown in minutes or provide access to the Don Valley Parkway and a network of connecting highways leading into and out of the city.

HISTORY:
Crescent Town can trace its roots back to 1887 when Walter Massey – son of Hart Massey, Canada's first major industrialist – purchased a 240-acre country property centered around Dawes Road and Victoria Park Avenue.

The Massey farm was named "Detonia," after Mrs. Massey's family, whose surname was Denton. The Massey farm sold fresh eggs and poultry, as well as fresh trout caught in the many streams and rivulets that criss-crossed the farm. The Massey farm was also the home of the City Dairy Company, which produced the first pasteurized milk in Canada.

In 1933 Susan Massey generously gave 40 acres of Detonia to Crescent School, where her grandsons were educated. Crescent School operated at Detonia until 1969, when this property was sold to the developers who built the present-day Crescent Town neighbourhood.

Hollywood actor Kiefer Sutherland was among the first Crescent Town residents. He spent part of his childhood in Crescent Town and attended the Crescent Town Elementary School.

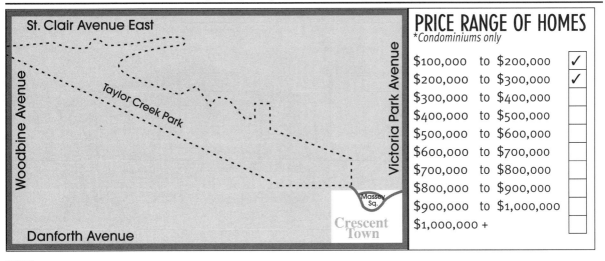

PRICE RANGE OF HOMES
Condominiums only

$100,000 to $200,000	✓
$200,000 to $300,000	✓
$300,000 to $400,000	
$400,000 to $500,000	
$500,000 to $600,000	
$600,000 to $700,000	
$700,000 to $800,000	
$800,000 to $900,000	
$900,000 to $1,000,000	
$1,000,000 +	

OVERVIEW:

Crescent Town is a self-contained community of approximately 10,000 people tucked away in a sylvan like setting in the east Don Valley Parklands.

Crescent Town is an interesting experiment in community planning, in that all of its pedestrian walkways are located above the street level. These walkways safely usher Crescent Town residents to their own community school, recreation centre, market place and town hall.

HOMES:

Crescent Town contains a mix of condominium apartment buildings, stacked condominium townhouses, and low- and high-rise rental apartment buildings. The condominiums are located on Massey Square and the rental apartment buildings are situated on Crescent Town Road. The building of Crescent Town was completed in 1971.

SHOPPING:

Crescent Town has its own "Market Place" located in a concourse strolling area situated in the centre of the Crescent Town neighbourhood. The Market Place includes a grocery store, a variety store, a bank, a drug store, a dry cleaner, a hair salon, a neighbourhood restaurant and medical and professional offices.

Crescent Town residents can also walk to the bustling shopping district on Danforth Avenue, including Shoppers World at the corner of Danforth and Victoria Park Avenues.

RECREATION:

The Crescent Town Hall, which occupies the ground floor of building #5, is the social hub of this neighbourhood. It contains a library, a church, and meeting rooms for various clubs and social functions.

The Crescent Town Club, located at 2A The Market Place, is a modern multi-recreational complex. Its facilities include a 25-metre swimming pool, an indoor track, a full-size gymnasium, squash, racquetball and handball courts.

The Crescent Town Club also doubles as a community centre and offers a myriad of programs for children, teens, adults, and seniors.

Taylor Creek Park is conveniently located at the north end of the Crescent Town neighbourhood. This long and narrow valley is thickly wooded and is perfect for walking, bird watching and photography. Taylor Creek Park also has a popular exercise trail and numerous picnic sites. Access to the park is located off Dawes Road.

Crescent Town residents can literally walk with their clubs in hand to the Detonia Park Golf Course on the east side of Victoria Park Avenue. This scenic 18-hole golf course is rated as "moderately difficult" by the City of Toronto Parks Department.

SCHOOLS:

(P) Crescent Town Elementary School, 4 Massey Square, (416) 396-2340
(P) D.A. Morrison Junior High, 271 Gledhill Ave., (416) 396-2400
(PH) Alternative School House, 670 Cosburn Ave., (416) 396-2925
(PH) East York Collegiate, 650 Cosburn Ave., (416) 396-2355
(C) St. Bernadette, 90 Balfour Ave., (416) 393-5327

TRANSPORTATION:

Crescent Town residents can access the Victoria Park subway station on the Bloor-Danforth subway line via an internal pedestrian walkway that connects directly to the station. The Dawes Road and Victoria Park buses also make connections to this station.

Danforth Avenue is the main arterial roadway in this district. Danforth Avenue ends at the Bloor Street Viaduct, which connects motorists into the downtown core.

SW

HISTORY: The Township of East York was incorporated on January 1, 1924. At that time East York comprised mostly market gardens, a handful of brick-making yards, and a racehorse track that was located in the area bound by Oak Park, Lumsden, Chisholm and Danforth avenues.

In its early years, East York's population consisted mostly of employees of the local market gardens and brickyards, as well as returning First World War veterans and their families. East York's period of largest growth took place between 1946 and 1961, when the housing supply nearly doubled in size.

East York held the distinction of being Canada's only borough until 1998 when it was amalgamated into the City of Toronto. The fact that East York chose to remain a borough for so long, rather than incorporate as a city, speaks volumes for the neighbourliness and small-town friendliness that has been an East York trademark ever since its formation in 1924.

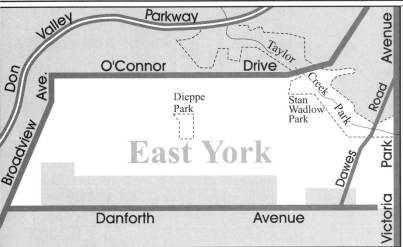

PRICE RANGE OF HOMES	
$100,000 to $200,000	
$200,000 to $300,000	✓
$300,000 to $400,000	✓
$400,000 to $500,000	✓
$500,000 to $600,000	✓
$600,000 to $700,000	
$700,000 to $800,000	
$800,000 to $900,000	
$900,000 to $1,000,000	
$1,000,000 +	

OVERVIEW:

For many years East York has held the distinction of having the highest percentage of senior citizens in Metropolitan Toronto. These demographics are changing, however, as many young families are now moving into this neighbourhood. Home buyers are finding East York attractive because the houses are relatively affordable and the location offers quick and easy access to downtown Toronto.

HOMES:

The majority of East York's housing stock was built in stages, beginning in the 1890s and continuing right up until the early 1960s. With the houses having been built over such a wide period of time, a myriad of different housing styles is evident from one street to the next.

East York includes two-storey or one-and-a half-storey detached and semi-detached houses, as well as an abundance of bungalows and some newer, custom designed homes. There are also a large number of high-rise rental apartment buildings concentrated along Cosburn Avenue between Broadview and Donlands avenues.

SHOPPING:

The majority of shopping in East York is located on the main north-south arterial roadways including Pape, Donlands, Greenwood, Coxwell and Woodbine avenues.

At the south end of East York, Danforth Avenue provides shoppers with a colourful array of fruit markets, bakeries, coffee shops, clothing and accessory stores and Toronto's best selection of Greek restaurants.

RECREATION:

East York is brimming with both indoor and outdoor recreational facilities.

The East York Tennis Club on Roosevelt Road has five tennis courts, Dentonia Park Tennis Club off Dawes road has four courts and East York Collegiate has four courts. The Dentonia Park Golf Course located off Victoria Park Avenue is a challenging 18-hole public course with a moderately difficult rating.

Stan Wadlow Park off Cosburn Avenue features five baseball diamonds and a batting cage. The excellent baseball facilities at this park helped produce the likes of Rich and Rob Butler, two native East Yorkers that went on to play major league baseball. Stan Wadlow Park also contains two outdoor swimming pools, a handball wall and picnic areas. It also serves as an access point to Taylor Creek Park, part of a nine-kilometre paved trail that is ideal for nature walks, jogging and cycling.

Adjacent to Stan Wadlow Park is the East York Memorial Arena, which provides recreational and league hockey programs as well as public skating. Across the street from Stan Wadlow Park is the East York Curling Club. The Dieppe Park Sports Complex at Greenwood and Cosburn has an outdoor ice rink, sports fields and a baseball diamond.

The newly refurbished East York Community Centre at 1081 Pape Avenue has an indoor pool, a multi-purpose gymnasium, a weight room and a small public library. The S. Walter Stewart Library at 170 Memorial Park Avenue features a large auditorium for storytelling and puppet shows. The Dawes Road Library at 416 Dawes Road also has children's programming.

The Secord Community Centre at 91 Barrington Avenue and the Terry Fox Community Centre at 2 Gledhill Avenue have gymnasiums as well as community meeting rooms.

SCHOOLS:

(P)	Chester School, 115 Gowan Ave.,	(416) 396-2325
(P)	Cosburn Middle School, 520 Cosburn Ave.,	(416) 396-2335
(P)	D.A. Morrison J.H., 271 Gledhill Ave.,	(416) 396-2400
(P)	Diefenbaker, 175 Plains Rd.,	(416) 396-2350
(P)	Parkside, 401 Cedarvale Ave.,	(416) 396-2425
(P)	R.H. McGregor, 555 Mortimer Ave.,	(416) 396-2390
(P)	Secord, 101 Barrington Ave.,	(416) 396-2490
(P)	William Burgess School, 100 Torrens Ave.,	(416) 396-2490
(PH)	East York Collegiate, 650 Cosburn Ave.,	(416) 396-2355
(PH)	Alternative School Programme, 670 Cosburn Ave., (416) 396-2925	
(C)	Canadian Martyrs, 520 Plains Rd.,	(416) 393-5251
(C)	Holy Cross, 299A Donlands Ave.,	(416) 393-5242
(C)	St. Aloysius, 80 Queensdale Ave.,	(416) 393-5287

TRANSPORTATION:

East York residents are conveniently located within a 10- to 15-minute drive of Toronto's financial and entertainment districts.

Bus service on O'Connor Drive and Pape, Donlands, Coxwell, Mortimer, Cosburn and Lumsden avenues provide passengers with a quick connection to subway stations on the Bloor-Danforth line.

HISTORY:
The Governor's Bridge neighbourhood was subdivided in 1912 by William Douglas and Wallace Nesbitt. Douglas and Nesbitt were distinguished lawyers at the Toronto law firm of McCarthy, Osler and Company, and both men were elected president of the Osgoode Legal and Literary Society during their careers.

The actual building of homes in this neighbourhood did not take place until after 1923, when the Governor's Bridge was opened. This bridge spanned a section of the Moore Park Ravine and received its name due to the close proximity of the Lieutenant Governor's residence, which was located where Chorley Park is today.

The same year that the Governor's Bridge opened, Wallace Nesbitt and the estate of William Douglas altered their original plan of subdivision for this neighbourhood. All of the original street names were changed in the new plan. Southview Avenue became Nesbitt Drive, Oakdale Crescent became Douglas Crescent and Hawthorne Avenue was changed to Governor's Road.

In the early years this neighbourhood was affectionately referred to as "Little Hollywood" because many of the first houses built in Governor's Bridge featured Spanish architectural accents.

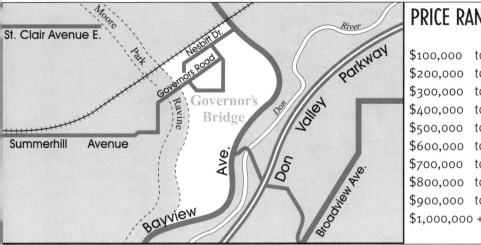

PRICE RANGE OF HOMES

$100,000	to	$200,000	
$200,000	to	$300,000	
$300,000	to	$400,000	
$400,000	to	$500,000	
$500,000	to	$600,000	
$600,000	to	$700,000	
$700,000	to	$800,000	✓
$800,000	to	$900,000	✓
$900,000	to	$1,000,000	✓
$1,000,000 +			✓

OVERVIEW:

Governor's Bridge is an exclusive enclave of approximately 115 homes nestled in a wooded ravine valley, which hides the fact that this neighbourhood is just five minutes from downtown Toronto.

There is very little turnover of homes in this highly sought-after neighbourhood, and it's easy to see why once you experience the peace and tranquility that this idyllic setting offers to its residents.

HOMES:

The Governor's Bridge neighbourhood features an eclectic mix of houses that come in all sizes, shapes and architectural styles. These houses were built in the 1920s, 1930s and 1940s. Many of the original bungalows are being torn down and replaced by new custom-designed houses that fit well on the generous lots that are characteristic of this neighbourhood.

For those seeking the ultimate in privacy the houses on Douglas Crescent sit perched atop the wooded slopes of the Moore Park Ravine. Blue jays, raccoons and even the occasional fox are some of the wildlife to be spotted from the backyards of these homes.

The Governor's Manor, located at 67-93 Douglas Crescent, is the only apartment complex in Governor's Bridge. This English-Tudor-style apartment, built in the 1920s, is a stately looking building that adds to the grandeur of this exclusive neighbourhood.

The Governor's Bridge Estates, a collection of executive homes, are the newest editions to this neighbourhood. These custom homes are situated on a high plateau of table land overlooking the Don Valley.

SHOPPING:

The closest shopping district to the Governor's Bridge neighbourhood is a cluster of stores and a shopping plaza located at the intersection of Bayview and Moore avenues. This group of stores includes a national grocery store, a pharmacy, a dry cleaner and a bank.

Further north on Bayview Avenue is the Leaside shopping district. This upscale shopping area includes fashion boutiques, antique stores, gift shops, professional services, gourmet coffee shops, specialty food stores, and a number of restaurants and cafés.

RECREATION:

Nesbitt Park is the quintessential neighbourhood park. This park is especially popular with families who have young children, as it features an excellent children's playground.

The Moore Park Ravine can be accessed from Chorley Park, which is situated within a short walk of this neighbourhood. The Moore Park Ravine walking trail is popular with bird watchers and nature enthusiasts. This trail follows the route of the old Belt Line Railway Company, a commuter railway train which ran through the Moore Park Ravine and through the City of Toronto from 1892 until 1894. The Belt Line tracks were removed during the First World War and used in the war effort in France.

SCHOOLS:

(P) Bennington Heights, 76 Bennington Heights Dr., (416) 396-2310
(P) Bessborough Drive, 211 Bessborough Dr., (416) 396-2315
(PH) Rosedale Heights, 711 Bloor St. E., (416) 393-1580
(PH) Leaside H.S., 200 Hanna Rd., (416) 396-2380
(PR) Branksome Hall, 10 Elm Ave., (416) 920-9741

TRANSPORTATION:

Governor's Bridge residents can catch the Rosedale bus on Summerhill Avenue. This bus route connects to the Rosedale station on the Yonge-University-Spadina subway line.

Motorists can quickly access the Bayview Extension at the northeast section of this neighbourhood. The Bayview Extension provides motorists with a quick passage into the downtown core.

HISTORY: Leaside was first settled by John Lea, a pioneer farmer who emigrated to Canada from Philadelphia in 1819. In the 1850s, Lea's oldest son William built an eight-sided octagonal-shaped house — appropriately named Leaside – near the present day site of Leaside Memorial Gardens. This neighbourhood has been called Leaside ever since.

The Canadian Northern Railway incorporated the Town of Leaside in 1913 on land formerly owned by the Lea family. Leaside's development was historically significant in that it was the first town in Ontario to be completely planned on paper before any homes were actually built.

Leaside's residential development was stalled due to the outbreak of the First World War, however Leaside was an important contributor to the war effort. Heavy artillery was manufactured at the Leaside Munitions Company. Leaside was also the location of an airfield used for the training of Canadian pilots.

In 1918 the Leaside Airfield made Canadian aviation history as the terminus of the first airmail flight in Canada, from Montreal to Toronto. Leaside's status as a town came to an end in 1967 when it became part of the Borough of East York, which has since amalgamated with the City of Toronto.

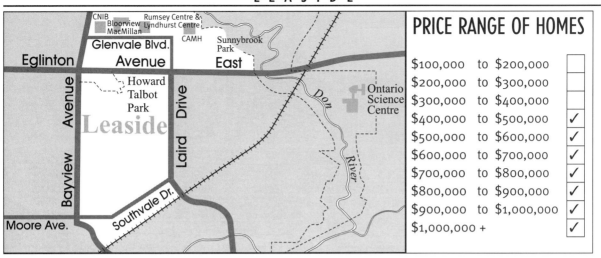

PRICE RANGE OF HOMES

$100,000 to $200,000	
$200,000 to $300,000	
$300,000 to $400,000	
$400,000 to $500,000	✓
$500,000 to $600,000	✓
$600,000 to $700,000	✓
$700,000 to $800,000	✓
$800,000 to $900,000	✓
$900,000 to $1,000,000	✓
$1,000,000 +	✓

OVERVIEW:

Leaside is in especially high demand with upper-middle-income families who value this neighbourhood as an ideal place to raise children. Leaside has abundant greenspace and parkland, a fine selection of schools, one of Toronto's best shopping districts on Bayview Avenue, and excellent access to public transit.

South Leaside, south of Eglinton Avenue, is the older section of this neighbourhood. South Leaside has the quaint, small-town feel of an older Toronto neighbourhood. You can easily access the local shops and restaurants from this location.

North Leaside, north of Eglinton Avenue, is more spacious and has a more suburban feel. This part of the neighbourhood was developed later and is still undergoing changes. A new public street, Kilgour Road, has recently opened in north Leaside to service the Kilgour Estate, which features a collection of Georgian-style townhomes overlooking the Burke Brook Ravine.

HOMES:

The typical Leaside house is situated on a generous size lot with a private drive and a garage. Most of the houses contain beautiful wood trim, hardwood floors and a working fireplace.

Leaside's Tudor-style houses were mostly built in the 1930s and 1940s. There is a good mix of two-storey detached homes, bungalows and semi-detached houses. A growing number of Leaside bungalows have had second-storey additions, while others have been replaced by new, custom designed homes.

Recently, a handful of exclusive condominium and townhouse projects have been built on the periphery of the neighbourhood. Leaside also contains some of Toronto's nicest rental apartment buildings, located on the east side of Bayview Avenue and on Leacrest Road overlooking the Don Valley Ravine.

SHOPPING:

Bayview Avenue features a wonderful collection of shops and restaurants. Many of these stores are geared towards children, reflecting the demographics of this neighbourhood. Bayview Avenue is also known for its antique shops, specialty stores, and neighbourhood pubs that attract a clientele from all over the city.

Leaside residents shop at the local stores along Eglinton Avenue. This shopping district is anchored by the Sunnybrook Plaza at the northeast corner of Bayview and Eglinton avenues. There are also some small shops and services located in the interior of the Leaside neighbourhood, on McRae Drive and Millwood Road.

Leaside's newest shopping destination is the Leaside Centre, a collection of large national retailers located at the southeast corner of Laird Drive and Eglinton Avenue. Adjacent to the Leaside Centre is the Leaside Business Park, which combines light industrial businesses with specialty retail stores.

RECREATION:

Few Toronto neighbourhoods can match Leaside when it comes to recreation. The Leaside Memorial Community Gardens at Millwood Road and Laird Drive is a multi-recreational complex that includes an indoor ice arena, an indoor swimming pool, a curling rink and an auditorium.

Leaside residents can enjoy nature and fitness activities in Serena Gundy Park and Sunnybrook Park. In addition to offering ideal picnic spots, Sunnybrook Park features top-notch sports fields, an exercise trail, horseback riding stables and a licensed snack bar operated by the Parks and Property Department.

Trace Manes Park, located in south Leaside off McRae Drive, is the home of the Leaside Tennis Club which has six tennis courts. Trace Manes Park also has a tots' playground, a baseball diamond and an outdoor natural ice rink which, is in use from late December until the end of February. The Leaside Public Library is situated adjacent to this park off McRae Drive.

Howard Talbot Park, situated in a picturesque valley at the southeast corner of Bayview and Eglinton avenues, features two baseball diamonds that are popular with local baseball leagues.

SCHOOLS:

(P)	Bessborough Dr., 211 Bessborough Dr.,	(416) 396-2315
(P)	Northlea, 305 Rumsey Rd.,	(416) 396-2395
(P)	Rolph Rd., 31 Rolph Rd.,	(416) 396-2435
(PH)	Leaside High School, 200 Hanna Rd.,	(416) 396-2380
(C)	St. Anselm, 770 Millwood Rd.,	(416) 393-5243
(PR)	Junior Academy, 235 McRae Dr.,	(416) 425-4567
(PR)	Crescent School, 2365 Bayview Ave.,	(416) 449-2556

TRANSPORTATION:

Bus service winds its way through the interior of the Leaside neighbourhood south of Eglinton Avenue, and connects to the St. Clair subway station on the Yonge-University-Spadina subway line. Bus routes on Bayview and Eglinton avenues connect to the Davisville and Eglinton stations, also on the Yonge-University-Spadina subway line.

Motorists can be downtown in 10 minutes via the Bayview Extension, which also links up with the Don Valley Parkway and a myriad of commuter highways.

HISTORY: Parkview Hills was once part of the vast Taylor family estate.

The Taylors moved to the Don Valley in the 1820s and built up a business empire that included a complex of mills and the Don Valley Brick Works.

While the Taylors never settled on this part of their estate, they were involved in the subdivision of land in Parkview Hills. The Taylor family is said to have named Hackberry, White Pine, Alder and Aspen streets after trees that once grew in this area. Presteign Avenue, Presteign United Church, and Presteign School are all named after the Welsh hometown of William Pugh, who, along with the Taylor family, subdivided the present-day neighbourhood.

When Parkview Hills first opened in 1947, three-bedroom bungalows were sold for around $9,950. The foundations of these houses were dug using teams of horses. There were no paved roads until 1950. Local residents recall swimming and fishing in nearby Taylor Creek up until 1955, when it was deemed to be to polluted for recreational use.

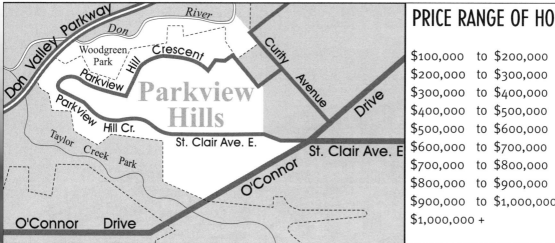

PRICE RANGE OF HOMES

$100,000 to $200,000		
$200,000 to $300,000		
$300,000 to $400,000		
$400,000 to $500,000	✓
$500,000 to $600,000	✓
$600,000 to $700,000	✓
$700,000 to $800,000	✓
$800,000 to $900,000	✓
$900,000 to $1,000,000	✓
$1,000,000 +		

OVERVIEW:
Parkview Hills is a quiet, secluded neighbourhood consisting of a few hundred homes surrounded by lush ravine and park land. The entrance to this neighbourhood would be easy to miss if not for the Parkview Hills stone gates, set-in from St. Clair Avenue. The gold letter inscription on these gates reads "Parkview Gardens," which is the name of the pretty little park at this entranceway.

Parkview Hills has an excellent mix of professionals, young families and retired couples. In particular, there is a large Greek community in this neighbourhood.

HOMES:
Parkview Hills houses range in style from bungalows to modest two-storey homes, English-cottage-style houses and newer, custom-designed houses.

The original Parkview Hills housing stock was built in the late 1940s and early 1950s. All the houses in Parkview Hills are detached with private drives. The lot sizes, on average, are among the most generous in the city and there are many spectacular ravine properties in this neighbourhood.

SHOPPING:
The O'Connor and St. Clair Avenue retail district is home to a variety of businesses including restaurants, banks, beauty salons, hardware stores, a pharmacy, a travel agency, variety stores and professional and medical offices.

RECREATION:
The Presteign Heights school, located in the centre of this neighbourhood off Parkview Hills Crescent, features a sports field, a baseball diamond and a children's playground. There is also an outdoor natural ice rink on the school grounds that is maintained by community volunteers from late December until the end of February. The Presteign Heights school gymnasium is the venue for a myriad of programs offered by the Toronto parks and recreation department.

Taylor Creek Park, accessed of Alder Road is part of a nine-kilometre paved trail that winds its way through the scenic wilderness of the Don River Valley. This nature trail is ideal for walking, jogging and cycling and includes many nice picnic spots.

SCHOOLS:
(P) Presteign Heights, 2570 St. Clair Ave. East, (416) 396-2430
(P) Gordon A. Brown Middle School, 2800 St. Clair Ave. East, (416) 396-2440
(PH) East York Collegiate, 650 Cosburn Ave., (416) 396-2355
(PH) Leaside High School, 200 Hanna Rd., (416) 396-2380

TRANSPORTATION:
Parkview Hills residents enjoy exclusive bus service along Parkview Hills Crescent that connects passengers to the Woodbine station on the Bloor-Danforth subway line.

Motorists can access the Don Valley Parkway in five to 10 minutes. The Don Valley Parkway provides quick and easy access to the downtown core and the commuter highways north of the city.

SW

HISTORY:
The Thorncliffe Park area was originally settled by George Taylor in the early 1800s. The tradition at this time was to give your house a name and Taylor named his home "Thorn Cliff." In 1888, George Taylor's daughter Margaret and her husband Robert Davies – a prominent brewer – purchased the Taylor property and created Thorncliffe Farms, which became one of the leading breeders of racehorses in Canada.

After Robert Davies's death in 1916 his sons sold Thorncliffe farms to a group of investors from Baltimore, Maryland. Thorncliffe's new owners operated a popular race track on this site from 1920 until 1952, when Thorncliffe was purchased by the Ontario Jockey Club. Thorncliffe was then resold to Thorncliffe Park Ltd., which developed the present-day neighbourhood in the late 1950s and early 1960s.

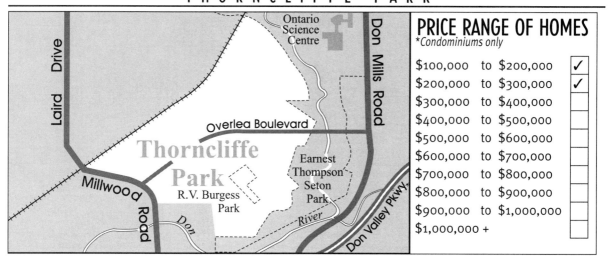

PRICE RANGE OF HOMES
Condominiums only

$100,000 to $200,000	✓
$200,000 to $300,000	✓
$300,000 to $400,000	
$400,000 to $500,000	
$500,000 to $600,000	
$600,000 to $700,000	
$700,000 to $800,000	
$800,000 to $900,000	
$900,000 to $1,000,000	
$1,000,000 +	

OVERVIEW:
Located along the Don River Valley corridor, Thorncliffe Park is a self-contained, multi-cultural community that includes its own shopping mall, school, library, park, community centre, churches and business centre.

Thorncliffe Park has traditionally been a starting point for many new Canadians. To help these new residents adjust, Thorncliffe Park has its own neighbourhood office, located inside the Thorncliffe Park Plaza. This neighbourhood resource centre provides multilingual, social and recreational programs and services for members of the Thorncliffe Park community.

HOMES:
Thorncliffe Park has traditionally been one of Toronto's largest rental districts. This neighbourhood contains over 30 low- and high-rise rental apartment buildings, close to 6,000 apartment units, and more than 13,000 residents.

Thorncliffe Park also offers home-ownership opportunities with new condominium apartment buildings and townhouses located on Overlea Boulevard.

SHOPPING:
The East York Town Centre is located right in the middle of the Thorncliffe Park neighbourhood, on Overlea Boulevard. This large shopping centre has over 70 stores in addition to a large number of professional and medical offices. The East York Town Centre also features a popular bowling alley.

The Overlea Mews, adjacent to the East York Town Centre, is a small strip plaza that includes local convenience-type stores.

RECREATION:
Nature lovers and fitness enthusiasts can enter the scenic Don Valley trail system via Ernest Thompson Seton Park. This park can be accessed between 71 and 75 Thorncliffe Park Drive. The E.T. Seton Park trail links up with both Sunnybrook Park and Edwards Gardens.

The Jenner Jean-Marie Community Centre on Thorncliffe Park Drive is a modern facility that includes a gymnasium, meeting rooms, and a public library.

Leaside Park, located at the south end of the neighbourhood, features a large sports field, two baseball diamonds, an outdoor heated pool and six tennis courts.

SCHOOLS:
(P) Thorncliffe Park, 80 Thorncliffe Park Dr., (416) 396-2460
(P) William Burgess, 100 Torrens Ave., (416) 396-2490
(PH) Marc Garneau Collegiate, 135 Overlea Blvd., (416) 396-2410

TRANSPORTATION:
Bus service on Overlea Boulevard and Thorncliffe Park Drive connect passengers to the Pape station on the Bloor-Danforth subway line.

Thorncliffe Park commuters travelling by car enjoy easy access to the Don Valley Parkway/ Highway 404 corridor which quickly connects motorists to downtown Toronto, and to a network of highways at the north end of the city.

HISTORY: Todmorden Village grew up around a complex of mills and
a brewery that operated near the banks of the Don River beginning in 1795.
Many of Todmorden's original families, including the Helliwells and
Eastwoods, came from Todmorden Village in Yorkshire, England. It is this
English village that Todmorden is named after. The Todmorden Mills Heritage
Museum, situated at the foot of Pottery Road, and a small number of work-
ers houses east of Broadview Avenue are vivid reminders of this pioneer
community.

The history of the Todmorden area north of O'Connor is dominated by the
Taylor family who came to the Don Valley in 1834. The Taylors owned all of
the land north of O'Connor between Broadview and Woodbine avenues. The
Taylors' business empire in the Don Valley included paper mills, saw mills,
grist mills and the Don Valley Pressed Brick Works, which supplied the bricks
for many of Toronto's houses and commercial buildings.

The Taylor estates were subdivided in the 1920s, 1930s and 1940s, which
led to the residential development of the north end of Todmorden Village.

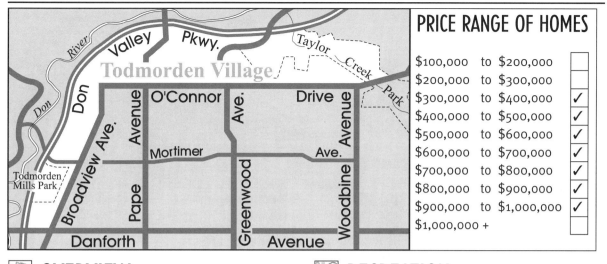

PRICE RANGE OF HOMES

$100,000	to	$200,000	
$200,000	to	$300,000	
$300,000	to	$400,000	✓
$400,000	to	$500,000	✓
$500,000	to	$600,000	✓
$600,000	to	$700,000	✓
$700,000	to	$800,000	✓
$800,000	to	$900,000	✓
$900,000	to	$1,000,000	✓
$1,000,000 +			

OVERVIEW:

The Todmorden Village neighbourhood is a mature, established community with quiet, tree-lined streets and solid-brick family homes. The rustic beauty of this neighbourhood is shaped by its location atop the ancient slopes of the Don Valley ravine. The vast amount of urban forest that shapes the western and northern boundaries of this neighbourhood make Todmorden Village one of the more peaceful and tranquil settings in Toronto.

HOMES:

The houses west of Broadview Avenue consist primarily of Tudor- and cottage-style brick homes from the 1930s and 1940s. Sprinkled into this mix are Victorian cottages and row houses that date from the late 1800s and early 1900s. These homes are holdovers from the old Todmorden Village. Many of the houses in this part of the neighbourhood back onto the Don Valley Ravine and enjoy a marvellous view of the city. There are also a handful of low- and high-rise apartment buildings situated in this part of the neighbourhood.

The six streets north of O'Connor between Pape and Donlands avenues have been coined "The Golden Triangle" by real estate agents. These charming Tudor-style homes were built in the late 1920s and early 1930s and include many decorative accents like front porches, leaded glass windows, wood burning fireplaces, beautiful wood trim and hardwood floors.

The northeast pocket of Todmorden Village around Four Oaks Park contains some of the prettier stone and brick bungalows in the city. These cosy homes are ideal for singles, couples and empty nesters.

SHOPPING:

The Pape Village shopping district south of O'Connor is brimming with local retailers that cater to the homeowners in the surrounding area. This busy shopping district includes everything from hardware stores and pharmacies to grocery stores, bakeries and restaurants.

The retail district located at Broadview Avenue and Pottery Road includes a large grocery store, restaurants, a health centre and professional offices. On a hot summer day it's worth a stop at the local Dairy Queen at the northwest corner of Broadview and Pottery Road. At the back of this Dairy Queen is an observation platform that provides a spectacular view of the Don River Valley.

RECREATION:

Todmorden Village residents enjoy convenient access to the Central Don network of parks that follow the valleys of the West Don River and Taylor Creek. These parks are linked together by a nine-kilometre paved trail that is ideal for nature walks, picnics, jogging and cycling.

The Todmorden Mills Heritage Museum and Arts Centre is located off Pottery Road. This heritage museum offers year-round programs for the whole family including art classes, a lecture series, a nature program, theatrical plays and special pioneer festivals.

Access to the Lower Don Valley nature trail is located off Pottery Road and at Beechwood Avenue. On your way into this parkland you might want to catch a glimpse of the charming red brick house at 20-22 Beechwood Avenue. This house was built in 1840 by the Taylor family, and is the oldest privately owned residence in Todmorden Village.

The newly renovated East York Community Centre, located at 1081½ Pape Avenue, offers year-round recreational programs for the whole family. This community centre features a swimming pool, a gymnasium, a weight room and a small public library.

SCHOOLS:

(P)	William Burgess School, 100 Torrens Ave., (416) 396-2490
(P)	Chester School, 115 Gowan Ave., (416) 396-2325
(P)	Westwood Junior High School, 994 Carlaw Ave., (416) 396-2480
(PH)	Leaside High School, 200 Hanna Rd., (416) 396-2380
(PH)	Massey Centre Secondary School, 1102 Broadview Ave., (416) 425-6348
(C)	Holy Cross, 299A Donlands Ave, (416) 393-5242

TRANSPORTATION:

Bus services on Broadview Avenue and O'Connor Drive connect passengers to the Broadview station on the Bloor-Danforth subway line, while the Pape Avenue bus connects passengers to the Pape station, also on the Bloor-Danforth subway line.

Motorist can drive downtown in five to 10 minutes via either the Bloor Viaduct or the Bayview Extension. Commuters are just a few minutes from the Don Valley Parkway, which connects motorists to a series of highways that span the Greater Toronto Area.

SW

HISTORY: Topham Park was an apple orchard in 1944, when the

crown purchased this property for war veterans' housing. The Topham Park neighbourhood was developed by the Canada Mortgage and Housing Corporation between 1944 and 1946.

Topham Park is named after Frederick Topham, who was a Victoria Cross recipient and a former resident of this neighbourhood. Some streets in Topham Park were given military-sounding names like "Warvet" and "Valor," and other streets were named after military men. For example, "Merritt" is named after Lieutenant Colonel Cecil Merritt, Canada's second Victoria Cross winner.

In the early days, Topham Park was known as "Sunshine Valley." This name was attributed to the local bus driver named Mac who used to holler, "All out for Sunshine Valley!" when making his stop in this neighbourhood. Original residents recall that Sunshine Valley was an appropriate name, as there were many children in the neighbourhood and it was a very happy place to live. Also, the sun shone down brightly on the homes, as there were few shade trees around at that time.

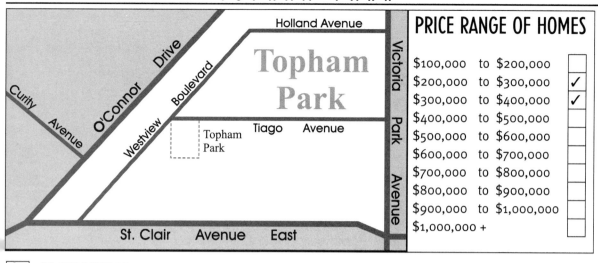

PRICE RANGE OF HOMES

$100,000	to $200,000	
$200,000	to $300,000	✓
$300,000	to $400,000	✓
$400,000	to $500,000	
$500,000	to $600,000	
$600,000	to $700,000	
$700,000	to $800,000	
$800,000	to $900,000	
$900,000	to $1,000,000	
$1,000,000 +		

OVERVIEW:

When you first come upon Topham Park you quickly sense the pride of ownership that is painted on the face of every home in the neighbourhood. This is a tightly knit community of only a few hundred homes, situated on quaint boulevards and pretty culs-de-sac. Its the type of neighbourhood where children have chosen to return as adults to raise their own families.

HOMES:

Topham Park's former war veterans' houses are located in the centre of this neighbourhood between Selwyn and Squires avenues from St. Clair Avenue north to Tiago Avenue. These houses were built between 1944 and 1946 and are easily distinguished by their bright frame siding and pretty front porches that look out over manicured lawns. Many of these houses have undergone significant upgrades and improvements since they were built. The renovations that have taken place have been careful to preserve the integrity and charm of these wartime houses.

The streets on the periphery of the neighbourhood include sturdy brick bungalows, and detached one-and-a-half- and two-storey houses. These homes were built mostly in the late 1940s.

SHOPPING:

Topham Park residents can easily walk to the Victoria Park and St. Clair Avenue intersection, which features a major grocery store and a cluster of smaller shops, restaurants, and medical and professional offices. Additional convenience-type stores catering to everyday household needs are located along St. Clair Avenue.

RECREATION:

Topham Park, located in the centre of this neighbourhood, features a baseball diamond that is the home field for men's, ladies' and children's softball leagues. This park also has two tennis courts, a clubhouse and a children's playground. In the wintertime, Topham Park has an outdoor natural ice rink that is used for pleasure skating and hockey. Recreational programs for the public are also held at Selwyn School located at 1 Selwyn Avenue.

SCHOOLS:

(P) Selwyn School, 1 Selwyn Avenue, (416) 396-2455
(P) Victoria Park School, 145 Tiago Ave., (416) 396-2475
(P) Gordon A. Brown Middle School, 2800 St. Clair Ave. E., (416) 396-2440
(PH) East York Collegiate, 650 Cosburn Ave., (416) 396-2355
(C) Canadian Martyrs, 520 Plains Rd., (416) 393-5251

TRANSPORTATION:

Bus lines on St. Clair Avenue and O'Connor Drive link up with the Coxwell station on the Bloor-Danforth subway line.

Motorists enjoy easy access to the downtown via the Don Valley Parkway. This commuter highway provides a direct link to Toronto's network of commuter highways.

SW

HISTORY: The Woodbine Gardens neighbourhood is located on the former site of the Woodbine Golf and Country Club which operated at this location during the 1930s. The Woodbine clubhouse was situated where Glenwood Crescent is today.

In 1932 the Woodbine Bridge was built across the Don Valley Ravine at a cost of $275,000. This bridge paved the way for the future development of Woodbine Gardens. The first house built in this neighbourhood was the Mary Pickford Bungalow situated at 90 Glenwood Crescent. This house was built in 1943 to raise money for the Canadian war effort. A raffle was held for the Pickford bungalow with tickets selling for only $1.00 a share. Mary Pickford, the Toronto-born Hollywood screen star, donated her time and money to this patriotic cause.

The building of the Woodbine Gardens subdivision in the early 1950s was a major engineering feat. Water courses had to be rerouted underground and 500,000 cubic yards of soil were removed in order to level many of the hills in this area. Woodbine Gardens houses originally sold for between $14,000 and $19,000.

Ed. Note: The Woodbine Bridge is one of Toronto's largest bridges. It measures 810 feet long and 46 feet wide.

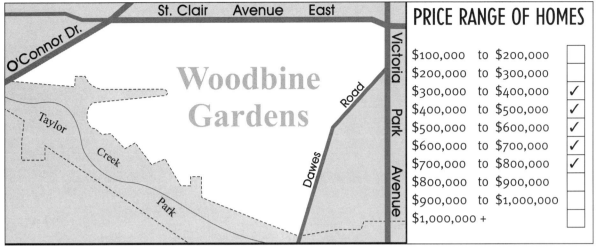

PRICE RANGE OF HOMES

$100,000	to $200,000	
$200,000	to $300,000	
$300,000	to $400,000	✓
$400,000	to $500,000	✓
$500,000	to $600,000	✓
$600,000	to $700,000	✓
$700,000	to $800,000	✓
$800,000	to $900,000	
$900,000	to $1,000,000	
$1,000,000 +		

OVERVIEW:

When you drive through Woodbine Gardens with its hills and dales, and winding and sloping crescents, it is easy to envision the fact that this neighbourhood was once an attractive golf course. The wonderful geography of the Woodbine Gardens neighbourhood is further complemented by Taylor Creek Park, which wraps itself around the southern reaches of this neighbourhood.

HOMES:

The charming brick and stone houses on Glenwood Crescent were built in the 1940s. All the other houses in the neighbourhood were built in the early 1950s. House styles range from Tudor- and ranch-style bungalows to solid brick two-storey houses. Most of these homes are situated on generous lots with private drives and garages.

Rexleigh Drive features some low-rise rental apartment buildings while Dawes Road has a number of high-rise rental apartment buildings that command a scenic view of Taylor Creek Park.

SHOPPING:

Woodbine Gardens residents have many shopping options to choose from. The O'Connor business area at St. Clair Avenue includes a major drug store, banks, variety stores, beauty shops, restaurants and medical and professional offices.

The shopping at Victoria Park and St. Clair avenues is anchored by a national grocery store and includes many handy retail stores that cater to everyday household needs.

Dawes Road also contains a large number of retail stores that draw their clientele mostly from the residents living in the nearby apartment buildings.

RECREATION:

Taylor Creek Park, located at the south end of this neighbourhood, is a picturesque woodland and wetland valley that is perfect for walking and exploring nature. Taylor Creek Park is part of a 10-kilometre walking trail that stretches from Warden Avenue in the east to Edwards Gardens in the west. Access points to Taylor Creek Park are located throughout this neighbourhood.

George Webster Park, situated along Chapman Avenue, has baseball diamonds, sports fields and a children's playground. There is also an outdoor natural ice rink that operates at this park during the wintertime. Donora Park, located east of Dawes Road, has a tots' playground. The moderate size hills in this park are good for tobogganing in the wintertime.

The Dawes Road branch of the East York public library is located at 416 Dawes Road. This library offers a variety of programs for children.

SCHOOLS:

(P)   George Webster, 2 Cedarcrest Blvd., (416) 396-2375
(P)   Gordon A. Brown Middle School, 2800 St. Clair Ave. E., (416) 396-2440
(PH) East York Collegiate, 650 Cosburn Ave., (416) 396-2355
(PH) Alternative School Program, 670 Cosburn Ave., (416) 396-2925
(C)   Canadian Martyrs, 520 Plains Rd., (416) 393-5251

TRANSPORTATION:

This neighbourhood is served by bus lines on Woodbine, Victoria Park and St. Clair avenues as well as on Dawes Road, Ferris Road and Rexleigh Drive. These bus routes connect to either the Coxwell, Main, Woodbine, or Victoria Park subway stations on the Bloor-Danforth subway line.

Motorists are approximately five minutes from the Don Valley Parkway on-ramp at O'Connor and Don Mills Road. This highway provides motorists with quick access to the downtown core as well as connecting routes to the major highways north of the city.

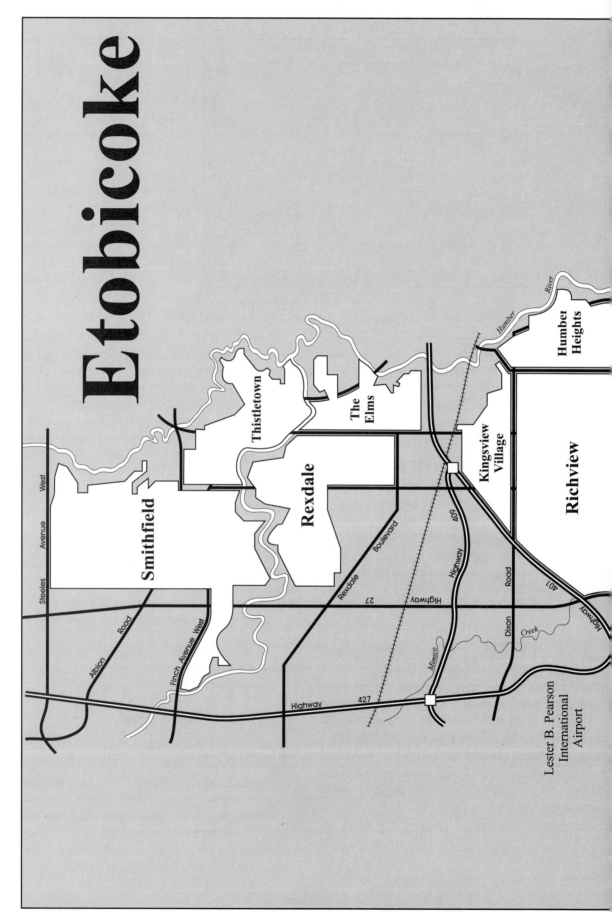

Etobicoke

Steeles Avenue West

Albion Road

Finch Avenue West

Smithfield

Thistletown

Rexdale

The Elms

Rexdale Boulevard

27

Highway

Highway 427

Mimico

Kingsview Village

Highway 409

Dixon Road

Creek

401

Richview

Humber River

Humber Heights

Highway 401

Lester B. Pearson International Airport

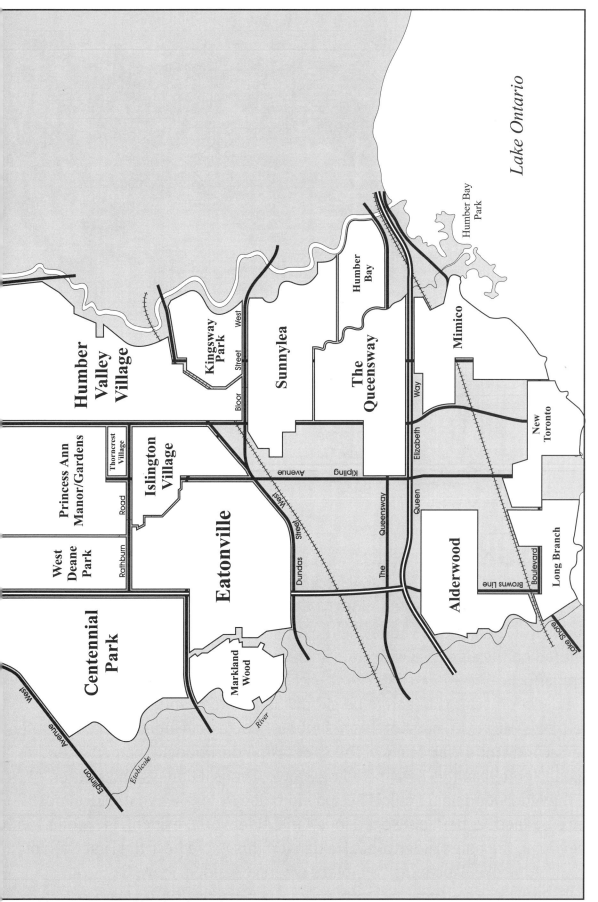

Lake Ontario

Humber Bay Park

Humber Bay

Humber Valley Village

Kingsway Park

Sunnylea

The Queensway

Mimico

New Toronto

Princess Ann Manor/Gardens

Thorncrest Village

Islington Village

West Deane Park

Eatonville

Alderwood

Long Branch

Centennial Park

Markland Wood

Bloor Street West

Avenue

Kipling

Elizabeth Way

Queen

The Queensway

Browns Line

Boulevard

Lake Shore

Dundas Street West

Rathburn Road

Eglinton Avenue West

Etobicoke River

HISTORY:
Alderwood was originally known as "New Toronto Park" or "New Toronto Heights," or simply as "the place above the tracks." Alderwood was the home of the six O'Connor sisters who achieved great fame in the 1910s touring North America's vaudeville theatres. The O'Connor sisters were often featured on the same bill with stars such as Jimmie Durante, Al Jolson and Sophia Tucker.

Alderwood's farms began to be subdivided for residential development in the 1920s. However, most of this neighbourhood's development occurred after the Second World War. Many of the streets in Alderwood are named after the original farmers in this area including Brown, Evans, Lunness and Horner.

The Alderwood name officially came into use in 1933 when the local post office opened. Robert Johnson, a long-time Alderwood resident, is credited with originating the name Alderwood. He derived this name from the First Nations word "Etobicoke," meaning "the place where the alders grow."

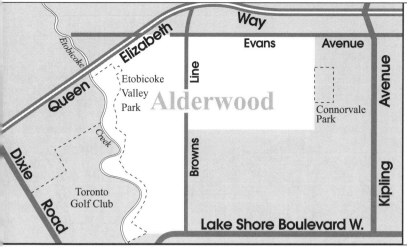

PRICE RANGE OF HOMES

$100,000	to $200,000	
$200,000	to $300,000	
$300,000	to $400,000	✓
$400,000	to $500,000	✓
$500,000	to $600,000	✓
$600,000	to $700,000	
$700,000	to $800,000	
$800,000	to $900,000	
$900,000	to $1,000,000	
$1,000,000 +		

OVERVIEW:

Alderwood is a well-established family-oriented neighbourhood, situated in the southwest part of Toronto. Alderwood has a strong home and school association and a privately run day-care facility called Alderwood Action Alliance, which operates out of Sir Adam Beck School. This neighbourhood is bordered on the west by the Etobicoke Creek Valley and on the east by light industry, which includes corporate giants such as Daimler-Chrysler Canada Ltd. and Domtar Packaging.

A new generation of Alderwood families have been instrumental in the opening of the recently completed Sir Adam Beck Centre, a multi-use facility situated on the Sir Adam Beck School grounds at 544 Horner Avenue. This ultra-modern neighbourhood centre combines a public library, a community room, a day-care centre, a fitness room and a swimming pool.

HOMES:

Alderwood's long, linear streets are lined with rows of bungalows and 1.5-storey houses. These houses were built during the 1920s, 1930s, 1940s and 1950s. Many of the older bungalows have been replaced with more modern semi-detached and detached homes.

The properties in Alderwood are well maintained with nicely manicured lawns. Each house has its own private driveway and most of the houses also have a garage.

SHOPPING:

Alderwood's main shopping street is located along Browns Line. This neighbourhood-oriented shopping district features fruit markets, home improvement stores, a medical centre, convenience stores and family restaurants. Alderwood Plaza is located at the north end of this shopping corridor. This small plaza includes a large food market as well as a traditional mix of stores and restaurants.

The Sherway Gardens Shopping Centre is located at the north end of this neighbourhood, off Evans Drive. This popular shopping centre is anchored by two major department stores, and includes over 200 shops and restaurants.

RECREATION:

Alderwood Pool at 520 Horner Avenue offers Aqua Tot, Aqua Quest and aquafit programs as well as Bronze Cross, snorkelling, and Junior Lifeguard programs, and recreational swims. The Alderwood Public Library offers children's and adult programming. The Horner Avenue Senior's Centre, located at 320 Horner Avenue, offers field trips, barbecues, workshops, information centres and special events.

Etobicoke Valley Park, located along the northwest border of Alderwood, is the finishing point for the Etobicoke Creek Interpretive Trail, a 2.5-kilometre trail that begins at the Marie Curtis Park on the shore of Lake Ontario. This nature trail was developed by the Alderwood Environmentalists in association with the city.

Alderwood Memorial Park, located in the centre of this neighbourhood, is a wide open greenspace with a children's playground. Connorvale Park, located off Valermo Drive, has a pretty baseball diamond and a children's playground.

SCHOOLS:

(P)   Lanor, 450 Lanor Ave., (416) 394-7800
(P)   Sir Adam Beck, 544 Horner Ave., (416) 394-7670
(PH) Lakeshore C.I., 350 Kipling Ave., (416) 394-7650
(C)   Christ the King, 432 Horner Ave., (416) 393-5257
(C)   St. Ambrose, 20 Coules Crt., (416) 393-5259
(CH) Father John Redmond, 300 Valermo Dr., (416) 393-5540

TRANSPORTATION:

Bus service on Browns Line and Evans and Horner avenues connects passengers to the Long Branch Go Transit and TTC station located on Lakeshore Boulevard.

Motorists can reach downtown Toronto in approximately 20 minutes via Lakeshore Boulevard and the Gardiner Expressway. Commuters heading out of the city have convenient access to the Highway 427 north on-ramps at Browns Line and Evans Avenue, and the Queen Elizabeth Way on-ramp off Evans Avenue.

HISTORY:

The Centennial Park neighbourhood was one of the last areas where working farms operated within Toronto. In fact, it wasn't until 1968, when the Hirons farm was sold to developers, that this area was completely urbanized.

Author Ester Heyes, in her book *Etobicoke: From Furrow to Borough*, remembers the Hirons farm. "Harold Hirons and his father before him had owned the 88.5-acre property fronting on Elmcrest Road at Rathburn Road from the days of the Furrow to a time well beyond the establishment of a Borough." When all around him the land had been turned into modern residential communities Harold Hirons continued to carry on a highly successful dairy farm, shipping milk to Toronto daily.

Heyes then quotes Mrs. Hirons as saying, "We felt sorry for our new neighbours who could not go out and gather their own strawberries, and the fruit from their own orchards, fresh picked vegetables from their kitchen gardens and eggs warm from the nest." Certainly this was the end of a simpler way of life.

In 1967, the former Borough of Etobicoke created Centennial Park as a centennial project to celebrate Canada's 100th birthday. It is this landmark park after which this neighbourhood is named.

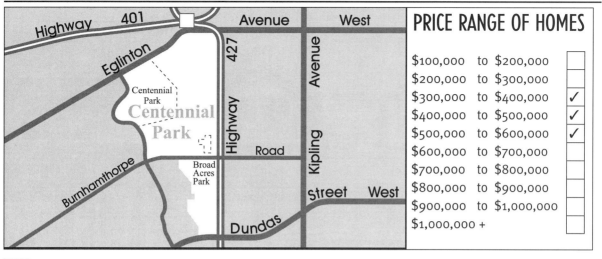

PRICE RANGE OF HOMES

$100,000	to	$200,000	
$200,000	to	$300,000	
$300,000	to	$400,000	✓
$400,000	to	$500,000	✓
$500,000	to	$600,000	✓
$600,000	to	$700,000	
$700,000	to	$800,000	
$800,000	to	$900,000	
$900,000	to	$1,000,000	
$1,000,000 +			

OVERVIEW:
The Centennial Park neighbourhood is located at the western edge of the City of Toronto. It is bordered on the east by Highway 427, on the north by Pearson International Airport and on the west by Centennial Park and the Etobicoke River Valley.

This neighbourhood is home to people from a wide range of cultural backgrounds and levels of income. It has many fine attributes including an abundance of parkland, a diverse housing stock, a local library, an excellent selection of public and Catholic schools and convenient access to shopping and transportation.

HOMES:
The majority of houses in this neighbourhood were built during the 1960s. These homes include ranch-style and contemporary-style bungalows on suburban-sized lots with private driveways and a garage or a carport.

Centennial Park also contains a subdivision of larger detached and semi-detached houses in the area around Elmbrook Park. Many of these houses feature Tudor-revival designs with steeply pitched roofs and Tudor accents.

SHOPPING:
Eringate Mall features a large supermarket, a bank, and some smaller retailers. The Renforth Mall at Rathburn and Renforth is highlighted by a large food market and also contains an assortment of smaller retail stores.

RECREATION:
Centennial Park is a regional park that includes 525 acres of recreational facilities. This enormous park has indoor hockey arenas, ski hills, a public golf course, a mini-Indy track,

tennis courts, a 2,200-seat stadium, playing fields, a pond with paddleboats, picnic sites and a greenhouse. Centennial Park is also the home of the Etobicoke Olympium, a multi-purpose recreational facility that is known for its aquatics, rhythmic gymnastics and aerobics programs. The Etobicoke Olympium also features its own fitness club and pro shop.

Local parks in this community include Elmbrook Park, which has a large children's playground and is also the home of the Elmbrook Public Library. Wellsworth Park and Broadacres Park each contain children's playgrounds and a baseball diamond. Eringate Park has baseball diamonds, a children's playground and an outdoor pool.

SCHOOLS:
(P)   Briarcrest, 60 Wellesworth Dr., (416) 394-6180
(P)   Broadacres, 45 Crendon Dr., (416) 394-7030
(P)   Hollycrest, 630 Renforth Dr., (416) 394-7050
(P)   Wellesworth, 225 Wellesworth Dr., (416) 394-7080
(PH) Burnhamthorpe C.I., 500 The East Mall, (416) 394-7130
(C)   Mother Cabrini, 720 Renforth Dr., (416) 393-5340
(C)   Nativity of Our Lord, 35 Saffron Cres., (416) 393-5288
(C)   Michael Power/St. Joseph, 105 Eringate Dr., (416) 393-5529

TRANSPORTATION:
Bus Service along Eglinton Avenue, The West Mall, and Rathburn and Burnhamthorpe roads provide passengers with connecting routes to Go Transit and TTC stations.

Motorists enjoy convenient access to Highway 427 from the Eglinton, Rathburn, and Burnhamthorpe on-ramps. This highway provides connecting routes to Toronto's network of commuter highways. The Pearson International Airport on-ramps are also located off Highway 427, just a few minutes from this neighbourhood.

HISTORY: Eatonville began as a farming community in the early 1800s. One of its first residents was Peter Shaver, who donated a portion of his property at Bloor Street and Highway 27 for the local school. This school was affectionately known as the "Swamp School" because of all the frogs that lived in the bushes and marshes nearby.

Peter Shaver's homestead and adjoining farms were purchased in the 1890s and early 1900s by Timothy Eaton, the patriarch of Eaton's department store. Eaton donated a portion of his land to the local school, which was renamed Eatonville in his honour. Eventually this entire area also became known as Eatonville.

The Eaton farm provided meat, poultry, vegetables and dairy products for Eaton's stores right up until the early 1950s when it was subdivided for residential development. In 1955, the rapid growth of this community led to the building of the present-day Eatonville School on Rossburn Drive, near the site of the original "Swamp School" where it all began.

Ed. Note: Peter Shaver's Applewood House was relocated in 1980 to 450 The West Mall, where it now stands as a historic museum.

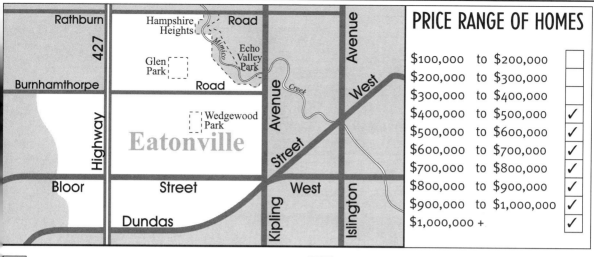

PRICE RANGE OF HOMES

$100,000	to	$200,000	
$200,000	to	$300,000	
$300,000	to	$400,000	
$400,000	to	$500,000	✓
$500,000	to	$600,000	✓
$600,000	to	$700,000	✓
$700,000	to	$800,000	✓
$800,000	to	$900,000	✓
$900,000	to	$1,000,000	✓
$1,000,000 +			✓

OVERVIEW:

Eatonville is a family-oriented neighbourhood that is home to people of a wide mix of incomes and cultural backgrounds. Residents of this neighbourhood still refer to their home as being in Etobicoke, which is not surprising; the former Etobicoke City Hall and City Centre are located within Eatonville's boundaries on the West Mall, south of Burnhamthorpe Road. The only two references to the pre-subdivision Eatonville are the Eatonville Public School on Rossburn Drive and the Eatonville Public Library located at 430 Burnhamthorpe Road.

HOMES:

Eatonville houses east of Highway 427 were built in the late 1940s and the 1950s. These houses consist of detached bungalows, 1.5-storey homes, and Cape-Cod-style two-storey houses. Many of the bungalows in this part of the neighbourhood are being torn down and replaced by custom designed new homes.

The houses west of Highway 427 were built in the 1960s and 1970s. This part of the neighbourhood contains a mix of brick bungalows, semi-detached houses, and large, detached two-storey homes. Eatonville's main arterial streets, including The West Mall, The East Malls and Burnhamthorpe Road, contain a mix of rental and condominium high-rise apartments and townhouses.

SHOPPING:

The Bloor Street shopping district west of Kipling Avenue is a small neighbourhood retail corridor that includes local shopping plazas, food markets, restaurants and independent owner-operated stores. The Westmall Bloor Plaza is located further west on Bloor Street at The West Mall. This community shopping plaza features a popular discount store and a mix of owner-operated shops including a flower shop, a hairstylist, convenience stores, a dry cleaner, a bank, professional offices and a fish and chips restaurant.

Dundas Street attracts a regional clientele to its many new car dealerships, restaurants and home improvement stores. Dundas Street also features two shopping malls. Cloverdale Mall is an indoor mall anchored by major department stores and includes over 100 retailers. This mall has special events going on throughout the year including a craft show, home show, antique shows, a seniors' show, and sidewalk sales. The outdoor Honeydale Mall is anchored by a department store with a dozen or so smaller retailers included in this shopping mix.

RECREATION:

The Neilson Park Creative Centre, located at 56 Neilson Drive, is a volunteer-operated, non-profit community arts centre. This centre is the home of the Etobicoke Art Group, the Humber Valley Art Club, the Heritage Rugcrafters of Etobicoke, the Etobicoke Quilters Guild and the Etobicoke Handweavers and Spinner Guild. Special events are held at this centre throughout the year including gallery exhibits, art festivals and craft sales.

Applewood — otherwise known as The Shaver Homestead — is located at 450 The West Mall. This circa-1850s house was occupied by the Shaver Family, one of Eatonville's original families. This historic house is now a museum and community reception hall.

The Eatonville Public Library, located at 430 Burnhamthorpe Road, offers a baby-time program, "Tales for Twos," and a preschool storytime. For the adults there is the Tea and Books program, where library staff lead an informal chat about books and authors.

The West Mall and The East Mall parks, Wedgewood Park and Cloverdale Park each contain tennis courts, a baseball diamond, and a children's playground. The West Mall Park also has an artificial ice rink and an outdoor swimming pool.

SCHOOLS:

(P)	Bloorlea, 4050 Bloor St.,	(416) 394-7140	
(P)	Eatonville, 15 Rossburn Dr.,	(416) 394-7040	
(P)	Wedgewood, 5 Swan Ave.,	(416) 394-7150	
(PH)	Burnhamthorpe C.I., 500 The East Mall,	(416) 394-7130	
(C)	Our Lady of Peace, 70 Mattice Ave.,	(416) 393-5253	
(C)	St. Elizabeth, 5 Redcar Ave.,	(416) 393-5278	

TRANSPORTATION:

Bus services on Bloor and Dundas streets, The West Mall, The East Mall and Burnhamthorpe Road connect passengers to the Kipling station located off Auckland Road just south of Bloor Street. This station serves both TTC and Go Transit commuters.

Motorists are within minutes of Highway 427 on-ramps at Dundas and Bloor streets and Burnhamthorpe and Rathburn roads. Bloor Street provides motorists with an alternative route into downtown Toronto. The Pearson International Airport is within a 10-minute drive of this neighbourhood.

HISTORY: The history of the Humber Bay neighbourhood began in 1888 with the opening of the first Humber Bay schoolhouse on High Street. Approximately 35 children attended the school in its first year. The Humber Bay school was gradually expanded and eventually became the focal point of this community, hosting ratepayers meetings, school concerts, movies and a variety of sports activities.

When the Humber Bay schoolchildren were not cracking the books they were tending to their families' market gardens. Humber Bay farmers grew mostly vegetables but there were also a few apple and pear orchards and the occasional strawberry and raspberry patch. It was appropriate that the first farmers market for the Toronto area began in Humber Bay, at Parklawn Road and The Queensway where the Ontario Food Terminal is situated today.

By the 1920s, Humber Bay had grown to include a brick yard, a cement block factory, a piggery, a library association, a volunteer fire brigade, and a couple of churches. There was also an 18-hole golf course where the Humber Sewage Treatment Plant and South Humber Park are located today.

In 1986 the old Humber Bay school was demolished to make room for a new housing development. Even though the cornerstone of this neighbourhood was lost, its sense of history and community spirit live on.

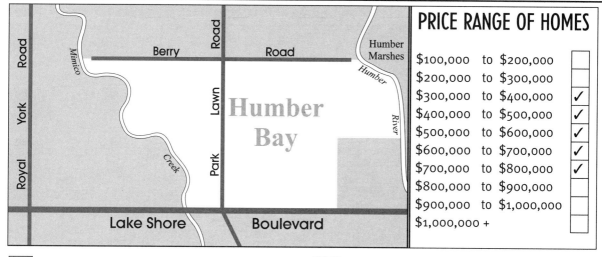

PRICE RANGE OF HOMES

$100,000 to $200,000		
$200,000 to $300,000		
$300,000 to $400,000	✓
$400,000 to $500,000	✓
$500,000 to $600,000	✓
$600,000 to $700,000	✓
$700,000 to $800,000	✓
$800,000 to $900,000	
$900,000 to $1,000,000	
$1,000,000 +	

OVERVIEW:

The Humber Bay neighbourhood is bounded on the west by the Mimico Creek and on the east by the Humber River Valley. These natural boundaries have shaped the topography of this area, which features rolling hills and many mature trees.

The former motel strip situated at the south end of this neighbourhood along Lake Shore Boulevard is currently being redeveloped as a luxury condominium community called Humber Bay Shores. When complete, some 2,500 condominium suites will have been added to this neighbourhood.

HOMES:

Humber Bay contains pockets of whimsical older houses from the early 1900s. Many of these homes were the former dwellings of the market gardeners who once flourished here. Humber Bay's more recently developed areas include a selection of bungalows, split-level houses, multiplex dwellings, low-rise apartment buildings and newer, custom designed homes. Many of Humber Bay's homes are situated on a hill and back onto either the Mimico Creek or the Humber River Valley.

The Humber Bay Shores development is located along Lake Shore Boulevard between the Humber River and Mimico Creek. At present this waterfront community consists of a handful of luxury, gated condominium apartment buildings. Many new condominium apartment buildings and townhomes are scheduled to be built at Humber Bay Shores during the next few years.

SHOPPING:

The Stonegate Plaza on Berry Road is the principal source of shopping for this neighbourhood. This community plaza includes a large supermarket, a pharmacy, a video store, a dry cleaners, variety and discount stores, restaurants, a dental office and a community health centre.

RECREATION:

Humber Bay residents enjoy convenient access to South Humber Park located off Stephen Drive. This park features open spaces and wooded areas overlooking the Humber Marshes. South Humber Park has a paved trail that is enjoyed by walkers, joggers, cyclists and in-line skaters. This trail links up with the Martin Goodman Trail on Toronto's waterfront.

Humber Bay Park, located at the foot of Park Lawn Road south of Lakeshore Boulevard, offers spectacular views of downtown Toronto. This park is located on the shores of Lake Ontario and includes a yacht club, boat launching facilities, a model boat pond and a fly casting pond.

Park Lawn Park, located north of Berry Road, is a multi-use recreational facility with an outdoor pool, a baseball diamond and a winter ice arena that is converted to tennis courts in the summertime.

The Humber Bay Public Library, located at 200 Park Lawn Road, is a small community oriented library that features books, as well as videos and tapes. This library also offers Internet access.

SCHOOLS:

(P)   Etienne Brule, 50 Cloverhill Rd., (416) 394-7850
(P)   Park Lawn, 71 Ballacaine Dr., (416) 394-7120
(PH) Lakeshore C.I., 350 Kipling Ave., (416) 394-7650
(C)   St. Mark, 45 Cloverhill Rd., (416) 393-5332

TRANSPORTATION:

Bus service on Berry and Park Lawn roads and on Stephen Drive connect passengers to the Old Mill station on the Bloor-Danforth subway line.

Motorists can get downtown in approximately 10 minutes via The Queensway. For commuters travelling outside the city, Lake Shore Boulevard is just a short drive from here and can be accessed from Park Lawn Road.

HISTORY: The area now known as Humber Heights was originally part of the Village of Weston. This hamlet was located along the west bank of the Humber River and revolved around a grist mill, a saw mill and a distillery. In 1852, this settlement was washed away by a torrential spring rain which saw the water level of the Humber River rise by about 20 feet. Only St. Philips Church and Cemetery and a handful of houses remain from this early settlement.

Humber Heights next established itself as a farming community centred along Scarlett Road. These farms began to be subdivided during the First World War in order to provide housing for the workers at the nearby munitions factories in Weston. A housing boom after the war resulted in the further urbanization of this community.

In 1921 the Humber Heights Consolidated School was opened and it soon became the focal point of this neighbourhood. Humber Heights school is still standing today at 2245 Lawrence Avenue West, where it is now operated by the Toronto District School Board as a resource centre and adult education centre.

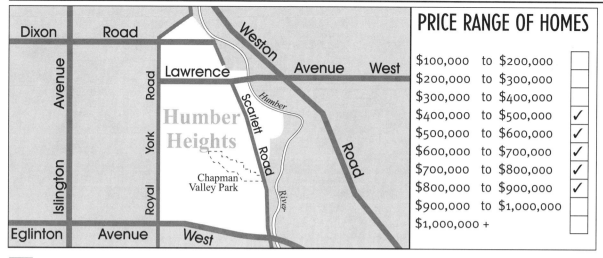

PRICE RANGE OF HOMES

$100,000	to	$200,000	
$200,000	to	$300,000	
$300,000	to	$400,000	
$400,000	to	$500,000	✓
$500,000	to	$600,000	✓
$600,000	to	$700,000	✓
$700,000	to	$800,000	✓
$800,000	to	$900,000	✓
$900,000	to	$1,000,000	
$1,000,000 +			

OVERVIEW:
Humber Heights is set in the enchanted Humber River Valley with its gently rolling hills and abundance of mature trees. Humber Creek, a tributary of the Humber River, winds its way through the centre of this neighbourhood. This small creek flows in a southeasterly course from Sun Row Park at Islington Avenue into the Humber River. The pedestrian bridge on Royal York Road, across from the shopping plaza, offers a picturesque view of the creek and the surrounding ravine valley.

HOMES:
Humber Heights has a very diverse mix of houses ranging from the impressive mansions on Yorkleigh Avenue and Westmount Park to the bungalow and split-level houses that are scattered throughout this neighbourhood.

The residential pocket east of Scarlett Road contains quaint Victorian cottages from the early 1900s, Edwardian-style houses from the 1910s and 1920s, Tudor-designed homes from the 1930s and 1940s, and 1.5-storey houses from the 1950s. The Scarlettwood apartment and townhouse complex, owned by Toronto Community Housing, is located in this section of the neighbourhood at the top of the valley.

On the west side of Scarlett Road you will find a large number of back-split and side-split-level houses from the 1960s, as well as a wide assortment of larger new homes built in the 1970s, 1980s and 1990s. This neighbourhood is fortunate to have a fine collection of historical houses including 11 Yorkleigh Avenue circa 1850, 85-89 Yorkleigh Avenue circa 1855, 5 Hill Garden Road circa 1840, 15 La Rush Drive circa 1850, and 581 Scarlett Road circa 1875.

SHOPPING:
There is a large neighbourhood shopping plaza located at 1500 Royal York Road. This plaza includes a supermarket, a bike and ski shop, fashion stores, a dry cleaners, a drug store, a bakery and deli, a dollar store, a travel agency, an indoor children's playground, a billiard hall and a bowling alley.

Dixon Road has a diverse mix of retail stores including a Somalian meat and grocery store and a Somalian clothing boutique.

RECREATION:
Humber Heights residents are conveniently located near the Humber River Valley nature and recreational trail. Access to this trail is available off Raymore Drive which leads into Raymore Park. A plaque in Raymore Park serves as a memorial to the 32 residents of Raymore Drive who were victims of Hurricane Hazel's wrath in 1954, when 14 homes were swept down a raging Humber River.

Riverlea Park, located at 99 Scarlett Road, is home to the Riverlea Italian Seniors Club, the Elm Jr. and Sr. Club, and the only greenhouse allotment gardens in Toronto. This allotment garden operates from October to May. It is a private facility run by the city which rents out greenhouse space to non-commercial applicants on a first-come, first-served basis.

SCHOOLS:
((P)   Westmount, 95 Chapman Rd., (416) 394-7720
(P)   Hilltop, 35 Trehorne Dr., (416)394-7730
(PH) Scarlett Heights C.I., 15 Trehorne Dr., (416) 394-7750
(C)   St. Demetrius, 125 La Rose Ave., (416) 393-5384

TRANSPORTATION:
The Royal York and Scarlett Road buses connect to stations on the Bloor-Danforth subway line while the Eglinton Avenue and Lawrence Avenue buses connect to stations on the Yonge-University-Spadina subway line.

Motorists are approximately five minutes from the Highway 401 on-ramp, north of Dixon Road off Islington Avenue.

HISTORY:

The Humber Valley Village neighbourhood was developed as part of Home Smith and Company's "Humber Valley Surveys." The Humber Valley Surveys included 3,000 acres of prime real estate stretching along the Humber River from The Queensway north to Eglinton Avenue. This large land assembly included the building of the Humber Valley Village neighbourhood as well as The Kingsway, Baby Point, Old Mill and Princess Anne Manor/Princess Gardens neighbourhoods. The St. George's Golf Club off Islington Avenue was also developed by Home Smith and Company.

The president of Home Smith and Company was Robert Home Smith, a graduate of law from the University of Toronto. Robert Home Smith was a multi-talented individual who served as Chairman of the Toronto Harbour Commission, helped to pioneer the development of Northern Ontario Mines, and was president of many North American railway companies.

The first homes in Humber Valley Village were built in the 1930s near James Gardens, along the Humber Valley. Unfortunately Robert Home Smith died in 1935, long before the Humber Valley Village neighbourhood was completed in the 1960s.

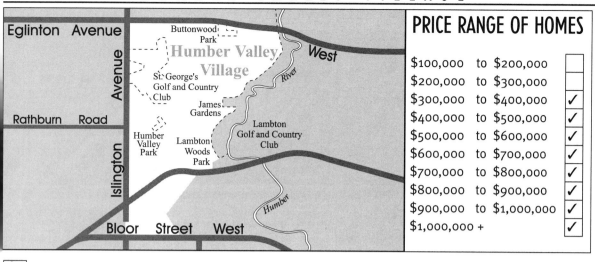

PRICE RANGE OF HOMES	
$100,000 to $200,000	
$200,000 to $300,000	
$300,000 to $400,000	✓
$400,000 to $500,000	✓
$500,000 to $600,000	✓
$600,000 to $700,000	✓
$700,000 to $800,000	✓
$800,000 to $900,000	✓
$900,000 to $1,000,000	✓
$1,000,000 +	✓

OVERVIEW:

Humber Valley Village is an upper middle-income family oriented neighbourhood. Its distinctive rolling topography, curvilinear streets and abundance of mature trees are a byproduct of the Humber River Valley Ravine, which forms the eastern boundary of this neighbourhood.

The two dominant geographical landmarks in Humber Valley Village are the St. George's Golf and Country Club, which stretches across Islington Avenue, and James Gardens, a picturesque strolling garden located along the banks of the Humber River Valley.

Signature streets within this neighbourhood that denote an exclusive address include Chestnut Hills, Valecrest and North Drive, among others.

HOMES:

Humber Valley Village contains a wide range of housing styles, which can be attributed to the fact that this neighbourhood was built in stages from the 1930s up to the 1960s. Thus, one can find handsome English brick and stone manor houses on streets like Edenbridge and North Drive, and then just a few streets away come upon a pocket of modest split-level and ranch-style bungalows.

In fact, exploring the architecture of the Humber Valley housing stock provides a glimpse at most of the house designs made popular in Toronto from the 1930s onward. These styles include Georgian, colonial, Tudor, English Cottage, Cape Cod, ranch bungalows, split-level, contemporary and modernist designs.

Humber Valley Village also contains a large number of rental apartment buildings on The Kingsway and on Anglesey Boulevard west of The Kingsway.

SHOPPING:

The residents of this neighbourhood do most of their shopping at the Humbertown Shopping Centre located off Royal York Road just north of Dundas Street. This upscale shopping centre is anchored by a grocery store, a liquor store, and a popular bakery and café restaurant.

The exclusive shops at Humbertown include a jewellery store that is manned by a uniformed police officer; a meat boutique that sells wild caribou, venison, mascovy duck, wild boar, ostrich, quail, bison and more; and a well-appointed interior design store. There are also two ice cream shops, a camera shop, gift stores, specialty food stores, a nutrition centre, fashion and shoe stores, a travel shop, a frame shop and children's clothing, shoe, and toy stores.

RECREATION:

The St.George's Golf and Country Club off Islington Avenue has been described as "one of the most difficult, historic and interesting courses in the world." This private golf club has hosted the Canadian Open and has been rated as one of the five best golf courses in Canada. James Gardens, located off Edenbridge Drive, features one of Toronto's loveliest strolling gardens highlighted by spring-fed pools, rustic bridges and colourful floral displays. James Gardens also features a rustic woodland trail that follows the banks of the Humber River.

There are public tennis courts at the Buttonwood, Central, Scarlett Mills and Humber Valley parks. Baseball diamonds are located at Central and Humber Valley Park. Humber Valley Park also has an artificial ice rink. For cyclists the off-street cycling path on the south side of Eglinton Avenue connects to the Humber River Valley trails, which link up with the Martin Goodman Trail on Toronto's waterfront.

SCHOOLS:

(P) Humber Valley Village, 65 Hartfield Rd., (416) 394-7860
(PH) Etobicoke C.I., 86 Montgomery Rd., (416) 394-7840
(PR) Kingsway College School, 4600 Dundas St. W., (416) 234-5073

TRANSPORTATION:

Bus service on Royal York Road and on Islington Avenue connects passengers to stations on the Bloor-Danforth subway line. The Eglinton bus connects passengers to Eglinton station on the Yonge-University-Spadina subway line.

Motorists are 20 minutes from downtown Toronto via Bloor Street, five minutes from the Highway 401 on-ramp off Islington Avenue and 10 minutes from Pearson International Airport.

HISTORY: Islington Village began in the early 1800s with stores, church-

es, a school and a post office, centred along Dundas Street West. The focal
point of this village was Thomas Montgomery's Inn. The Montgomery Inn was a
popular meeting place for the local villagers as well as the thirsty farmers taking their grain to the mills on the Humber River. Montgomery's Inn, located at
4709 Dundas Street West, is now a local museum. It is one of the few buildings
from the old Village of Islington to survive the residential subdivision of this
neighbourhood which took place shortly after the Second World War.

It is interesting to note that Islington was originally known as Mimico, but
that its name was changed in 1858 to avoid confusion with the postal station at
Toronto's Mimico Lakeshore neighbourhood. The Islington name was chosen
by Elizabeth Smith, whose husband Thomas was proprietor of the local hotel.
Elizabeth Smith chose the name Islington after her birthplace in England.

*Ed. Note: The Islington Burial Grounds on Dundas Street is one of the oldest
cemeteries in Toronto. It was opened around 1807.*

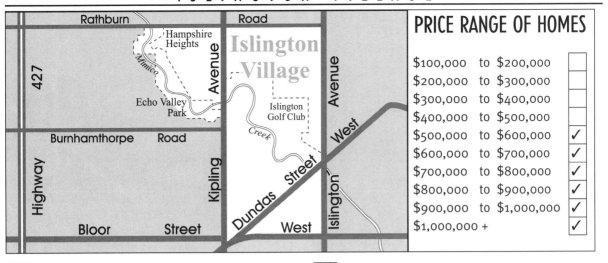

PRICE RANGE OF HOMES	
$100,000 to $200,000	
$200,000 to $300,000	
$300,000 to $400,000	
$400,000 to $500,000	
$500,000 to $600,000	✓
$600,000 to $700,000	✓
$700,000 to $800,000	✓
$800,000 to $900,000	✓
$900,000 to $1,000,000	✓
$1,000,000 +	✓

OVERVIEW:

This countrified west-end neighbourhood has many fine attributes including an excellent selection of homes situated on mature lots, an historic shopping district on Dundas Street, an abundance of greenspace and parkland and convenient access to TTC and Go Transit stations. A major condominium apartment and townhouse building boom is currently underway in the Kipling Avenue and Bloor Street area. These homes vary widely in size and price. The development along this corridor, which provides convenient access to the subway, is expected to add approximately 2,400 dwelling units to this neighbourhood over the next few years.

HOMES:

Islington's housing stock dates from the 1930s, 40's, and 50's. The older houses in this neighbourhood represent some of the best examples of Georgian-, colonial-, English cottage- and Tudor-style houses in the city. There is also a nice mix of Cape Cod-style houses, ranch-style bungalows and split-level homes. Many of these houses are situated on premium size lots that either front or back onto the Islington Golf Course.

Islington also has a growing number of custom built new homes. Most of these houses are well designed and blend in well with the older houses in the neighbourhood.

SHOPPING:

The Islington Village shopping district on Dundas Street has an upscale tone with a small town feel. The list of stores here includes a gourmet food shop, a wine making establishment, a deli, a drug store, a hardware store, a flower store, a coffee house and a good selection of restaurants and cafés.

Further west along Dundas Street, in the Dunbloor area, are a cluster of small retail plazas, family restaurants, professional and medical offices and specialty stores including a ladies golf shop, a lingerie store, and a leather store.

RECREATION:

The historic Montgomery's Inn located at 4709 Dundas Street West, is now a museum. This Georgian Loyalist Inn with its handsome riverstone exterior is one of the most beautiful and alluring buildings in Toronto. Montgomery's Inn hosts a number of festivals year round, a lecture series, and an afternoon tea in its cosy and comfortable tea room.

The Islington Golf Club features a par-72, 6,400-yard course that was designed by renowned golf course architect Stanley Thompson. This private club has a friendly atmosphere and is geared towards families.

If tennis is your game you will want to head to Rosethorn Park located just north of the Islington Golf Club. This park has three tennis courts and a children's playground.

The Islington Baseball League has been in operation since 1952. This club operates out of Rosethorn Park. Programs include Co-ed T-Ball, Boys and Girls Rookie Ball, Clinics and Rep teams.

SCHOOLS:

(P)   Islington, 44 Cordova Ave., (416) 394-7870
(P)   Rosethorn, 2 Remington Dr., (416) 394-6360
(PH) Etobicoke C.I., 86 Montgomery Rd., (416) 394-7840
(C)   St. Gregory, 126 Rathburn Rd., (416) 393-5262

TRANSPORTATION:

Bus service on Islington and Kipling Avenues connect passengers to stations on the Bloor-Danforth subway line. The Kipling station also provides service to the Go Transit Line.

Motorists are approximately 20 minutes from downtown Toronto via Bloor Street. Commuters are within a 10-minute drive of the Islington Avenue and Kipling Avenue on-ramps to Highway 401, which connects to all of Toronto's major highways.

HISTORY:

The documented history of the Kingsview Village area dates back to the 1850s. The first settler in this area was Thomas Madill, who owned a farm on the north side of Dixon Road that stretched from Islington Avenue over to Kipling Avenue. The Madill farmhouse was a 1.5-storey dwelling constructed of fieldstone. This house stood on Islington Avenue. It was demolished in 1973 and with it went the last trace of the pre-subdivision history of this neighbourhood.

The present-day Kingsview Village neighbourhood was developed during the late 1950s and the early 1960s. The small brick entrance pillars for the Kingsview Village subdivision can be seen on the west side of Islington Avenue at Kingsview, St. Andrews and St. Georges boulevards. The letter "K" is inscribed on the face of one of these pillars and the letter "V" is inscribed on the other two pillars. These inscriptions stand for Kings-View-Village.

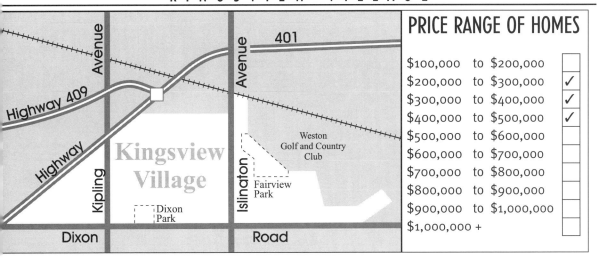

PRICE RANGE OF HOMES

$100,000	to	$200,000	
$200,000	to	$300,000	✓
$300,000	to	$400,000	✓
$400,000	to	$500,000	✓
$500,000	to	$600,000	
$600,000	to	$700,000	
$700,000	to	$800,000	
$800,000	to	$900,000	
$900,000	to	$1,000,000	
$1,000,000 +			

OVERVIEW:

Kingsview Village is a strong, family-oriented neighbourhood with an active ratepayers' association and its own community school and recreational facility. There is also a community church and a park conveniently located in the centre of this neighbourhood, off Kingsview Boulevard.

The single-family houses in the interior of this neighbourhood are occupied by a diverse mix of people from a variety of backgrounds and incomes. The high-rise apartment buildings along Dixon Road are home to a very large Somalian population, which has established a solid community in this neighbourhood.

HOMES:

Kingsview Village contains a mix of ranch- and contemporary-style bungalows, split-level houses, 1.5-storey homes, and newer two-storey homes. These houses feature front porches with elaborate accents including fanciful stair railings and arched entranceways. All these houses are situated on suburban-sized lots and include a garage or car-port. The properties are well maintained and professionally landscaped with the occasional ornamental statue decorating the front lawn.

The residential pocket east of Islington Avenue, in the Fairhaven Drive-Golfwood Heights area, was formerly part of the Weston Golf and Country Club Grounds. The golf club sold this land to developers in the 1950s and 1960s at which time most of these houses were built. The houses in this part of the neighbourhood include some charming Colonial-revival-style homes as well as an assortment of bungalows and modern two-storey houses. Many of these houses are located on premium lots that either face or back onto the Weston Golf Course.

Kingsview Village also contains a cluster of high-rise apartment buildings on Dixon Road and more high-rise buildings and townhouses on Islington Avenue.

SHOPPING:

The basic household needs of Kingsview Village residents are well served by the Westway Centre, located at the southeast corner of Dixon Road and Kipling Avenue. This small shopping plaza includes a large supermarket, a bakery and deli, a video store, a drug store, a McDonald's restaurant, a dollar store, a beer store, a hardware store, a jewellery store, professional and medical offices and a bowling alley and billiards hall. There is also a small but very busy Somalian meat and grocery store tucked away at the back of this plaza.

The Loblaws superstore located at the southeast corner of Dixon Road and Islington Avenue includes a bakery and deli, a photo finishing shop, a dry cleaners and a take-out restaurant.

RECREATION:

The Kingsview Village Community School, located at 1 York Road off Kingsview Boulevard, offers a variety of services and programs for the entire family. Some of these programs include aerobics, Tae Kwon Do and yoga. This facility also provides room rentals, community meeting space, special events, field trips and camps. Kingsview Park, located across from the community school off Kingview Boulevard, includes tennis courts, bocce ball and a children's playground.

Fairhaven Park, located east of Islington Avenue off Fairhaven Drive, is a pretty park that contains a baseball diamond, a sports field, an outdoor swimming pool and a children's playground. The Weston Golf and Country Club property is adjacent to this park.

SCHOOLS:

(P)   Kingsview Village, 1 York Rd., (416) 394-7950
(P)   Valleyfield, 35 Saskatoon Dr., (416) 394-7590
(PH)   Kipling C.I., 380 The Westway, (416) 394-7930
(PH)   School of Experiential Education, 40 McArthur St., (416) 394-6990
(C)   St. Maurice, 45 Kingsview Blvd., (416) 393-5379
(CH)   Don Bosco, 2 St. Andrews Blvd., (416) 393-5525

TRANSPORTATION:

The Dixon Road, Islington Avenue and Kipling Avenue buses connect passengers to stations on the Bloor-Danforth subway line. The Islington station provides a connecting route to the Mississauga Transit service and an express bus service to the Pearson International Airport. The Kipling station is also part of the Go Transit system.

Motorists are just a few minutes from the Highway 401 on-ramps at Islington and Kipling Avenues. Pearson International Airport is approximately a five-minute drive from this neighbourhood.

HISTORY:
Kingsway Park is situated on former Clergy Reserve lands that were deeded to the Church of England in the early 1800s. The church leased this property to farmers until 1908, when it was acquired by Robert Home Smith, the visionary who planned the Kingsway Park neighbourhood.

Home Smith and Company began marketing this subdivision in 1912. However the sale of homes in Kingsway Park was stalled by the outbreak of the First World War, as well as inadequate transportation routes across the Humber River Valley. It wasn't until 1924, when the Bloor Street bridge was built, that the sale of houses in Kingsway Park began.

Many of the first Kingsway Park residents were northern Ontario mining executives and Toronto businessmen, who were personally acquainted with Robert Home Smith and were encouraged by him to purchase houses here. Home Smith's motto for Kingsway Park was "a little bit of England far from England." His lofty ideal was to establish an English-style garden suburb of the highest integrity and beauty. It is Robert Home Smith's legacy that Kingsway Park endures today as one Toronto's finest neighbourhoods.

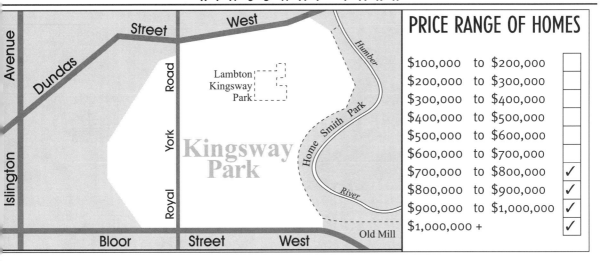

PRICE RANGE OF HOMES	
$100,000 to $200,000	
$200,000 to $300,000	
$300,000 to $400,000	
$400,000 to $500,000	
$500,000 to $600,000	
$600,000 to $700,000	
$700,000 to $800,000	✓
$800,000 to $900,000	✓
$900,000 to $1,000,000	✓
$1,000,000 +	✓

OVERVIEW:

Kingsway Park is the premier neighbourhood in Toronto's west end. This well-planned community was designed for families. The houses and properties are a good size, the streets are pedestrian friendly, and the schools, shopping, churches, and recreation are all within walking distance.

Kingsway Park is known for its idyllic setting, nestled in the forest of the Humber River Valley. The streets are lined with majestic oak and maple trees that provide the perfect backdrop for the stately homes that grace this neighbourhood.

HOMES:

The houses located between Kingsway Crescent and Royal York Road, and from Bloor Street north to Kings Garden Road, were developed as part of a separate plan of subdivision called "Kingsway Park." These houses were built between 1924 and 1947 and include some of the finest examples of Old English classical and vernacular architecture in Toronto.

Many houses in Kingsway Park feature handsome stone exteriors, intricate tapestry brick patterns, and elaborate stucco and half-timbering designs. These homes also feature solid oak doors, leaded glass windows, fanciful bay and oriel windows, and decorative wrought iron railings and porch lamps.

Kingsway Park's oldest houses are located along Government Road near Dundas Street. These homes where originally part of the Lampton community and were already built when the Kingsway Park subdivision was being developed. Here you will find some excellent examples of Victorian and Edwardian architecture built during the later half of the 1800s and the early 1900s. Mixed in with these older houses are contemporary bungalow designs from the 1940s and 1950s.

SHOPPING:

The gentrified Kingsway Village shopping district on Bloor Street West has an excellent mix of small specialty shops, chain stores, restaurants and professional and medical services. The village theme for this shopping district is a natural extension of the neighbourhood with park benches placed all along this route, and the use of black painted cast-iron street lamps. Even the garbage bins are framed in cast iron. The boulevard in the middle of this street is adorned with flag poles that proudly wave the Canadian flag alongside the Kingsway Village flag.

Dundas Street West at the north end of the Kingsway is a less dressed-up version of the aforementioned Kingsway Village shopping district. Most of the shopping here is located in strip plazas and includes a number of home furnishing/design and landscaping shops. There are also some interesting hobby and craft stores, an antique store and an art gallery. This street also features a rarity: a drive through dry cleaner that offers in-car drop-off and pick-up service. The Kingsway Mills outdoor shopping plaza at 4242 Dundas Street West is a collection of small chain stores, specialty shops, and a fine food store.

RECREATION:

The Etobicoke Memorial Pool and Health Club located at 44 Montgomery Road offers a myriad of aerobic and aquafit programs for adults. Next door to the pool and health club is the Central Arena which offers public skating and organized ice and ball hockey leagues for children and adults.

Central Park located off Islington south of Dundas, is the home of the Etobicoke Lawn Bowling Club which includes two bowling greens. Central Park also has tennis courts and a large baseball diamond.

Home Smith Park accessed off Dundas Street follows the Humber River and is part of a 10-kilometre paved trail that links cyclists, in-line skaters, walkers and joggers to the Martin Goodman Trail on Toronto's waterfront.

The Brentwood Public Library at 36 Brentwood Road North offers Kingsway Park residents a variety of children's and adult programming. The Kingsway movie theatre at 3030 Bloor Street West screens old and new films and offers membership privileges for a nominal annual fee.

SCHOOLS:

(P)	Lambton-Kingsway, 525 Prince Edward Dr., N., (416) 394-7890
(PH)	Etobicoke C.I., 86 Montgomery Rod., (416) 394-7840
(C)	Our Lady of Sorrows, 32 Montgomery Rd., (416) 393-5246
(PR)	Kingsway Montessori School, 85 The Kingsway (416)-233-1491
(PR)	Kingsway College School, 4600 Dundas St. West, (416) 234-5073

TRANSPORTATION:

Most Kingsway Park residents can walk to either the Royal York or Islington subway stations on Bloor Street. These stations are part of the Bloor-Danforth subway line. The Islington station is also a connecting route for the Mississauga Transit system as well as providing an express bus service to Pearson International airport.

Motorists are approximately 20 minutes from downtown Toronto's business and entertainment districts via either Bloor Street or Lakeshore Boulevard. The airport is approximately a 10-minute drive from Kingsway Park.

HISTORY:

Long Branch was first settled in 1797 by Colonel Samuel Smith, a loyalist officer with the Queens Rangers. Smith's 500-acre tract of land spanned the entire present-day neighbourhood. Smith, who served two terms as administrator of Upper Canada, built a modest regency-style cottage at the southeast corner of 41st Street and Lake Shore Boulevard, where Parkview Public School is situated today.

Smith passed away in 1826. His children retained possession of his estate until 1871, when it was sold to James Eastwood. The industrious Eastwood timbered the pine and oak forest that covered this land. He then rafted the logs from the mouth of the Etobicoke Creek to the Toronto Harbour where the lumber was sold for a tidy profit.

In 1883, Eastwood sold the eastern 64 acres of his property to the developers who created Long Branch Park, a summer resort modelled after its namesake in New Jersey. Ferry boats ushered thousands of Toronto vacationers each year to Long Branch, which boasted fanciful summer cottages, a grand hotel, a boardwalk and numerous amusement rides including a Coney Island carousel.

Long Branch became more accessible in 1916 when Lake Shore Boulevard was paved. This transportation corridor helped turn Long Branch into a year-round community. This neighbourhood was developed largely from the 1920s up to the 1950s.

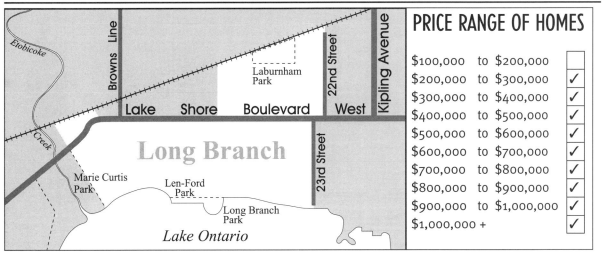

PRICE RANGE OF HOMES

$100,000	to $200,000	
$200,000	to $300,000	✓
$300,000	to $400,000	✓
$400,000	to $500,000	✓
$500,000	to $600,000	✓
$600,000	to $700,000	✓
$700,000	to $800,000	✓
$800,000	to $900,000	✓
$900,000	to $1,000,000	✓
$1,000,000 +		✓

OVERVIEW:

Long Branch is a well-established neighbourhood located along the Toronto waterfront at the extreme southwest part of the city. This neighbourhood is in transition, with many new home developments being built along Lake Shore Boulevard.

This lakeside village is blessed with many fine attributes, including picturesque waterfront parks, a local arena, a public library, a waterfront trail, a Go Transit station and a vibrant shopping district.

HOMES:

Long Branch's oldest houses are located on Lake Promenade between Long Branch Avenue and 38th Street. A handful of these houses date back to the days when Long Branch was a resort community. These houses have undergone numerous renovations and additions over the years however they retain some of their original features including whimsical turrets and front porch verandas.

Lake Promenade also features prime waterfront properties and a handful of small apartment buildings. The rest of the houses north to Lake Shore Boulevard were built from the 1920s up to the 1950s. These brick and frame houses include Edwardian- and Tudor-style bungalows and two-storey homes, modern semi-detached homes and duplexes. There are also a growing number of new custom designed houses in this part of the neighbourhood.

North of Lake Shore Boulevard the houses are much smaller and the lots are narrower. However the pride of ownership of these residents is evident on their well-kept properties, a handful of which proudly fly the Canadian flag.

Long Branch currently has a number of new townhouse and condominium projects being built along Lake Shore Boulevard.

SHOPPING:

The Long Branch Village shopping district, located along Lake Shore Boulevard, includes an eclectic mix of shops, restaurants and professional services. Also included in this mix are new car dealerships, billiards halls, a tattoo parlour, an adult entertainment hotel, a bowling alley and the Moose Lakeshore Lodge which has been active in this community for over 40 years.

RECREATION:

Marie Curtis Park, located at the mouth of the Etobicoke Creek, has a supervised sandy beach with picnic areas in addition to a wading pool and a children's playground. This park is where the Toronto Waterfront Trail and the Etobicoke Creek Trail connect. This waterfront trails offer miles of fitness and leisure activities. The Waterfront trail passes through Colonel Samuel Smith Park which features a wetland habitat interpretive trail, as well as spectacular views of Lake Ontario.

The scenic Waterfront Trail that skirts the south end of this neighbourhood passes through Len Ford Park, an ideal spot for picnics, and Long Branch Park which hosts the Lakeshore Summer Concert Series in the park gazebo.

Birch Park, located south of Lake Shore Boulevard between 28th and 29th streets, features two tennis courts and a children's playground. Adjacent to this park is the Long Branch Centennial Arena which offers public skating as well as ice hockey and ringette programs.

The James S. Bell Community School, located at 90-31st Street hosts Youth Dances, a Teen Zone, adult fitness programs and a variety of children and family events.

The Long Branch Public Library is a friendly, community-oriented library that offers pre-school story time programs and a Tea and Books program for adults and seniors.

SCHOOLS:

(P) James S. Bell, 90-31st St., (416) 394-7680
(PH) Lakeshore C.I., 350 Kipling Ave., 94160 394-7650
(U) Humber College, 3199 Lakeshore Blvd. W., (416) 675-3111

TRANSPORTATION:

Long Branch has its own Go Transit station located at the west end of this neighbourhood on the north side of Lake Shore Boulevard. Bus service at this station links passengers to Union Station and the Yonge-University-Spadina subway line.

Motorists can access downtown Toronto's entertainment and financial districts in approximately 15 minutes via Lake Shore Boulevard. Commuters also enjoy quick access to the Queen Elizabeth Way and Highway 427 on-ramps at Browns Line north of Lake Shore Boulevard.

HISTORY: The land on which the Markland Wood neighbourhood is built
was originally granted to John Silverthorn in 1810. Silverthorn was an experienced millright and immediately built a saw mill and a grist mill on the banks of
the Etobicoke River skirting his property.

The Silverthorn Mills were the focal point of this community as local farmers
brought their grain to the grist mill to be ground into flour and their logs to the
saw mill to be cut into lumber. The present day Mill Road was a shortcut used by
the farmers on their way to the mills.

The Silverthorn Mills operated until 1870, when the water flow in the
Etobicoke River decreased to the point where it could no longer power the mills.
The Silverthorn family then turned their attention to farming. They proved to be
as adept at farming as they were at milling, and even sold tomatoes from their
farm to the nearby Campbell Soup Company.

The Silverthorn family saw the city at their doorstep when they decided to sell
their farm to developer Mark Cavotti in 1958. Cavotti's associates honoured him
by naming this development Markland Wood. Thus a neighbourhood was born.

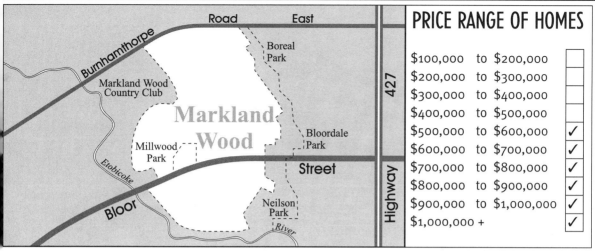

PRICE RANGE OF HOMES	
$100,000 to $200,000	
$200,000 to $300,000	
$300,000 to $400,000	
$400,000 to $500,000	
$500,000 to $600,000	✓
$600,000 to $700,000	✓
$700,000 to $800,000	✓
$800,000 to $900,000	✓
$900,000 to $1,000,000	✓
$1,000,000 +	✓

OVERVIEW:

The Markland Home Association is one of the strongest ratepayers' associations in Toronto. There are approximately 1,200 homes in Markland Wood and 85 to 90 per cent of the homeowners support their residents' association.

The Markland Homes Association organizes and promotes many worthwhile endeavours including the annual Christmas Caravan, all-candidates' meetings, and a scholarship program for residents of Markland Wood who are going on to University. The Markland Home Association also publishes a monthly newsletter called *The Marklander*, which keeps residents informed about the goings-on in their neighbourhood.

HOMES:

The Markland Wood housing stock was built between 1960 and 1962. These houses consist of detached two-storey Georgian- and regency-revival designs mixed in with contemporary bungalow and split-level designed houses.

Markland Wood houses are situated on good-sized lots with private driveways and double garages. There are many mature trees surrounding these properties and some of the backyards even contain apple trees from the old Silverthorn farm. The houses on Markland Drive back onto the Markland Wood Country Club and the Etobicoke River Valley.

SHOPPING:

The Markland Wood Plaza is located at the southwest corner of Bloor Street and Mill Road. This local shopping plaza is anchored by a national supermarket and a McDonald's restaurant that was specially designed with input from the Markland Homes Association. This shopping plaza also has a drug store, dry cleaner, pastry shop, bank, hairstylist, flower shop and a veterinarian clinic.

The Burnhamthorpe Mall, located at 666 Burnhamthorpe Drive, features a popular food market, a post office, a pet store, medical and dental clinics and a family restaurant.

RECREATION:

The Bloordale Community School, located at 10 Toledo Road, offers a myriad of programs for children as well as adults. The adjoining Bloordale Park is the home field of the Bloordale Baseball League which offers house league, inter-league, inter-county and all-star programs. Bloordale Park also has tennis court facilities.

Millwood Park, located off Bloor Street, has tennis courts and a baseball diamond. This park is scheduled to receive a new playground area.

The Markland Wood Country Club borders Markland Drive and, together with the Etobicoke River Valley, forms a nice natural barrier for this neighbourhood. This club offers golf as well as social memberships.

SCHOOLS:

(P)   Bloordale, 10 Toledo Rd., (416) 394-7020
(P)   Millwood, 222 Mill Rd., (416) 394-7070
(PH) Silverthorn C.I., 291 Mill Rd., (416) 394-7010
(C)   St. Clement, 4319 Bloor St., (416) 393-5307

TRANSPORTATION:

Bus service along Mill Road, Markland Drive and Bloor Street connect passengers to the Kipling TTC and Go Transit stations.

Motorists can quickly access the Burnhamthorpe on-ramp to Highway 427 which links up with other Toronto commuter highways. For those travelling out of the city, Pearson International Airport is only five minutes away.

SW

HISTORY:
Mimico was originally known by the First Nations people as "Omimeca," meaning "the resting place of the wild pigeons." The passenger pigeon is now an extinct species whose memory lives on in the name of this community.

The present day Mimico neighbourhood began to be developed in the 1890s south of Lake Shore Boulevard, where many of Toronto's wealthiest families built their summer homes. Some of these estates are still intact, however, most were lost to development after the Second World War.

Mimico began to emerge as a year-round community in 1906, when the Grand Trunk Railway opened the Mimico Yard. This led to a building boom, as houses were needed to accommodate the influx of workers who found employment at the Mimico Yard.

Mimico's meteoric growth led to its incorporation as a Town in 1917. Mimico retained its town status until 1967, when it was amalgamated with the Township of Etobicoke, which is now part of the City of Toronto.

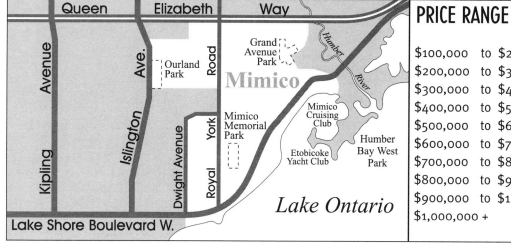

PRICE RANGE OF HOMES		
$100,000	to $200,000	
$200,000	to $300,000	✓
$300,000	to $400,000	✓
$400,000	to $500,000	✓
$500,000	to $600,000	✓
$600,000	to $700,000	✓
$700,000	to $800,000	✓
$800,000	to $900,000	✓
$900,000	to $1,000,000	
$1,000,000 +		

OVERVIEW:
Mimico is the gateway to Toronto's west-end waterfront neighbourhoods. This established community is well known for its scenic lakefront parks and excellent recreational facilities. Mimico is within a short commute of downtown Toronto and features its own Go Transit train station located on Royal York Road.

Mimico residents come out in droves to show their community spirit at a number of local events, including the annual Lakeshore Community Festival and the Etobicoke-Lakeshore Christmas Parade. There is also an annual Mimico Festival held every August in Amos Waites Park. This event is always followed by a kite-flying contest the next day at Humber Bay Park.

HOMES:
Mimico's grand Edwardian and Tudor mansions on the south side of Lake Shore Boulevard are holdovers from the 1890s and early 1900s, when Mimico was the summer home of Toronto's wealthiest families. These homes are set well back from the road and feature elaborate stone and iron gateways. The cobblestone craftsman-style houses are particularly noteworthy.

The houses south of Lake Shore Boulevard include an eclectic mix of custom-built new homes, modern bungalow designs, and a large number of low-rise rental apartment buildings. Many of these homes feature a full or partial view of Lake Ontario. The houses north of Lake Shore Boulevard include a mix of Edwardian- and Victorian-style houses from the 1910s and 1920s, as well as Tudor-style bungalows and two-storey houses from the 1930s and 1940s. There are also some multiplex apartment houses in this part of the neighbourhood.

SHOPPING:
Mimico residents are well served by the shopping districts on Lake Shore Boulevard and on Royal York Road. These shopping areas feature an excellent variety of small locally owned stores and restaurants.

RECREATION:
Mimico is well known for its sports clubs and recreational facilities. Much of this activity takes place at the Mimico Arena located off Royal York Road at Drummond Street. During the winter this arena is used extensively for hockey and skating programs and in the summer by the Mimico Minor Lacrosse Club.

National Hockey League star Brendan Shanahan grew up in Mimico and played hockey and lacrosse at the Mimico Arena.

The John English Community School, located at 95 Mimico Avenue, offers preschool programs as well as a variety of sports and arts programs for children and adults. The Mimico Tennis Club, located at 29 George Street, is unique in that it has Toronto's only red clay surface tennis courts. The Lakeshore Lawn Bowling Club is located in Coronation Park off Royal York Road. Amos Waites Park at 2445 Lake Shore Boulevard West has an outdoor swimming pool. The Mimico Centennial Public Library is located at 47 Station Road. This library offers children's programming.

The Metropolitan Toronto Region Conservation Authority has recently established a wetland habitat in Humber Bay Park, located along Lake Shore Boulevard West at Park Lawn Road. This peninsula park, joined together by a pedestrian bridge, is teeming with birds including Canada geese, swans, mallard ducks, seagulls, and red-winged blackbirds. Humber Bay Park also features a pond for model boats and a fly casting pond. The Mimico Cruising Club, Etobicoke Yacht Club and Humber College Sailing School are all based in Humber Bay Park.

SCHOOLS:
(P)   David Hornell, 32 Victoria St., (416) 394-7690
(P)   George R. Gauld, 200 Melrose St., (416) 394-7830
(P)   John English, 95 Mimico Ave., (416) 394-7660
(PH) Lakeshore C.I., 350 Kipling Ave., (416) 394-7650
(C)   St. Leo, 165 Stanley Ave., (416) 393-5333

TRANSPORTATION:
The Royal York bus connects to the Bloor-Danforth subway line, while the Lake Shore Boulevard bus connects to Union station and the Yonge-University-Spadina subway line. Mimico also has its own Go Transit train station located off Royal York Road. It is approximately a 15-minute ride from Mimico station to downtown Toronto's Union station.

Motorists can reach downtown Toronto in approximately 10 minutes via Lake Shore Boulevard or the Gardiner Expressway.

HISTORY:

New Toronto's history dates back to the 1890s when it was planned as a working town. This plan became a reality in 1906 when the Grand Trunk Railway opened repair shops, a roundhouse and a freight yard in New Toronto. The railway attracted industry to New Toronto. The areas largest employer was the Goodyear Tire and Rubber Company, which established a plant here in 1917.

New Toronto's rapid growth led to its incorporation as a Town in 1920. Frank Longstaff, in *Villages of Etobicoke*, recalls that during this period of prosperity, New Toronto touted itself as having the "highest value of manufacturing per square mile in North America." Thanks to this strong industrial base New Toronto was able to maintain one of the lowest residential tax rates in the Toronto area throughout much of its history.

In 1967, New Toronto was amalgamated with the former Township of Etobicoke, however it never lost its sense of identity as a working-class town. In recent years, the local industry has gradually been replaced with new home developments, which are attracting new families to this neighbourhood.

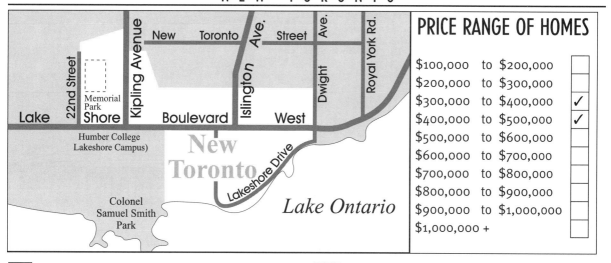

PRICE RANGE OF HOMES

$100,000 to $200,000		
$200,000 to $300,000		
$300,000 to $400,000	✓
$400,000 to $500,000	✓
$500,000 to $600,000	
$600,000 to $700,000	
$700,000 to $800,000	
$800,000 to $900,000	
$900,000 to $1,000,000	
$1,000,000 +	

OVERVIEW:
New Toronto is located along Toronto's western beaches. It is a neighbourhood in transition, as the industrial corridor located at the north end of the neighbourhood has recently been converted to residential zoning. Industry is gradually moving out of New Toronto and plans are underway for new home developments in this part of the neighbourhood.

At present New Toronto is home to residents from a wide mix of cultures and incomes and includes a large seniors population. Some of the selling features of this neighbourhood are the waterfront bicycle trail, convenient TTC and Go Transit service, affordable homes and quick access to downtown Toronto via Lake Shore Boulevard.

HOMES:
New Toronto's small frame-and-brick bungalows and modest two-storey houses were built largely between the 1910s and the 1950s. Larger single-family homes are located closer to the lake, south of Lake Shore Boulevard.

A fairly recent addition to this neighbourhood is the Lakeshore Village subsidized housing development, situated between 10th and 13th streets north of Lakeshore Blvd. This housing complex features an artists co-op, which accounts for its funky appearance.

New home buyers will want to visit the area north of Birmingham Road, between Islington and Kipling Avenues, for new home developments.

SHOPPING:
The Lakeshore Village shopping district, located along Lake Shore Boulevard West, is a busy retail corridor that features fast food and family-style restaurants, and a wide mix of stores including food markets, bakeries, delis, coffee shops, bargain stores, drug stores and convenience stores.

The Lakeshore Village shopping district is often lined with television and movie production crews that film on-site in New Toronto. Many of the *Police Academy* movies where filmed here.

RECREATION:
New Toronto is blessed with a bevy of waterfront parks, including Colonel Samuel Smith Park. This park includes the first Wetlands-Wildlife Restoration trail on the Great Lakes. This wetland habitat is home to a large variety of fish and birds, as well as frogs, garter snakes, painted turtles and a vast array of wildflowers. The Lakeshore Yacht Club is also based in this park. New Toronto's smaller waterfront parks, east of Colonel Samuel Smith Park, include Cliff Lumsden Park, Prince of Wales Park and Rotary Peace Park. Cliff Lumsden and Prince of Wales Parks offer magnificent views of the Toronto waterfront. The Prince of Wales Park also features an artificial ice rink, a wading pool and a children's playground. Rotary Peace Park features a new outdoor swimming pool, a large baseball diamond, two tennis courts, and a children's playground. Adjacent to this park, overlooking Lake Ontario, is the New Toronto Lawn Bowling Club.

The New Toronto Seniors Centre, located at 105 4th Street, hosts the Etobicoke Seniors Games every year from March to June. This seniors' centre for ages 55 and older offers a variety of programs including ceramics, computers, euchre and Slo-Pitch baseball. The New Toronto Public Library is located on 11th Street, south of Lake Shore Boulevard.

SCHOOLS:
(P)	Second Street School, 71-2nd., (416) 394-7640
(P)	Seventh Street School, 101-7th St., (416) 394-7820
(P)	Twentieth Street School, 3190 Lakeshore Blvd., (416) 394-7810
(PH)	Lakeshore C.I., 350 Kipling Ave., (416) 394-7650
(C)	St. Teresa, 110 Tenth St., (416) 393-5266
(U)	Humber College, 3199 Lakeshore Blvd. W., (416) 675-3111

TRANSPORTATION:
Bus service along Lake Shore Boulevard West provides connecting routes to the Mimico and Long Branch Go Transit service and to downtown Toronto's Union Station which is part of the Yonge-University-Spadina subway line.

Motorists are only a 15-minute drive along Lake Shore Boulevard or the Gardiner Expressway to downtown Toronto's Harbourfront district.

HISTORY: Princess Anne Manor and Princess Gardens were the last subdivisions to be developed by Home Smith and Company, whose earlier developments included the building of neighbourhoods such as Kingsway Park, Baby Point, Old Mill, and Humber Valley Village. Home Smith and Company also built the Brule Gardens subdivision in Swansea and the Foxwell subdivision in Lampton.

The following excerpt is taken from a 1955 Home Smith Properties Ltd. advertising brochure promoting the sale of homes in Princess Anne Manor and Princess Gardens: "Rapid acceptance of Princess Anne Manor and Princess Gardens by the builders and homeowners has been unprecedented. More than 45 discriminating families have moved into the area since May 1955...If you are looking for the kind of home you and your wife have planned, come to us for advice on a house or a lot in Princess Anne Manor or Princess Gardens."

Princess Anne Manor and Gardens proved to be very popular with families seeking an idyllic suburban lifestyle, and by the early 1960s this neighbourhood was completely developed.

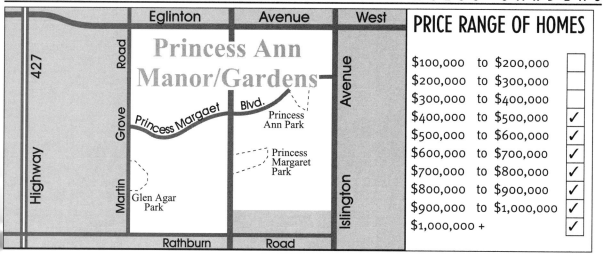

PRICE RANGE OF HOMES	
$100,000 to $200,000	
$200,000 to $300,000	
$300,000 to $400,000	
$400,000 to $500,000	✓
$500,000 to $600,000	✓
$600,000 to $700,000	✓
$700,000 to $800,000	✓
$800,000 to $900,000	✓
$900,000 to $1,000,000	✓
$1,000,000 +	✓

OVERVIEW:

Princess Anne Manor and Princess Gardens are virtually one neighbourhood. However, east of Kipling Avenue has always been referred to as Princess Anne Manor while west of Kipling Avenue is known as Princess Gardens.

This is a quiet, family-oriented community that is the epitome of suburban living. Here you will find wide open spaces, tall stands of mature trees, spacious houses, excellent schools, an abundance of parks, nearby golf courses and neighbourhood shopping plazas.

HOMES:

The mix of houses in this neighbourhood includes ranch-style bungalows, 1.5-storey houses, split-level homes, contemporary-style bungalows and Georgian-revival family homes. Most of these houses were built between 1955 and 1965.

It is noteworthy that all of the houses in this neighbourhood are detached single-family homes and the lots are exceptionally large, with many streets offering 80- and 90-foot frontages.

SHOPPING:

The Lloyd Manor Plaza at Eglinton Avenue is anchored by a large grocery store, a photo shop, a wine shop, a drug store, a dry cleaners, a hair salon, an optical store, a large convenience store, and medical and professional offices.

Residents of this neighbourhood also shop at the nearby Thorncrest Plaza, on Islington Avenue at Rathburn Road, and the Humbertown Shopping Centre on The Kingsway.

RECREATION:

The main recreational facility in this neighbourhood is the John G. Althouse Community School located at 130 Lloyd Manor Road. This community school offers a variety of sports, music and arts programs for children and adults. This community school is also a venue for a spring flea market and a summer camp.

Tennis courts, sports fields and baseball diamonds are available for public use at the John G. Althouse School and Princess Anne Park. Lloyd Manor Park is a wide open green space that has been the site of many exciting touch football games over the years.

SCHOOLS:

(P)   John G. Althouse, 130 Lloyd Manor Rd., (416) 394-7580
(P)   Princess Margaret, 65 Tromley Dr., (416) 394-6350
(P)   St. George's, 70 Princess Anne Cres., (416) 394-7990
(PH)   Martingrove C.I., 50 Winterton Dr., (416) 394-7110
(PH)   Richview C.I., 1738 Islington Ave., (416) 304-7980
(C)   St. Gregory, 126 Rathburn Rd., (416) 393-5262

TRANSPORTATION:

Bus services along Lloyd Manor Road, Kipling Road and Islington Avenue connect passengers to stations on the Go Transit line and the Bloor-Danforth subway line. The Eglinton bus connects passengers to the Yonge-University-Spadina subway line.

Motorists are approximately 25 minutes from downtown Toronto, and five minutes from the Islington Avenue and Kipling Road on-ramps to Highway 401.

HISTORY: Rexdale was still farmland in the 1950s when developer
Rex Heslop began the land assembly that led to the building of this neighbourhood. Heslop predicted that the completion of Highway 401 and the
creation of jobs at the nearby Toronto International Airport would bring a
strong demand for houses in Rexdale. Heslop's prediction proved to be
correct, as the Rexdale subdivision was sold out in a relatively short period
of time between the mid 1950s and the early 1960s.

The former Township of Etobicoke granted certain concessions to Heslop
on the condition that he also develop the farmland around what is now
Rexdale Boulevard. Etobicoke wanted this land changed from rural to industrial use to help ease the rising residential tax rate in the township. Heslop
was more than willing to accommodate Etobicoke's demands, realizing that
more industry meant more jobs and therefore more buyers for his Rexdale
homes. Upon its completion the Rexdale industrial area would become one
of the city's largest industrial corridors.

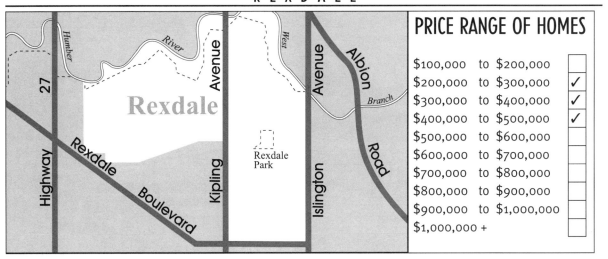

PRICE RANGE OF HOMES

$100,000	to	$200,000	
$200,000	to	$300,000	✓
$300,000	to	$400,000	✓
$400,000	to	$500,000	✓
$500,000	to	$600,000	
$600,000	to	$700,000	
$700,000	to	$800,000	
$800,000	to	$900,000	
$900,000	to	$1,000,000	
$1,000,000 +			

OVERVIEW:

The Rexdale neighbourhood is buffered by the picturesque West Humber River Valley to the north and an industrial corridor forms the southern boundary. Rexdale's housing stock is very diverse with owner-occupied single-family houses located on the interior of the neighbourhood and subsidized and rental housing located on the periphery of this community.

HOMES:

Rexdale's winding streets are well shaded by mature trees. The front lawns are meticulously maintained and include a variety of smaller ornamental trees. The mix of housing here includes raised and ranch-style bungalows, contemporary-style bungalows with attached car-ports, split-level homes, 1.5-storey houses, semi-detached houses, and basic two-storey detached houses.

The houses in the Kipling Heights subdivision east of Kipling Avenue were built mostly in the mid to late 1950s while the houses west of Kipling date mostly from the early 1960s. There are a number of properties located at the north end of this neighbourhood that feature spectacular views of the West Humber River Parkland.

Rexdale also contains a large number of walk-up apartment buildings and multiplex dwellings in the Islington Avenue and Rexdale Boulevard area. These include publicly and privately owned buildings that provide affordable rental apartments.

SHOPPING:

The Rexdale Plaza located off Islington Avenue at Rexdale Boulevard is anchored by a large Asian supermarket and contains a nice mix of independent and franchise stores. This plaza also features a women's health club, professional offices, a language centre for new Canadians and the Northern Elms Public Library.

The shopping corridor along Rexdale Boulevard is an interesting mix of retail stores, car dealerships, a big box store, a bowling alley and professional offices. North on Kipling Avenue you will find a myriad of fast food franchise restaurants and two neighbourhood shopping plazas that cater to the everyday needs of the Rexdale homeowners.

The Woodbine Centre located at Rexdale Boulevard and Highway 27 features nearly 200 specialty shops. This shopping centre is also known for its popular indoor amusement park that is highlighted by an antique carousel, a ferris wheel, a train, and a children's play village.

RECREATION:

There are plenty of recreational opportunities for the whole family in Rexdale. The Sunnydale Acres, Rexdale, and Rexlington Parks all contain wading pools, Falstaff Park has an outdoor swimming pool. Tennis courts are located at Sunnydale Acres, Flagstaff and Rexlington Parks. The tennis courts at Rivercrest School are used as an artificial ice rink in the wintertime.

The Rexdale baseball league operates out of several Rexdale parks and offers T-Ball and house league programs for children.

Esther Lorrie Park and Kipling Heights Park, located at the north end of Rexdale, offer spectacular views of the West Humber River Valley. These parks provide access to the West Humber Parkland that is highlighted by a paved trail used extensively by walkers, joggers and bicyclists.

The West Acres Seniors Centre, located at 65 Hinton Road, hosts a variety of special events and programs including monthly birthday parties, dances, field trips, bowling and crafts. This recreation centre is also the home of the Rexdale Lawn Bowling Club.

Horse racing fans are just minutes from the Woodbine Race Track located at the west end of this neighbourhood off Rexdale Boulevard. This horse track features thoroughbred racing during the daytime and harness racing in the evenings.

SCHOOLS:

(P)	Rivercrest, 30 Harefield Dr.,	(416) 394-7920
(P)	West Humber, 15 Delsing Dr.,	(416) 394-7760
(PH)	Thistletown C.I., 20 Fordwich Cres.,	(416) 394-7710
(C)	St. Benedict, 2202 Kipling Ave.,	(416) 393-5267
(C)	Msgr., Percy Johnson, 2170 Kipling Ave.,	(416) 393-5535

TRANSPORTATION:

Bus service along West Humber Boulevard and Elmhurst Drive connects passengers to the Wilson station on the Yonge-University-Spadina subway line. The Rexdale Boulevard, Islington Avenue and Kipling Avenue bus lines link up with stations on the Bloor-Danforth subway line. The Kipling subway station is also part of the Go-Transit system.

Motorists are less than five minutes from a network of commuter highways, including highways 401, 427, 409 and 27 . Many of these provide direct routes to the Pearson International Airport, which is located just a few minutes from Rexdale.

HISTORY:

The Richview name originated in 1852 when a post office called Richview opened in this area. By the 1870s, Richview had its own school, church and tavern. The Richview neighbourhood was more clearly defined in the 1880s when it was designated as School Section 4 in the former Township of Etobicoke.

Richview had a proud farming tradition that dated back to the 1850s, when Richview farmers participated in the Etobicoke Agricultural Society Fair and the Provincial Exhibition. Richview farmers sold their produce at the St. Lawrence Market in Toronto and their surplus beef cattle to the former Union Stockyards on St. Clair Avenue.

In the early 1900s, Richview farmers shifted their focus from agriculture to dairy farms to satisfy the demand for milk in the burgeoning City of Toronto. In 1956, Richview's last dairy farm was sold to developers. This brought to a close a tradition of farming in Richview that endured for over 100 years.

The former Dixon homestead, located at 1671 Kipling Avenue, and the former La Rose homestead, located at 322 La Rose Avenue, are reminders of Richview's rural past.

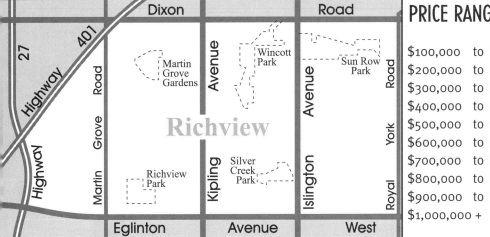

PRICE RANGE OF HOMES	
$100,000 to $200,000	
$200,000 to $300,000	✓
$300,000 to $400,000	✓
$400,000 to $500,000	✓
$500,000 to $600,000	✓
$600,000 to $700,000	✓
$700,000 to $800,000	
$800,000 to $900,000	
$900,000 to $1,000,000	
$1,000,000 +	

OVERVIEW:

Richview is a large, diverse neighbourhood that is home to people of a wide range of incomes and cultural backgrounds. This neighbourhood includes a multitude of parks, shopping plazas and excellent transportation routes. Richview is located just minutes from Pearson International Airport.

Real estate agents will sometimes refer to the area between Royal York Road and Islington Avenue as "Royal York Gardens" and the area between Islington Avenue and Kipling Avenue as "Richmond Gardens," although these two pockets are historically part of the greater Richview community.

HOMES:

Richview's housing stock consists primarily of ranch- and contemporary-style bungalows, split-level homes, and Georgian revival style houses built during the 1950s and 1960s. The typical Richview property features 40-, 50-, or 60-foot-plus frontages, with most properties having a private drive and garages. Many Richview properties back onto prime ravine or parkland.

Richview also includes a handful of new townhouse and condominium projects along its main streets. There are also a number of rental apartment buildings and row-houses located on the periphery of this neighbourhood.

SHOPPING:

Richview Square, located on the southwest corner of Eglinton Avenue and Wincott Drive, is a medium-size shopping plaza that includes fashion boutiques, a bakery and deli, a gift shop, a bank, a jeweller, a photo shop, a drug store, a travel agency, a health food store, a florist, an animal hospital, beer and liquor stores and professional and medical offices.

Martingrove Plaza, located at the southeast corner of Martingrove Road and The Westway, is anchored by a supermarket and also includes a drug store, hardware store, discount store, florist, bakery and deli, video store, travel agency, an ice cream shop, a liquor store, a post office and professional and medical offices.

Westway Centre, located at the southeast corner of Kipling Avenue and Dixon Road, features a large supermarket, fast food restaurants, a hardware store, professional and medical offices and a bowling alley.

The shopping plaza known simply as 1500 Royal York Road is more exciting than its name might imply. This large retail complex features a bicycle and ski shop, a bulk food store, a bowling alley and billiards hall, an indoor children's playground and a wide selection of shops that serve the everyday needs of the local residents.

RECREATION:

Richview Park, located next to the Richview Water Reservoir at Eglinton Avenue and Martin Grove Road is the largest recreational park in this neighbourhood. This wide open green space contains sports fields, baseball diamonds, tennis courts and a children's playground. The smaller West Grove, Martin Grove, Valley Field and Silver Creek parks each have tennis courts, a baseball diamond and a children's playground. West Grove Park also has an outdoor swimming pool and an artificial ice rink.

Sun Row Park, located in the northeast part of Richview, features an interpretive nature trail along the Humber River Watershed. Here hikers can explore fish habitats, wildflowers and a variety of wildlife. Richview residents can also enjoy the bicycle trail along Eglinton Avenue that merges with the Canadian Ukrainian Memorial Park and the paved South Humber trail which winds it's way down to Toronto's waterfront.

SCHOOLS:

(P)	Dixon Grove, 315 The Westway, (416) 394-7940
(P)	Hilltop, 35 Treehorne Dr., (416) 394-7730
(P)	Parkfield, 31 Redgrave Dr., (416) 394-7960
(P)	Valleyfield, 35 Saskatoon Dr., (416) 394-7590
(P)	Westway, 25 Poynter Dr., (416) 394-7970
(PH)	Central Etobicoke H.S., 10 Denfield St., (416) 394-7090
(PH)	Kipling C.I., 380 The Westway, (416) 394-7930
(PH)	Scarlett Heights C.I., 15 Treehorne Dr., (416) 394-7750
(C)	All Saints, 1435 Royal York Rd., (416) 393-5290
(C)	Father Serra, 111 Sun Row Dr., (416) 393-5391
(C)	St. Eugene, 30 Westroyal Rd., (416) 393-5337
(C)	St. Marcellus, 15 Denfield St., (416) 393-5311
(C)	Transfiguration, 55 Ludstone Dr., (416) 393-5276

TRANSPORTATION:

Bus service along Eglinton Avenue, The Westway, and Dixon Road connects passengers to the Eglinton station on the Yonge-University-Spadina subway line. The Islington bus connects to Islington Station on the Bloor-Danforth subway line. This station also provides a connecting route to the Mississauga Transit system as well as providing an express bus service to the Pearson International Airport. The Kipling Avenue bus connects to the Kipling station which is the westernmost station on the Bloor-Danforth subway line. This station also provides service to the Go Transit line.

Motorists can access Toronto's network of commuter highways off Eglinton Avenue west of Martingrove Road or Islington Avenue.

sW

HISTORY:

Smithfield is named after Robert Smith, who was a major landowner in this area dating back to the 1830s. It was Smith who donated the land for the first community church at the corner of Albion and Martin Grove roads. Smithfield Church is described in the *Story of Etobicoke* by Robert Given as a "simple log structure...When it was torn down the logs were taken to Rowntree's saw-mill on the Humber for lumber which was used in the building of a church in Thisletown in 1873."

From 1874 onwards this pioneer community revolved around the Smithfield school that was situated on Albion Road, west of Martin Grove. This two-room schoolhouse was designated as School Section 7 by the former Township of Etobicoke. The original Smithfield school was closed in 1954, however, when the present-day neighbourhood was developed in the 1960s, a new Smithfield school was opened on Mount Olive Drive. The School Section #7 plaque from the original Smithfield school is mounted in the foyer wall of the present-day Smithfield school.

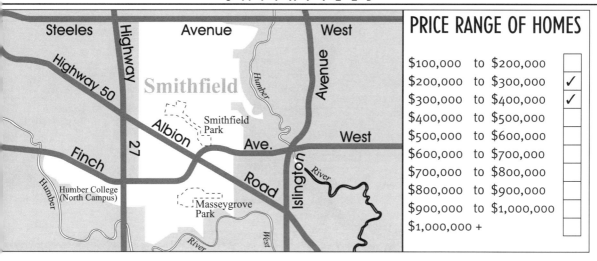

PRICE RANGE OF HOMES

$100,000	to $200,000	
$200,000	to $300,000	✓
$300,000	to $400,000	✓
$400,000	to $500,000	
$500,000	to $600,000	
$600,000	to $700,000	
$700,000	to $800,000	
$800,000	to $900,000	
$900,000	to $1,000,000	
$1,000,000 +		

OVERVIEW:

Smithfield is located at the far northwest boundary of the City of Toronto. It is bordered on the south, east and west by the Humber River Valley. Neighbourhood landmarks include Etobicoke General Hospital and Humber College (North Campus).

Smithfield is home to many new residents of Canada and includes one of the largest concentrations of subsidized housing in Toronto. This neighbourhood has recently received a tremendous boost with the $10-million North Kipling Junior-Middle School and Community Centre project situated at 2 Rowntree Road.

HOMES:

Smithfield's housing stock was built up during the 1960s, 1970s and 1980s, and includes a handful of recent new home developments located along Finch Avenue, west of Highway 27. Smithfield houses feature concrete and clay brick exteriors or frame siding and are situated on decent size lots with private drives. The style of houses found here includes split-level houses, bungalows and detached, two-storey houses.

Smithfield also contains a large number of private and subsidized townhouse complexes and high-rise apartment buildings. There are a handful of high-rise condominium buildings on Kipling Avenue, at Rowntree Road.

SHOPPING:

Shoppers World Albion, located at the intersection of Albion Road and Kipling Avenue, is a large indoor mall anchored by a department store and a supermarket. This mall contains a mix of franchise stores and independent retailers. Smaller shopping plazas can be found scattered throughout the Smithfield neighbourhood.

The retail corridor along Highway 27 north of Finch Avenue includes a large garden centre, a car dealership, big box stores, a discount mall, a bingo hall and the Albion Flea Market which includes over 400 vendors.

RECREATION:

Smithfield residents can exercise or take a leisurely stroll in the West Humber Parkland trail that skirts this neighbourhood. This nine-kilometre paved trail extends from Albion Road through the valley to Finch Avenue west of the Humber Arboretum. Entrances and parking to this trail are located west off Albion Road or off Westhumber Boulevard between Martin Grove Road and Kipling Avenue. It's worth a visit to the Humber Arboretum — a large botanical garden highlighted by extensive ornamental gardens, a hillside of roses and over 100 species of flowering rhododendrons and azaleas.

Smithfield residents of all ages can enjoy a variety of recreational activities at the Smithfield Community School, located at 175 Mount Olive Drive, the Albion Pool and Health Club, located at 1485 Albion Road, and the Humberwood Community Centre, located at 850 Humberwood Boulevard.

SCHOOLS:

(P)	Albion Heights, 45 Lynmont Rd.,	(416) 394-7520
(P)	Claireville, 350 Silverstone Dr.,	(416) 394-7500
(P)	Elmbank, 10 Pittsboro Dr.,	(416) 394-7560
(P)	Greenholme, 10 Jamestown Cres.,	(416) 394-7700
(P)	Highfield, 85 Mount Olive Dr.,	394-7510
(P)	John D. Parker, 202 Mount Olive Dr.,	(416) 394-7530
(P)	Melody Village, 520 Silverstone Dr.,	(416) 394-7620
(P)	Smithfield, 175 Mount Olive Dr.,	(416) 394-7540
(PH)	North Albion C.I., 2580 Kipling Ave.,	(416) 394-7550
(PH)	West Humber C.I., 1675 Martin Grove Rd.,	(416) 394-7570
(C)	Holy Child Jesus, 155 John Garland Blvd.,	(416) 393-5433
(C)	Msgr. John Corrigan, 100 Royalcrest Rd.,	(416) 393-5399
(C)	St. Andrew, 2533 Kipling Ave.,	(416) 393-5295
(C)	St. Dorothy, 155 John Garland Blvd.,	(416) 393-5341
(CH)	Father Henry Carr, 21 Panorama Crt.,	(416) 393-5521
(CH)	Marian Academy, 1760 Martin Grove Rd.,	(416) 393-5548

TRANSPORTATION:

There is bus service along the major streets and many of the secondary streets in the Smithfield neighbourhood. These bus lines connect passengers to either the Yonge-University-Spadina subway line or the Bloor-Danforth subway line.

Highway 27 runs through the centre of this neighbourhood and is easily accessed as is Highway 401 with on-ramps at Kipling Avenue. Both of these highways connect motorists to Toronto's network of commuter highways.

HISTORY: The history of the Sunnylea neighbourhood revolves around

Alexander Thompson, who purchased 200 acres of land in this area in 1803, after his discharge from the Kings Rangers.

Alexander Thompson lived in a distinguished residence, just south of Bloor Street at Royal York Road, that was known as "Rose Bank Cottage." His son Archibald lived in a country Georgian farmhouse, just to the south of his father, which was called "Spring Bank Cottage." Spring Bank Cottage is still standing today at 7 Meadowcrest Road.

The Thompson property was renowned for its apple, cherry, pear and plum orchards. In the latter part of the 1800s the Thompsons were joined in Sunnylea by families who cultivated thriving market gardens filled with fruits and vegetables. A handful of these old Sunnylea farmhouses are still standing both on Prince Edward Drive and on Islington Avenue.

In 1907, the first Sunnylea School – a two room white brick schoolhouse – was built on Prince Edward Drive. Edna G. Whitworth, a pupil at the school won a contest in coming up with the Sunnylea name which also became the name of this community.

Sunnylea's old farms were subdivided in the 1930s and 1940s, when the present-day neighbourhood was developed. The influx of new families to this community led to the opening of the second Sunnylea school in 1942.

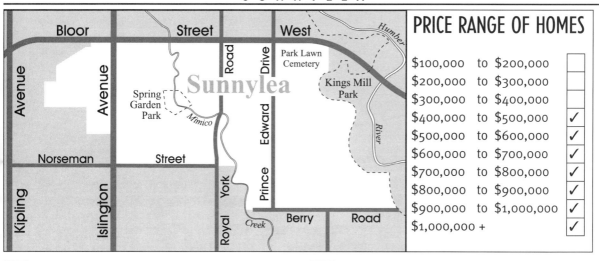

PRICE RANGE OF HOMES	
$100,000 to $200,000	
$200,000 to $300,000	
$300,000 to $400,000	
$400,000 to $500,000	✓
$500,000 to $600,000	✓
$600,000 to $700,000	✓
$700,000 to $800,000	✓
$800,000 to $900,000	✓
$900,000 to $1,000,000	✓
$1,000,000 +	✓

OVERVIEW:
Sunnylea is a highly sought-after neighbourhood that is especially popular with young families. There is a country charm here thanks to the Mimico Creek which gently meanders through the centre of this neighbourhood. Sunnylea's many mature trees and the exclusion of sidewalks add to its country-like ambience.

Sunnylea is known for its excellent schools which are a popular drawing card for this neighbourhood. The elementary schools have definite enrolment boundaries that serve different parts of this neighbourhood. You can phone the schools listed below to see which one your child would attend.

HOMES:
Sunnylea's bungalow, split-level, and one-and-a-half- and two-storey houses were built mostly in the 1940s and 1950s. All of these houses are detached and include at least a 30-foot frontage and a private drive.

The Tudor-style houses closer to Bloor Street are the older houses in this neighbourhood. Many of these houses feature handsome Riverstone exteriors, bay windows, stone chimneys, wrought iron railings and decorative front porches.

Sunnylea residents in the area bound by Bloor Street, Royal York Road, and the Mimico Creek have been progressive in forming the Thompson Orchard Community Association. This association has been successful in getting the city to pass site specific zoning by-laws designed to protect the residential character of this neighbourhood.

SHOPPING:
Sunnylea residents enjoy convenient access to the Kingsway Village shopping district on Bloor Street West. This well-planned retail corridor has a festive, pedestrian friendly atmosphere and features comfortable park benches, evergreen trees, and expensive-looking cast iron street lamps. Even the garbage bins are wrapped in ornate cast-iron frames. There is plenty of meter parking along Bloor Street and many of the side streets which make it easy to explore this vibrant shopping district.

The shops in the Kingsway Village include high-end fashion shops, children's stores, book shops, specialty stores, upscale restaurants, fruit and vegetable markets, bakeries and coffee shops. There is also a myriad of professional services located on this street, led by a large number of travel shops and real estate offices that serve the high-profile neighbourhoods in this district.

RECREATION:
The Norseman Community School, located at 105 Norseman Street, and the Park Lawn Community School, at 71 Ballacaine Drive, offer a large variety of recreational programs for children, teens, adults and seniors. Norseman has an indoor pool which is extensively used for aquafit and instructional swim programs. Park Lawn has a winter ice arena that converts to tennis courts in the summertime. The outdoor pool at Park Lawn is used for recreational swimming.

Sunnylea Park and Laura Hill Park each have two tennis courts and a children's playground. Spring Garden Park is nestled on the west bank of Mimico Creek. This idyllic park has a children's playground and is well shaded by many old trees. The Brentwood Public Library is located at 36 Brentwood Road, one block west of Royal York Road and one block north of Bloor Street. This library offers year-round programs for children. The 55-years-plus Fairfield Seniors' Centre is located at 80 Lothian Avenue. The facilities here include a seniors' lounge, a library, workshops, support groups, and a variety of special events including fashion shows, pub nights, a flea market and summer barbecues.

SCHOOLS:
(P)	Norseman, 105 Norseman St.,	(416) 394-7880
(P)	Park Lawn, 71 Ballacaine Dr.,	(416) 394-7120
(P)	Sunnylea, 35 Glenroy Ave.,	(416) 394-3850
(PH)	Etobicoke C.I., 86 Montgomery Rd.,	(416) 394-7840
(PH)	Etobicoke School of the Arts, 675 Royal York Rd.,	(416) 394-6910
(C)	Sainte-Margueritte-d'Youville, 755 Royal York Rd.,	(416) 393-5418

TRANSPORTATION:
Bus lines on Prince Edward Drive, Royal York Road and Islington Avenue provide Sunnylea residents with connecting routes to stations on the Bloor-Danforth subway line.

Motorist are approximately 15 minutes from Toronto's downtown financial and entertainment districts via Lake Shore Boulevard or the Gardiner Expressway, which also provide commuters with connecting routes to the all of the major highways leading out of the city.

HISTORY:

The Elms neighbourhood is named after the former Elms Golf Club, which occupied all of the land between Islington Avenue and Albion Road north of Hadrian Drive. Another large golf course named Pine Point was located just south of the Elms course. The Pine Point clubhouse is still standing in Pine Point Park, where it now serves as the home of the Thistletown Lions Club.

The Pine Point Golf Course was sold in the early 1950s to the same developers who built the Rexdale neighbourhood. In fact, the area south of Hadrian Drive is still sometimes referred to as "Old Rexdale." The Elms Golf course site was developed much later in the mid 1960s.

The Elms Ratepayers Association was formed in the 1970s in opposition to the Wilson Avenue extension, which would have cut a wide swath through the ravine valley in the centre of this neighbourhood. The residents' association won this battle. Their most recent accomplishment was their successful lobbying for the Northern Elms Public Library, which opened in the Rexdale Plaza in 1995.

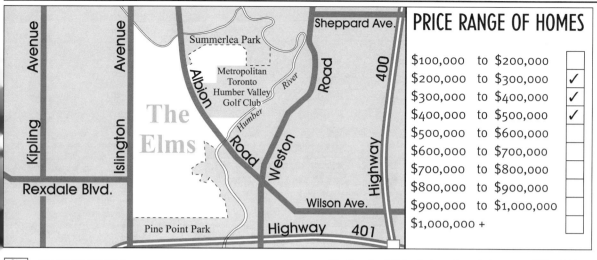

PRICE RANGE OF HOMES	
$100,000 to $200,000	
$200,000 to $300,000	✓
$300,000 to $400,000	✓
$400,000 to $500,000	✓
$500,000 to $600,000	
$600,000 to $700,000	
$700,000 to $800,000	
$800,000 to $900,000	
$900,000 to $1,000,000	
$1,000,000 +	

OVERVIEW:

The Elms is a diverse community made up of people from a wide variety of economic and cultural backgrounds. The Elms neighbourhood is located next to the very scenic Humber River Valley corridor. As a result there are plenty of parks, mature trees and a varied topography. The peaceful tranquility of this area is intermittently broken by the roar of airplanes which fly above The Elms neighbourhood enroute to nearby Pearson International Airport.

HOMES:

The Elms neighbourhood contains a large assortment of houses built mostly during the 1950s and 1960s. These houses are generally well-kept and nicely landscaped. Many of these properties back onto ravine or parkland. The various house styles found in this neighbourhood include ranch, contemporary and raised bungalows, split-level homes, 1.5-storey houses, detached, two-storey Georgian-revival homes and some newer custom built housing.

The residential pocket east of Albion Road around Summerlea Park has some continuity in housing from the west side of Albion Road. However, this residential pocket also features low-rise rental apartment buildings and townhouses that are owned and operated by the Toronto Community Housing Authority.

SHOPPING:

Rexdale Plaza located off Islington Avenue at Rexdale Boulevard, features a large Asian Supermarket, lots of bargain and discount stores, sports and children's wear, professional offices, a women's health club and the Northern Elms Public Library.

Islington Avenue and Albion Road both contain clusters of small shopping plazas that include a vast array of food shops and restaurants from a cross-section of cultures.

RECREATION:

The Elms Community School, located at 45 Goldown Road, has an indoor swimming pool and gymnasiums. During the school year this centre offers preschool, children, youth and adult programming. Some of these programs include dance classes, piano lessons, gymnastics, cartooning, ballet and drama classes. Programming is halted during the summer when The Elms summer camp program begins. Every year in June The Elms Community School hosts an annual "Fun Day" where neighbourhood residents come together to enjoy games, a garage sale, entertainment and a barbecue.

The Berry Creek Valley that runs through the centre of this neighbourhood is a watershed of the Humber River Valley. Elms Park is located in the section of the Berry Creek Valley between Islington Avenue and Norfield Crescent. This park contains a paved walking trail and a children's playground.

The West Humber Parkland Trail can be accessed off Albion Road at the north end of this neighbourhood. This 5.5-kilometre paved trail follows the valley to the Humber Arboretum where a large variety of plants and wildlife can be discovered. Across the street from the West Humber Trail parking lot is Summerlea Park. This pretty park includes a baseball diamond, a children's playground and tennis courts which are used as an artificial ice rink in the wintertime.

Pine Point Park is a long linear park that forms the southern boundary of this neighbourhood. This multi-use recreational park includes the Pine Point Indoor Arena which is the home of the Etobicoke Hockey League, a figure skating club, and a ball hockey league. Next to the arena is the Pine Point Banquet Hall which hosts a variety of social, cultural, and business events. Pine Point Park also includes four clay surface tennis courts, an outdoor pool, an outdoor hockey rink, a sports field, and a children's playground. In addition this park is also the starting point for a 1.7-kilometre paved trail with bridges across the Humber River and nearby Berry Creek.

The Humber Valley Golf Course located at Albion Road and Beattie Avenue is a par-70 course with a combination of links and valleyland holes.

SCHOOLS:

(P)	Braeburn, 15 Tanridge Dr., (416) 394-7770
(P)	Elmlea, 15 Hadrian Dr., (416) 394-7910
(P)	The Elms, 45 Golfdown Dr., (416) 394-7900
(PH)	Thistletown C.I., 20 Fordwich Cres., (416) 394-7710
(C)	St. Stephen, 55 Golfdown Dr., (416) 393-5284
(PR)	Timothy Christian School, 28 Elmhurst Dr., (416) 741-5770

TRANSPORTATION:

Bus lines both on Islington Avenue and on Albion Road connect passengers to the Islington station on the Bloor-Danforth subway line.

Motorists are less than five minutes from the Islington Avenue and the Weston Road on-ramps to Highway 401, which links drivers to Toronto's network of commuter highways.

HISTORY:
The Queensway began as a small farming community in the late 1800s. One of the few reminders of the Queensway's rural past is the little white stucco cottage that sits in an old farmers field at 694 Royal York Road.

In 1912, the urbanization of The Queensway led to the creation of the two-room Queensway Public School. This school was expanded in 1923 and then again in 1948. After a long period of growth, The Queensway experienced a decline in population during the 1960s, which led to the closing of the Queensway Public School in 1969.

The former Queensway School was demolished in the 1990s to make room for the giant Costco retail complex south of The Queensway, at Taymall Avenue. Ironically, like the school before it, Costco has become a landmark in The Queensway and has helped jump-start a revitalization of this neighbourhood, which has seen an influx of new retailers and condo developments.

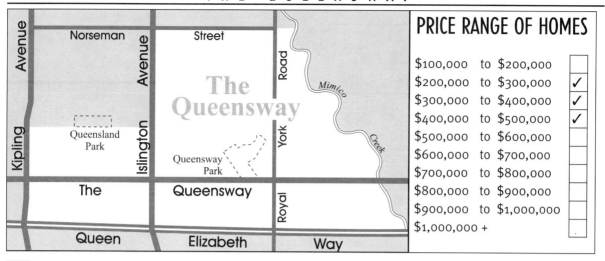

PRICE RANGE OF HOMES

$100,000	to $200,000	
$200,000	to $300,000	✓
$300,000	to $400,000	✓
$400,000	to $500,000	✓
$500,000	to $600,000	
$600,000	to $700,000	
$700,000	to $800,000	
$800,000	to $900,000	
$900,000	to $1,000,000	
$1,000,000 +		

OVERVIEW:

The Queensway is an affordable west-end neighbourhood that offers convenient access to downtown Toronto and numerous recreational opportunities at the nearby South Humber Parklands.

This relatively low-profile neighbourhood has quietly earned celebrity status, with many television, movie and commercial productions having taken place in the residential pocket around Queensway Park.

HOMES:

The oldest houses in The Queensway neighbourhood include a handful of former market-garden cottages and pre-subdivision houses located in the northeast pocket of this neighbourhood, near the Mimico Creek and Woodford Park.

The majority of the houses in The Queensway are two-bedroom brick bungalows and 1.5-storey houses built in the 1940s and 1950s. These houses are situated on good-sized lots with private driveways and garages.

The quaint looking frame houses located around Queensway Park were originally built as war veterans' housing during the 1940s. These houses have provided the backdrop for television and movie productions as well as commercials.

The area east of Royal York Road and south of The Queensway features a large number of newer townhomes and condominiums.

SHOPPING:

The Queensway is a shopping lover's delight. This retail district is anchored by the Kipling Queensway Mall which features Don Cherry's Sports Grill. Don Cherry is said to check in regularly at this sports emporium to personally sample the food and chat with the patrons and staff. The Kipling Queensway Mall is also known for its large department store and supermarket.

The shopping core of this neighbourhood has been revitalized by major retailers like Costco, Ikea, Sobey's supermarket, and Canadian Tire, as well as an 18-theatre Cineplex Odeon movie complex.

RECREATION:

Queensway residents can access South Humber Park, north of The Queensway at Stephen Drive. This park features a mix of open spaces and wooded areas that overlook the Humber Marshes. This park also provides a link with the Martin Goodman Trail which spans Toronto's waterfront and is enjoyed by walkers, joggers, cyclists and in-line skaters.

Queensway Park, located off Avon Park Drive just north of The Queensway, has a field-of-dreams baseball diamond, two tennis courts and a children's playground. Woodford Park is situated next to the Mimico Creek and includes a baseball diamond, a children's playground and two tennis courts.

SCHOOLS:

(P)   Norseman, 105 Norseman St., (416) 394-7880
(PH) Etobicoke School of the Arts, 675 Royal York Rd., (416) 394-6910
(C)   St. Louis, 11 Morgan Ave., (416) 393-5331
(C)   St. Margueritte-d'Youville, 755 Royal York Rd., (416) 393-5418
(CH) Bishop Allen Academy, 721 Royal York Rd., (416) 393-5549

TRANSPORTATION:

Queensway motorists can travel to downtown Toronto's financial and entertainment districts in approximately 10 minutes via the Gardiner Expressway. For commuters heading west of the city the Queen Elizabeth Way can be immediately accessed off Islington Avenue.

Bus service on Royal York Road and on Islington Avenue connect passengers to stations on the Bloor-Danforth subway line. The Islington station also provides an express bus service to the airport and a connection to the Mississauga Transit service.

HISTORY:
Thistletown was originally named "Coonats Corners" after the Coonat family, who settled here in the early 1800s. The next major landowner to settle in this area was John Grubb. Grubb's colonial riverstone home, built in 1832, is still standing today in a picturesque woodlot at 19-23 Jason Road.

John Grubb was a successful businessman who built many of the roads in this area, including Albion Road. When a post office was established on Albion Road in 1847, it was named St. Andrews in honour of Grubb's birthplace in Scotland. However, confusion with St. Andrews in New Brunswick led to the post office being renamed Thistletown, in honour of Dr. William Thistle, who was a well respected member of this community. His son John Thistle was Thisletown's first postmaster.

In the early 1900s, a few summer cottages and some year-round residences were built in Thistletown. However, Thistletown would remain primarily farmland until the Toronto real estate boom of the 1950s and 1960s led to the complete urbanization of this neighbourhood.

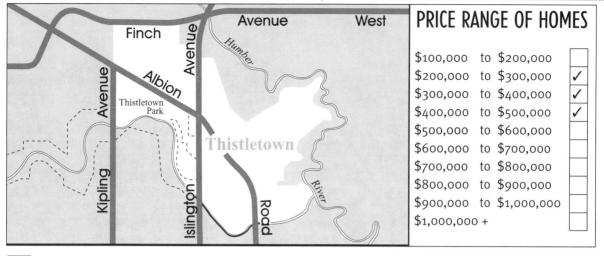

PRICE RANGE OF HOMES

$100,000 to $200,000		
$200,000 to $300,000	✓
$300,000 to $400,000	✓
$400,000 to $500,000	✓
$500,000 to $600,000	
$600,000 to $700,000	
$700,000 to $800,000	
$800,000 to $900,000	
$900,000 to $1,000,000	
$1,000,000 +	

OVERVIEW:

Thistletown is nestled amidst the rustic beauty of the Humber River Valley lands. This picturesque neighbourhood is home to a wide mix of people from many different cultural backgrounds. Thistletown's unique charm has led many second- and third-generation Thistletowners to raise their families here.

Thistletown has many outstanding neighbourhood landmarks, including the Anga's Farm at 89 Benfield Drive. This privately owned farm is popular with Thistletown residents who regularly stop here in the summertime to purchase fruit and vegetables. Anga's Farm also makes and sells its own honey.

Another Thistletown landmark is the Village Green, which is situated behind the Thistletown Multi-Service Centre on Albion Road. The Village Green was deeded to the residents of Thistletown in the 1890s by Jonathan Farr. The Village Green is the site of the very popular Thistletown Fair, which is held the first Saturday in June and includes a flea market, local entertainment, a baking contest, a children's carnival, and a barbecue hosted by the Thistletown Lions Club.

HOMES:

"Old Thistletown," situated between Islington Avenue and Albion Road, has a forest setting with many of the properties located on premium ravine lots overlooking the Humber River Valley. These houses are highlighted by Elmbank, the circa-1832 house of Thistletown pioneer John Grubb. Elmbank is located at 19-23 Jason Road. The Century houses at 32 and 34 Jason Road were also part of the Grubb farm. Old Thistletown also features a handful of former summer cottages built in the 1910s, as well as bungalows from the 1940s and 1950s, and a small number of recently designed, custom-built homes.

The newer pockets of Thistletown, around Albion Gardens Park and Beaumonde Heights Park, were built up during the 1950s and 1960s. The houses here include ranch-style bungalows, split - level houses, and 1.5-storey homes.

SHOPPING:

The retail district centred around Islington Avenue and Albion Road is one of the most culturally diverse shopping areas in the City of Toronto. Included in this mix are a plethora of East and West Indian, African, Middle Eastern and Asian food shops and restaurants. Convenience-type shops including supermarkets, drug stores and banks can be found at the Thistletown Plaza on Albion Road.

RECREATION:

The Thistletown Multi-Service Centre, located at 925 Albion Road, offers a variety of programs for the entire family. Some of these programs include men's and women's basketball, ballroom dancing, jazz, ballet, painting, and gardening. The Thistletown Seniors Centre, for seniors aged 55 and up, is based in this multi-service centre and offers a variety of programs including "Fit For Life," computer courses, woodworking, shuffleboard, bridge, euchre, ceramics and badminton.

The Franklin Carmichael Art Centre, located at 34 Riverdale Drive, is situated in a picturesque woodlot setting overlooking the Humber River Valley. This arts centre offers watercolour, oil and acrylic classes for children and adults. Studio time is also available for artists at designated times.

The West Humber Parkland, located off Albion Road, features a 5.5-kilometre paved walking and cycling trail that links up with the Humber Arboretum, a 100-hectare botanical garden where a variety of plants, trees, and wildlife can be explored. Recreational parks in Thistletown include Albion Gardens and Beaumonde Heights. Both of these neighbourhood parks contain tennis courts and a baseball diamond.

SCHOOLS:

(P)   Beaumonde Heights, 70 Monterrey Dr., (416) 394-7790
(PH) Thistletown C.I., 20 Fordwich Cres., (416) 394-7710
(C)   St. John Vianney, 105 Thistle Down Blvd., (416) 393-5392

TRANSPORTATION:

Bus service along Finch Avenue West and on Albion Road connect passengers to stations on the Yonge-University-Spadina subway line, while the Islington Avenue bus provides a connecting route to the Islington station on the Bloor-Danforth subway line.

Motorists are just a couple of minutes away from the Islington Avenue and Weston Road on-ramps to Highway 401. This highway provides quick connections to Toronto's network of commuter highways leading into and out of the city.

HISTORY: Thorncrest Village is named after the former summer home of Sir William Pearce Howland, Ontario's first Lieutenant Governor. Howland's rambling country estate was purchased in 1944 by developer Marshall Foss, who built the Thorncrest Village neighbourhood. Thorncrest Village was modelled after the renowned Kansas City Country Club subdivision in the United States.

Thorncrest Village is credited with being Toronto's first modern suburb. It introduced the idea of a strong homeowners' association, neighbourhood zoning and building restrictions, curvilinear street patterns and culs-de-sac, as well as an emphasis on the preservation of trees. Thorncrest Village is recognized as Canada's first planned, private co-operative housing community. Residents enjoy shared ownership of a neighbourhood clubhouse, pool, playground and tennis courts.

Thorncrest Village was designed by Dr. Eugene Faludi, an internationally renowned architect and town planner. Faludi received high praise for his work on Thorncrest Village and was subsequently hired to design many other Toronto neighbourhoods, including Don Mills, Humber Valley Village, Bayview Village and Lawrence Manor.

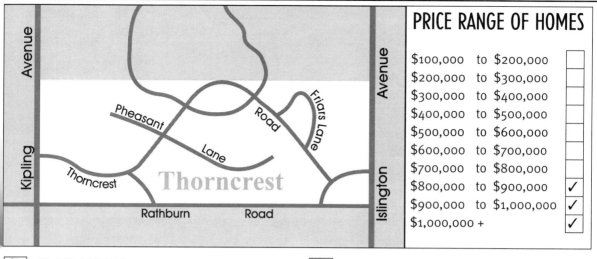

PRICE RANGE OF HOMES	
$100,000 to $200,000	
$200,000 to $300,000	
$300,000 to $400,000	
$400,000 to $500,000	
$500,000 to $600,000	
$600,000 to $700,000	
$700,000 to $800,000	
$800,000 to $900,000	✓
$900,000 to $1,000,000	✓
$1,000,000 +	✓

OVERVIEW:
Thorncrest Village is one of Toronto's most exclusive neighbourhoods, with just over 200 homeowners. It is also one of Toronto's prettier neighbourhoods, with winding, tree-lined roads that are whimsically decorated with cast-iron street lamps and wood post signs that combine to create a countrified charm.

It is interesting to note that all of the streets in Thorncrest Village have an east-west orientation. This was planned intentionally so that all of the houses in this neighbourhood would benefit from a direct south exposure.

HOMES:
Thorncrest's sweeping, tree-lined streets and expansive lots provide an idyllic backdrop for its varied collection of houses. The original Thorncrest houses include ranch-style bungalows and modernist-style homes from the late 1940s and the 1950s. These houses are gradually being replaced by larger brick and stone custom homes.

Thorncrest Village houses are subject to three site-specific zoning by-laws that are the legacy of a former building covenant, which was deeded to every Thorncrest property owner. Detailed information on Thorncrest Village's bylaws can be obtained by phoning the City of Toronto's Etobicoke planning office.

SHOPPING:
The immediate shopping needs of the residents of this neighbourhood are well served by the Thorncrest Plaza located on the northwest corner of Islington Avenue and Rathburn Road. This small shopping plaza includes a supermarket, bank, barber shop, coffee shop, hardware store, drug store, framing shop, dry cleaner, tailor, wine shop and a couple of professional offices.

Thorncrest residents are less than five minutes by car from the upscale Humbertown Shopping Centre located on The Kingsway, as well as the Kingsway Village and Bloor West Village shopping districts, situated along Bloor Street West.

RECREATION:
The Thorncrest Homeowners Association is the only homeowners' association in Toronto that owns and operates its own clubhouse and recreational facilities. The Thorncrest clubhouse, located at 35 Thorncrest Road, hosts many neighbourhood social events including family barbecues, bridge, theme dinners and a children's christmas show. There is also a family fun day that coincides with a pool-opening party. This annual event features pony rides, a bake sale, carnival food, a clown and games.

The Thorncrest community facilities include a 25-metre outdoor swimming pool which is a popular cooling-off spot in the summertime. Swim lessons from qualified instructors are offered at this site. The Thorncrest Homeowners Association also operates two tennis courts and a children's playground that are adjacent to the clubhouse and pool. The tennis courts are busy all summer with lessons, clinics, leagues, round robins and spring and fall tournaments.

SCHOOLS:
(P)   Rosethorn, 2 Remington Dr., (416) 394-6360
(P)   St. George's, 70 Princess Anne Cres., (416) 394-7990
(P)   Humber Valley Village, 65 Hartfield Rd., (416) 394-7860
(PH) Richview C.I., 1738 Islington Ave., (416) 394-7980
(C)   St. Gregory, 126 Rathburn Rd., (416) 393-5262

TRANSPORTATION:
The bus service along Islington Avenue connects passengers to the Islington station on the Bloor-Danforth subway line. Islington station also provides express bus service to the airport as well as being a connecting route to the Mississauga Transit system.

Motorists are 20 minutes from downtown Toronto via Bloor Street and 10 minutes from the Highway 401 on-ramp off Islington Avenue.

HISTORY:
The West Deane Park neighbourhood was still farmland when it was purchased by construction magnate Percy Law in the 1930s. Law raised prize cattle and race horses on this property, which also served as a storage depot for his construction equipment.

In keeping with his love for race horses, Law built a Colonial Revival "Old Kentucky" style home over an existing brick farmhouse that had stood on his property. This impressive white house with its large Corinthian-style pillars is still standing today, set back from the street at number 59 Beaverbend Road. On the property surrounding his house Law also built a coach house, a farm manager's house and stables. The farm manager's house is still standing at 18 Deanewood Crescent.

Law sold his hobby farm in the early 1960s to developer Edmund Peachey, who built the present-day neighbourhood. Peachey named this subdivision West Deane Park, in honour of his wife whose maiden name was Deane.

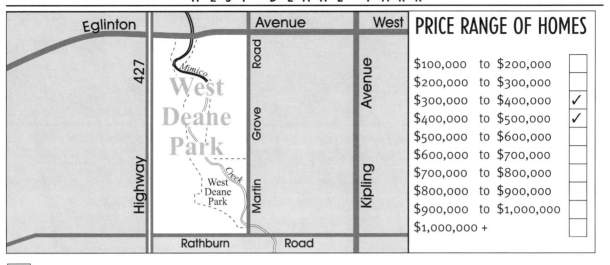

PRICE RANGE OF HOMES

$100,000	to $200,000	
$200,000	to $300,000	
$300,000	to $400,000	✓
$400,000	to $500,000	✓
$500,000	to $600,000	
$600,000	to $700,000	
$700,000	to $800,000	
$800,000	to $900,000	
$900,000	to $1,000,000	
$1,000,000 +		

OVERVIEW:

West Deane Park is an extremely quiet neighbourhood with a good mix of long-time residents and newcomers. The country feel of this neighbourhood is derived from the Mimico Creek Valley, which cuts a wide swath through the centre of the West Deane Park neighbourhood. The Mimico Creek Valley is home to a variety of wildlife including fox, beaver, deer, pheasants, ground hogs, skunks, raccoons, coyotes, red tailed hawks, and blue birds — all of which have been spotted by residents of this neighbourhood. If you love nature and animals, you will love the West Deane Park neighbourhood.

HOMES:

The majority of West Deane Park houses were built in the 1960s. These ranch-style bungalows, split-level homes, and Georgian-revival centre-hall designs are all situated on generous-sized lots with private driveways and an attached garage. There are also a small number of row-houses and multiplex homes located on the periphery of this neighbourhood.

The area around Beaverbend Road was developed later than the rest of this neighbourhood, and therefore includes some larger and more modern family-style houses built in the 1980s.

SHOPPING:

The Rathburn Medical Centre on The East Mall is part of a shopping plaza that includes a supermarket, pharmacy, hair salon and convenience store.

RECREATION:

West Deane Park is situated in the scenic Mimico Creek Ravine Valley. This park is highlighted by a paved exercise and bicycle trail that winds its way along the course of the Mimico Creek. West Deane Park also includes a children's playground, two baseball diamonds and a shaded picnic area. The Martingrove Tennis Club is located at the north end of this park. These four tennis courts double as an artificial ice rink in the wintertime.

SCHOOLS:

(P) Princess Margaret, 65 Tromley Dr., (416) 394-6350
(PH) Martingrove C.I., 50 Winterton Dr., (416) 394-7110
(C) Josyf Cardinal Slipyj, 35 West Deane Park, (416) 393-5413

TRANSPORTATION:

Bus services on the East Mall and on Martingrove Road connect passengers to Go Transit stations. The Eglinton Avenue and Rathburn Road buses provide connecting routes to the Yonge-University-Spadina subway line.

Motorists can gain immediate access to Highway 427 South, Highway 27 North and Highway 401, which provide connecting routes to Toronto's network of commuter highways.

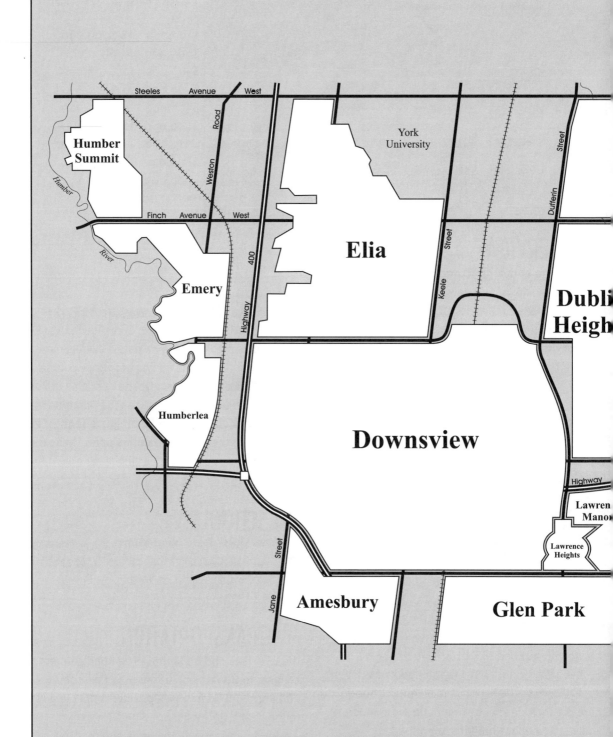

Steeles Avenue West

York University

Humber Summit

Weston Road

Dufferin Street

Finch Avenue West

Elia

Keele Street

Highway 400

Emery

Humber River

Dubli Heigh

Humberlea

Downsview

Highway

Lawren Mano

Lawrence Heights

Jane Street

Amesbury

Glen Park

North York

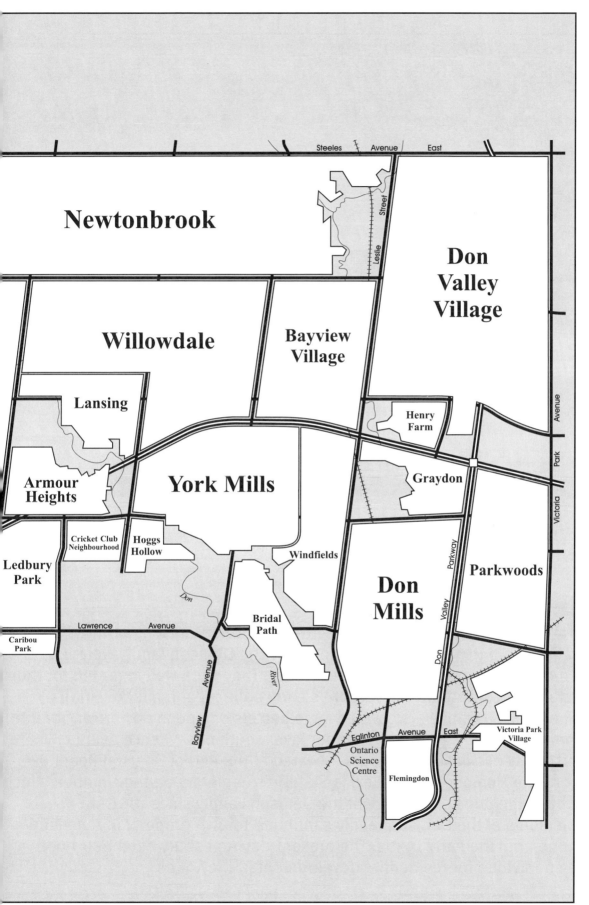

Newtonbrook

Don
Valley
Village

Willowdale

Bayview
Village

Lansing

Henry
Farm

Armour
Heights

York Mills

Graydon

Cricket Club
Neighbourhood

Hoggs
Hollow

Windfields

Parkwoods

Ledbury
Park

Don Mills

Caribou
Park

Bridal
Path

Victoria Park
Village

Eglinton

Ontario
Science
Centre

Flemingdon

Steeles Avenue East

Leslie Street

Victoria Park Avenue

Don Valley Parkway

Don

Lawrence Avenue

Bayview Avenue

River

Avenue East

HISTORY: Amesbury's first settler was John Denison, a United Empire Loyalist who purchased land here in 1804. The Denison family were influential members of the Toronto establishment. They were well regarded for their outstanding contribution to Toronto's early political and military affairs.

The Denison Family also owned large parcels of land in downtown Toronto, Richmond Hill, and along the Humber River south of Lawrence Avenue where Denison Avenue is situated today. Located at the end of Denison Road, overlooking the Humber River Valley, is St. John's Cemetery-on-the-Humber, which has been the private cemetery of the Denison Family since 1861.

Members of the Denison family continued to own property in Amesbury right up until the early 1930s. The present-day Amesbury neighbourhood was subdivided for residential development in the 1940s.

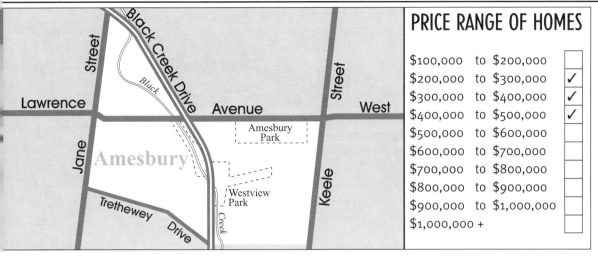

PRICE RANGE OF HOMES	
$100,000 to $200,000	
$200,000 to $300,000	✓
$300,000 to $400,000	✓
$400,000 to $500,000	✓
$500,000 to $600,000	
$600,000 to $700,000	
$700,000 to $800,000	
$800,000 to $900,000	
$900,000 to $1,000,000	
$1,000,000 +	

OVERVIEW:
Amesbury is a family-oriented middle-income neighbourhood. Even though this neighbourhood is fairly small in size, it has its own schools, community centre, public library and sports clubs.

Amesbury is divided in the middle by Black Creek Drive and the Black Creek Valley. The geography of the Amesbury neighbourhood includes pockets of ravine woodlots, many hills and an abundance of mature trees which all contribute to the natural beauty of this neighbourhood.

HOMES:
Amesbury, east of Black Creek Drive, features curvilinear streets and numerous culs-de-sac that are complimented by well-kept bungalows and 1.5-storey brick houses. There are only a small number of semi-detached houses in this part of the neighbourhood. These houses were built in the 1950s and early 1960s.

The older homes west of Black Creek Drive include smaller two-bedroom bungalows, an abundance of semi-detached housing, and a handful of newer homes. The streets circling Harding Park are lined with "Veterans Housing" or "Victory Housing." These cosy dwellings were built in the late 1940s and early 1950s for returning Second World War veterans and their families.

SHOPPING:
The North Park Plaza situated at the southeast corner of Keele Street and Lawrence Avenue has a Wal-Mart department store, a large supermarket, a popular video store, small independent retailers, fast food restaurants, and professional and medical offices. The Lawrence and Black Creek Plaza includes restaurants, a dry cleaner, a photo shop, and professional and medical offices.

Jane Street provides street level shopping with a wide assortment of food stores, retail shops and professional offices.

RECREATION:
The Amesbury Community Centre at 1507 Lawrence Avenue West is an ultra-modern facility with a gymnasium and meeting rooms. This centre offers kinder-gym, music, art and dance programs for preschoolers. Some of the other programs offered at this community centre include a Junior Kids Club, senior youth basketball, family karate, and country, ballroom and square dancing.

Amesbury Park, located adjacent to the Amesbury Community Centre, includes sports fields, a baseball diamond, tennis courts, and a children's playground. The Amesbury Sports Complex at 155 Culford Drive is located to the west of the community centre, and has four indoor bocce courts, an outdoor hockey rink, a swimming pool and a basketball court. The Amesbury Park Public Library located at 1565 Lawrence Avenue West offers programs for adults, children and preschoolers.

SCHOOLS:
(P)   Brookhaven, 70 Brookhaven Dr., (416) 395-2110
(P)   George Anderson, 30 George Anderson Dr., (416) 395-5000
(P)   Amesbury M.S., 201 Gracefield Ave., (416) 395-2000
(PH) Nelson Boylen C.I., 155 Falstaff Ave., (416) 395-3270
(C)   Immaculate Conception, 23 Comay Rd., (416) 393-5281
(C)   St Bernard, 12 Duckworth St., (416) 393-5261
(CH) Chaminade, 490 Queens Dr., (416) 393-5509

TRANSPORTATION:
Amesbury is well served by public transit with north-south bus routes on Keele and Jane streets and east-west bus lines on Trethewey Drive and along Lawrence Avenue. There is also a rush-hour bus service that runs along Maple Leaf Drive, Culford Road and Gulliver Road. All of the aforementioned bus routes provide connections to either the Bloor-Danforth or the Yonge-University-Spadina subway lines.

For motorists, Black Creek Drive runs through the centre of this neighbourhood. This scenic thoroughfare connects commuters to highways 400 and 401.

HISTORY:

Armour Heights was originally settled in the 1830s by John Armour, after whom this neighbourhood is named. The Armour homestead was situated where Armour Heights Community Centre is located today.

The Armour family sold its farm in 1911 to Colonel F.B. Robins, who planned the Armour Heights neighbourhood. Robins envisioned Armour Heights as a high-class address with its own polo field and bridle path. The polo field was never built, however the bridle path has become today's Yonge Boulevard.

When the First World War broke out Colonel Robins put his subdivision on hold and, instead, donated land in Armour Heights to the air force as a training school for American and Canadian pilots. American Aviatrix hero Amelia Earhardt was a regular visitor to the airfield during the latter part of the war, when she was stationed in Toronto as a nurses' aid with the Canadian Red Cross. In 1929 Robins and fellow developer W.P. Mulock sold all their interest in Armour Heights to R. J. Lillico & Associates. This sale was described in local papers at the time as one of the largest real estate transactions ever in Toronto.

The new owners attempted to change the name of this subdivision to Beverley Hills but it is the original Armour Heights name that has stood the test of time.

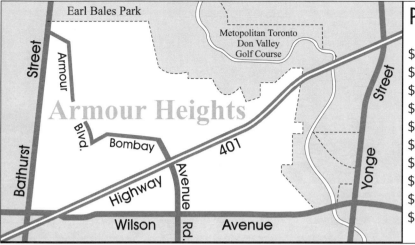

PRICE RANGE OF HOMES

$100,000 to $200,000		
$200,000 to $300,000		
$300,000 to $400,000		
$400,000 to $500,000	✓
$500,000 to $600,000	✓
$600,000 to $700,000	✓
$700,000 to $800,000	✓
$800,000 to $900,000	✓
$900,000 to $1,000,000	✓
$1,000,000 +	✓

OVERVIEW:

Armour Heights is an established Toronto neighbourhood with a rich history. The Don River Valley, Earl Bales Park and the Don Valley Golf Course form a natural boundary along the north and east end of this neighbourhood. Highway 401, one of Toronto's main commuter highways, winds its way discreetly through the centre of this neighbourhood.

The Armour Heights Community Centre is well known for its excellent selection of children's programs, while Armour Heights School and Summit Heights School are highly regarded as the top public schools in Toronto.

HOMES:

The residential tone of Armour Heights was inspired by Strathrobyn, the magnificent Tudor stone mansion set back from the street at the northeast corner of Yonge Boulevard and Wilson Avenue. Strathrobyn was built in 1914 for Colonel Frederick B. Robins. It is now owned and operated by the Canadian Armed Forces as a staff college.

Armour Heights houses were built over time from the 1920s to the 1970s. These houses range in size from modest two-storey, three-bedroom homes to the impressive Tudor Manor houses situated on the spectacular ravine lots along Sandringham Drive.

The homes at the north end of Armour Heights, just south of Earl Bales Park, are located on the former site of the York Downs Golf Club, which operated in Armour Heights from the early 1920s until 1968. The houses in this area represent excellent examples of the modernist architectural designs that were in vogue in North America during the 1960s and 1970s.

SHOPPING:

Avenue Road has a plethora of shops and restaurants catering to every taste and budget. Included in this shopping mix are food markets, drug and health food stores, gift shops, bookstores, convenience stores, fashion stores, home furnishing shops, hairstylist and beauty salons, children's clothing and toy shops, banks, fast food outlets and upscale restaurants.

Bathurst Street forms the western boundary of this neighbourhood. This street contains drug stores, banks, a large supermarket, Jewish specialty shops, delicatessens and bakeries.

RECREATION:

The Armour Heights Community Centre, located at 2141 Avenue Road, offers dance and fitness programs for adults, tiny tots programs and an after school children's program. The Armour Heights public library is also located in this community centre.

The Don Valley Golf Course is conveniently located at the southeast boundary of this neighbourhood. This 18-hole public course provides beautiful scenery and spectacular golfing. The entrance to this course is off Yonge Street, just north of York Mills.

Earl Bales Park is located at the north end of Armour Heights off Bathurst Street. This expansive park is home to the North York Ski Centre which offers lessons, clinics and rentals for skiers and snowboarders of all ages and ability. Earl Bales Park also includes a community centre with a parent and tot activity centre, games and meeting rooms and a banquet hall. In addition, this multi-faceted park includes a seniors' centre, an amphitheatre and many fine picnic spots. Access to the West Don River Parkland trails is available at the north end of Earl Bales Park off Don River Boulevard.

SCHOOLS:

(P)	Armour Heights, 148 Wilson Ave.,	(416) 397-2950
(P)	Summit Heights, 139 Armour Blvd.,	(416) 395-2920
(PH)	York Mills C.I., 490 York Mills Rd.,	(416) 395-3340
(C)	St. Margaret, 85 Carmichael Ave.,	(416) 393-5249
(CH)	Loretto Abbey, 101 Mason Blvd.,	(416) 393-5510
(PJ)	Toronto Cheder School, 3600 Bathurst St.,	(416) 789-9933

TRANSPORTATION:

The Avenue Road and Wilson Avenue buses connect to stations on the Yonge-University-Spadina subway line while the Bathurst Street bus connects to the Bloor-Danforth subway station. The York Mills subway station located inside the York Mills Centre at the northwest corner of Yonge Street and York Mills Road also provides Go Transit service with an express bus to the airport.

Motorists can travel directly downtown in approximately 25 minutes by way of Avenue Road. The Avenue Road on-ramp to Highway 401 can be immediately accessed at the south end of this neighbourhood.

HISTORY:
Bayview Village began as a small farming community in the 1800s. One of this area's first settlers was Thomas Clark, a father of seven children and an influential member of the community. The Clark house, built circa 1885, and located at 9 Barberry Place, is the only dwelling that remains from Bayview Village's pioneer days.

The present-day Bayview Village neighbourhood was planned in 1954 by a group of developers led by Farlinger Development Ltd. Bayview Village was hailed as "contemporary living in the countryside, at the doorstep of the urban concentration of Metropolitan Toronto."

The town planner for Bayview Village was Dr. E. G. Faludi, who also designed the Rexdale, Thorncrest Village, and Humber Valley neighbourhoods in Toronto. Faludi's trademark curvilinear street pattern that follows the natural contours of the land was designed to highlight the beautiful topography of this neighbourhood.

Bayview Village's novel approach to neighbourhood building combined with affordable house prices, which ranged from $16,000 to $40,000, helped make this subdivision an instant success. A residents' association was formed in 1956 and by the early 1960s Bayview Village was completely developed.

Ed. Note: A number of Bayview Village streets such as Citation, Candida, and Bunty Lane are named after famous race horses.

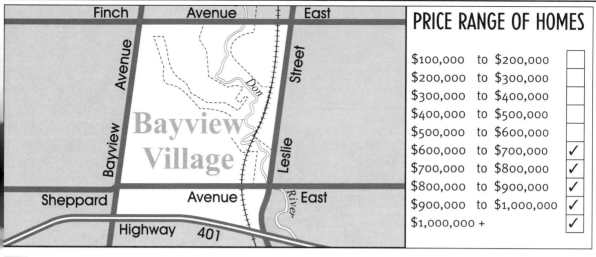

PRICE RANGE OF HOMES

$100,000 to $200,000		
$200,000 to $300,000		
$300,000 to $400,000		
$400,000 to $500,000		
$500,000 to $600,000		
$600,000 to $700,000		✓
$700,000 to $800,000		✓
$800,000 to $900,000		✓
$900,000 to $1,000,000		✓
$1,000,000 +		✓

OVERVIEW:
The Bayview Village community revolves around three popular local landmarks – the Bayview Village Shopping Centre, the North York YMCA, and the East Don Valley Parklands – each of which is an integral part of this family-oriented neighbourhood.

The design and layout of Bayview Village is very much influenced by the East Don Valley Parklands. Dr E.G. Faludi, the town planner who designed Bayview Village, recognized the importance of the East Don Valley Parklands when he said, "We will fit the community into the landscape and not the landscape into the community." This lofty ideal was met in the interior of Bayview Village.

Bayview Village has recently undergone a dramatic transformation. Massive condominium and townhouse projects have sprung up along Sheppard Avenue, dramatically increasing the density in this formerly sleepy hollow.

HOMES:
Bayview Village's winding streets and culs-de-sac are decorated with mature birch, cedar, willow, spruce, and pine trees. Many of the Bayview Village houses are situated on spectacular ravine lots that feature glorious views of the East Don River Valley Parklands.

Most Bayview Village homes were built between 1954 and 1964. The mix of housing here includes raised and ranch-style bungalows, split-level houses, and Georgian-revival-style homes. There are also a large number of affordable condominium townhouse communities along the west side of Leslie Street that feature playful street names like Tangle Briarway, Thorny Vineway, and Peach Willoway.

SHOPPING:
Bayview Village residents do most of their shopping at the Bayview Village Shopping Centre, located at the northeast corner of Bayview and Sheppard Avenues. Bayview Village is a nicely designed, intimate shopping centre anchored by a large upscale supermarket. This popular shopping centre also contains an excellent selection of fashion, gift, and specialty stores, as well as family restaurants.

Sheppard and Finch avenues and Leslie Street all contain small outdoor shopping plazas that feature mostly small, independent retailers, restaurants, and professional offices. Many of these businesses include English and Chinese on their signage, reflecting the large Chinese population living in and around Bayview Village.

Sheppard Avenue also has a number of well-known big box stores and a large medical centre.

RECREATION:
The North York YMCA, located at 567 Sheppard Avenue East, is the largest recreational facility serving this neighbourhood. Some of the programs being offered at this YMCA include playgym and swim lessons for preschoolers, gymnastics, karate, swimming and basketball programs for children, and aerobics, yoga and aquafit for adults. Facilities at this centre include a gymnasium, a dance studio, a conditioning room, a main swimming pool with lanes and a training swimming pool.

The East Don Parklands Trail winds its way through the centre of this neighbourhood from Finch Avenue down to Sheppard Avenue. From Sheppard Avenue south to Duncan Mills Road this trail is paved and is known as the Betty Sutherland trail, named after a long-serving municipal councillor from this area.

The Bayview Village Shopping Centre is a popular recreation spot for residents of this neighbourhood. This shopping centre stages a variety of special events throughout the year including a fashion show and an antique and collectible show. The Bayview Village Shopping Centre also has a public library, a health spa, and four movie theatres.

SCHOOLS:
(P)   Bayview M.S., 25 Bunty Lane, (416) 395-2050
(P)   Elkhorn, 10 Elkhorn Dr., (416) 395-9500
(PH) Avondale Alternative, 171 Avondale Ave., (416) 395-3130
(PH) Earl Haig S.S., 100 Princess Ave., (416) 395-3210
(C)   Blessed Trinity, 3205 Bayview Ave., (416) 393-5289
(C)   St. Gabriel, 396 Spring Garden Ave., (416) 393-5256
(C)   St. Martha, 1865 Sheppard Ave., (416) 393-5344

TRANSPORTATION:
The new Sheppard subway line facilitates quick and easy access to the Yonge subway line. There is regular bus service on Finch and Sheppard avenues and limited bus service on Bayview Avenue and Leslie Street. All these bus lines provide connecting routes to stations on the Yonge-University-Spadina subway line.

Motorists are approximately 25 minutes from downtown via Yonge Street or Bayview Avenue. On-ramps to Highway 401 are located off of Bayview Avenue, Yonge Street and Leslie Street.

HISTORY: The Bridle Path could hardly have been envisioned by Alexander
Milne, who settled on what is now Edwards Gardens in 1827. Milne operated
woolen and saw mills on the banks of Wilket Creek until 1832, when a dwindling
water supply forced Milne to move east to a mill site along the Don River.

The Bridle Path inconspicuously spent the rest of the 1800s and early 1900s
as farmland. It wasn't until 1929, when the Bayview Bridge was built over the
steep Don River Valley, that this area was considered for residential development.

Hubert Daniel Bull Page, a Toronto-based land developer, was one of the
founders of the present-day neighbourhood. Page envisioned the Bridle Path as
an exclusive enclave of estate homes. In 1929, Page built the Cape Cod-colonial-
style house at 2 The Bridle Path, in an effort to spark interest in his subdivision.

Early plans for this neighbourhood called for an elaborate system of equestrian bridle paths. These bridle paths have long since been paved over. However,
their legacy remains in the Bridle Path's unusually wide streets and in the name
of this neighbourhood.

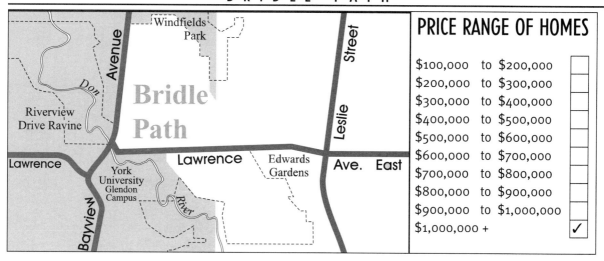

PRICE RANGE OF HOMES

$100,000	to	$200,000	
$200,000	to	$300,000	
$300,000	to	$400,000	
$400,000	to	$500,000	
$500,000	to	$600,000	
$600,000	to	$700,000	
$700,000	to	$800,000	
$800,000	to	$900,000	
$900,000	to	$1,000,000	
$1,000,000 +			✓

OVERVIEW:

The Bridle Path has often been referred to as "Millionaires Row." Indeed, houses in this neighbourhood sell for well in excess of $1 million. This exclusive enclave of homes is surrounded by the Don River Valley and lush parkland, which provide the perfect backdrop for the Bridle Path's stately homes.

Bridle Path residents shop, play, and educate their children along Bayview Avenue, whose landmarks include the upscale York Mills Shopping Plaza, the posh Toronto Granite Club, and the private Crescent School for boys. The Toronto French School is located just off of Bayview at Lawrence Avenue.

HOMES:

The Bridle Path's largest mansions located between Post Road and Park Lane Circle are among the largest homes in Toronto. These grand homes are situated on one- to six-acre lots, and feature stone and cast-iron gateways with elaborate built-in security systems. The houses south of Park Lane Circle are somewhat smaller in scale, still with very generous 100-foot frontages.

The houses in the Bridle Path were built mostly in the 1930s, 1950s and 1960s, which accounts for the eclectic mix of architectural styles found here. This mix of designs includes Georgian, colonial, Greek- and Tudor-revival, Italianate, neo-Gothic, California bungalows and futuristic modernist-style houses.

The typical Bridle Path estate offers a wide range of luxury features, ranging from pools, tennis courts, gazebos and cabanas, to greenhouses and waterfalls. Interior features range from gold fixtures and marble finishes to dance floors, saunas, personal gyms, and home theatres.

The French-chateau-inspired luxury condominium at One Post Road is an exclusive building with only 42 units, all with private elevator access. Also noteworthy are the European-design Chedington Place Condominiums, situated on the northeast corner of Bayview and Lawrence avenues. These exclusive condominiums feature private elevators and spectacular ravine views.

SHOPPING:

York Mills Plaza, located at the southwest corner of Bayview Avenue and York Mills Road, was once described by Toronto Mayor Mel Lastman as the Tiffany's of shopping centres. Here you will find vintage wines, imported cigars, swiss chocolate, decadent desserts, Cartier eyeglasses, designer lingerie, and a glittering coffee shop serving up espresso, cappuccino, and caffe lattes.

Situated at the northeast corner of Bayview and Sheppard avenues is the Bayview Village Shopping Centre, which features designer clothing stores and an excellent selection of restaurants. A massive Loblaws supermarket anchors this shopping centre.

RECREATION:

Bridle Path residents can walk to beautiful Edwards Gardens, the home of the Civic Garden Centre, one of Canada's finest public gardening resource centres. Edwards Gardens contains rockeries, perennial gardens, a pond, waterfalls, a rose garden and the beginning of a nine-kilometre paved trail that extends through the Don River Valley all the way to Warden Woods Park in Scarborough.

The Edwards Gardens trail passes through Sunnybrook Park, which features top quality sports fields for cricket, field hockey, rugby and soccer. Sunnybrook park also has riding stables which offers lessons to the public. It is appropriate that these equestrian facilities are located on the border of the Bridal Path neighbourhood which has such a rich horse-riding history.

SCHOOLS:

(P) Rippleton, 21 Rippleton Rd., (416) 395-2810
(PH) York Mills C.I., 490 York Mills Rd., (416) 395-3340
(C) St. Bonaventure, 1340 Leslie St., (416) 393-5263
(PR) Crescent School, 2365 Bayview Ave., (416) 449-2556
(PR) Toronto French School, 296 Lawrence Ave., E., (416) 484-6533
(PR) Crestwood School, 411 Lawrence Ave, (416) 444-5858
(PR) Bayview Glen, 275 Duncan Mill Rd., (416) 443-1030

TRANSPORTATION:

The Bayview Avenue bus connects passengers to the Davisville station on the Yonge-University-Spadina subway line and also provides passengers with a connecting route to the Lawrence Avenue subway station.

Motorists can get directly downtown to Toronto's business and entertainment districts in approximately 20 minutes from nearby arterial roadways including Mount Pleasant Road and Yonge Street. The Highway 401 on-ramp off Bayview Avenue and the Don Valley Parkway on-ramp off Lawrence Avenue are both approximately a five-minute drive from here.

HISTORY: Caribou Park was formerly part of a farm owned by a pioneer named Thomas Snider, who resided here from the 1830s to the 1870s. The Snider farm took in the entire present-day neighbourhood, and also included land west of Bathurst Street. Remarkably, the Snider farm house is still standing just outside this neighbourhood at 519 Glengrove Avenue. The Snider house is hidden from the street by two towering blue spruce trees that stand guard over this historic house.

Following Thomas Snider, the next name to appear on city maps of this area is that of John H. Watson, whose family resided here from the 1870s up until the early 1900s.

Another house which was built when this area was still farmland is 43 Kimbark Boulevard. This cobblestone house was built in 1906 by a stone mason from Scotland, and is listed on the Toronto Historical Board's Inventory of Heritage Properties.

The rest of the present-day neighbourhood was laid out in two separate plans of subdivision registered in 1910 and 1912. However, the actual building of houses in Caribou Park did not commence until the 1930s.

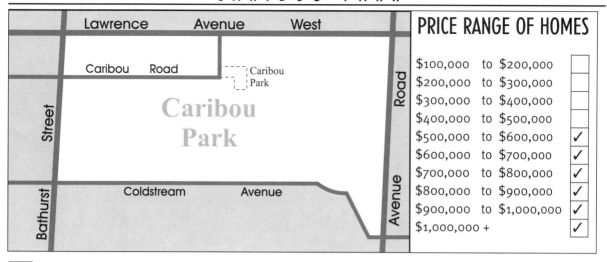

PRICE RANGE OF HOMES

$100,000 to $200,000	
$200,000 to $300,000	
$300,000 to $400,000	
$400,000 to $500,000	
$500,000 to $600,000	✓
$600,000 to $700,000	✓
$700,000 to $800,000	✓
$800,000 to $900,000	✓
$900,000 to $1,000,000	✓
$1,000,000 +	✓

OVERVIEW:

Caribou Park street names – including Otter, Caribou, and Kimbark (originally called Beaver Street) – are appropriate for a neighbourhood that features many mature trees, lush landscapes and a small ravine with a creek running through it. Discovering this neighbourhood for the first time, one can't help but feel that one has taken a surprise turn out of the city and into the country.

This neighbourhood is in big demand for its rustic charm, fine selection of houses, close proximity to private schools, convenience to the upscale Avenue Road shopping district and close proximity to downtown.

HOMES:

Caribou Park has two very distinct residential pockets. The Georgian-, Tudor-, and English-cottage-style houses closer to Avenue Road and east of Caribou Park were built in the 1930s and 1940s. The houses along Otter Crescent that back onto the ravine and the Otter Creek are generally situated on premium lots that command the highest prices in the neighbourhood.

The split-level houses and ranch style bungalows located west of Caribou Park and closer to Bathurst Street were built in the 1950s and 1960s. Some of these houses have been replaced by modern custom built homes. Many of the homeowners in this area are members of Toronto's orthodox Jewish community that is centred along Bathurst Street.

SHOPPING:

Caribou Park residents enjoy the luxury of being able to walk to the popular shops and restaurants on Avenue Road, north of Lawrence Avenue. This shopping district is anchored by the Pusateri's food shop which attracts shoppers from all over the city. The mix of stores along Avenue Road includes children's shops, home decorating and furniture stores, clothing stores, a garden nursery, and neighbourhood pubs and restaurants.

Caribou Park residents can also walk to the Bathurst and Lawrence shopping district which is anchored by the Lawrence Plaza at the northwest corner of Bathurst and Lawrence. This shopping plaza attracts shoppers from far and wide to its outstanding collection of discount and outlet stores. Bathurst Street itself contains many fine Jewish food shops and bakeries featuring some of the finest bagels in town.

RECREATION:

The Caribou neighbourhood park is conveniently located right in the centre of this neighbourhood off Caribou Drive. This park features a popular children's playground.

Otter Creek Park is located just east of Avenue Road off Cheritan Avenue. This fitness-oriented park includes four tennis courts that are retrofitted for use as an artificial ice rink in the wintertime. Otter Creek also provides access to the Chatsworth ravine which contains a nature trail.

The ultra-modern Barbara Frum Public Library at 20 Covington Road includes a children's storyroom, French and multicultural collections, and an auditorium with a 150-person seating capacity. This library is combined with a 10,000 square foot recreation centre that contains multi-purpose rooms, a kitchen/craft room and meeting rooms.

SCHOOLS:

(P)	John Ross Robertson Jr., 130 Glencairn Ave. W., (416) 393-9400
(P)	Glenview Sr., 401 Rosewell Ave., (416) 393-9350
(P)	Ledbury Park M.S., 95 Falkirk Ave., (416) 395-2630
(PH)	Lawrence Park C.I., 125 Chatsworth Dr., (416) 393-9500
(C)	St. Margaret, 85 Carmichael Ave., (416) 393-5249
(PR)	Havergal College, 1451 Avenue Rd., (416) 483-3519
(PJ)	Bais Yakov, 15 Saranac Blvd., (416) 256-4436
(PJ)	Yeshiva Yesodei Hatorah, 77 Glen Rush Blvd., (416) 787-1101
(PJ)	Beth Jacob, 410 Lawrence Ave., W., (416) 787-4949
(PJ)	Yeshiva Nachalas Zvi, 475 Lawrence Ave., W., (416) 782-8912

TRANSPORTATION:

Caribou Park is a centrally located neighbourhood that is well served by public transit. The Lawrence and Avenue Road buses connect passengers to stations on the Yonge-University-Spadina subway line. The Lawrence subway station is within walking distance for those seeking a bit of exercise.

Avenue Road provides motorists with a direct route downtown in approximately 20 minutes. A five-minute drive north on Avenue Road will link commuters to Highway 401.

HISTORY: Cricket Club Neighbourhood was originally settled by a Scotsman named Andrew McGlashan, who settled here with his family in the early 1800s. The McGlashans operated a tannery on the southwest corner of Yonge Street and York Mills Road up until the 1860s.

In 1876 the McGlashan property was purchased by Andrew Bathgate. Bathgate's heirs sold the family homestead in 1907 to William George Gooderham, the owner of the Gooderham and Worts distillery.

Gooderham fortuitously discovered a spring of fresh water on the Yonge Street hillside of his property where the York Mills Gardens apartments are now located. He then set up Mineral Springs Ltd., which bottled and sold this water around the world up until the 1920s.

Gooderham played a key role in the residential subdivision of this neighbourhood during the early 1900s. He also helped form the Toronto Cricket Skating and Curling Club, which opened in 1925 and has been a neighbourhood landmark ever since.

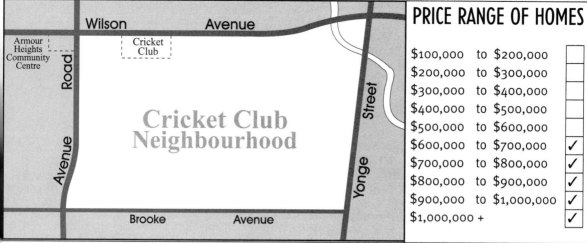

PRICE RANGE OF HOMES

$100,000	to	$200,000	
$200,000	to	$300,000	
$300,000	to	$400,000	
$400,000	to	$500,000	
$500,000	to	$600,000	
$600,000	to	$700,000	✓
$700,000	to	$800,000	✓
$800,000	to	$900,000	✓
$900,000	to	$1,000,000	✓
$1,000,000 +			✓

OVERVIEW:

Many families in this neighbourhood are members of the Cricket Club, and so the neighbourhood has adopted its name. The local residents display a pride of ownership that can be seen on the manicured lawns and pretty gardens found throughout this neighbourhood. There is a relaxed, country charm ambience here thanks to an abundance of mature trees and the fact that many of the streets do not have sidewalks.

Cricket Club homes are in great demand because of all the amenities that this location has to offer, including upscale shopping districts, excellent schools, and close proximity to public transportation and to Highway 401.

HOMES:

The Cricket Club neighbourhood contains a mix of housing including two- and three-bedroom bungalows, Tudor-revival houses, and larger Georgian-revival-style homes with spacious centre-hall plans. All of the houses in this neighbourhood have private drives and the lot frontages are generous, varying in size from 30 to 50 feet.

The majority of homes originally built in this neighbourhood were constructed in the 1920s, 1930s and 1940s. These houses include many decorative features such as pretty bay windows, hardwood floors, fireplaces, french doors, wood trim, and built-in cabinetry.

In recent years a large number of these houses, especially the bungalows, have been torn down and replaced with custom-built homes.

SHOPPING:

Cricket Club residents enjoy some of the best shopping found anywhere in Toronto along Yonge Street and on Avenue Road. The shops, restaurants, and professional offices on these two streets are located in small two-storey brick buildings that blend in nicely with the residential tone of this neighbourhood.

The shopping mix on Yonge Street and on Avenue Road includes designer clothing stores, home furnishing and decorating stores, hairstylists, beauty salons, children's clothing and toy shops, video stores, antique shops, art shops, gourmet coffee shops, bakeries, gift shops, hardware stores, banks, convenience stores, supermarkets, drug and health food stores, dry cleaners, fast food outlets, a grocery store, restaurants and professional and medical offices.

RECREATION:

The Armour Heights Community Centre, located at 2141 Avenue Road, offers dance and fitness programs for adults, a tiny tots program, and a children's after-four program. The Armour Heights public library is located in this community centre.

For golf enthusiasts, the Don Valley Golf Course is located just north of York Mills off Yonge Street. This public course is set amongst the beautiful scenery of the Don River Valley.

Many residents of this neighbourhood spend their recreational time at the Toronto Cricket Skating and Curling Club, located at 141 Wilson Avenue. The Cricket Club is one of Toronto's premier private clubs. Its facilities include tennis, squash, skating, curling, cricket, croquet, lawn bowling, aerobics, and swimming, as well as a snack bar and dining facilities.

SCHOOLS:

(P)   Armour Heights, 148 Wilson Ave., (416) 397-2950
(P)   St. Andrew's, 131 Fenn Ave., (416) 395-3090
(PH) York Mills C.I., 490 York Mills Rd., (416) 395-3340
(C)   St. Margaret, 85 Carmichael Ave., (416) 393-5249
(C)   Loretto Abbey, 101 Mason Blvd., (416) 393-5510

TRANSPORTATION:

Cricket Club Neighbourhood residents are well served by public transit. Bus services on Avenue Road and Yonge Street connect to the Yonge-University-Spadina subway line. The York Mills subway stations is within reasonable walking distance of the homes in this neighbourhood.

Motorists can get downtown to Toronto's business and entertainment districts via Yonge Street or Avenue Road in approximately 25 minutes. For commuters the Yonge Street and the Avenue Road on-ramps to Highway 401 are conveniently located just beyond the north boundary of this neighbourhood.

HISTORY:
The Don Mills name makes reference to the historic Don River, and the fact that several mills were operating in this part of the Don Valley during the 1800s. The historic residences of pioneer miller William Gray are still in their original location overlooking the Don River on the Donalda Golf Club grounds.

The Gray property was purchased in 1914 by David Dunlap, who made his fortune in the mining business. The Dunlap family established a prize winning "model farm" here in Don Mills. Donalda Farm was visited by farming experts from around the world who came to inspect and marvel at its livestock and equipment.

In 1952 David's son, Moffat Dunlop, sold the 600-acre Donalda Farm to the Don Mills Development Company, which was headed by Canadian business legend E.P. Taylor. Donalda House was originally used as a sales office by the developers, and now serves as the clubhouse for the Donalda Golf Club.

Don Mills is recognized as the first planned and fully integrated post-war community in North America. It is credited with laying out the blueprint for Toronto's post-war suburban development and the building of contemporary neighbourhoods.

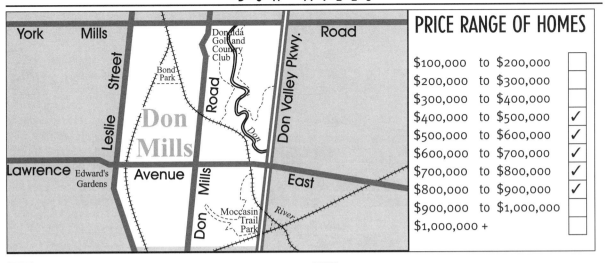

PRICE RANGE OF HOMES		
$100,000	to $200,000	
$200,000	to $300,000	
$300,000	to $400,000	
$400,000	to $500,000	✓
$500,000	to $600,000	✓
$600,000	to $700,000	✓
$700,000	to $800,000	✓
$800,000	to $900,000	✓
$900,000	to $1,000,000	
$1,000,000 +		

OVERVIEW:
Don Mills is one of Toronto's best known and most popular neighbourhoods. Neighbourhood landmarks include the picturesque Donalda Golf and Country Club, scenic Edwards Gardens, and the Don Mills Shopping Centre, which is currently being redeveloped (see Shopping, below). The commercial/industrial sector of Don Mills serves as the head office for IBM Canada Ltd., Global Television Station, the Toronto Real Estate Board and many other prominent companies.

HOMES:
Don Mills is one of Toronto's most-treed neighbourhoods. The spacious front lawns in Don Mills are covered with a great variety of trees including birch, willow, spruce, pine, maple and a myriad of ornamental and fruit trees. The ravine lots situated in east Don Mills back onto the Don River Valley and a virtual forest of trees.

Don Mills houses were built between 1953 and 1967. The mix of housing here includes detached and semi-detached homes, executive ranch-style bungalows, luxury condominium apartment buildings, low-rise rental apartment buildings, terraced row housing and seniors' residences.

All Don Mills houses were designed by an architect whose plans had to meet the approval of the Don Mills Development Company before any house could be built. Don Mills's contemporary-style architectural designs earned many Canadian Housing Design Council awards. Typical of this style of housing are shallow roof lines, multi-dimensional facades, expansive picture windows and the use of a carport as an alternative to a garage.

SHOPPING:
The Don Mills Shopping Centre is conveniently located right in the centre of Don Mills, at 939 Lawrence Avenue West. The former indoor mall is being replaced by a dynamic open-air centre that will have the look and feel of a town square. The new Don Mills Centre is scheduled to be completed in 2008.

RECREATION:
Many of Don Mills smaller local parks are connected by a paved walkway that runs behind Don Mills' houses. Another path inside Edwards Gardens is part of a nine-kilometre paved trail that follows the valley of the West Don River all the way to Warden Woods Park in Scarborough.

Bond Park, located off Duncairn Road, is Don Mills largest park. It includes extensive baseball facilities and organized leagues, and is also home to the North York Winter Tennis Club. Three Valleys Park, located next to Three Valleys School, has a large children's playground and tennis courts.

The Don Mills Civitan Arena located at 1030 Don Mills Road has a children's house league program and offers pleasure skating at designated times throughout the week.

The Don Mills Public Library at 881 Lawrence Avenue East has regular programming for babies, toddlers, preschoolers, and school children. Don Mills is close to the Ontario Science Centre, located at 770 Don Mills Road.

SCHOOLS:
(P)   Greenland, 15 Greenland Rd., (416) 395-2500
(P)   Norman Ingram, 50 Duncairn Rd., (416) 395-2720
(P)   Three Valleys, 76 Three Valleys Dr., (416) 395-2930
(P)   Don Mills M.S., 17 The Donway E., (416) 395-2320
(PH) Don Mills C.I., 15 The Donway E., (416) 395-3190
(C)   St. Bonaventure, 1340 Leslie Rd., (416) 393-5263
(PR) Bayview Glen, 275 Duncan Mill Rd., (416) 443-1030

TRANSPORTATION:
Bus routes on York Mills Road, Lawrence Avenue East and Leslie Street connect passengers to stations on the Yonge-University-Spadina subway line. The Don Mills Road bus connects to the Pape station on the Bloor-Danforth subway line.

Don Mills Road provides commuters with a quick and easy access route to downtown Toronto. North and south on-ramps to the Don Valley Parkway are located east of Don Mills Road, off Eglinton and Lawrence avenues and off York Mills Road.

HISTORY:

The Don Valley Village neighbourhood was developed in the 1960s and 1970s. However, the pre-subdivision history of this area dates back to the early 1800s, when Don Valley Village was comprised of a collection of small farming hamlets. Only three historical landmarks remain from the pioneer days of Don Valley Village. These vestiges include the Zion Primitive Methodist Church, circa 1873, located at 1650 Finch Avenue East and the charming little red brick Zion Schoolhouse, circa 1869, located at 1091 Finch Avenue East. The only pioneer home still standing in this area is the Alexander Muirhead Victorian-style farmhouse, circa 1853, located at 179 Old Sheppard Street. This house was originally part of the former O'Sullivan's Corners, a crossroads community that once thrived at the corner of Victoria Park and Sheppard avenues.

Ed. note: The neo-colonial MacDougald mansion just north of Sheppard Avenue and east of Leslie Street, which now provides the backdrop for the posh Green Meadows subdivision, hosted at various times: the Queen, the Queen Mother, Princess Anne and Prince Philip during royal visits to Toronto.

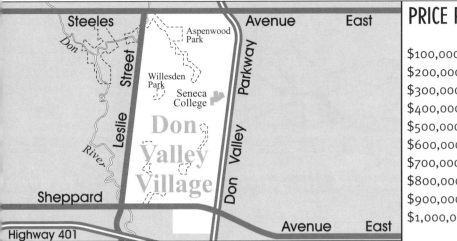

PRICE RANGE OF HOMES

$100,000	to $200,000	
$200,000	to $300,000	
$300,000	to $400,000	✓
$400,000	to $500,000	✓
$500,000	to $600,000	✓
$600,000	to $700,000	✓
$700,000	to $800,000	✓
$800,000	to $900,000	✓
$900,000	to $1,000,000	✓
$1,000,000 +		✓

OVERVIEW:

Don Valley Village is a low- to middle-income neighbourhood that includes many new Canadian citizens of Armenian, Chinese, East Indian and Middle Eastern backgrounds. The outstanding feature of Don Valley Village is its hill-and-dale topography, which is formed from the nearby Don River Valley situated along the eastern boundary of this neighbourhood.

Don Valley Village landmarks include Fairview Mall (one of Toronto's largest shopping centres), North York General Hospital located at the southwest corner of Sheppard Avenue and Leslie Street, and the Cummer Park Fitness Centre, which is one of Toronto's largest municipally operated recreational facilities.

HOMES:

The majority of Don Valley Village houses and apartments were built during the 1960s and 1970s. The mix of housing here includes a large selection of condominium townhouse and apartment buildings, split-level houses, semi-detached homes, and family-sized detached houses that feature Georgian-, Tudor-, and contemporary-style designs.

The recently built Green Meadows subdivision, situated off Leslie Street north of Sheppard Avenue, is an exclusive collection of stately homes built around the magnificent neo-colonial estate home of former Canadian business establishment icon Bull MacDougald. The former MacDougald home is still a private residence. The apple orchard, magnificent trees and ornamental gardens that surround this grand home provide a streetscape that is enjoyed by all who live here.

There are also a large number of high-rise rental apartment buildings in Don Valley Village that are concentrated along the peripheral streets that border this neighbourhood.

SHOPPING:

Fairview Mall is a large regional shopping centre located at the northeast corner of Sheppard Avenue and Don Mills Road. Fairview Mall has recently been remodelled and includes over 150 stores plus professional and medical offices. Don Valley Village's other indoor shopping mall is The Shops on Steeles and the 404. This mid-size shopping centre is anchored by a national department store and a medical and health centre.

Don Valley Village also has a number of excellent shopping plazas, including The Pickle Barrel Plaza at Finch Avenue and Leslie Street, Skymark Plaza at Don Mills Road and Finch Avenue, the Finch and Leslie Square and Cliffwood and Peanut plazas, both on Don Mills Road.

RECREATION:

The Cummer Park Fitness Centre, located at 6000 Leslie Street near Steeles Avenue, features squash and racquetball courts, fitness classes, an indoor jogging/walking track, two weight rooms, outdoor tennis courts, whirlpools and saunas.

The Oriole Community Resource Centre is located at 2975 Don Mills Road West features a gymnasium, meeting rooms, and a seniors' lounge. This centre is also the home of the Oriole Arena, which offers pleasure skating, shinny and organized hockey programs for the public. Next door to Oriole Centre is Oriole Park, home of the North York Tennis Association. This club features a tennis bubble and offers year round tennis.

Victoria Park Village is also filled with an abundance of local parks that feature children's playgrounds, sports fields, tennis courts, baseball diamonds and outdoor hockey rinks.

The Fairview Library and Theatre located at 35 Fairview Mall is the cultural and entertainment centre of this neighbourhood. This theatre has been running since 1976 and features regular performances produced by local theatre groups. The Fairview Public Library offers a myriad of programs for preschoolers, children, and adults. Some of the programs at this library include English as a second language, seniors' socials and children's storytime in various languages including Cantonese, Persian and Tamil.

SCHOOLS:

(P)	Arbor Glen, 55 Freshmeadow Dr., (416) 395-2020	
(P)	Brian, 95 Brian Dr., (416) 395-2080	
(P)	Cherokee, 390 Cherokee Blvd., (416) 395-2190	
(P)	Cliffwood, 140 Cliffwood Rd., (416) 395-2230	
(P)	Cresthaven, 46 Cresthaven Dr., (416) 395-2240	
(P)	Crestview, 101 Seneca Hill Dr., (416) 395-2250	
(P)	Don Valley J.H.S., 3100 Don Mills Rd, (416) 395-3010	
(P)	Ernest, 150 Cherokee Blvd., (416) 395-2380	
(P)	Seneca Hill, 625 Seneca Hill Dr., (416) 395-2840	
(PH)	A.Y. Jackson, 50 Francine Dr., (416) 395-3140	
(PH)	George Vanier, 3000 Don Mills Rd., (416) 395-3250	
(C)	Holy Redeemer, 111 Aspenwood Dr., (416) 393-5353	
(C)	Our Lady of Guadalupe, 3105 Don Mills Rd., (416) 393-5342	
(C)	St. Martha, 1865 Sheppard Ave., (416) 393-5344	
(U)	Seneca College-Newnham Campus, 1750 Finch Ave., W., (416) 491-5050	

TRANSPORTATION:

Don Valley Village residents are well served by bus routes on Steeles, Finch and Sheppard avenues that provide direct connections to stations on the Yonge-University-Spadina subway line. Bus services along Don Mills Road and Victoria Park Avenue connect passengers to stations on the Bloor-Danforth subway line.

Motorists can get downtown and out of town very quickly via on-ramps to the Don Valley Parkway, which are conveniently located off Sheppard and Finch avenues.

HISTORY: Downsview derives its name from John Perkins Bull, a justice of the peace who settled in this area around 1842. Bull named his farm "Downs View" as his property was situated on one of the highest elevations in Toronto.

In what must surely have been one of the first home offices, the Bull farmhouse included a courtroom addition and a jail, which was located in the basement of the house. The John Perkins Bull house is still standing today at 450 Rustic Road where it is presently in use as a nursing home.

For over 100 years Downsview was a thriving agricultural community with its own general store, schoolhouse and post office. The pillar of this community was the red brick Downsview United Church. Built in 1870, this church is still standing in its original location at 2822 Keele Street.

Downsview began a new chapter in its history in 1928 when the world-famous De Havilland Aircraft Company chose Downsview as its home. The Canadian Armed Forces followed De Havilland to Downsview, setting up an important military base in Downsview during the Second World War. Once the war was over Downsview experienced a building boom that saw the entire neighbourhood developed by the early 1970s.

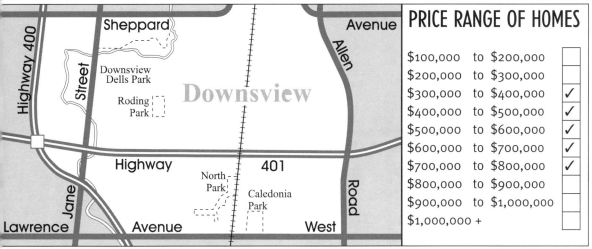

PRICE RANGE OF HOMES	
$100,000 to $200,000	
$200,000 to $300,000	
$300,000 to $400,000	✓
$400,000 to $500,000	✓
$500,000 to $600,000	✓
$600,000 to $700,000	✓
$700,000 to $800,000	✓
$800,000 to $900,000	
$900,000 to $1,000,000	
$1,000,000 +	

OVERVIEW:
Downsview is one of Toronto's largest neighbourhoods. It has a large Italian community centred around Keele Street as well as a large Jewish community centred around Bathurst Street and Wilson Avenue.

The dominant landmark in this neighbourhood is the former Downsview Canadian Armed Forces Base, which occupies a huge swath of land from Keele Street to Wilson Heights and from Wilson Avenue to Sheppard Avenue. This property is currently being transformed into Downsview National Park, the first urban national park in Canada. Its 400-plus hectares will make it one of the world's largest urban parks.

HOMES:
Downsview's original housing stock dates from the 1950s and 1960s. These detached, semi-detached and split-level houses are situated on suburban-sized lots with private driveways. Balmoral, a subdivision of newer custom-designed brick and stone houses, is located in the northeast pocket of Downsview, off Wilson Heights Boulevard.

Downsview contains a number of residential streets that back on to greenbelts and parkland. Many of these houses are custom-built to take advantage of their lush surroundings. Over 300 new townhomes and semi-detached houses have recently been built, east of Keele Street on the former Canadian Forces Base.

SHOPPING:
Downsview contains some of the best shopping in the Toronto area. The Yorkdale shopping centre is conveniently located at Dufferin and Highway 401. This large indoor shopping mall attracts shoppers from all over Toronto to its high-profile retail stores. Yorkdale also contains movie theatres, a public library, professional offices, restaurants and a fitness facility.

North York Sheridan Mall, at Jane Street and Wilson Avenue, is a local indoor mall with a nice mix of big department stores and independent retailers. Further east the Downsview Plaza at Keele Street and Wilson Avenue features a large Italian supermarket, and professional and medical offices. The Lawrence Square shopping centre located at Lawrence Avenue West and the Allen Expressway includes big department stores, small retailers and professional and medical offices.

The Wilson Avenue and Bathurst Street shopping district includes Jewish gift shops, bakeries and restaurants.

RECREATION:
When it's complete, Downsview Park will include nature areas, walking paths, sports fields, skating rinks, concert venues, and museums.

Downsview Dells Park, located at the north end of this neighbourhood, is part of a scenic 4.7-kilometre paved trail that follows the Black Creek Valley north to Black Creek Pioneer Village, a restored pre-Confederation village at Steeles Avenue West. Downsview also contains a number of smaller recreational parks whose facilities range from tennis courts and baseball diamonds to children's playgrounds.

The Downsview Arena at 1630 Wilson Avenue offers public skating and hockey league programs to the local community. To the south of the arena is the Downsview Lawn Bowling Green.

The Downsview Public Library at 2793 Keele Street offers a myriad of programs for adults, children and preschoolers.

Yorkdale Mall and North York Sheridan Mall both have movie theatres.

SCHOOLS:
(P) Calico, 35 Calico Dr., 395-2130
(P) Chalkfarm, 100 Chalkfarm Dr., (416) 395-2160
(P) Beverley Heights M.S. 26 Troutbrooke, (416) 395-3000
(P) Dellcrest, 1633 Sheppard Ave., (416) 395-2290
(P) Pierre Laporte M.S. (416) 1270 Wilson Ave., (416) 395-3070
(P) Downsview, 2829 Keele St., (416) 395-2340
(P) Maple Leaf, 301 Culford Rd., (416) 395-2670
(PH) Downsview S.S., 7 Hawksdale Rd., (416) 395-3200
(PH) Nelson A. Boylen, 155 Falstaff Ave., (416) 395-3270
(C) St. Conrad, 610 Roding St., (416) 393-5396
(CH) Madonna, 20 Dubray Ave., (416) 393-5506
(PR) St. James Academy, (416) 781-7900

TRANSPORTATION:
Toronto Transit Commission bus lines along Wilson, Lawrence and Sheppard avenues connect to stations on the Yonge-University-Spadina subway line. Bus routes on Jane, Keele and Dufferin streets connect to stations on the Bloor-Danforth subway line.

Motorists can get downtown in 25 to 30 minutes via Bathurst Street. Highway 401 is a short drive from any spot in this neighbourhood, with on-ramps at Keele and Dufferin streets and the Allen Expressway.

SW

HISTORY: Dublin Heights began as a farming hamlet in the early 1800s. It is named after Dublin Farm, which was located near Sheppard Avenue and Dufferin Street. Dublin Farm was owned by William Duncan, who emigrated to Canada from Ireland in 1827 and paid $3.50 an acre for his 200-acre farm.

William Duncan had a significant impact on the growth of Dublin Heights. He personally oversaw the building of Dublin Heights's first school and hired the first schoolmaster. Duncan also served as a highly respected justice of the peace for York Township.

The Watson family, also from Ireland, opened the first general store and post office in Dublin Heights in 1854. This post office was originally called "Carronbrook," however, that name was changed in 1878 to "Dublin" in recognition of William Duncan and his landmark Dublin Farm.

The Dublin post office was closed in 1955 when the present-day neighbourhood was being developed. The only tangible reminder of the history of Dublin Heights is the cornerstone from the circa-1872 Dublin Schoolhouse. This cornerstone is mounted on the main entrance wall of the present-day Dublin Heights School, located on Bainbridge Avenue.

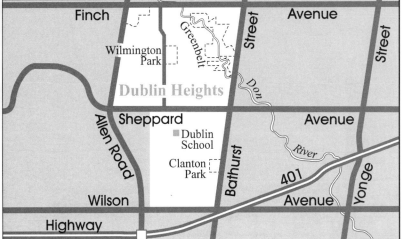

PRICE RANGE OF HOMES

$100,000	to	$200,000	
$200,000	to	$300,000	
$300,000	to	$400,000	✓
$400,000	to	$500,000	✓
$500,000	to	$600,000	✓
$600,000	to	$700,000	✓
$700,000	to	$800,000	✓
$800,000	to	$900,000	✓
$900,000	to	$1,000,000	
$1,000,000 +			

OVERVIEW:

Dublin Heights is a quiet neighbourhood located in the north-central part of Toronto. Dublin Heights's large Jewish population revolves around the many Jewish cultural and learning centres as well as synagogues situated throughout this neighbourhood. There are also many families of Italian heritage in this neighbourhood whose children attend St. Robert Separate School on Sheppard Avenue. In addition to excellent public and separate schools Dublin Heights also includes six local parks, two greenbelts, two hospitals, a community centre, local bus service and close proximity to Toronto's commuter highways. The Dublin Heights public school is a major drawing card for this neighbourhood, as it is considered to have one of the very best arts programs in the Toronto public school system.

HOMES:

The majority of Dublin Heights houses were built in the 1950s and the 1960s. The mix of housing in this neighbourhood includes ranch-style bungalows, split-level and semi-detached homes, townhouses, and contemporary-style houses. Dublin Heights housing stock is situated on suburban-sized lots with an average of 50- to 60-foot frontages.

The Balmoral subdivision located at Faywood and Joel Swirsky boulevards is a nice collection of newer, custom built homes with smart-looking stone and brick exteriors. The entrance to this exclusive subdivision is marked by a stone pillar gateway at Faywood Boulevard.

Dublin Heights also contains rental apartment buildings although these are located on the periphery of the neighbourhood.

SHOPPING:

Sheppard Plaza, located at the northwest corner of Bathurst Street and Sheppard Avenue, is anchored by a large supermarket and includes a Jewish bakery, a drug store, a dry cleaner, banks, fast food outlets and a post office.

The Bathurst Manor shopping plaza, located on Wilmington Avenue, is anchored by a large grocery store and includes drug, liquor and hardware stores, a Kosher bakery and deli, a jewellery store, and a party planning store.

The strip shopping plazas that line Wilson and Sheppard avenues feature a large variety of food stores, restaurants, beauty salons, fashion wear, convenience stores and professional offices. The Jewish food shops are known for their pita, chalah and rye breads, Montreal-style bagels, smoked fish, and prepared foods. The Filipino food shops carry various exotic delicacies such as imported noodles and rices, coconut milk, and an assortment of dried fish including herring, anchovies and squid.

RECREATION:

The North York Centennial Centre, located at 580 Finch Avenue West, features a popular ice arena that is used for figure and pleasure skating and hockey programs. In the summer this rink is used for in-line skating.

The Irving Chapley Community Centre is located in Wilmington Park off Wilmington Avenue. This community centre features a tots' play area, meeting rooms and an outdoor pool and water play area. Wilmington Park, located next to the community centre, features tennis courts and a baseball diamond.

The Bathurst Jewish Centre at 4588 Bathurst Street is a multi-purpose facility with 5,000 square feet of state-of-the-art cardiovascular conditioning equipment, 50 fitness classes a week, indoor and outdoor pools, weight training, indoor and outdoor track, tennis, basketball, and a myriad of children's and adults programs. This centre is also the home of the Leah Posluns Theatre and the Koffler Gallery.

The Forest Valley Outdoor Education Centre located at 60 Blue Forest Drive is operated by the Toronto District School Board. This centre is located in a wilderness setting in the West Don River Valley and provides school children with an opportunity to explore and to learn about Toronto's natural habitat.

SCHOOLS:

(P)	Dublin Heights, 100 Bainbridge Ave.,	(416) 395-2360
(P)	Faywood, 95 Faywood Blvd.,	(416) 395-2390
(P)	C.H. Best, 330 Wilmington Ave.,	(416) 395-2180
(PH)	WM. Lyon Mackenzie C.I., 20 Tillplain Rd.,	(416) 395-3330
(C)	St.Robert, 819 Sheppard Ave., W.,	(416) 393-5297
(PJ)	Toronto Heschel, 55 Yeomans Rd.,	(416) 635-1876
(PJ)	She'arim Hebrew Day School, 100 Elder St.,	(416) 633-8247
(PJ)	Zareinu Educational Centre, 100 Elder St.,	(416) 633-8247
(PJ)	Community Hebrew Academy, 200 Wilmington Ave.,	(416) 636-5984
(PJ)	Yeshivat Or Chaim, 159 Almore Dr.,	(416) 630-6772

TRANSPORTATION:

Bus service in the interior of this neighbourhood along Wilmington Avenue and Faywood Boulevard connects passengers to stations on the Yonge-University-Spadina subway line. The Wilson Heights, Wilson Avenue, Sheppard Avenue and Finch Avenue buses also connect to stations on the Yonge-University-Spadina subway line.

Bathurst Street is the main arterial roadway serving this neighbourhood. It provides motorists with a direct route downtown and also provides southbound commuters with access to Highway 401.

HISTORY: The earliest inhabitants in what is now known as Elia were
the First Nations tribe that established a village along the banks of the
Humber River, just north of present-day Finch Avenue. This First Nations village was in existence from 1400 to 1550.

The pioneers who arrived in Elia in the late 1700s and early 1800s were of
German descent. These pioneers travelled from Pennsylvania in oxen-led
Conestoga wagons with their cattle in tow. They were followed by English
and Scottish families who settled in Elia in the 1820s.

The Elia name originated with the post office of William Snider which,
opened in 1878 at the southwest corner of Keele Street and Finch Avenue in
Sniders general store. The two focal points of this farming community were
the one-room Elia schoolhouse and the Elia church. Both of these former
landmarks were closed in 1956 when Elia's farms were sold to developers.

The Elia church, renamed "Elijah" and situated at 1130 Finch Avenue
West, is all that remains of this historic hamlet, whose landscape is now
dominated by residential subdivisions and shopping plazas.

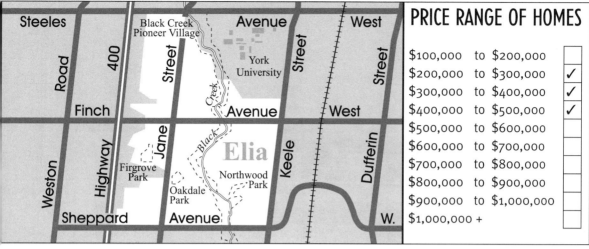

PRICE RANGE OF HOMES

$100,000	to	$200,000	
$200,000	to	$300,000	✓
$300,000	to	$400,000	✓
$400,000	to	$500,000	✓
$500,000	to	$600,000	
$600,000	to	$700,000	
$700,000	to	$800,000	
$800,000	to	$900,000	
$900,000	to	$1,000,000	
$1,000,000 +			

OVERVIEW:

Elia is a culturally diverse neighbourhood that has traditionally been home to many new Canadian families. Elia's plethora of high-rise apartment buildings in the Jane and Finch corridor help make it one of Toronto's most densely populated neighbourhoods.

York University and Black Creek Pioneer Village are located at the north end of this neighbourhood, off Steeles Avenue. The Black Creek meanders through a series of connecting parks in the centre of this community providing an ideal recreational greenspace for residents to enjoy.

HOMES:

Elia's housing stock includes bungalows, split-level and two-storey semi-detached houses. There are some small pockets of detached homes here as well. All of the houses in this neighbourhood were constructed in the 1960s and 1970s.

Elia has one of the highest concentration of apartment buildings in Toronto. Many of these apartment towers are located around the intersection of Jane Street and Finch Avenue. There are also many Ontario Housing apartment and townhouse complexes within this neighbourhood that offer rents geared towards income.

SHOPPING:

There are three shopping malls located at the crossroads of Jane Street and Finch Avenue. The Jane Finch Mall on the southeast corner is the largest of these three centres, with 70 retail shops and services highlighted by national department stores. York Gate Mall located on the northwest corner contains over 60 stores, including professional and medical offices. Norfinch Shopping Centre on the southwest corner is the place to eat, with numerous fast food franchises located here.

Keele Street is another shopping destination with many shopping plazas, value centres, and food markets. The Jane-Sheppard shopping plaza also serves this community.

RECREATION:

Elia residents have an abundance of recreational facilities to choose from. There are three community centres in this neighbourhood. The Driftwood Centre at 4401 Jane Street and the Northwood Centre at 15 Clubhouse Court offer numerous programs for children and adults. Both of these community centres have a gymnasium and an outdoor pool. The Yorkwood Community Recreation Centre at 20 Yorkwoods Gate is a small facility that runs tiny-tot and after-school programs. The Jane Finch Boys and Girls Club also operates out of this centre.

The Boake Greenbelt can be accessed from Northwood Park off Sheppard Avenue, just west of Keele Street. This parkland runs through the centre of the Elia neighbourhood and features a scenic 4.7-kilometre bicycle and walking trail. This trail finishes at Black Creek Pioneer Village, which gives Elia residents a glimpse of what their community was like back in the 1800s. Black Creek Pioneer Village has over 35 restored pioneer buildings, a visitors' centre and exhibit gallery, a restaurant, banquet facilities and seasonal events such as the spring fair and Christmas in the Village.

Elia is also filled with smaller parks that have various recreational facilities including tennis courts, sports fields, swimming pools, and children's playgrounds. Fountainhead Park at 445 Sentinel Road has an artificial ice rink. Indoor hockey and pleasure skating arenas are located at 23 Grandravine Drive and 230 Gosford Boulevard.

The York Woods Regional Library at 1785 Finch Avenue West offers programs for children and adults. Adjacent to the library is the York Woods Library theatre, a state-of-the-art multi-purpose theatre that is used extensively by the local community.

An outdoor Fun Park located next to York Gate Mall includes mini-golf, batting cages and bumper cars, as well as a licensed restaurant with a patio and bar.

SCHOOLS:

(P)	Blacksmith, 45 Blacksmith Cres.,	(416) 395-2060
(P)	Derrydown, 120 Derrydown Rd.,	(416) 395-2310
(P)	Driftwood, 265 Driftwood Ave.,	(416) 395-2350
(P)	Firgrove, 270 Firgrove Cres.,	(416) 395-2420
(P)	Gosford, 30 Gosford Blvd.,	(416) 395-2470
(P)	Shoreham, 31 Shoreham Dr.,	(416) 395-2870
(P)	Stanley, 75 Stanley rd.,	(416) 395-2890
(P)	Stilecroft, 50 Stilecroft Dr.,	(416) 395-2910
(P)	Topcliff, 65 Topcliff Ave.,	(416) 395-2940
(P)	Yorkwoods, 20 Yorkwoods Gate,	(416) 395-2990
(P)	Brookview M.S., 4505 Jane St.,	(416) 395-2120
(P)	Elia M.S., 215 Sentinel Rd.,	(416) 395-3020
(P)	Oakdale Park M.S., 315 Grandravine Dr.,	(416) 395-3060
(PH)	C.W. Jefferys C.I., 340 Sentinel Rd.,	(416) 395-3170
(PH)	Westview Centennial S.S., 755 Oakdale Rd.,	(416) 395-3320
(C)	St. Augustine, 98 Shoreham Dr.,	(416) 393-5328
(C)	St. Charles Garnier, 20 Stong Crt.,	(416) 393-5363
(C)	St. Camillo, 77 Stanley Rd.,	(416) 393-5388
(C)	St. Francis de Sales, 333 Firgrive Cres.,	(416) 393-5366
(C)	St. Wilfrid., 1685 Finch Ave., W.,	(416) 393-5313
(CH)	James Cardinal Mcguigan, 1440 Finch Ave. W.,	(416) 393-5527
(CH)	Regina Pacis, 45 Norfinch Dr.,	(416) 393-5526

TRANSPORTATION:

Bus services along Sheppard, Finch and Steeles avenues connect passengers to stations on the Yonge-University-Spadina subway line. The Keele Street and Jane Street buses travel south to subway stations on the Bloor-Danforth subway line.

Motorists are approximately five minutes from highways 400 and 401, which link up with all the major highways leading into and out of the city.

SW

HISTORY: Emery was originally settled by Issac Devins, a German pioneer who came to Canada from Pennsylvania in the 1790s. Emery's second settler, John Crosson, walked here from Pennsylvania in 1799. The Crosson family belongings were carried on the back of a two-year-old horse that Crosson sold to Devins in exchange for half of the latter's 200-acre farm lot.

By the 1870s, Emery had emerged as a farming hamlet at the crossroads of Finch Avenue and Weston Road. Emery had its own school, church, blacksmith shop and general store. A local post office opened in 1879 under the name "Dayton." The Toronto Grey and Bruce Railway adopted the Dayton name for their flag station on Finch Avenue.

The post office and railway station later changed their names to Emery, to avoid the inevitable confusion that arose between Dayton, Ontario and Dayton, Ohio. No one is certain why the name Emery was chosen, but it was readily adopted by the whole community.

Emery's rural existence came to an end in the 1960s when developers built residential subdivisions and industry where farms once dotted this landscape. The former Emery School bell mounted in a cairn on the grounds of Emery Collegiate serves as a lonely reminder of the small-town origins of this community.

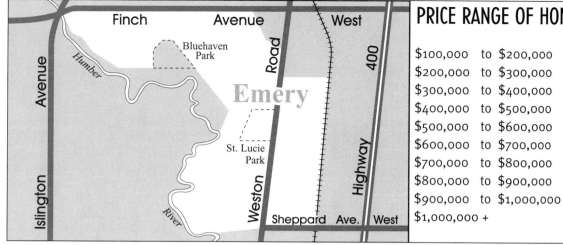

PRICE RANGE OF HOMES	
$100,000 to $200,000	
$200,000 to $300,000	✓
$300,000 to $400,000	✓
$400,000 to $500,000	
$500,000 to $600,000	
$600,000 to $700,000	
$700,000 to $800,000	
$800,000 to $900,000	
$900,000 to $1,000,000	
$1,000,000 +	

OVERVIEW:

Emery is located in the northwest pocket of Toronto. It is bordered to the west by the majestic beauty of the Humber River Valley and to the east by the Canadian Pacific freight railway line. At the north end of this neighbourhood is the Milvan Drive commercial and industrial corridor, which encompasses an eclectic mix of automobile sales and service shops, a church, wholesalers and importers, a shopping plaza with a Latin American theme, and a variety of specialty-type businesses.

Emery is one of Toronto's most culturally diverse neighbourhoods. The local high school has students from 45 different cultural backgrounds and the shopping districts are filled with a plethora of food shops that specialize in various cuisines from around the world.

HOMES:

Emery's housing stock dates mostly from the 1960s. The north and east pockets of the neighbourhood are filled with bungalow and two-storey solid brick semi-detached homes. All of these houses have private driveways and most also have a garage.

The houses west of Weston Road and south of St. Lucie Park are situated on streets named after places in Florida. Some of the street names here include: Coral Gable, Gulfstream, Hibiscus, Royal Palm, Tampa, Vero Beach and West Palm. Maybe it's the street names, but these detached, ranch-style bungalows on the Humber Valley side of the neighbourhood have a certain Floridian ambience and appeal.

SHOPPING:

If you are a food connoisseur and want to sample a variety of foods from around the world, Emery is a good place to shop. The strip malls on Finch Avenue and Weston Road are lined with food shops and restaurants that specialize in East and West Indian, African, Jamaican, Asian, European, Italian and Spanish foods.

The largest mall in the neighbourhood is the Finch West Mall at the corner of Finch Avenue and Weston Road. This mall has a McDonald's, a Canadian Tire, bargain stores, and medical and professional offices.

RECREATION:

Emery residents can access the West Humber parkland at designated points south of Finch Avenue and east of Islington Avenue. This park contains a 5.5-kilometre paved trail that follows the Humber River Valley to the Humber Arboretum, which features a variety of plants and wildlife. There are also a number of pretty strolling parks found throughout this neighbourhood.

The Habitant Arena at 3383 Weston Road has a house hockey league for children, as well as shinny hockey and public skating. The Woodview Park public library is located at 16-18 Bradstock Road, at the Woodview Plaza.

SCHOOLS:

(P)   Daystrom, 25 Daystrom Dr., (416) 395-2280
(P)   Gulfstream, 20 Gulfstream Rd., (416) 395-2520
(PH) Emery C.I., 3395 Weston Rd., (416) 395-3220
(C)   St. Jude, 3251 Weston Rd., (416) 393-5279

TRANSPORTATION:

The Finch Avenue bus connects passengers to the Finch station on the Yonge-University-Spadina subway line. The Weston Road bus connects to the Weston Go Train station and the Keele station on the Bloor-Danforth subway line.

Weston Road and Finch Avenue are the main arterial roadways in the neighbourhood. Weston Road will link motorists to the central corridor of the city, while Finch Avenue links up with Toronto's major north-south arterial roadways. For those travelling out of the city highways 400 and 401 are each approximately five minutes away.

HISTORY:

The Flemingdon Park neighbourhood is built on the former farm of R.J. Fleming after whom this neighbourhood is named. "Don" makes reference to the Don River, which forms the eastern boundary of Flemingdon Park.

Flemingdon Park was first proposed to North York (now Toronto) city councillors in 1958. It was touted as Canada's first completely planned "apartment city," and was based on similar developments already built in Europe and Scandinavia.

The initial response to Flemingdon Park was one of apprehension and concern. North York residents and politicians alike were concerned about the high density of the development. There were also questions about how city services would be provided and who would pay for them. Five North York councillors went so far as to fly to "apartment city" projects in England, Sweden and Copenhagen in order to view first-hand this novel approach to neighbourhood building.

In 1959, after much debate, the Flemingdon Park development was approved by city council. There were some obstacles along the way but Flemingdon Park was finally completed in the early 1970s.

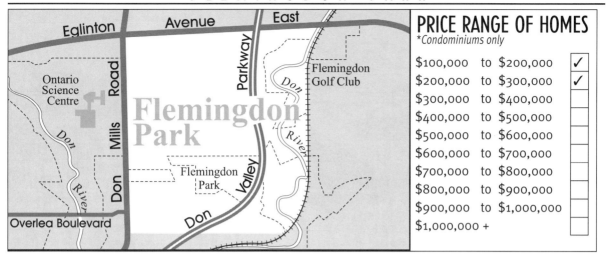

PRICE RANGE OF HOMES
*Condominiums only

$100,000	to	$200,000	✓
$200,000	to	$300,000	✓
$300,000	to	$400,000	
$400,000	to	$500,000	
$500,000	to	$600,000	
$600,000	to	$700,000	
$700,000	to	$800,000	
$800,000	to	$900,000	
$900,000	to	$1,000,000	
$1,000,000 +			

OVERVIEW:
Flemingdon Park is a multicultural neighbourhood that has traditionally served as the first home for many new Canadians seeking affordable housing in the City of Toronto. A recent Flemingdon Park Public Library study places the total population of this neighbourhood at approximately 35,000 people, with over 100 different languages being spoken within the community.

Flemingdon Park residents have their own community information centre and health centre, a non-profit legal services clinic and a number of support programs for children, women and families.

HOMES:
Flemingdon Park's residential housing west of the Don Valley Parkway consists of a sea of high-rise rental apartment buildings and blocks of row house apartments. Most of these buildings offer marketplace rents, however, there are also subsidized housing units where the rent is geared to income. There is also seniors' housing located in this part of the neighbourhood.

Flemingdon Park east of the Don Valley Expressway contains affordable condominium apartment buildings. Many of the units in these apartments command spectacular views of the Flemingdon Park Golf course and the Don River Valley.

SHOPPING:
The Flemingdon Park shopping centre, located off Don Mills Road, includes a large supermarket, bakery, deli, restaurants, flower shop, dry cleaner, drug store, hairstylist, medical centre, a bingo parlour and a community information centre.

RECREATION:
The Flemingdon neighbourhood is well served by two excellent community centres. The Flemingdon Resource Centre at 29 St. Dennis Drive is a multi-faceted facility that includes an indoor pool, a gymnasium, a day-care centre and a busy public library.

The Flemingdon Community Centre at 150 Grenoble Drive features the only municipally funded indoor children's play ground in Canada. This "Playground Paradise" features a two-storey play structure, a huge spiral slide, a track ride, cargo elevator, talk tube, crawl tubes, construction zone, and ball pool with 8,000 balls, all set in a meadow-like atmosphere. There is also a party room in this centre that can accommodate up to 35 people.

Across the street from the Flemingdon Community Centre is the Flemingdon Ice Arena, which offers organized hockey league programs and pleasure skating. Adjacent to the arena and community centre is Flemingdon Park, a long linear park that spans almost the entire length of the neighbourhood. This park has soccer fields, a baseball diamond and a large basketball court. On the east side of the neighbourhood is another large park known as Linkwood Lane Park. This park features a children's playground, a soccer field and a baseball diamond. North of Linkwood Lane Park is the Flemingdon Park golf course, a pay-as-you-play course set in the very scenic Don River Valley.

The Ontario Science Centre located at 770 Don Mills Road is an interactive museum of science and technology that features more than 800 exhibits. One of the Science Centre's most popular attractions is the Shoppers Drug Mart OMNIMAX theatre, which features a 24-metre domed screen with a powerful hi-fidelity sound system.

SCHOOLS:
(P)   Gateway, 55 Gateway Blvd., (416) 397-2970
(P)   Grenoble, 9 Grenoble Dr., (416) 397-2900
(PH) Marc Garneau C.I., 135 Overlea Blvd., (416) 396-2410
(C)   John XXIII, 175 Grenoble Dr., (416) 393-5348

TRANSPORTATION:
Bus service on Eglinton Avenue connects passengers to the Eglinton station on the Yonge-University-Spadina line. The Don Mills bus and another bus that runs on Flemingdon Park's interior streets both connect to the Broadview station on the Bloor-Danforth subway line.

Don Mills Road and Eglinton Avenue provide quick passage to the Don Valley Parkway, a popular commuter highway that ushers motorists into and out of the city.

HISTORY: One of Glen Park's first settlers was Sir Sanford Fleming,
the father of standard time and the chief engineer of the Ontario, Simcoe
and Huron railways. Fleming's property was located just south of Lawrence
Avenue between Dufferin and Keele streets. In 1856, Fleming subdivided his
farm into the Balmoral subdivision, which was the first planned subdivision
in North York. Unfortunately, Fleming was ahead of his time – pardon the
pun – and Balmoral never got past the marketing stage.

Fleming's son Colonel Fred Fleming took over the family farm in 1881 and
began importing and breeding Hereford cattle. Under the young Fleming's
guidance "Park Farm" rose to prominence as one of the finest stock breeding
farms in Canada.

Glen Park's transition from farmland to residential neighbourhood began
in the 1920s. Its largest period of growth occurred after the Second World
War, when many returning war veterans and their families settled in Glen
Park. This increased population led to the building of the Glen Park Public
School in 1948.

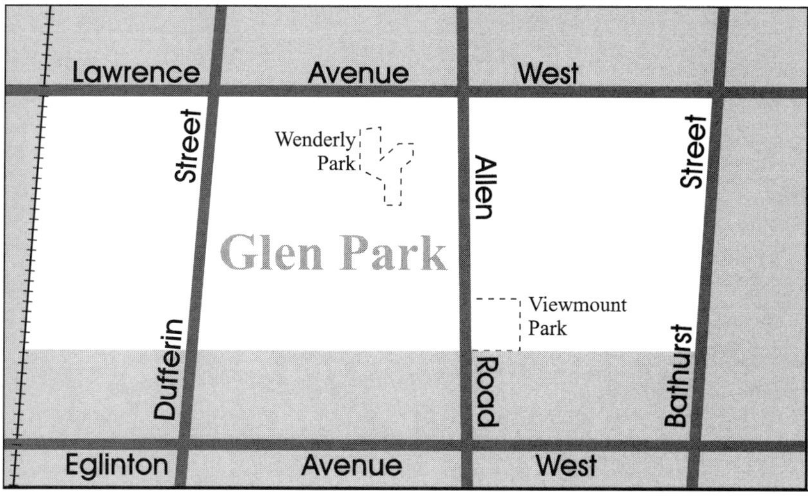

Map

Lawrence Avenue West

Street (Dufferin Street)

Wenderly Park

Glen Park

Allen

Viewmount Park

Road

Street (Bathurst Street)

Eglinton Avenue West

PRICE RANGE OF HOMES

Price Range			
$100,000	to	$200,000	
$200,000	to	$300,000	
$300,000	to	$400,000	✓
$400,000	to	$500,000	✓
$500,000	to	$600,000	✓
$600,000	to	$700,000	✓
$700,000	to	$800,000	✓
$800,000	to	$900,000	✓
$900,000	to	$1,000,000	✓
$1,000,000 +			

OVERVIEW:

Glen Park is a diverse community bringing together people from broad socio-economic backgrounds. Italian-Canadian families own many of the homes around Dufferin Street, while a large Jewish orthodox community resides closer to Bathurst Street.

Glen Park also has a low-income district that is located in the centre of this neighbourhood near the Allen Expressway. This pocket of Glen Park is home to many new Canadians and contains geared-to-income rental housing.

The Glen Park Public School recently received the Canada Award of Excellence from the National Quality Institute. This award recognizes the improved standards and above average test results achieved at this school, which also boasts a strong French Immersion program.

HOMES:

Glen Park contains an eclectic mix of houses that come in a variety of shapes, colours and sizes. The oldest homes in this neighbourhood are the cosy-looking white or pastel painted bungalows. These homes were built mostly in the late 1940s and contain pleasing decorative accents such as front bay windows and accent octagonal shaped windows. Note that while many of these bungalows are framed with aluminum siding, there are also a fair number of houses framed with asbestos siding which was popular during this era for its fire-resistant features.

The slightly larger brick bungalows that are also common in this neighbourhood were built mostly between 1955 and 1972. They include ranch-style, split-level, and raised-bungalow designs.

Since the early 1990s a growing number of Glen Park's original housing stock has been replaced by new custom-built homes that are well suited to the expansive lots found in this neighbourhood.

SHOPPING:

The Lawrence Square Shopping Centre, situated on Lawrence Avenue West at the Allen Expressway, is anchored by two national department stores and a large Italian supermarket. This shopping centre also includes many smaller independent retailers as well as professional and medical offices.

The Lawrence Plaza at the northwest corner of Lawrence Avenue and Bathurst Street is anchored by a popular discount department store and a 24-hour food market. This plaza is filled with discount and outlet stores that attract a local and regional clientele.

Street shopping on both Dufferin Street and Marlee Avenue ranges from Italian food markets and Chinese restaurants to car dealerships and auto body shops. Bathurst Street has a Jewish flavour with Kosher food shops and restaurants mixed in with professional and medical offices, a large supermarket and a prominent drug store.

RECREATION:

The Glen Long Community Centre at 35 Glen Long Avenue has an indoor gymnasium and two indoor bocce courts as well as preschool and meeting rooms. This community centre is adjacent to Glen Long Park which has an outdoor hockey rink, a swimming pool, a bocce ball court, and a children's playground. Viewmount Park and Wenderly Park are also located in this neighbourhood. Both these parks feature baseball diamonds and children's playgrounds. Viewmount Park also has tennis courts and a tennis club.

The Columbus Centre at 901 Lawrence Avenue West is a vibrant community centre that brings together art, culture, food, fitness, and friends. The Columbus Centre is recognized as the Italian Canadian contribution to multiculturalism in the Metropolitan Toronto area. The Columbus Centre has a cultural wing, an athletic wing with over 80,000 square feet of multi-purpose facilities and an art gallery that features modern art and historical exhibits by local, national and international artists. This centre also has an Italian restaurant, a café and meeting rooms.

SCHOOLS:

(P) Glen Park, 100 Dalemount Ave., (416) 395-2460
(P) Joyce, 26 Joyce Pkwy., (416) 395-2600
(PH) Bathurst Heights, 640 Lawrence Ave., W., (416) 395-3160
(C) Our Lady of the Assumption, 125 Glenmount Ave.,(416) 393-5265
(C) Regina Mundi, 70 Playfair Ave., (416) 393-5362
(C) St. Charles, 50 Claver Ave., (416) 393-5250
(C) St. Cosmas and Damian, 111 Danesbury Ave., (416) 393-5398
(CH) Dante Alighieri, 60 Playfair Ave., (416) 393-5522
(PJ) Bialik Hebrew Day School, 14 Viewmount Ave, (416) 783- 3346
(PJ) Eitz Haim, One Viewmount Ave., (416) 789-4366
(PJ) Beth Jacob High School, 41 Lawrence Ave., W., (416) 787-4949
(U) Seneca College, 2999 Dufferin St,(416) 491-5050

TRANSPORTATION:

Many Glen Park residents are within walking distance of either the Glencairn or the Lawrence West subway stations, which are located between Bathurst and Dufferin streets on overpasses above the Allen Expressway. These stations are part of the Yonge-University-Spadina subway line.

For those commuting by car, Bathurst and Dufferin Streets are major north-south arterial roadways that provide a direct link south to the Toronto waterfront and north to the suburbs. Motorists can access Toronto's network of commuter highways from the Allen Expressway interchange located along Lawrence Avenue West at the north end of this neighbourhood.

SW

HISTORY:
Graydon's first landowners were the Duncan, family who put down roots in this area during the mid-1800s. Henry Duncan, the family patriarch, was elected to the York Township Council in 1870 and served as the town reeve for a number of years. It was Henry's son David who farmed the land where the Graydon neighbourhood is now located.

David Duncan was a well known dairy farmer and breeder of Jersey cattle. His gingerbread style farmhouse, known as Moatfield, was built in 1865. It was moved to its current location at 125 Moatfield Drive in the 1970s when the present-day neighbourhood was being developed.

The other historic house in this neighbourhood is Graydon Hall, from which this neighbourhood derives its name. Graydon Hall is located at 185 Graydon Hall Drive. This English-manor-style house was built in 1936 by financier Henry Rupert Bain. It's quite likely Graydon Hall was named after the "Gray" family who, from the 1830s until 1914, operated a grist mill on the banks of the "Don" River where the Donalda Golf Course is located today.

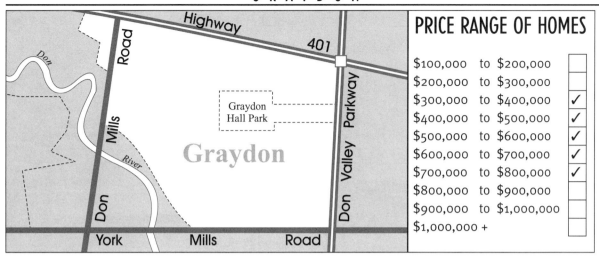

PRICE RANGE OF HOMES

$100,000	to	$200,000	
$200,000	to	$300,000	
$300,000	to	$400,000	✓
$400,000	to	$500,000	✓
$500,000	to	$600,000	✓
$600,000	to	$700,000	✓
$700,000	to	$800,000	✓
$800,000	to	$900,000	
$900,000	to	$1,000,000	
$1,000,000 +			

OVERVIEW:

The Graydon neighbourhood is built on a high plateau of land that is part of the wondrous hills and dales produced by the natural contours of the Don River Valley. The hilly terrain that forms the western reaches of this neighbourhood overlooks the picturesque Donalda Golf Course. The east boundary of this neighbourhood is bordered by the Don Valley Parkway.

Middle-income families occupy the houses on the crest of the hill at the southern half of this neighbourhood. The apartments at the north end of this neighbourhood, off of Graydon Hall Drive, are tenanted by lower-income families, many of whom have recently immigrated to Canada.

HOMES:

Graydon's winding streets and culs-de-sac are well-treed and contain a wide mix of housing, which was built in the 1970s. Viewing this neighbourhood from Don Mills Road the houses appear as if they are wrapped around the hillside. Front and back porch balconies are common features of these houses, designed to take advantage of the magnificent views and lush greenery in the valley below.

Graydon Hall Drive and Fenelon Drive are ringed with high-rise rental apartment buildings. The only condominium apartment building is 75 Graydon Hall Drive.

SHOPPING:

Graydon residents are a short drive from the Parkwoods Village Shopping Centre, located at 1277 York Mills Road. The mix of stores here includes food shops, a flower and fruit market, a bakery, a hairstylist , a dry cleaner, drug, video, bargain and dollar stores, a shoe repair shop a bank, restaurants and professional offices.

The Don Mills Shopping Centre, located at the intersection of Don Mills Road and Lawrence Avenue, is currently being redeveloped as an open-air shopping destination with a town square and public walkways.

RECREATION:

Graydon Park provides a large island of green space at the summit of this neighbourhood above Graydon Hall Drive. This park features tennis courts and a children's playground.

The Graydon Hall Manor Club is accessed from the courtyard of Graydon Hall Manor. Admission to this club is free for tenants in some of the local buildings. Facilities include a large swimming pool, an exercise room and a sauna.

The Duncan Mill, Spinney and Silverdale greenbelts, located on the periphery of this neighbourhood, feature scenic trails that are enjoyed by walkers, joggers and cyclists.

SCHOOLS:

(P) Rene Gordon, 20 Karen Rd., (416) 395-2790
(P) Don View M.S., 20 Evermede Dr., (416) 395-2330
(P) George S. Henry Academy, 200 Graydon Hall Dr., (416) 395-3240

TRANSPORTATION:

Bus service runs along Graydon Hall Drive and York Mills Road, connecting passengers to the York Mills station on the Yonge-University-Spadina subway line. The Don Mills Road bus connects passengers to the Pape station on the Bloor-Danforth subway line.

On-ramps to the Don Valley Parkway are located at the south end of this neighbourhood along York Mills Road. Motorists travelling south on the Don Valley Parkway can get to downtown Toronto in approximately 20 minutes. The Don Valley Parkway north is ideal for commuters travelling outside the city as well as providing a quick link to Highway 401.

SW

HISTORY:
The Henry Farm neighbourhood is situated on property that was originally settled in 1806 by Henry Mulholland, a native of Clones County, Monaghan, Ireland. Henry Mulholland sold this farm in the early 1800s, however, it was reacquired in 1898 by his great grandson George S. Henry.

George S. Henry was a distinguished politician whose 40 years of public service were highlighted by a term as Premier of Ontario from 1930 to 1934. While Henry made his mark in politics his great passion was his dairy farm which, in its peak years boasted 90 head of prize Holstein cattle. Henry's rambling brick farmhouse was known as Oriole Lodge, so called because of the numerous orioles that nested around here in the summertime.

In 1958, at the age of 77, Henry sold his farm for $2 million to the developers of the present-day neighbourhood. One day after this historic transaction George S. Henry passed away at Oriole Lodge.

Ed. Note: Henry Farm's major historical landmarks include Oriole Lodge, which is still standing in its original location at 17 Manorpark Crescent and is still a private residence. Further up the street from Oriole Lodge, situated in a small parkette, is the Henry Mulholland Cairn, which is maintained by descendants of the Mulholland family.

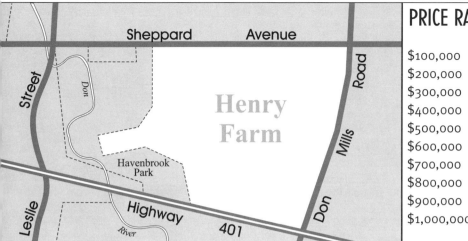

PRICE RANGE OF HOMES	
$100,000 to $200,000	
$200,000 to $300,000	
$300,000 to $400,000	
$400,000 to $500,000	✓
$500,000 to $600,000	✓
$600,000 to $700,000	✓
$700,000 to $800,000	✓
$800,000 to $900,000	
$900,000 to $1,000,000	
$1,000,000 +	

OVERVIEW:

Henry Farm is a small, family-oriented neighbourhood with a strong sense of community spirit. Henry Farm has always had an active community association which oversees Neighbourhood Watch and Block Parent programs, and organizes recreational activities including fitness classes at the Shaugnessey Public School and an annual "neighbours night out" barbecue and picnic, also held at the school. The Henry Farm Residents Association publishes a regular newsletter called he *Henry Farmer*, which keeps residents up to date with all of the goings-on in the neighbourhood.

HOMES:

Henry Farm's housing consists of a good mix of Georgian- and Tudor-revival-style houses, split-level houses and bungalows. There are also a couple of condominium townhouse complexes and high-rise apartment buildings located on the periphery of this neighbourhood.

Henry Farm houses were built in the late 1950s and early 1960s. A large percentage of these houses include brick veneer on the ground floor and aluminum siding on the second storey. Henry Farm houses are well landscaped with nice gardens. These houses are located on suburban-sized lots and many of the homes back onto the Don River Valley.

SHOPPING:

Henry Farm residents do most of their shopping at the nearby Fairview Mall Shopping Centre, located at the northeast corner of Don Mills Road and Sheppard Avenue. Fairview Mall is one of Toronto's largest shopping centres. The shopping mix at this mall includes national department stores, a large supermarket, well known national and international chain stores, restaurants, fast food outlets and professional and medical offices.

Fairview Mall also features a regular calender of special events and mall promotions. One of Fairview Malls most popular programs is the daily "Fitness at Fairview Indoor Walking Program" which is offered free to all participants. Fairview Mall also features six movie theatres.

RECREATION:

The Fairview Public Library and Theatre, located next to Fairview Mall at 35 Fairview Mall Drive, is the cultural and entertainment centre of this neighbourhood. The Fairview Library Theatre stages evening and weekend performances by local theatre groups. Yearly adult, senior, student and family subscriptions are available at this theatre. The library has recently been remodelled and now offers 10 computers with Internet access and an expanded multilingual program.

The East Don Valley Parkland trail can be accessed off Havenbrook Boulevard and at Manorpark Court. This nature trail passes through Moatfield Farm Park where a recent archaeological find uncovered evidence of a former First Nations village that flourished here about 600 years ago.

Havenbrook Park, located at the south end of Henry Farm, includes a baseball diamond, a children's playground, tennis courts and popular tobogganing hills.

SCHOOLS:

(P) Shaughnessy, 30 Shaughnessy Blvd., (416) 395-2850
(PH) George S. Henry Academy, 200 Graydon Hall Dr., (416) 395-3240
(PH) Georges Vanier, 3000 Don Mills Rd., (416) 395-3250
(C) St. Timothy, 25 Rochelle Cres., (416) 393-5298

TRANSPORTATION:

Henry Farm residents can take the Sheppard Avenue bus to the Sheppard station on the Yonge-University-Spadina subway line and the Don Mills Road bus to the Pape station on the Bloor-Danforth subway line.

Motorists have immediate access to Highway 401 and the Don Valley Parkway on-ramps located off Sheppard Avenue. These commuter highways provide quick and easy access to all parts of Toronto.

HISTORY:
Hogg's Hollow is named after James Hogg, a Scotsman from Lanarkshire, who settled here in 1824. Hogg operated a whisky distillery and a grist mill, and was considered the most successful of all the millers in the valley.

In 1856 James Hogg's sons John and William subdivided their late father's estate under the name Hogg's Hollow. The Hogg's Hollow subdivision included 141 lots, however, only a handful of houses were actually built at this time.

Four of the original Hogg's Hollow houses are still standing. These include two former mill workers' cottages that were relocated in 1986 to 4150 Yonge Street, where they now serve as the entrance to the Auberge du Pommier restaurant. The other two original houses are located at 1 and 5 Old Yonge Street. Both of these houses have undergone extensive renovations. The Jolly Miller tavern, circa 1857, situated at 3885 Yonge Street, and the George S. Pratt House, circa 1886, located at 17 Mill Street, are the other historic landmarks in this neighbourhood.

The present-day Hogg's Hollow neighbourhood began to be subdivided in the 1920s. This neighbourhood grew in stages and was finally completed in the 1960s.

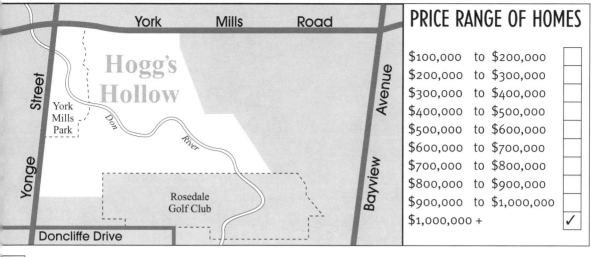

PRICE RANGE OF HOMES	
$100,000 to $200,000	
$200,000 to $300,000	
$300,000 to $400,000	
$400,000 to $500,000	
$500,000 to $600,000	
$600,000 to $700,000	
$700,000 to $800,000	
$800,000 to $900,000	
$900,000 to $1,000,000	
$1,000,000 +	✓

OVERVIEW:

Heading north on Yonge Street, past the prominent Loblaws superstore with the cedar shingled roof, motorists begin a descent down a steep valley. As you make your way down into the valley, you will see blue and white Hogg's Hollow street signs that beckon you to discover where they might lead. Follow these signs and you will be in the storybook neighbourhood of Hogg's Hollow.

Hogg's Hollow is an enchanted place set in the rustic beauty of the Don River valley. Here you will find winding crescents and private culs-de-sac lined with a colour guard of majestic maple, birch, pine, spruce and willow trees. There is even a stone bridge in the middle of this neighbourhood under which the Don River gently flows on its winding course towards Lake Ontario.

HOMES:

Hogg's Hollow's idyllic charm comes with a huge price tag, as this is one of Toronto's most expensive neighbourhoods. Hogg's Hollow houses are set in a lush landscape with a hill-and-dale topography that is left unfettered and in its original state without the intrusion of sidewalks.

Hogg's Hollow houses were built over a long period of time between the 1920s and 1960s, which accounts for the curious mixture of English-cottage, Tudor, colonial, Georgian and modernist architecture found here. Freshly painted window shutters adorn many of these houses and picket fences are also popular.

Hogg's Hollow also contains luxury condominium townhouses and apartment buildings on the brow of the Yonge Street hill, overlooking the valley.

SHOPPING:

Hogg's Hollow residents can walk to the York Mills Centre located at the northeast corner of Yonge Street and York Mills Road. This centre includes retail shops and services, medical offices and a food court.

The Yonge Street shopping district to the south of Hogg's Hollow is anchored by a Loblaws Superstore, which features a garden centre and a take out restaurant. Continuing south on Yonge Street you will find clothing stores, professional and medical offices, restaurants and basic household services.

RECREATION:

Hogg's Hollow residents host an annual "Community Fair" where the families in the neighbourhood get together and enjoy rides, races, food, and good times. This fair is held in Brookfield Park, which is a small neighbourhood park with a playing field that doubles as an outdoor ice rink in the wintertime.

Hogg's Hollow community events are announced on the "Notices" sign posts at Mill street and at the community bulletin board in the Millstone Parkette on Plymridge Road.

York Mills Park, off of Yonge Street, is a large linear park that is traversed by the historic Don River. This park contains a walking path, a children's playground and tennis courts.

Golf enthusiasts can walk to the scenic Don Valley Golf Course, just north of York Mills, off Yonge Street.

SCHOOLS:

(P)   Armour Heights, 148 Wilson Ave., (416) 397-2950
(P)   Owen, 111 Owen Blvd., (416) 395-2740
(P)   St.Andrews, J.H.S., 131 Fenn Ave., (416) 395-3090
(PH)   York Mills C.I., 490 York Mills Rd., (416) 395-3340
(PR)   Hillcrest Progressive School, 59 Plymridge Rd., (416) 489-8355
(PR)   Havergal College, 1451 Avenue Rd., (416) 483-3519
(PR)   Crescent School, 2365 Bayview Ave., (416) 449-2556
(CH)   Loretto Abbey, 101 Mason Blvd., (416) 393-5510

TRANSPORTATION:

Hogg's Hollow residents can walk to the York Mills subway station entrances at either Old York Mills Road or inside the York Mills Centre. The York Mills station is also a Go Transit station that includes an express bus service to the Pearson International Airport.

Yonge Street provides motorists with a direct route downtown in only 20 minutes. For commuters the Yonge Street on-ramp to Highway 401 is just a few minutes north of Hogg's Hollow.

SW

HISTORY: From the 1800s until the mid-1900s Humberlea was a
thriving farming community. The north half of this neighbourhood above
Wallasey Avenue and Flindon Road was owned by the Griffith brothers, who
operated farms on both sides of Weston Road. In the 1940s, the Griffith farms
were sold to the federal government for the development of the Humberlea
War Veterans subdivision. Second World War veterans were given a quarter-
acre property on which they erected simple frame dwellings. These properties
have since been subdivided, however, many of the original houses still
remain.

The streets around the present day Acacia Park are part of a small residential enclave built up in the early 1900s. This community was formerly known
as Albion Park and is now considered part of the Humberlea neighbourhood.
At the south end of Humberlea was the Caulfield dairy farm. The cattle grazed
on fields west of Weston Road while the Caulfield barn stood on the east side
of Weston Road. This farm operated up until the 1950s when it was sold to
developers. The subdivision of the old Caulfield farm led to the completion of
the present-day neighbourhood.

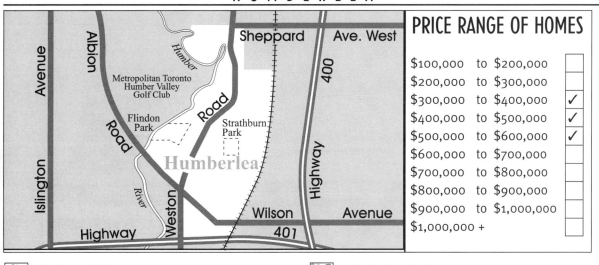

PRICE RANGE OF HOMES	
$100,000 to $200,000	
$200,000 to $300,000	
$300,000 to $400,000	✓
$400,000 to $500,000	✓
$500,000 to $600,000	✓
$600,000 to $700,000	
$700,000 to $800,000	
$800,000 to $900,000	
$900,000 to $1,000,000	
$1,000,000 +	

OVERVIEW:

Humberlea is a quiet, family-oriented community. Weston Road runs through the centre of this neighbourhood, which is sheltered by the Humber River Valley to the west, Highway 401 to the south and the Canadian Pacific railway and industry to the east. Humberlea's original population was of British background. These residents have been joined in recent years by a large Italian community that now calls this neighbourhood home.

HOMES:

Humberlea's oldest houses are situated around Acacia Park. These cottage-style houses were built in the early 1900s.

Humberlea has a large number of war veterans' houses from the late 1940s and early 1950s. These simple frame houses are situated on very large lots. However the growing trend has been to replace these small houses with large, custom-built homes.

There are also a fair number of brick ranch-style bungalows to be found in this neighbourhood. These houses are situated on generous-sized lots with private drives.

SHOPPING:

Humberlea residents do most of their shopping on Weston Road, just south of Highway 401. The Crossroads Centre is a regional shopping centre that contains one of Toronto's largest selections of big-box national chain stores. Included in this mix are a home improvement store, furniture, appliance and computer stores, and fashion stores.

RECREATION:

Strathburn Park, located in the centre of this neighbourhood, is a large, open greenspace with tennis courts, a basketball court, a baseball diamond and a children's playground. Acacia Park is situated on flat table land just above the Humber escarpment. This quaint neighbourhood park has a small baseball diamond and a children's playground.

The Humber Valley Golf Course at the western edge of this neighbourhood is a par-70 course known for its challenging links and valleyland holes.

SCHOOLS:

(P)   Gulfstream, 20 Gulfstream Rd., (416) 395-2520
(PH)   Emery C.I., 3395 Weston Rd., (416) 395-3220
(C)   St. Simon, 20 Wallasey Ave., (416) 393-5383
(CH)   St. Basil, 3100 Weston Rd., (416) 393-5513,
       St. Basil South Campus, 24 Strathburn Blvd.,
       (416) 393-5547

TRANSPORTATION:

Bus service on Weston Road connects passengers to the Weston Go Train station as well as providing links to the Royal York and the Keele stations on the Bloor-Danforth subway line. The Sheppard and Wilson Avenue buses connect passengers to their respective stations on the Yonge-University-Spadina subway line.

Weston Road is the main arterial roadway serving the Humberlea neighbourhood. This city street will take motorists as far south as St. Clair Avenue. For commuters, Highways 400 and 401 are located just a few minutes from this neighbourhood.

HISTORY: Humber Summit began as a pioneer settlement in the 1840s. This community revolved around the Rowntree grist and saw mills, which operated on the banks of the Humber River where Rowntree Mills Park is situated today. Many of Humber Summit's first settlers are buried in the historic Pine Ridge Methodist Church Cemetery on Islington Avenue.

By the early 1900s, Humber Summit settlers had turned their attention to farming. Then in the 1940s, with the city encroaching at its doorstep, Humber Summit was transformed into a popular summer resort known as Riverbank Park.

Riverbank Park was popular with Toronto residents who built cottages overlooking the Humber River. These cottages had been converted to year-round use by the time Hurricane Hazel struck in 1954. Hurricane Hazel was the worst hurricane in Toronto's history, and its deadly fury wrecked havoc on the Humber Summit community as 10 houses were swept away by the raging river.

Hurricane Hazel's toll on this community would have been much worse if not for the heroic deeds of the Humber Summit Fire Brigade. This volunteer bucket brigade consisting of 12 men worked valiantly in the dark to safely rescue all of Humber Summit's residents. The Humber Summit Fire Brigade closed down in 1966, however, a plaque commemorating its service hangs in the Humber Summit Public Library, which is located on the site of the former fire hall.

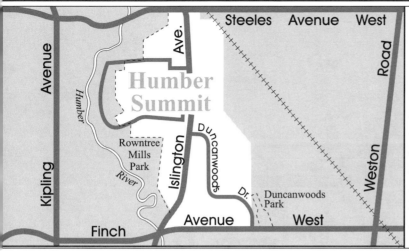

PRICE RANGE OF HOMES	
$100,000 to $200,000	
$200,000 to $300,000	✓
$300,000 to $400,000	✓
$400,000 to $500,000	✓
$500,000 to $600,000	✓
$600,000 to $700,000	
$700,000 to $800,000	
$800,000 to $900,000	
$900,000 to $1,000,000	
$1,000,000 +	

OVERVIEW:

Humber Summit is a small, middle-class community located in the northwest pocket of North York. This neighbourhood is bordered to the west by the Humber River and to the east by industry. Humber Summit's northern boundary is Steeles Avenue, which also serves as the border between the City of Toronto and the City of Vaughan.

Humber Summit is a close-knit neighbourhood with an established Italian community. In recent years, Humber Summit has welcomed many new families of East Indian and Asian background into the neighbourhood.

HOMES:

Humber Summit's winding roads and rolling hills west of Islington Avenue contain a curious mix of old frame cottages from the 1940s and 1950s together with newer two-storey custom-designed homes. Houses on Riverside Drive and Rowntree Mill Road feature beautiful views of the Humber River Valley.

The houses east of Islington Avenue consist of semi-detached backsplits with built-in garages and front porches decorated with cast iron railings. Elaborate front archways also add to the character of these post-war suburban houses which were built largely in the 1960s.

SHOPPING:

There is a small pocket of shops and services located on Islington Avenue. This retail district includes Italian bakeries, cafés, pizzerias and food markets.

The closest shopping plaza is Finchdale, which has a large discount store, banks, a bakery, a beer store and an Italian restaurant. There is also a large Italian supermarket brimming with fresh fruits and vegetables.

RECREATION:

Rowntree Mill Park, accessed off Islington Avenue from Rowntree Mill Road, is part of the North Humber watershed and contains many nice picnic spots set amidst open meadows and woodlands. Hiking and nature walks are popular activities in this park.

To the east of Islington Avenue and south of Finch Avenue are access points to the West Humber Parkland trail. This 5.5-kilometre paved trail follows the Humber Valley to the Humber Arboretum. The Humber Arboretum is operated by the City of Toronto and features a wide variety of plants and wildlife with demonstration gardens, self-guided trails and a visitor interpretation centre.

Golf enthusiasts are just minutes from the Humber Valley public golf course off Beattie Avenue at Albion Road. This par-70 course challenges golfers with its combination of links and valleyland holes.

SCHOOLS:

(P)   Humber Summit, 60 Pearldale Ave., (416) 395-2570
(P)   Gracedale, 186 Gracedale Blvd., (416) 395-2480
(PH) Emery C.I., 3395 Weston Rd., (416) 395-3220
(C)   St. Gaspar, 135 Plunkett Rd., (416) 393-5349
(C)   St. Roch, 174 Duncanwoods Dr., (416) 393-5320
(C)   Ven. John Merlini, 123 Whitfield Ave., (416) 393-5397

TRANSPORTATION:

Humber Summit is well served by public transit. The Islington Avenue bus connects passengers to the Islington Go Train and Bloor-Danforth subway stations on Bloor Street. The Finch Avenue bus connects to the Finch station on the Yonge-University-Spadina subway line.

Motorists are approximately 10 minutes from highways 400 and 401, which can be accessed off Islington Avenue.

HISTORY:
Lansing was first settled by Joseph Shepard, who built a log house on Yonge Street at Sheppard Avenue in 1798. Shepard was a swashbuckling character who traded furs with the First Nations people, fought in the battle of York against the Americans and operated saw and grist mills on the banks of the Don River.

Shepard was a close friend of William Lyon Mackenzie, who led the Toronto Rebellion in 1837. Shepard passed away just prior to the rebellion, however his four sons were active participants in this revolt. Joseph and Jacob were captured and spent time in prison, while Thomas and Michael escaped from the Kingston Penitentiary and fled to the United States.

In 1843 the Shepard brothers were pardoned by the Queen and returned to Lansing to carry on their fathers business. In 1860 Joseph Shepard built a general store and residence on the northwest corner of Yonge Street and Sheppard Avenue. He added a post office in 1866. This post office was given the name "Lansing" by Shepard's daughter Saida.

The Lansing general store and post office – later known as Dempsey Brothers Hardware Store – was a fixture in this neighbourhood until 1996 when it was moved to its present location at 250 Beecroft Road, where it now serves as a public museum and office for the North York Archives.

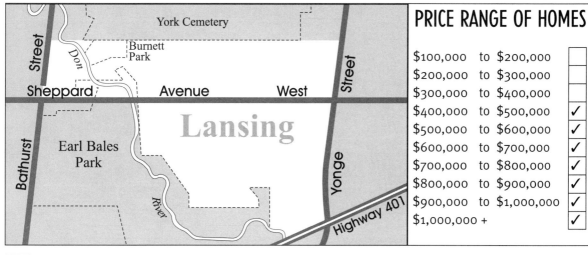

PRICE RANGE OF HOMES

$100,000 to $200,000		
$200,000 to $300,000		
$300,000 to $400,000		
$400,000 to $500,000	✓
$500,000 to $600,000	✓
$600,000 to $700,000	✓
$700,000 to $800,000	✓
$800,000 to $900,000	✓
$900,000 to $1,000,000	✓
$1,000,000 +	✓

OVERVIEW:

Lansing is conveniently located along the Yonge Street corridor near the former North York City Hall and the North York Civic Centre. Lansing is a surprisingly peaceful and quiet neighbourhood, considering its central location. This neighbourhood is sheltered from outside traffic by its borders which include the Don River Valley, York Cemetery, and Beecroft Road.

HOMES:

Lansing houses are surrounded by gently swaying pine trees and grand old maple trees that compliment the whimsical mix of Edwardian-, Tudor-, English-cottage- and craftsman-style houses found in this neighbourhood. Lansing's original housing stock dates from the 1920s up to and including the 1950s. There is also a considerable amount of new home construction going on in this neighbourhood. A fair number of Lansing houses are situated on ravine lots that offer spectacular views of the Don River Valley.

Historical houses in this neighbourhood include the Joseph Shepard house, circa 1835, located at 90 Burndale Avenue; the Michael Shepard house, circa 1859, which now serves as the York Cemetery office; the Joseph Shepard House/Dempsey Brothers Store, circa 1860, at 250 Beecroft Road; and the former house of Canadian artist and Group of Seven member Frank Carmichael, circa 1918, located at 21 Cameron Avenue.

SHOPPING:

Lansing residents can walk to the Yonge and Sheppard retail district which is anchored by the recently renovated Sheppard Shopping Centre, situated on the northeast corner of Yonge Street and Sheppard Avenue. The Willowdale Plaza is located directly south of the shopping centre and includes a large grocery store, a national sports chain store, and an assortment of smaller retailers. Street-level shopping on Yonge Street and Sheppard Avenue provide Lansing residents with a good selection of restaurants, retail services and professional and medical offices.

RECREATION:

The North York Civic Centre at Beecroft Drive is one of Toronto's finest sports and entertainment centres. This complex includes the massive North York Central Library and the Douglas Snow Aquatic Centre, which is recognized as one of Canada's top all-purpose aquatic facilities. Across the street from the civic centre on Beecroft Drive is the Willowdale Lawn Bowling Club.

Adjacent to the civic centre is Mel Lastman Square, a multi-faceted civic square that is equipped with a spacious amphitheatre, intimate wedding pavilion, a garden court and a reflecting pool which doubles as a skating rink in the wintertime. Mel Lastman Square is also the site of many ceremonies, festivals and annual events including the very popular North York Winter Carnival.

The Toronto Centre for the Performing Arts, located at 5040 Yonge Street, includes the Art Gallery of North York, the George Weston Recital Hall and the Studio Theatre.

The very scenic Gwendolen Park has an active community tennis club, a baseball diamond and a children's playground. Earl Bales Park located south of Sheppard Avenue is the home of the North York Ski Centre which offers downhill skiing and snowboarding at reasonable rates from December to March.

SCHOOLS:

(P) Cameron, 211 Cameron Ave., (416) 395-2140
(P) Willowdale M.S., 225 Senlac Rd., (416) 395-2970
(PH) Avondale E. & S. Alternative, 171 Avondale Ave., (416) 395-3130
(PH) Earl Haig S.S., 100 Princess Ave., (416) 395-3210
(C) St.Edward, 21 Eddfield Ave., (416) 393-5255

TRANSPORTATION:

Bus service on Sheppard Avenue, Bathurst Street, Yonge Street, and Senlac Road connects passengers to the Sheppard subway station on the Yonge-University-Spadina subway line. This Sheppard subway station is within walking distance of most Lansing residents.

Yonge Street provides a direct route to downtown Toronto in approximately 25 minutes. Lansing commuters can gain immediate access to the Yonge Street on-ramp to Highway 401, located just south of Sheppard Avenue.

SW

HISTORY: Lawrence Heights is located on the old Mulholland farm.
Henry Mulholland was one of North York's earliest pioneers, settling in this
area in 1814. Mulholland's heirs continued to live on the family farm until
the 1940s when it was sold to developers.

In the early 1950s Lawrence Heights was transformed from farmland into
one of Toronto's largest public housing developments. The Canada Mortgage
and Housing Corporation oversaw the design and building of this entire
neighbourhood. The Canada Mortgage and Housing Corporation head office
was formerly located next door to Lawrence Heights, on Lawrence Avenue
West.

John Sewell, in *The Shape of the City,* writes that Lawrence Heights was
originally slated to include high-rise apartment towers. This was before Jack
Brown, a government official and Second World War pilot, took a reconnais-
sance flight over the project site, and recognized that Lawrence Heights was
too close to the Downsview Airport to permit high-rise apartments within this
development. The revised plan incorporated the row houses and low-rise
buildings that the present-day neighbourhood comprises.

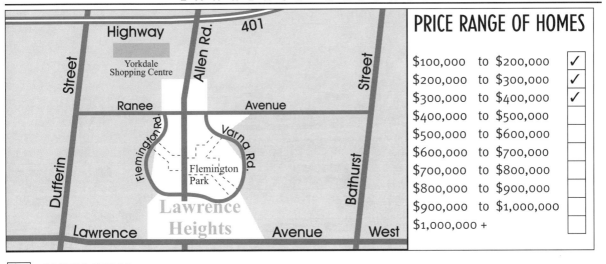

PRICE RANGE OF HOMES

$100,000 to $200,000	✓
$200,000 to $300,000	✓
$300,000 to $400,000	✓
$400,000 to $500,000	
$500,000 to $600,000	
$600,000 to $700,000	
$700,000 to $800,000	
$800,000 to $900,000	
$900,000 to $1,000,000	
$1,000,000 +	

OVERVIEW:

Lawrence Heights is a low-income neighbourhood managed by the Metro Toronto Housing Authority. The backbone of this community is the Lawrence Heights Area Alliance, a team of volunteers comprised of local church members as well as Lawrence Heights residents. The Lawrence Heights Area Alliance has been very active in developing local Youth and Seniors programs.

The Lawrence Heights Community Health Centre is also an integral part of this community. This centre offers a range of outreach and educational programs. It also includes a clinic with doctors, nurses and a chiropodist, and a team of community development workers, social workers and dietitians.

HOMES:

There are approximately 6,000 residents in Lawrence Heights. Most of the housing is publicly owned and the rents are geared to the income of the tenants. The public housing is contained in row houses with one-, two-, three-, and four-bedroom apartments. There are also a limited number of single-family five-bedroom houses. Lawrence Heights's two-storey apartment buildings are reserved as housing for senior citizens.

Privately owned townhouse and condominium apartments are now being built on the former site of Canada Mortgage and Housing Corporation at 650 Lawrence Avenue West. These buildings are foregoing luxury building amenities and upgrades to the interior of the homes in favour of affordable prices.

SHOPPING:

Lawrence Heights residents can walk to Lawrence Square, which features national department stores as well as small independent retailers and medical and professional offices. Lawrence Square merchants participate in a retail education program for Lawrence Heights Youth that is sponsored by the Lawrence Heights Area Alliance. Lawrence Square also hosts the annual Lawrence Heights Multi-Cultural Fair.

Lawrence Plaza, situated at the northwest corner of Bathurst Street and Lawrence Avenue, includes many discount and outlet stores that attract shoppers from all over the city.

RECREATION:

The Lawrence Heights Community Centre at 5 Replin Road offers a myriad of programs including children's art and dance, children's martial arts, Bell Raptorball, instructional basketball, youth afternoon programs, girls' basketball house leagues, leisure games, youth dance and music, seniors' clubs and aerobics.

The ultra-modern Barbara Frum Public Library at 20 Covington Road features a children's storyroom, French and multicultural collections, private study rooms, a meeting room, and an auditorium with a 150-person seating capacity. Combined with the library is a 10,000-square-foot recreation centre with multi-purpose meeting rooms, and a kitchen/craft room.

SCHOOLS:

(P) Flemington, 10 Flemington Rd., (416) 395-2430
(P) Lawrence Heights M.S., 50 Highland Hill, (416) 395-2620
(PH) Bathurst Heights, 640 Lawrence Ave., W., (416) 395-3160

TRANSPORTATION:

The Lawrence Heights neighbourhood is well served by public transit. Bus service on Lawrence and on Wilson avenues connect to stations on the Yonge-University-Spadina subway line. The Bathurst Street bus travels south to the Bathurst station on the Bloor-Danforth subway line.

Motorists are approximately 25 minutes, via Bathurst Street, from downtown. The Allen Expressway, which runs through the centre of this neighbourhood, is easily accessed from Lawrence Avenue West and provides a connecting route to Highway 401.

HISTORY: Lawrence Manor was farmland from the early 1800s until the 1940s, when the Canada Mortgage and Housing Corporation purchased this property for residential development. CMHC serviced this entire subdivision, putting in water service, sewers, and roads, before selling off individual lots to a number of small builders in the early 1950s. The first Lawrence Manor buyers had to qualify for a CMHC mortgage. These mortgages were for 25 years at a rate of only 4.5 per cent.

Cows were still grazing on the northwest corner of Bathurst Street and Lawrence Avenue in 1951 when the first residents began moving into this neighbourhood. Lawrence Plaza was built on the site of this former cow patch in 1960. Lawrence Plaza was the largest shopping centre in Toronto when it first opened. It attracted shoppers from all over Toronto and helped put the Lawrence Manor neighbourhood on the map.

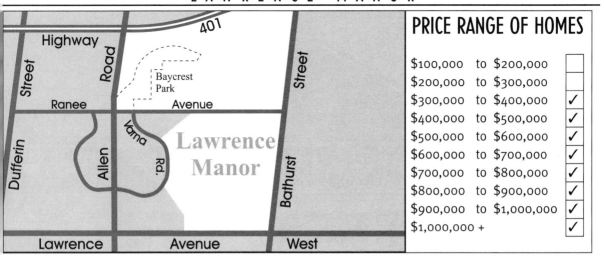

PRICE RANGE OF HOMES

$100,000	to	$200,000	
$200,000	to	$300,000	
$300,000	to	$400,000	✓
$400,000	to	$500,000	✓
$500,000	to	$600,000	✓
$600,000	to	$700,000	✓
$700,000	to	$800,000	✓
$800,000	to	$900,000	✓
$900,000	to	$1,000,000	✓
$1,000,000 +			✓

OVERVIEW:

Lawrence Manor is a family-oriented neighbourhood with a predominantly Jewish Orthodox community. Bathurst Street, which forms the eastern boundary of this neighbourhood, includes Jewish schools and cultural centres, synagogues, restaurants and retail shops.

The dominant landmark in this neighbourhood is the Baycrest Centre for Geriatric Care, which provides hospital and nursing-home care. Baycrest has recently undergone a major renovation and expansion of its highly regarded nursing home facilities.

HOMES:

Lawrence Manor's original housing stock was built largely between 1951 and 1955. These houses include detached brick two-storey houses as well as split-level homes and bungalows. There are also some newer custom-built houses in this neighbourhood. The lots in Lawrence Manor are at least 30 feet wide and all the houses have a private drive.

Bathurst Street is lined with low and high-rise apartment buildings as well as a recently built luxury condominium apartment building.

SHOPPING:

The Bathurst Street and Lawrence Avenue intersection is one of the premiere Jewish shopping districts in Toronto. Included in this mix are gift shops, bookstores, kosher food shops, bakeries selling "Montreal-style" bagels, delicatessens and restaurants. A handful of Chinese restaurants are also included in this retail corridor.

The Bathurst Street and Wilson Avenue shopping area is centred around smaller shopping plazas. This retail district also features many stores and restaurants that cater to the local community.

Lawrence Plaza, situated on the northwest corner of Bathurst Street and Lawrence Avenue, is a popular shopping destination that attracts a local and regional clientele. This plaza is especially well known for its many outlet and discount stores.

RECREATION:

Prince Charles Park is an island of greenspace conveniently located right in the middle of this neighbourhood. Prince Charles Park has a children's playground that is well used by the many young children in Lawrence Manor.

The ultra-modern Barbara Frum Library at 20 Covington Road features a children's storyroom, French and multicultural collections, private study rooms, a meeting room, and an auditorium with a 150-person seating capacity. Combined with the library is a 10,000-square-foot recreation centre that contains multi-purpose rooms for use by local community groups.

SCHOOLS:

(P) Baycrest, 145 Baycrest Ave., (416) 395-2040
(P) Ledbury Park, E. & M.S., 95 Falkirk Ave.,
     (416) 395-2630
(PH) Sir Sanford Fleming Academy, 50 Ameer Ave.,
     (416) 395-3300
(PJ) Associated Hebrew Schools, 18 Neptune Dr.,
     (416) 494-7666
(PJ) Beth Jacob, 410 Lawrence Ave., W., (416) 787-4949

TRANSPORTATION:

Bus routes on Lawrence and Wilson avenues connect passengers to stations on the Yonge-University-Spadina subway line. The Bathurst Street bus travels south to Bathurst station on the Bloor-Danforth subway line.

By taking Bathurst Street south motorists can access Toronto's financial and entertainment districts in 25 to 30 minutes. At the north end of this neighbourhood Bathurst Street provides commuters with an on-ramp to Highway 401.

HISTORY: Ledbury was a small farming community up until the early 1900s, when the first houses in this neighbourhood were built along Bedford Park and Woburn avenues on the site of the old Lawrence Farm.

The Ledbury area north of Woburn Avenue had been the former hobby farm of Alfred St. Germain, the successful publisher of the old *Toronto Evening Journal*. The St. Germain property was subdivided in 1922 by the Melrose Realty Company under the name Melrose Park.

Melrose Realty president H.A. Clark selected the street names for the Melrose Park subdivision. St. Germain was chosen for obvious reasons, while Old Orchard Grove recalls the St. Germain apple orchard. Deloraine, Melrose, Marmion, and Falkirk are street names adopted from the works of Sir Walter Scott, of whom Clark was an avid fan.

Ledbury's residential development was not fully complete until the 1950s when Ledbury school and Ledbury Park were added to this neighbourhood.

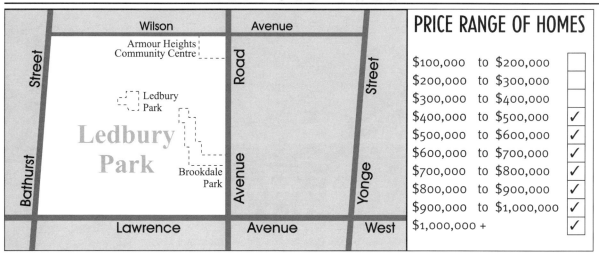

PRICE RANGE OF HOMES

$100,000 to $200,000	
$200,000 to $300,000	
$300,000 to $400,000	
$400,000 to $500,000	✓
$500,000 to $600,000	✓
$600,000 to $700,000	✓
$700,000 to $800,000	✓
$800,000 to $900,000	✓
$900,000 to $1,000,000	✓
$1,000,000 +	✓

OVERVIEW:

Ledbury is a neighbourhood in transition. The first generation of Ledbury families have been gradually moving out of the neighbourhood and young urban professional families are moving in. The ripple effect in this change in demographics can be seen in the flurry of building activity currently taking place in this neighbourhood, as the original housing stock is gradually being replaced with expensive custom-built homes. The local parks have also undergone recent improvements and Avenue Road has emerged as one of Toronto's finest shopping districts.

HOMES:

Ledbury Park is checkered with an abundance of real estate signs, reflecting the large amount of new home construction taking place within this neighbourhood.

Ledbury Park's original housing stock dates from the 1910s to the 1950s. These houses include Tudor-style bungalows on prime 30- to 50-foot-wide lots. Ledbury's bungalows are rapidly being replaced by new homes. The original Ledbury houses also include small pockets of two-storey detached and semi-detached homes.

The custom-built new homes in this neighbourhood range in size from approximately 2,000 to 4,000 square feet. These homes generally include lavish interior custom finishings. The exteriors are generally brick, stone or stucco and feature many decorative accents such as large bay windows, juliet balconies, professional landscaping, interlock driveways and elaborate front porches decorated by columns, and fanciful wrought iron railings.

SHOPPING:

Avenue Road is one of Toronto's most popular shopping districts. There is a tremendous mix of shopping here including gourmet food shops, video stores, gift shops, fashion stores, home design and furnishing shops, a discount supermarket, pharmacies, children's stores, sports stores, beauty salons, antique shops, professional offices and a large variety of restaurants.

The Bathurst Street shopping district is much different in tone than Avenue Road. This shopping district includes Jewish food and gift shops, delicatessens, restaurants, and a handful of popular bakeries that serve up freshly baked Montreal-style bagels.

RECREATION:

Ledbury Park, located in the centre of this neighbourhood, has recently been redesigned and has earned a Canadian Architect Award of Excellence for its innovative approach to neighbourhood park planning. The focal point of this park is a rectangular reflecting pool and skating rink that is linked to a swimming pool, and a water play area designed specifically for young children. There are also a number of smaller children's playgrounds contained within the Ledbury neighbourhood.

The Armour Heights Community Centre, located at 2141 Avenue Road, has dance and fitness programs for adults and a myriad of programs for toddlers and preschoolers. The Armour Heights Public Library is located inside the community centre.

The Morris Winchevsky Centre located at 585 Cranbrooke is a secular Jewish organization that has a children's Sunday school and a seniors' club; it also hosts a variety of educational and cultural events. The ultra-modern Barbara Frum Public Library at 20 Covington Road has a wide range of facilities including a 150-seat auditorium.

SCHOOLS:

(P) Ledbury Park E. & M.S., 95 Falkirk Ave., (416) 395-2630
(PH) Lawrence Park C.I., 125 Chatsworth Dr., (416) 393-9500
(C) St. Margaret, 85 Carmichael Ave., (416) 393-5249
(PR) Havergal College, 1451 Avenue Rd., (416) 483-3519
(PR) Associated Hebrew, 18 Neptune Dr., (416) 787-1872

TRANSPORTATION:

Ledbury residents are well served by public transit. The Bathurst bus connects passengers to the Bloor-Danforth subway line, while the Avenue Road bus connects passengers to the Yonge-University-Spadina subway line. The Lawrence station on the Yonge subway line is a good exercise walk from this neighbourhood.

Ledbury residents can drive downtown in approximately 25 minutes via Avenue Road. The Avenue Road on-ramp to Highway 401 is located just beyond the northern boundary of this neighbourhood. Highway 401 links up with a network of major highways leading into and out of the greater Toronto area.

HISTORY: Newtonbrook was first settled in the early 1800s. This
hamlet revolved around saw and grist mills that operated on the east and
west branches of the Don River. The spiritual centre of this hard-working
pioneer community was the Newton Brook Wesleyan Church, which was
named after Reverend Robert Newton. One of Newtonbrook's earliest settlers
was Lieutenant Colonel William S. Durie of the Queens Own Rifles. Durie
subdivided part of his Newtonbrook property in 1847, creating what is now
known as Drewry Avenue. At first Drewry Street was given the name "Pope's
Lane" because so many Roman Catholics built houses here. The Rueter
House at 270 Drewry is the only house still standing from this early
Newtonbrook subdivision.

When Newtonbrook was subdivided for large-scale residential development
in the 1950s most of the former village landmarks were demolished. The two
notable exceptions are the Newtonbrook Schoolhouse, circa 1878, located at
43 Drewry Avenue, and the second Newtonbrook General Store, circa 1907,
located on the northwest corner of Yonge Street and Drewry Avenue.

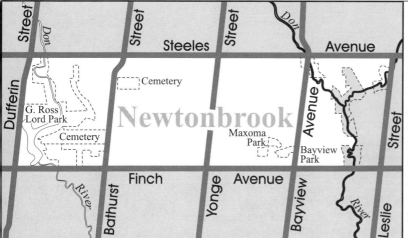

PRICE RANGE OF HOMES

$100,000	to	$200,000	
$200,000	to	$300,000	
$300,000	to	$400,000	✓
$400,000	to	$500,000	✓
$500,000	to	$600,000	✓
$600,000	to	$700,000	✓
$700,000	to	$800,000	✓
$800,000	to	$900,000	✓
$900,000	to	$1,000,000	✓
$1,000,000 +			✓

OVERVIEW:

Newtonbrook is located at the north end of the City of Toronto. It is situated between the east and west branches of the Don River Valley, which serve to provide an attractive natural backdrop for this neighbourhood in addition to providing residents with plenty of recreational opportunities.

Newtonbrook's most famous native son is the late Lester B. Pearson, who became prime minister of Canada in 1963 and won the Nobel Peace Prize for his role in diffusing the Suez Canal crisis. The local Lester B. Pearson school is named in his honour.

HOMES:

Newtonbrook's original housing stock was built from the 1920s up to the 1960s. This mix of housing includes split-level and 1.5-storey houses as well as bungalows. There is also an increasing number of new custom built-homes in this neighbourhood.

Newtonbrook contains a good selection of newer, luxury condominium apartment buildings that are mostly concentrated along Steeles Avenue. Bayview Avenue has traditionally been a hot spot for modern townhouse and new home developments.

Bathurst Street has a large number of high-rise rental apartment buildings for people seeking an option to home ownership but who still want to live in this conveniently located neighbourhood.

SHOPPING:

CentrePoint Mall is, as its name implies, conveniently located in the centre of this neighbourhood on the southwest corner of Yonge Street and Steeles Avenue. This indoor shopping mall is anchored by two national department stores, a popular family-style restaurant and a large grocery store.

Newtonbrook's Yonge Street shopping district is checkered with shopping plazas and new car dealerships. This section of Yonge Street also contains a dizzying array of fast food restaurants, coffee shops, and convenience-type stores.

Dufferin Street is Toronto's largest discount warehouse district featuring a wide selection of well known brand name clothing, high-tech items, and home furnishing products. Steeles Avenue is a higher-end retail district with numerous shopping plazas, big-box chain stores, and smaller specialty shops and restaurants.

RECREATION:

Newtonbrook contains over 20 neighbourhood parks and children's playgrounds. Many of these parks offer tennis courts, baseball diamonds, sports fields, and fitness trails. Newtonbrook also has two community centres and four indoor ice arenas.

Cummer Park Fitness Centre, located at 6000 Leslie Street, features squash and racquetball courts, fitness classes, an indoor jogging/walking track, two weight rooms, outdoor tennis courts, whirlpools and saunas.

Esther Shiner stadium located at 5720 Bathurst Street has a 2,000-seat stadium that hosts a myriad of sport and track and field competitions.

SCHOOLS:

(P)	Cummer Valley M.S., 70 Maxome Ave.,	(416) 395-2260
(P)	Lester B. Pearson, 500 Cummer Ave.,	(416) 395-2650
(P)	Lillian, 1059 Lillian St.,	(416) 395-2660
(P)	R. J. Lang E. & M.S., 227 Drewry Ave.,	(416) 395-2780
(P)	Rockford, 60 Rockford Rd.,	(416) 395-2820
(PH)	Drewry, 70 Drewry Ave.,	(416) 395-3260
(PH)	Newtonbrook, 155 Hilda Ave.,	(416) 395-3280
(PH)	Northview Heights, 55 Finch Ave.,	(416) 395-3290
(C)	St. Agnes, 280 Otonabee Ave.,	(416) 393-5345
(C)	St. Antoine Daniel, 160 Finch Ave. W.,	(416) 393-5339
(C)	St. Paschal Baylon, 15 St. Paschal Crt.,	(416) 393-5283
(CH)	Brebeuf College, 211 Steeles Ave. E.,	(416) 393-5508
(CH)	St. Joseph Morrow Park, 3377 Bayview Ave.,	(416) 393-5516
(CH)	Mgr-de-Charbonnel, 110 Drewry Ave.,	(416) 393-5537
(PJ)	Associated Hebrew Schools, 252 Finch Ave. W.,	(416) 223-4845
(PJ)	Eitz Chaim Day Schools, 475 Patricia Ave.,	(416) 225-1187

TRANSPORTATION:

Newtonbrook's location along the Yonge street corridor provides its residents with quick and easy access to stations on the Yonge-University-Spadina subway line. Regular bus service is available on Finch, Steeles, Bayview, Cummer and Drewry avenues and on Bathurst and Dufferin streets.

Bayview Avenue and Yonge, Bathurst and Dufferin streets provide motorists with direct access to Highway 401 on-ramps, south of Sheppard Avenue. These major arterial roadways also usher commuters into the downtown core.

HISTORY:
The Parkwoods name was given to this neighbourhood by city planners who were making obvious reference to Parkwoods Village Drive – one of the main thoroughfares in this neighbourhood. Parkwoods United Church and Parkwoods Village Shopping Centre also share this name.

Parkwoods Village Drive also has an historical significance. In approximately 1833, a teenager named John Coulson emigrated to Canada from England and built a log house on what is now the northwest corner of Parkwoods Village Drive and Victoria Park. Incredibly, the Coulson log cabin remained standing until 1956, when this neighbourhood began to be developed.

One of Coulson's long-time neighbours to the south was Charles D. Maginn, a Welshman who arrived in this area around 1832. Maginn was a general merchant in the community and is described by Patricia Hart in *Pioneering in North York* as having "had a reputation for being very adept at spearing salmon in the Deer Lick, a small stream running near his farm."

The Maginns often lent out their grove to the Wesleyan Methodist Church for field meetings. In 1841 this church established a cemetery at the southwest corner of Lawrence Avenue East and Victoria Park Avenue. Many of Parkwoods first settlers are buried in this cemetery, which has been declared a heritage property by the city.

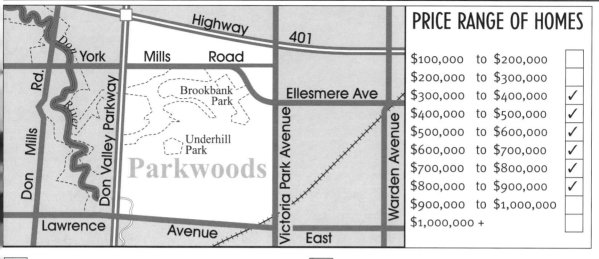

PRICE RANGE OF HOMES		
$100,000	to $200,000	
$200,000	to $300,000	
$300,000	to $400,000	✓
$400,000	to $500,000	✓
$500,000	to $600,000	✓
$600,000	to $700,000	✓
$700,000	to $800,000	✓
$800,000	to $900,000	✓
$900,000	to $1,000,000	
$1,000,000 +		

OVERVIEW:

Parkwoods's boundaries are formed by the Don Valley Parkway to the west, Victoria Park Avenue to the east, Highway 401 to the north, and Lawrence Avenue and the Canadian Pacific railway tracks to the south. With all these thoroughfares skirting the neighbourhood, one could easily get the impression that Parkwoods is a loud and busy place when in fact the opposite is true.

Parkwoods has a natural beauty that is derived from its location on the eastern edge of the Don River Valley. Gently rolling hills and well-treed streets are common in this quiet middle-income neighbourhood.

HOMES:

Parkwoods's modest two-storey houses, split-level homes and ranch-style bungalows were built in the 1960s. The architecture is varied and incorporates elements of Tudor- and Georgian-revival as well as contemporary-style housing.

Parkwoods also contains a large number of semi-detached starter homes north of York Mills Road as well as a large concentration of rental and condominium townhouses south of York Mills Road. A new luxury condominium is situated on Brookbanks Drive.

SHOPPING:

Parkwoods residents have many shopping options. These include Victoria Terrace situated at Lawrence and Victoria Park Avenues. This shopping plaza features a huge toy shop, a food market, a bank, postal services, restaurants, and professional and medical offices.

Donwood Plaza at Underhill Drive and Lawrence Avenue is a small local plaza with a food market, professional offices, and restaurants. Victoria Park also contains some small local shopping plazas with an assortment of retailers and restaurants.

Parkway Mall located at the southeast corner of Victoria Park and Lawrence Avenues is anchored by a supermarket and a department store. This large indoor shopping mall features ladies and mens wear, specialty apparel, sporting goods, hobbies and toys, footwear, jewellery and gifts, home furnishings, stationary and books, restaurants, and professional and medical offices.

RECREATION:

Parkwoods contains an abundance of recreational opportunities. For the fitness enthusiast there is pleasure skating available at the Fenside Arena, year-round tennis at Cassandra Park, and an outdoor pool at the Broadlands community centre. There are also a myriad of local parks with a wide range of facilities including baseball diamonds, indoor and outdoor pools, basketball, tennis courts and children's playgrounds.

Brookbanks Park, which winds its way through the centre of this neighbourhood, is a lush ravine valley with a thick cover of trees and a wood chip nature trail that is used frequently by neighbourhood residents. This park is accessible year-round and also features a paved path that is ideal for walking, jogging, in-line skating and cycling. During the winter residents cross-country ski and snowshoe in this winter wonderland.

The Victoria Terrace shopping centre at Lawrence and Victoria Park avenues is anchored by six Famous Players movie theatres that screen all of the newest Hollywood pictures. The Brookbanks Public Library at 210 Brookbanks Drive includes an auditorium that is available for both children and adult programs.

SCHOOLS:

(P)	Broadlands, 106 Broadlands Blvd.,	(416) 395-2090
(P)	Cassandra, 45 Cassandra Blvd.,	(416) 395-2150
(P)	Fenside, 131 Fenside Dr.,	(416) 395-2400
(P)	Ranchdale, 60 Ranchdale Cres.,	(416) 395-2800
(P)	Roywood, 11 Roywood Dr.,	(416) 395-2830
(P)	Milne Valley M.S., 100 Underhill Dr.,	(416) 395-2700
(PH)	Victoria Park, 15 Wallingford Rd.,	(416) 395-3310
(C)	Annunciation, 65 Avonwick Gate,	(416) 393-5299
(C)	St.Catherine, 30 Roanoke,	(416) 393-5316
(C)	St.Issac Jogues, 1330 York Mills Rd.,	(416) 393-5315
(C)	Sainte-Madelaine, 1 Ness Dr.,	(416) 393-5312
(CH)	Senator O'Connor, 5 Avonwick Gate,	(416) 393-5505

TRANSPORTATION:

Local bus service along Parkwoods Village Drive, York Mills Road and Lawrence Avenue provide connecting routes to stations on the Yonge-University-Spadina subway line. The Victoria Park Avenue bus links up to the Victoria Park station on the Bloor-Danforth subway line.

Motorists enjoy convenient access to the downtown core and Toronto's network of commuter highways via the Don Valley Parkway, which has north and south on-ramps off Lawrence Avenue and York Mills Road. The Highway 401 on-ramp is situated off Victoria Park Avenue.

HISTORY: Victoria Park Village was prime Don Valley farmland until 1952 when a syndicate of investors, led by Conservative member of Parliament R.H. McGregor, purchased the 600 acres that now make up this neighbourhood. In total, seven local farms were purchased for the assembly of this neighbourhood.

The largest individual deal involved the Fitzpatrick family, who had farmed this area for 120 years. Bob and Martin Fitzpatrick sold their 175-acre farm to the developers of this neighbourhood for the then-princely sum of $279,000.

The inspiration for Victoria Park Village came from the tremendously popular Don Mills subdivision, which was being developed on the west side of the Don Valley Parkway just prior to the creation of Victoria Park Village. Following Don Mills's lead, Victoria Park Village was planned as a self-contained community with its own schools, shops, parks and industry.

Victoria Park Village began welcoming its first residents in 1953. The Victoria Park Village name was chosen in reference to Victoria Park Avenue, the major street that borders this neighbourhood.

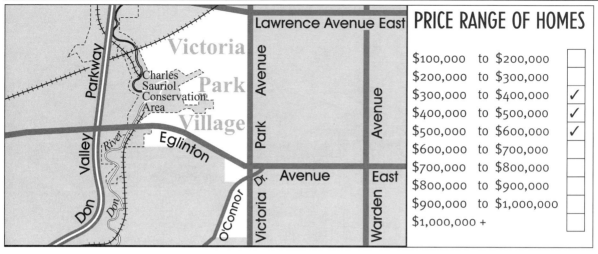

PRICE RANGE OF HOMES		
$100,000	to $200,000	
$200,000	to $300,000	
$300,000	to $400,000	✓
$400,000	to $500,000	✓
$500,000	to $600,000	✓
$600,000	to $700,000	
$700,000	to $800,000	
$800,000	to $900,000	
$900,000	to $1,000,000	
$1,000,000 +		

OVERVIEW:

Victoria Park Village is a quiet, middle-income neighbourhood that is bordered by the East Don River Valley, the Canadian Pacific Railway line, and light industry. Victoria Park Village is a community in transition as a steady stream of young families from a myriad of cultural backgrounds have begun moving into this affordable neighbourhood.

Many of Victoria Park Village's new residents have become active members of the Victoria Park Village Ratepayers Association. This association has been involved in shaping recent developments on the periphery of the neighbourhood as well as working on traffic calming issues and the improvement of local parks.

HOMES:

Victoria Park Village houses are located on gently sloping curvilinear streets. These houses were built in the 1950s and early 1960s and include detached and semi-detached two-storey brick homes, split-level houses and bungalows. Many Victoria Park Village homes back onto park or valley land that offers beautiful views and extra privacy.

The periphery of this neighbourhood is ringed by apartment buildings and newer condominium buildings.

SHOPPING:

Victoria Park Village is handy to a number of different shopping centres, including Golden Mile, Eglinton Square and Victoria Terrace. These shopping centres are located at the main intersections bordering this neighbourhood and feature large supermarkets, national department stores and small retailers.

Additional shopping is available on Eglinton and Victoria Park avenues, which together contain a handful of shopping plazas.

RECREATION:

The Conservation Area located on the eastern edge of this neighbourhood is named in memory of Charles Sauriol, an author and pioneer Toronto conservationist who was an important figure in the preservation of Toronto's Don Valley parklands.

The Charles Sauriol Conservation Area can be accessed from Wigmore Park, located off Wigmore Drive. Wigmore Park also features a baseball diamond and a children's playground. Sweeney Park, located off Sweeney Drive, has tennis courts and a baseball diamond.

The Victoria Village Arena at 190 Bermondsey Road offers children's hockey league programs, instructional skating and family pleasure skating.

The Victoria Village Public Library, tucked away in the middle of this neighbourhood at 184 Sloane Avenue, offers children's and adults' programs as well as a popular bridge club for seniors.

SCHOOLS:

(P)   O'Connor, 1665 O'Connor Dr., (416) 397-2980
(P)   Sloane, 110 Sloane Ave., (416) 397-2920
(P)   Victoria Village, 88 Sweeney Dr., (416) 397-2930
(PH) Victoria Park S.S., 15 Wallingford Rd., (416) 395-3310

TRANSPORTATION:

Many of the interior streets in this neighbourhood including Carnforth Road, Sweeney Drive, and Sloane Avenue have their own bus service that runs south to the Woodbine station on the Bloor-Danforth subway line. The Victoria Park bus also connects passengers to the Bloor-Danforth subway. The Eglinton and Lawrence Avenue buses connect passengers to stations on the Yonge-University-Spadina subway line.

Eglinton and Lawrence Avenue provide motorists with immediate access to the Don Valley Parkway, which ushers motorists downtown as well as providing a connecting route to other commuter highways.

HISTORY: Willowdale was originally settled by Jacob Cummer, who immigrated to Canada from the United States in 1797. Cummer was a mill owner on the nearby Don River, a proprietor of a tinsmith shop on Yonge Street, and a self trained doctor and veterinarian. Cummer was held in such high esteem by his neighbours that this area was originally known as "Kummer's Settlement."

David Gibson, a distinguished land surveyor, was another leader in this community. Like most of his neighbours, Gibson participated in the ill-fated Toronto Rebellion of 1837. He was thus charged with high treason and escaped to the United States, where he found employment as the first assistant engineer on the building of the Erie Canal.

Gibson returned to his Yonge Street farm in 1851, after being pardoned for his role in the rebellion. He then helped to establish the "Willow Dale" post office, named after the many willow trees that once graced this district. Members of the Gibson family were still living in Gibson House in the 1920s when the residential subdivision of Willowdale began to take place.

Ed. Note: The Gibson House, circa 1851, is still standing in its original location at 5172 Yonge Street, and is now a historic museum.

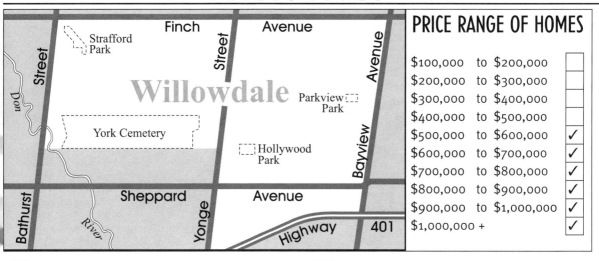

PRICE RANGE OF HOMES	
$100,000 to $200,000	
$200,000 to $300,000	
$300,000 to $400,000	
$400,000 to $500,000	
$500,000 to $600,000	✓
$600,000 to $700,000	✓
$700,000 to $800,000	✓
$800,000 to $900,000	✓
$900,000 to $1,000,000	✓
$1,000,000 +	✓

OVERVIEW:

Willowdale is a vibrant and cosmo-politan urban centre filled with luxury condominiums, custom-built homes, shining office towers, a newly renovated shopping mall and theatre complex, an ultra modern civic centre, a world-class aquatic centre and a highly acclaimed centre for the performing arts.

Willowdale is also the home of the newly rebuilt Earl Haig Secondary School, which has an outstanding academic reputation. Earl Haig is also highly regarded for its Claude Watson Arts program where students can major in either dance, drama, music or visual arts.

HOMES:

Willowdale's original housing stock was built from the 1920s through to the 1950s. In this neighbourhood you will find charming Edwardian- and Tudor-style houses (generally located near Yonge Street), rows of cosy brick and frame bungalows, and a fair number of split-level houses situated in the western section of Willowdale.

Willowdale has recently become a hot spot for new custom-built homes. These new homes on average provide 3,000 to 4,000 square feet of living space. The exterior of these homes typically includes double or triple garages, interlock driveways, wrought iron railings and balconies and professionally landscaped gardens. The lavish interior finishes range from marble and slate tiles, ceramic backsplash, rich hardwood floors, cornice mouldings, skylights, potlights, alarm and intercom systems, central air and central vacuum, and nine-foot ceilings.

Willowdale also includes a large number of newer luxury condominium apartment buildings and townhouses. These homes are located mainly on or near Yonge Street and feature convenient access to the subway station.

SHOPPING:

The Yonge Street shopping district, which runs through the centre of this neighbourhood, is a curious mix of small retailers, big box stores, one-of-a-kind specialty stores, fast food restaurants, small shopping plazas and a large shopping centre. This vibrant shopping mecca also features an international selection of restaurants including French, Italian, Greek, Chinese, Japanese and Middle Eastern foods. If you prefer making dinner at home there are numerous food markets along this street.

The Bayview Village Shopping Centre, located at the northeast corner of Bayview and Sheppard Avenues, is known for its excellent selection of clothing stores and restaurants. Willowdale Avenue provides residents in the east part of this neighbourhood with additional convenience-type shopping and also contains a number of specialty service stores and professional offices.

RECREATION:

The North York Civic Centre, located on Beecroft Road one block west of Yonge Street, is a multi-faceted facility that includes the Douglas Snow Aquatic Centre and the North York Central Library. Adjacent to the civic centre is Mel Lastman Square, a popular public promenade that is equipped with a spacious amphitheatre, intimate wedding pavilions, a garden court, and a reflecting pool which doubles as a skating rink in the wintertime. Next to Mel Lastman Square is the Toronto Centre for the Performing Arts which includes the Art Gallery of North York, the George Weston Recital Hall, and the Studio Theatre. The Willowdale Lawn Bowling Club is located across the street from the civic centre at 150 Beecroft Road.

The newly built Mitchell Field Community Centre located at 89 Church Avenue includes an ice arena, an indoor pool, a gymnasium and community meeting rooms. Tennis courts and baseball diamonds can be found at Bayview Village Park off Bayview Avenue and Edithvale Park on Edithvale Drive. Willowdale Park, located off Hollywood Avenue also has tennis courts. In addition, the Willowdale neighbourhood contains many children's parks, equipped with playgrounds, that are conveniently situated throughout the neighbourhood.

SCHOOLS:

(P)	Churchill, 188 Churchill Ave., (416) 395-2200
(P)	Finch, 277 Finch Ave., E., (416) 395-2410
(P)	Hollywood, 360 Hollywood Ave., (416) 395-2560
(P)	McKee, 44 McKee Ave., (416) 395-2680
(P)	Yorkview, 130 Yorkview Dr., (416) 395-2980
(P)	Willowdale M.S., 225 Senlac Rd., (416) 395-2970
(PH)	Earl Haig S.S., 100 Princess Ave., (416) 395-3210
(C)	St. Cyril, 18 Kempford Blvd., (416) 393-5270
(C)	St. Edward, 21 Eddfield, (416) 393-5255
(C)	St. Gabriel, 396 Spring Garden Ave., (416) 393-5256
(PJ)	United Synagogue Day School, 3080 Bayview Ave., (416) 225-1143

TRANSPORTATION:

Bus service along Sheppard, Finch and Bayview avenues connects passengers to stations on the Yonge-University-Spadina subway line. The Bathurst Street bus links up with the Bathurst station on the Bloor-Danforth subway line. A York Region GO Transit bus terminal is located at the Finch subway station for those commuters heading north of the city. The new Sheppard subway line extends from Yonge Street east to Don Mills and the Fairview Shopping Centre.

Yonge Street runs right through the centre of Willowdale, providing a quick and easy access route both into and out of the city. On-ramps to highway 401 are conveniently located off Bayview Avenue and Yonge Street, south of Sheppard Avenue.

HISTORY:
The Windfields neighbourhood is located on the former site of Windfields Farm, after which this neighbourhood is named. Windfields Farm was the former estate of E.P. Taylor, the legendary Canadian entrepreneur and philanthropist.

Windfields Farm was founded in 1937. It was Taylor's wife Winnifred who came up with the "Windfields" name while the couple were out walking on their property during a windy autumn day. In its heyday Windfields Farm was famous as one of the top thoroughbred racing stables in North America. Its stable of horses included Northern Dancer, the first Canadian horse to win the Kentucky Derby.

In 1963, an increasingly private E.P. Taylor moved his main residence to Lyford Cay in the Bahamas. In 1968, he sold most of his Windfields estate to developers. At the same time he donated 30 acres of land for what is now Windfields Park.

E.P. Taylor's Windfields mansion, located at 2489 Bayview Avenue, was also gifted to the city by the Taylor family in 1968. This colonial-revival-style mansion is now the home of the Canadian Centre for Advanced Film Studies, which opened its doors in 1988. E.P. Taylor passed away at his home in Lyford Cay in 1989.

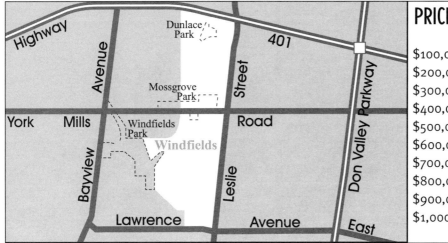

PRICE RANGE OF HOMES

$100,000 to $200,000	
$200,000 to $300,000	
$300,000 to $400,000	
$400,000 to $500,000	
$500,000 to $600,000	
$600,000 to $700,000	✓
$700,000 to $800,000	✓
$800,000 to $900,000	✓
$900,000 to $1,000,000	✓
$1,000,000 +	✓

OVERVIEW:
Windfields is a predominantly upper-middle-income neighbourhood that has traditionally been popular with young families. This neighbourhood has many fine attributes including well-treed streets, spacious family-sized houses, an abundance of parkland, a good selection of highly rated schools and convenient access to Highway 401.

Windfields includes a maze of curvilinear streets that twist and wind until they either abruptly end at a local park or ravine, or spill out onto one of the major arterial roads that skirt this neighbourhood. The net effect is that traffic is kept to a minimum and the streets have a suburban, child-friendly feel to them that suggests a game of road hockey could be played out reasonably uninterrupted by the intrusion of motorists.

HOMES:
Windfields's houses were built in the 1970s and 1980s. They range in size from modest split-level and ranch-style bungalows to 5,000-square-foot (or more) homes. Many of these houses feature decorative accents, including stone arch entranceways, exaggerated Tudor roof lines and half timbering, doric columns and even the occasional turret. Windfields also contains some of the most interesting and experimental modernist style housing in Toronto. These houses are characterized by asymmetrical designs, flat roofs, and large picture windows.

Windfields also contains entry level condominium townhouses on Leslie Street and a handful of high-rise apartment buildings on York Mills Road.

SHOPPING:
Leslie Street provides Windfields residents with a limited amount of street shopping and includes an interesting mix of restaurants, convenience stores, commercial businesses and professional offices.

The Bayview Village Shopping Centre at Bayview and Sheppard Avenues, York Mills Plaza located at Bayview Avenue and York Mills Road and the Don Mills Shopping Centre at Don Mills Road and Lawrence Avenue are all within a five-minute drive of this neighbourhood.

York Mills Road, east of Leslie Street, has a large shopping plaza anchored by a Longos supermarket. Fast food restaurants and national family-style restaurants proliferate along this stretch of York Mills.

RECREATION:
Windfields Park, which runs through the centre of this neighbourhood, contains a picturesque walking trail that follows the course of Wilket Creek. This nature park includes 200-year-old trees, a pond and marsh area, and many species of wild flowers, birds and other wildlife. This park is ideal for picnicking in the summer and cross-country skiing in the winter. Windfields Park can be accessed from York Mills Park situated at the southeast corner of York Mills Road and Bayview Avenue. This park is home to the York Mills Arena, which offers seasonal skating opportunities for all ages.

Edwards Gardens – one of Toronto's prettiest and most famous parks – forms the southern boundary of Windfields Park. Wilket Creek flows through the centre of this park, which is admired for its rockeries, perennial borders, rose gardens, and waterfalls. Edwards Gardens is also the home of the Civic Garden Centre, one of Canada's finest public gardening resource centres.

The Banbury Community Centre is located at 120 Banbury Road in a naturalized setting backing onto Windfields Park. This centre offers Banbury Kids and Banbury Fitness programs as well as dance, yoga, and arts programs. The Banbury Tennis Club is located behind the community centre.

SCHOOLS:
(P)   Dunlace, 20 Dunlace Dr., (416) 395-2370
(P)   Denlow, 50 Denlow Blvd., (416) 395-2300
(P)   Rippleton, 21 Rippleton Rd., (416) 395-2810
(P)   Windfields J.H.S., 375 Banbury Rd., (416) 395-3100
(PH) York Mills C.I., 490 York Mills Rd., (416) 395-3340
(C)   St. Bonaventure, 1340 Leslie St., (416) 393-5263
(PR) Crescent School, 2365 Bayview Ave., (416) 449-2556

TRANSPORTATION:
The York Mills Road bus connects passengers to the York Mills station on the Yonge-University-Spadina subway line. This station doubles as a Go Transit bus station and includes express bus service to the Pearson International Airport. Leslie Street and Lawrence Avenue also have limited bus service.

Motorists are approximately 25 minutes from downtown Toronto and five minutes from Highway 401, one of Toronto's main commuter highways.

HISTORY:

"York" makes reference to the former Town of York — the forerunner to modern day Toronto — and "Mills" refers to the grist and saw mills that churned in this valley from 1804 until 1926. During this period of industry York Mills was a busy place. It included a distillery, a tannery, a blacksmith shop, three churches, a school, a post office, a toll gate and the Jolly Miller Tavern, which is still standing today at 3885 Yonge Street. Another York Mills landmark is St. John's Anglican Church, which began in 1816. The original log church was replaced by the present-day white brick church in 1844. The church bells of St. John's still ring out over the valley every day at noon, cheerfully piercing the monotone roar of the traffic below on Yonge Street.

York Mills's transition from a rural hamlet to a residential neighbourhood began in the 1930s on the ridge of the hill near St. John's Church, and in the Hedgewood Road area south of York Mills Road. St. Andrew's College, a venerable boys private school, owned the land east of Old Yonge Street over to Bayview Avenue during the early 1920s before moving north to Aurora in 1924. The former St. Andrew's College grounds were then purchased by St. Andrew's Estates, which operated a championship golf course at this site until the 1950s when the club was sold to developers. St. Andrew's Park, Tournament Park and local street names, including Foursome and Lower Links, are reminders that this part of York Mills was once a golf course.

Ed. Note: E.P. Taylor, a giant in the archives of Canadian business, oversaw the development of York Mills Plaza in 1952 and was responsible for subdividing much of York Mills east of Bayview Avenue.

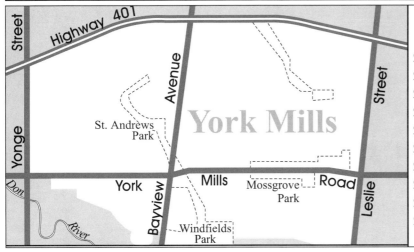

PRICE RANGE OF HOMES

$100,000	to	$200,000	
$200,000	to	$300,000	
$300,000	to	$400,000	
$400,000	to	$500,000	
$500,000	to	$600,000	
$600,000	to	$700,000	✓
$700,000	to	$800,000	✓
$800,000	to	$900,000	✓
$900,000	to	$1,000,000	✓
$1,000,000 +			✓

OVERVIEW:

York Mills is one of Toronto's most affluent neighbourhoods. Its mills are long gone, replaced by shining office towers and luxury condominiums. Its main arterial roadways, including Yonge Street and Bayview Avenue, which were once impassable by car, now serve as major roadways to and from the city core.

Yet, despite all these changes, York Mills has managed to maintain a peaceful tranquility and natural beauty that has helped make it one of Toronto's most desirable neighbourhoods.

HOMES:

York Mills is famous for its expansive properties, century-old trees and lush landscape. All of these trademarks form the perfect backdrop for the executive-style houses found in this neighbourhood.

The original York Mills housing stock dates from the late 1920s to the 1960s. There are pockets of Tudor-inspired manor houses, English-cottage-style designs, and contemporary designs. There are also large numbers of ranch-style bungalows and split-level houses which are gradually being replaced by large new custom-built homes.

York Mills also has its share of luxury condominium apartment buildings that have recently been built on the well-treed hills around the Yonge Street and York Mills Road intersection.

The Bayview Mills condominium townhouses located at the northeast corner of Bayview Avenue and York Mills Road provide entry-level prices into this exclusive neighbourhood.

Ed. Note: York Mills heritage properties include the charming red brick cottage located at 4111 Yonge Street. This house was built in the 1830s. From 1914 to 1941 it was the residence and studio of Canadian historical artist C.W. Jeffreys. The William and Elizabeth Harrison House at 111 Harrison Road was also built in the 1830s. The Harrisons were among the first settlers in the York Mills area.

SHOPPING:

York Mills Plaza is conveniently located at the southwest intersection of Bayview Avenue and York Mills Road. This popular outdoor shopping plaza is anchored by a large drug store and a supermarket. York Mills Plaza also features an international restaurant, a wine shop, small specialty retail stores and a fine selection of gourmet food shops.

The Bayview Village Shopping Centre is located at the northeast corner of Bayview and Sheppard avenues. This upscale shopping centre caters to the affluent York Mills market, with several designer clothing and accessory stores, gift shops, a magazine and book shop, jewellery stores, and an excellent selection of restaurants.

The York Mills Centre located on the northeast corner of Yonge Street and York Mills Road has about a dozen retail shops and professional services in addition to medical offices and a food court.

St. Andrew's Square on Tournament Drive is a handy little shopping plaza that features a quaint courtyard of stores including a bank, dry cleaners, a video store, a restaurant, a veterinary clinic and professional and medical offices.

RECREATION:

The multi-faceted York Mills Park, located at the southeast corner of York Mills Road and Bayview Avenue is well used in the summertime for a variety of pursuits. There is an outdoor pool for recreational swimming, a children's playground and a baseball diamond with recreational house leagues. This park also provides access to Windfields Park, which has an attractive footpath through a ravine valley that follows the winding course of Wilkett Creek, a tributary of the Don River.

York Mills Park is also the home of the York Mills Arena. This arena is busy year round with organized hockey leagues, as well as power and pleasure skating.

There are many parks located north of York Mills and west of Bayview Avenue. The largest of these neighbourhood parks is St. Andrew's Park, which features a mini-valley and lush greenspace that is popular for walks and light recreational pursuits. Tournament Park located next to St. Andrew's Square features tennis courts and an active tennis club program.

Golfers are very close to the scenic Don Valley Golf Course located west of Yonge Street and south of Highway 401.

SCHOOLS:

(P)	Harrison, 81 Harrison Rd., (416) 395-2530
(P)	Owen, 111 Owen Blvd., (416) 395-2740
(P)	St. Andrew's J.H.S., 131 Fenn Ave., (416) 395-3090
(PH)	York Mills C.I., 490 York Mills Rd., (416) 395-3340
(CH)	Loretto Abbey, 101 Mason Blvd., (416) 393-5510
(PR)	Crescent School, 2365 Bayview Ave., (416) 449-2556
(PR)	Toronto French School, 296 Lawrence Ave., E., (416) 484-6533
(PR)	Bayview Glen, 275 Duncan Mill Rd., (416) 443-1030
(PR)	Crestwood School, 411 Lawrence Ave., (416) 444-5858

TRANSPORTATION:

York Mills is extremely well served by public transit. Bus lines run on all of York Mills's main arterial roadways including York Mills Road, Yonge Street and Bayview Avenue. All of these routes connect to stations on the Yonge-University-Spadina subway line. The York Mills subway station located at the northeast corner of Yonge Street and York Mills Road also serves as a Go Transit station and provides express service to the Pearson International Airport.

Motorists can take Yonge Street directly downtown to Toronto's major business and entertainment districts. On-ramps to Highway 401 are quickly accessed from either Yonge Street or Bayview Avenue.

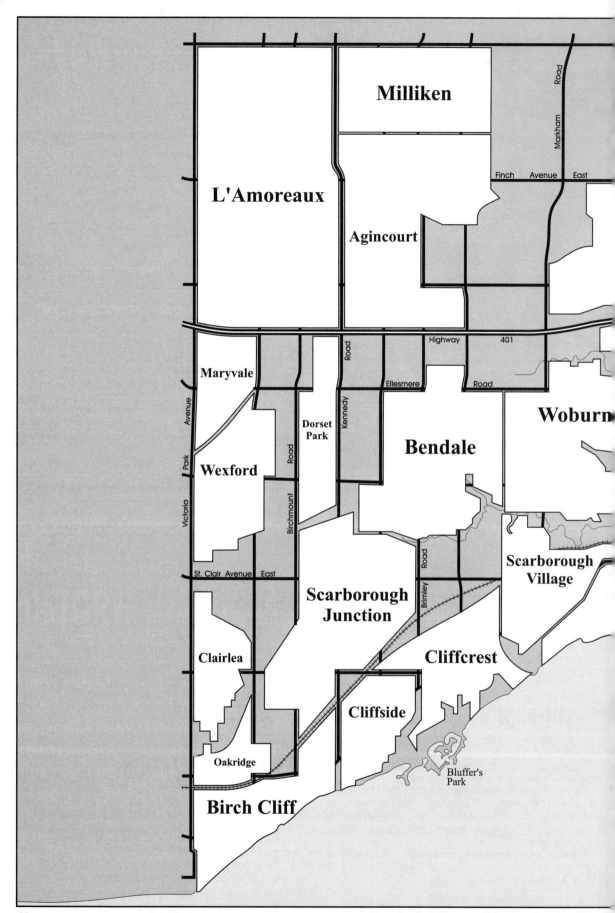

Milliken

L'Amoreaux

Agincourt

Markham Road

Finch Avenue East

Highway 401

Maryvale

Road

Dorset Park

Kennedy

Ellesmere Road

Woburn

Park Avenue

Bendale

Birchmount Road

Wexford

Victoria

St. Clair Avenue East

Road

Scarborough Village

Scarborough Junction

Brimley

Clairlea

Cliffcrest

Cliffside

Oakridge

Bluffer's Park

Birch Cliff

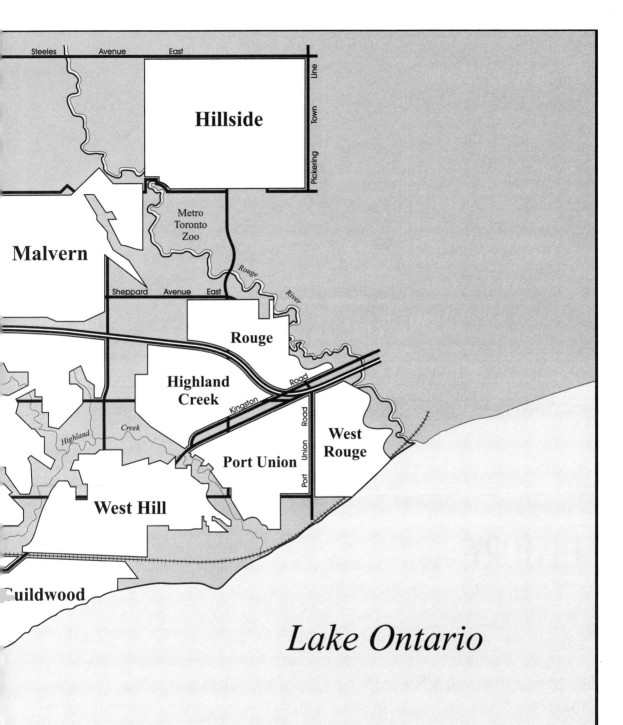

Hillside

Steeles Avenue East

Line

Town

Pickering

Metro
Toronto
Zoo

Malvern

Rouge

Sheppard Avenue East

River

Rouge

Highland
Creek

Road

Creek

Kingston

Highland

West
Rouge

Port Union Road

Port Union

West Hill

Guildwood

Lake Ontario

Scarborough

HISTORY: Agincourt began as a small village centred around the

Knox Presbyterian Church. The original frame Knox Church, built in 1846, was replaced in 1872 with the storybook brick church that still stands today on the the northwest corner of Sheppard and Midland avenues.

In 1858, the Agincourt post office opened in the general store of John Hill. Hill secured this post office with the help of a Quebec member of Parliament, who insisted the post office be given a French name. Hill's customers were mostly English and Scottish and so he chose the name "Agincourt" after the French town where King Henry V won his famous battle in 1415.

Agincourt began to boom in the late 1800s when two railway lines opened stations here. This led to the building of the first Agincourt subdivision in 1913, on the old Patterson farm north of Sheppard Avenue between Midland Avenue and the railway tracks. The most significant wave of development in Agincourt took place between 1945 and 1965, when most of the present-day neighbourhood was developed.

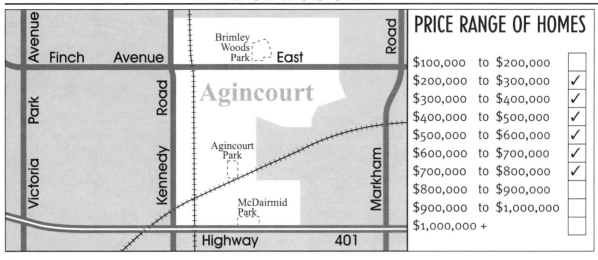

PRICE RANGE OF HOMES		
$100,000 to $200,000		
$200,000 to $300,000	✓	
$300,000 to $400,000	✓	
$400,000 to $500,000	✓	
$500,000 to $600,000	✓	
$600,000 to $700,000	✓	
$700,000 to $800,000	✓	
$800,000 to $900,000		
$900,000 to $1,000,000		
$1,000,000 +		

OVERVIEW:

Agincourt has one of the largest Asian communities in Toronto. This ethnic mix is visible in the signage of the many shopping malls that proliferate in this neighbourhood.

The East Indian and Indo-Pakistani community are also well established in Agincourt. The Woodside Cinemas, located at the Woodside Square Mall on McCowan Road, includes three theatres that screen East Indian, Indo-Pakistani and Chinese films, occasionally with English subtitles.

HOMES:

Old Agincourt, located between Midland Avenue and the railway tracks from Sheppard Avenue north to Lockie Avenue, contains one of the best collections of Edwardian-style houses in the City of Toronto. These charming brick houses were built in the 1910s and 1920s and include elegant front porches that are reminiscent of a bygone era.

The bulk of the houses in Agincourt were built in the 1940s, 1950s and 1960s. These houses include bungalows, split-level homes, detached two-storey homes and townhouses. These houses are situated on suburban-sized lots with private drives and attached garages.

SHOPPING:

Agincourt is filled with Asian shopping malls and shopping plazas, particularly along Sheppard Avenue and on McCowan Road north of Finch Avenue. The mix of shopping in these plazas includes Asian supermarkets, fruit stores, seafood restaurants, herbal stores, vegetarian shops, beauty salons, banks and bakeries.

The largest shopping mall in this neighbourhood is the Agincourt Mall on Sheppard Avenue. This mall is anchored by both a Wal-Mart department store and a Loblaws supermarket, and features mostly national retailers and chain stores.

Woodside Square, located at the northwest corner of Finch Avenue and McCowan Road, is a medium-sized indoor shopping mall anchored by discount department stores and a supermarket. This mall features a good mix of fashion, gift, home entertainment and food stores. There is also a large Chinese book store and a herbal and health food store.

RECREATION:

The Agincourt Community Centre, located at 31 Glen Watford Drive, offers indoor swimming programs, fitness classes and recreational skating. The Agincourt Lawn Bowling Club operates out of the park adjacent to the community centre.

The Agincourt Gardening Club meets regularly at the Christian Centre of Knox United Church, 2575 Midland Avenue. This gardening club recently erected a plaque at the Donalda Park on Donalda Drive commemorating the three varieties of lilacs developed in Agincourt. These species include the "Agincourt beauty," which is reputed to have the largest lilac flower in the world.

Brimley Woods Park, located just north of Finch Avenue, is renowned for its brilliant display of trillium flowers that bloom in early May. This park features a short, wood-chip nature trail underneath a tall canopy of maple trees. A chorus of bird calls serenades hikers through this beautiful trail.

The Woodside Square shopping centre, located at Finch Avenue and McCowan Road, features a public library that offers year-round programming for adults as well as children.

SCHOOLS:

(P) Agincourt Jr., 29 Lockie Ave., (416) 396-6010
(P) Alexmuir Jr., 95 Alexmuir Blvd., (416) 396-6025
(P) A.S Taylor Jr., 20 Placentia Blvd., (416) 396-6035
(P) Brimwood Blvd. Jr., 151 Brimwood Blvd., (416) 396-6085
(P) C.D. Farquharson, 1965 Brimley Rd., (416) 396-6110
(P) Chartland Jr., 109 Chartland Blvd., (416) 396-6140
(P) Iroquois Jr., 90 Ionview Rd., (416) 396-6355
(P) Henry Kelsey Sr., 1200 Huntingwood Dr., (416) 396-6315
(P) Sir Alexander Mackenzie Sr., 33 Heather Rd., (416) 396-6570
(PH) Agincourt C.I., 2621 Midland Ave., (416) 396-6675
(PH) Sir William Osler, 1050 Huntingwood Dr., (416) 396-6830
(C) Our Lady of Grace, 121 Brimwood Blvd., (416) 393-5372
(C) St. Bartholomew, 51 Heather Rd., (416) 393-5334
(C) Franciss Libermann, 4640 Finch Ave., (416) 393-5224

TRANSPORTATION:

Agincourt has its own Go Transit station on the north side of Sheppard Avenue, just east of Kennedy Road. This station provides commuters with morning train service to Union Station in downtown Toronto. This train returns to Agincourt in the late afternoon from Union Station.

Toronto Transit bus lines on Finch and Sheppard Avenues connect passengers to the Yonge-University-Spadina subway line. Bus services on Kennedy, Brimley, McCowan, Bellamy and Markham roads, as well as Midland Avenue, link passengers to stations on the Bloor-Danforth subway line.

HISTORY:
Bendale was settled in 1796 by David and Mary Thompson, who were the first Europeans to reside in the former Township of Scarborough. David Thompson's brothers, Andrew and Archibald, also settled nearby. Thompson Memorial Park is named in honour of this pioneer family.

Historical landmarks at Thompson Memorial Park include Springfield House, built in 1840 by Andrew Thompson's son James, and the St. Andrew's Presbyterian Church, built in 1849 on land donated by David Thompson. For directions to these historical sites visit the Scarborough Historical Museum located just inside the entrance to this park, off Brimley Road.

Bendale was originally known as "Benlomond," which was the name given to the local post office in 1878. However, the Benlomond name had already been in use elsewhere, and in 1881 this community was renamed Bendale. When the development of the present-day neighbourhood took place in the 1950s the Bendale name was adopted by Bendale Public School, Bendale Park and Bendale Boulevard.

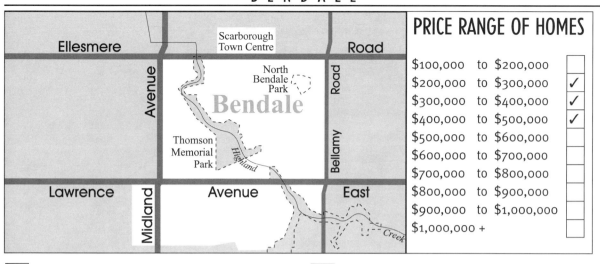

PRICE RANGE OF HOMES

$100,000	to	$200,000	
$200,000	to	$300,000	✓
$300,000	to	$400,000	✓
$400,000	to	$500,000	✓
$500,000	to	$600,000	
$600,000	to	$700,000	
$700,000	to	$800,000	
$800,000	to	$900,000	
$900,000	to	$1,000,000	
$1,000,000 +			

OVERVIEW:
Bendale is a culturally diverse, middle-income neighbourhood that is conveniently located near TTC and Go Transit lines. Neighbourhood landmarks include Thompson Memorial Park, Scarborough Town Shopping Centre, the Scarborough Civic Centre and Scarborough General Hospital.

HOMES:
Bendale's housing stock consists mostly of bungalows and split-level brick houses built in the 1950s and 1960s. These houses are situated on generous-sized lots with private driveways and either a garage or a carport. The houses here are well maintained and the lots are well treed, providing for a pleasing streetscape.

SHOPPING:
The Scarborough Town Shopping Centre, located off McCowan Road north of Ellesmere Road, is one of Toronto's largest shopping centres with over 200 shops and restaurants.

The busy shopping corridor along Lawrence Avenue includes a discount department store, a large supermarket, a home-care centre, a dollar store, fast food restaurants, an Asian supermarket, new car dealerships, a bingo club and an assortment of small shopping plazas.

Danforth Road south of Lawrence Avenue is highlighted by a country farm market, a large drug store, convenience stores and restaurants. The Birkdale Plaza, located off Ellesmere Road, features an East Indian restaurant, a grocery store, a clothing store and a video store.

RECREATION:
The Thompson Memorial Park, situated off Brimley Road, is the home of the Scarborough Historical Museum. This is one of Toronto's largest and most beautiful parks and has many fine picnic spots. There is also a children's zoo. Recreational facilities at this park include a paved trail, a sports field, tennis courts, a baseball diamond, a wading pool, a children's playground and a snack bar. Wintertime activities at Thompson Memorial Park include cross-country skiing, skating and tobogganing.

The Birkdale Community Centre, located at 1299 Ellesmere Road, offers neighbourhood meeting rooms. The adjacent park contains a paved recreation trail that connects with the Thompson Memorial Park.

SCHOOLS:
(P)   Bendale Jr., 61 Benshire Dr., (416) 396-6045
(P)   North Bendale Jr., 29 Aveline Cres., (416) 396-6495
(P)   Charles Gordon Sr., 25 Marcos Boulevard, (416) 396-6130
(P)   Donwood Park Jr., 61 Dorcot Ave., (416) 396-6201
(P)   Edgewood, 230 Birkdale Rd., (416) 396-6215
(P)   Hunters Glen Jr., 16 Haileybury Dr., (416) 396-6430
(P)   St. Andrews Jr., 60 Brimorton Dr., (416) 396-6545
(PH) Bendale P.T.I, 1555 Midland Ave., (416) 396-6695
(PH) David and Mary Thompson C.I., 2740 Lawrence Ave.,W. (416) 396-5525
(C)   St. Victor, 20 Bernadine St., (416) 393-5338

TRANSPORTATION:
Bus routes along Midland Avenue and McCowan Road connect passengers to stations on the Bloor-Danforth subway line. The Lawrence Avenue and Ellesmere Road buses provide connecting routes to the Yonge-University-Spadina subway line.

Motorists are approximately five minutes from the McCowan Road on-ramp to Highway 401.

HISTORY: The Birch Cliff area began to be developed in 1895, when
the Toronto Hunt Club relocated here. Fox Hunts were held at this club up
until the 1930s, when golf became the members' preferred activity. In the
late 1890s and early 1900s many Toronto residents built summer cottages
on the property adjacent to the Toronto Hunt Club. These cottagers were
attracted to the area by the magnificent Scarborough Bluffs.

The crest of the Scarborough Bluffs was lined with birch trees, which
prompted a cottager by the name of John Stark to name his cottage Birch
Cliff. The Birch Cliff name was adopted by the local post office, which
opened in 1907 in Arthur Mitchell's grocery store. This store formerly stood
at the corner of Kingston Road and Birchmount Avenue.

Birch Cliff emerged as a year-round residential community beginning in
the 1910s and 1920s. From 1922 to 1947, it held the distinction of being the
meeting place of the Scarborough Municipal Council. Birch Cliff's residential
development was completed shortly after the Second World War.

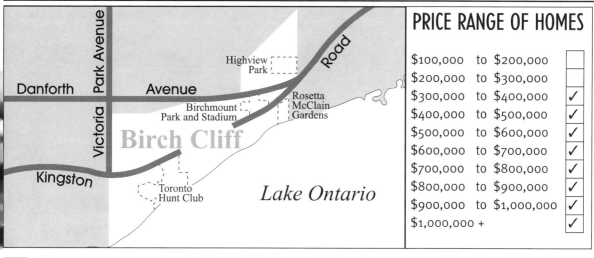

PRICE RANGE OF HOMES

$100,000	to $200,000	
$200,000	to $300,000	
$300,000	to $400,000	✓
$400,000	to $500,000	✓
$500,000	to $600,000	✓
$600,000	to $700,000	✓
$700,000	to $800,000	✓
$800,000	to $900,000	✓
$900,000	to $1,000,000	✓
$1,000,000 +		✓

OVERVIEW:

Birch Cliff is an established, family-oriented neighbourhood set amidst the idyllic backdrop of the Scarborough Bluffs and Lake Ontario. Drawing attention away from the lake is Kingston Road, a major thoroughfare that arches its way through the centre of this neighbourhood. The annual Birch Cliff community parade held in May takes place along Kingston Road.

Two distinct residential pockets within the greater Birch Cliff area include the exclusive Fallingbrook community, located west of the Toronto Hunt Club to the south of Kingston Road, and the Birch Cliff Heights community, situated on the north side of Kingston Road, between Birchmount and Kennedy roads.

HOMES:

Birch Cliff contains an excellent selection of bungalows, 1.5-storey houses and detached, two-storey homes that feature Tudor, Edwardian and Cape Cod designs. This neighbourhood's original housing stock dates from the 1910s all the way up to the 1950s. Birch Cliff also contains a fairly large number of homes built in the 1980s and 1990s.

The highly sought-after Fallingbrook district is known for its lush ravine topography and splendid manor houses that overlook Lake Ontario. Fallingbrook also contains a large number of houses that back onto the picturesque grounds of the Toronto Hunt Club.

SHOPPING:

The retail corridor along Kingston Road contains a mix of convenience-type stores, neighbourhood bars and restaurants, and professional and medical offices. Kingston Road west of the Toronto Hunt Club is more gentrified and includes an art gallery, a doggie daycare and apparel store, a party and play centre for children, and upscale restaurants and cafés. The artsy tone of this shopping district continues west past Victoria Park Avenue and into the Upper Beach neighbourhood.

RECREATION:

The Birchmount Community Centre, Birchmount Stadium, Birchmount Leisure Pool and Scarborough Gardens arena, located at Kingston and Birchmount roads, make up one of Toronto's largest multi-purpose recreational facilities. Birchmount Park itself contains baseball diamonds and sports fields while Birchmount Stadium is best known as the home of the Robbie International Soccer Tournament. The Scarborough Gardens indoor ice arena situated adjacent to Birchmount Stadium is the home of the Scarborough Wexford Raiders Jr. A hockey club.

The Birchmount Community Centre is located across from the arena. This centre offers a full range of adult, seniors' and children's programming. This modern community centre also features a large indoor pool that is used for recreational swims and lessons.

The Taylor Memorial Branch Toronto Public Library located at 1440 Kingston Road offers children's programming. The R.C. Harris Filtration Plant situated at the foot of Victoria Park Avenue is Toronto's largest water filtration plant. This art deco edifice has been declared a National Historic Civil Engineering Site. Free guided tours of this Toronto landmark are available to the public.

SCHOOLS:

(P)   Birch Cliff, 1650 Kingston Rd., (416) 396-6060
(P)   Birch Cliff Heights, 120 Highview Ave., (416) 396-6065
(P)   Blantyre, 290 Blantyre Ave., (416) 396-6070
(P)   Courcelette, 100 Fallingbrook Rd., (416) 396-6185
(P)   Birchmount Park C.I., 3663 Danforth Rd.,
       (416) 396-6704
(CH) Neil McNeil, 127 Victoria Park Ave., (416) 393-5502

TRANSPORTATION:

The Danforth Road bus connects passengers to stations on the Bloor-Danforth subway line. The Danforth Go Train station situated on Main Street shuttles commuters to Toronto's Union Station in approximately 10 minutes.

Motorists can access downtown Toronto in 15 minutes via Kingston Road, which links up with the Gardiner Expressway, Lakeshore Boulevard, and the Don Valley Parkway.

HISTORY:

Clairlea was formerly part of a pioneer crossroads village known as "Moffat's Corners." Moffat's Corners is best remembered for the Strangford post office, which opened in 1863. This post office was situated at the present-day intersection of St. Clair and Victoria Park avenues. The Strangford name given to the post office was probably taken from a small town in Northern Ireland, as most of this area's first settlers were of Irish descent.

When the Strangford post office closed in 1873, Moffat's Corners became part of the greater Scarborough Junction community. In the early 1900s, the children in this area attended the Scarborough Junction school, which was located at Kennedy and Danforth Roads.

The present-day neighbourhood began to take shape in the 1950s, when furrowed farm fields were replaced by rows of houses. This neighbourhood takes its name from the Clairlea Public School which opened in 1951.

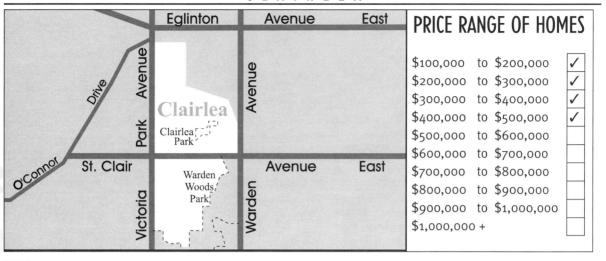

PRICE RANGE OF HOMES	
$100,000 to $200,000	✓
$200,000 to $300,000	✓
$300,000 to $400,000	✓
$400,000 to $500,000	✓
$500,000 to $600,000	
$600,000 to $700,000	
$700,000 to $800,000	
$800,000 to $900,000	
$900,000 to $1,000,000	
$1,000,000 +	

OVERVIEW:

Clairlea is a quiet, middle-income neighbourhood that features tree-lined streets and affordable homes. There is plenty of shopping on Warden, Victoria Park and Eglinton avenues. This is an ideal neighbourhood for commuters, as it is well served by public transit and is also within close proximity to the Don Valley Parkway.

Clairlea's major landmark is Warden Woods, a deep ravine valley that spans the southeast perimeter of this neighbourhood. The Warden Woods Ravine parkland has a paved trail which offers Clairlea residents a bit of nature close to home.

HOMES:

Clairlea's original housing stock dates from the 1940s and 1950s. The style of houses found here includes small bungalows, modest 1.5-storey houses, and two-storey detached houses.

The streets north of St. Clair have a curvilinear street pattern and the houses are fairly uniform in style. The residential pocket south of St. Clair features a steep-hill topography and smaller, older houses.

The new Warden Woods Ravine subdivision situated south off St. Clair Avenue offers a collection of new townhouses, semi-detached and detached, family-style houses.

SHOPPING:

The Warden Power Centre located at the northeast corner of St.Clair and Warden avenues is a modern day shopping centre that contains big box retail chain stores including Winners, Future Shop, and Hy & Zels.

Victoria Park contains a limited amount of shops, and a good variety of restaurants including Chinese, Mediterranean, Caribbean and East and West Indian foods.

RECREATION:

Warden Woods Park is a heavily wooded ravine valley containing a paved trail frequented by nature enthusiasts, joggers and cyclists. Access points to this park are located off St. Clair and Pharmacy avenues. To the south of Warden Woods Park is Byng Park and the West Scarborough N.C.C., which features a bocce club and horseshoe pits.

The Detonia Park Golf Course, located on the east side of Victoria Park Avenue, just north of Danforth Avenue, is a challenging scenic course that is ideal for beginners and advanced players looking to practice their short game.

The Warden Woods Power Centre situated off Warden Avenue has a Cineplex movie theatre with eight screens that feature all the latest movie releases.

SCHOOLS:

(P) Clairlea, 25 Rosalind Cres., (416) 396-6165
(P) Regent Heights Jr., 555 Pharmacy Ave., (416) 396-6535
(PH) W.A. Porter C.I., 40 Fairfax Cres., (416) 396-3365
(C) Our Lady of Fatima, 3176 St. Clair Ave. E., (416) 393-5252

TRANSPORTATION:

Bus routes along Warden, Pharmacy, Victoria Park and St. Clair avenues connect passengers to stations on the Bloor-Danforth subway line.

Motorists are just a few minutes from the Don Valley Parkway on-ramp, situated off Eglinton Avenue, west of Victoria Park.

HISTORY: The Cliffcrest neighbourhood was named in the 1960s by

city planners, who were making obvious reference to the Scarborough Bluffs land formation that skirts the southern boundary of this neighbourhood. The Scarborough Bluffs are a natural wonder that was formed following the last ice age, some 12,000 years ago. Archaeological evidence gathered in this area during the early 1900s shows that the First Nations people established settlements along the Scarborough Bluffs dating back 10,000 years, making this one of the oldest inhabited sites in Toronto.

The Toronto and York Radial Railway established the 60-acre Scarborough Heights Park on the crest of the Bluffs in 1912. This park was created for business purposes by the railway in order to attract more passengers to their line. Scarborough Heights Park closed in 1929 and the streetcar line was discontinued in 1936. Following the dismantling of the streetcar Kingston Road was widened to cater to the automobile age, which ultimately led to the residential development of Cliffcrest in the 1940s and 1950s.

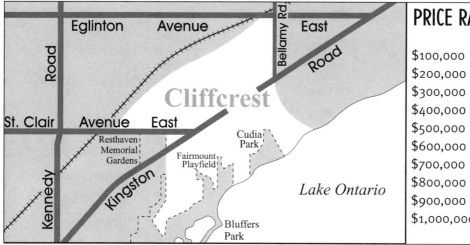

PRICE RANGE OF HOMES

$100,000	to $200,000	
$200,000	to $300,000	✓
$300,000	to $400,000	✓
$400,000	to $500,000	✓
$500,000	to $600,000	✓
$600,000	to $700,000	✓
$700,000	to $800,000	✓
$800,000	to $900,000	✓
$900,000	to $1,000,000	✓
$1,000,000 +		

OVERVIEW:

Cliffcrest is a family-oriented community that looks and feels more like cottage country than a big-city neighbourhood. The lushness and natural beauty of this area emanates from the spectacular Scarborough Bluffs, whose towering sandy cliffs peer out over the Lake Ontario shoreline.

HOMES:

Cliffcrest's bungalows, 1.5-storey houses, semi-detached homes and detached, two-storey houses were built in the late 1940s and the 1950s. There are also a number of newer, custom-built houses found throughout this neighbourhood.

The residential pocket south of Kingston Road is filled with cosy frame cottages that provide the ambience of a cottage community. Some of these houses offer beautiful views of Lake Ontario.

SHOPPING:

The retail shopping corridor situated along Kingston Road offers an interesting mix of small shopping plazas and restaurants, as well as auto service centres, motels, a Canadian Tire store and a large garden centre. Cliffcrest Plaza is anchored by a large supermarket and a discount department store. This plaza includes a video store, banks, a gift store, ice cream shops, restaurants, and professional and medical offices.

The retail strip along Eglinton Avenue contains a mix of neighbourhood plazas, a tropical food store, a fishing supplies store, home improvement stores, auto service centres and food markets.

RECREATION:

Bluffers Park, located along the Lake Ontario shoreline, features a large, sandy beach and many fine picnic areas. This lakeside park also features a marina, yacht clubs, and a popular waterfront restaurant. Bluffers Park can be accessed by car off Brimley Road South.

Tots Park, located at the south end of this neighbourhood features a children's playground and a baseball diamond. Halbert Park, in the north end of Cliffcrest has a wading pool and an outdoor pool. The R.H. King Academy has an indoor pool that is open to the public at designated times for recreational and instructional swims.

SCHOOLS:

(P)	Anson Park, 30 MacDuff Cres., (416) 396-6030
(P)	Bliss Carman Sr., 10 Bellamy Rd., South., (416) 396-6075
(P)	Fairmount Jr., 31 Sloley Rd., (416) 396-6240
(P)	H.A. Halbert Jr., 31 McCowan Rd., (416) 396-6300
(PH)	R.H. King Academy, 3800 St. Clair Ave., E., (416) 396-5550
(C)	St. Theresa Shrine, 2665 Kingston Rd., (416) 393-5248
(CH)	Cardinal Newman, 2675 Kingston Rd., (416) 393-5519

TRANSPORTATION:

Bus services along Cliffcrest's main streets connect passengers to either the Kennedy station on the TTC subway line or the Scarborough Go Transit Train station situated off St. Clair Avenue.

Motorists are approximately 25 minutes from downtown Toronto via Kingston Road.

HISTORY: Cliffside was formerly known as "Mortlake," in reference to
an English hamlet outside London. The Mortlake name came into use with
the opening of a post office in the Halfway House Hotel, which was situated
on Kingston Road. This hotel was moved in 1962, and now assumes a prominent role in Toronto's historic Black Creek Pioneer Village, located at 1000
Murray Ross Parkway.

An enduring Cliffside landmark is the St. Augustine Seminary, which
opened in 1910. St. Augustine was the first Canadian seminary for the
training of English-speaking clergy. This large edifice, with its beaux-arts-
style architecture and soaring dome, is a powerful visual landmark on
Kingston Road.

In the early 1900s, the land west of the St. Augustine Seminary began to
evolve as a summer cottage community. The first year-round residences were
built in the 1920s at the south end of Chine Drive. These charming arts-and-
crafts style houses set the tone for the present-day neighbourhood.

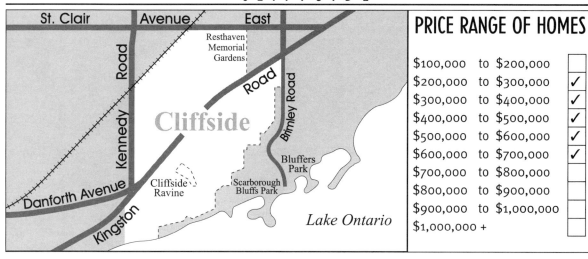

PRICE RANGE OF HOMES

$100,000	to $200,000	
$200,000	to $300,000	✓
$300,000	to $400,000	✓
$400,000	to $500,000	✓
$500,000	to $600,000	✓
$600,000	to $700,000	✓
$700,000	to $800,000	
$800,000	to $900,000	
$900,000	to $1,000,000	
$1,000,000 +		

OVERVIEW:

Cliffside is an established, family-oriented neighbourhood located along Toronto's eastern beaches, next to the majestic Scarborough Bluffs. Cliffside has many fine attributes including an appealing mix of older-style houses, tree-line streets, a vibrant shopping district located along Kingston Road, and beautiful waterfront parks.

The major landmark in this neighbourhood is the St. Augustine Seminary, whose soaring dome can easily be seen looking south towards the lake from Kingston Road. The St. Augustine Seminary has been training Roman Catholic priests since 1910.

HOMES:

Cliffside houses were built mostly in the 1920s, 1930s and 1940s. These houses include an eclectic mix of architectural styles including Tudor-, Cape Cod-, Edwardian-, craftsman-style bungalows and newer, contemporary homes.

Chine Drive south of Kingston Road is known for its fine collection of Tudor- and Elizabethan-style houses that are set back from the road in a forest-like setting. Fishleigh Drive, located at the south end of this neighbourhood, offers homeowners magnificent views of Lake Ontario.

SHOPPING:

The Cliffside Village shopping district, located along Kingston Road, is decorated with a series of colourful wall murals that depict the history of this community. The wide boulevard in the centre of Kingston Road is lined with flags and trees that add to the ambience of this busy neighbourhood shopping district.

Cliffside Village features a myriad of shops, including home improvement stores, household convenience stores, a variety of restaurants, and a good mix of small, independent retailers and company-owned stores.

RECREATION:

Scarborough Bluffs Park, located off Undercliff Drive, is a scenic lakefront park that offers many excellent picnic spots with panoramic views of Lake Ontario. The recreational facilities at this park include four tennis courts and a children's playground.

The Rosetta McClain Gardens, located south of Kingston Road off Glen Everest Road, features a pathway through a herb and scented garden, a perennial garden and a rose garden. This park is known for its spectacular views of Lake Ontario.

SCHOOLS:

(P)   Chine Drive, 51 Chine Dr., (416) 396-6155
(P)   Cliffside, 27 East Haven Dr., (416) 396-6170
(P)   John A. Leslie, 459 Midland Ave., (416) 396-6380
(P)   Norman Cook Jr., 725 Danforth Rd., (416) 396-6485
(PH) R.H. King Academy, 3800 St. Clair Ave., E., (416) 396-5550
(PH) Cardinal Newman, 2675 Kingston Rd., (416) 393-5519

TRANSPORTATION:

Toronto Transit bus service along St. Clair Avenue and Kennedy Road connects passengers to stations on the Bloor-Danforth subway line. The Scarborough Go Train station, located on St. Clair Avenue at Midland Avenue, connects passengers to downtown Toronto's Union Station in approximately 20 minutes.

Motorists can travel to downtown Toronto via Kingston Road and the Gardiner Expressway in approximately 20 minutes.

HISTORY:
Dorset Park was originally part of the Village of Ellesmere, a small farming hamlet that was centred around the intersection of Kennedy and Ellesmere roads during the 1800s. Ellesmere was named after the Village of Ellesmere, in England.

In the early 1900s, the focal point of this community was the Ellesmere Arena. This venue served as the home of the Maple Leaf Curling Club and the Ellesmere Maple Leaf Band, the latter of which performed at church garden parties, fall fairs and other public functions. Ellesmere was particularly well known for its sports clubs including the Maple Leaf Football Team that won the Ontario Championships in 1890.

In the early 1950s, Ellesmere's market gardens and dairy farms gave way to the present-day Dorset Park subdivision. Like Ellesmere, the Dorset Park neighbourhood is also named after a small village in England.

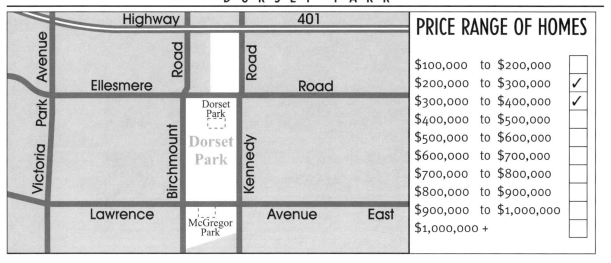

PRICE RANGE OF HOMES		
$100,000	to $200,000	
$200,000	to $300,000	✓
$300,000	to $400,000	✓
$400,000	to $500,000	
$500,000	to $600,000	
$600,000	to $700,000	
$700,000	to $800,000	
$800,000	to $900,000	
$900,000	to $1,000,000	
$1,000,000 +		

OVERVIEW:

Dorset Park is a middle-income family oriented neighbourhood comprised of people from a wide range of cultural backgrounds. This neighbourhood is currently in transition as a new generation of young families with children are gradually replacing the aging first-generation Dorset Park homeowners.

The Dorset Park neighbourhood is bound on the north by Highway 401 and on the east and west by a commercial corridor and light industry. Large companies like Kraft Foods and Laura Secord are based on the periphery of Dorset Park, off Birchmount Road.

HOMES:

Dorset Park's housing stock was built in the 1950s. These houses include well-kept bungalows, cosy 1.5-storey houses, and a few semi-detached homes.

The northeast corner of Birchmount and Ellesmere Roads is a modern subdivision community consisting of detached and semi-detached homes.

SHOPPING:

Kennedy Road is a regional shopping destination that is filled with home furniture and appliance stores, electronics and computer shops, and discount department stores. There are also many restaurants located along this street. The international mix of cuisines found here includes Chinese, Greek and Japanese restaurants.

A recent addition to Kennedy Road is Kennedy Commons, located just south of Highway 401 on the east side of Kennedy Road. This gigantic shopping area features a Rona home improvement store that encompasses 80,000 square feet of retail space. A Sears Furniture and Appliance store, the Brick and Dominion Supermarket are some of the other big name retailers in this shopping complex.

The neighbourhood-oriented Courtesy Plaza on Birchmount Road reflects the ethnic mix of this neighbourhood with its East and West Indian food market and family style restaurant.

RECREATION:

The Dorset public park located of Lewiston Road includes a baseball diamond and a children's playground. McGregor Park, situated off Lawrence Avenue East, is the largest recreational facility in this neighbourhood. It is the home of the McGregor Park Public Library and the McGregor Park Community Centre, which includes an outdoor pool and an indoor ice arena. This park also offers three tennis courts, a baseball diamond, sports fields and a children's playground.

SCHOOLS:

(P)	Dorset Park Jr., 28 Blaisdale,	(416) 396-6205
(P)	General Crerar, 30 McGregor Rd.,	(416) 396-6255
(P)	Ellesmere-Statton, 739 Ellesmere Rd.,	(416) 396-6225
(P)	Glamorgan Jr., 51 Antrim Cres.,	(416) 396-6275
(P)	Manhattan Park Jr., 90 Manhattan Dr.,	(416) 396-6445
(PH)	Winston Churchill C.I., 2239 Lawrence Ave. E.,	(416) 396-6883
(C)	St.Lawrence, 2216 Lawrence Ave., E.,	(416) 393-5264

TRANSPORTATION:

The Birchmount and Kennedy roads buses provide passengers with connecting routes to the Lawrence East station on the Scarborough Rapid Transit line. Scarborough Rapid Transit links up with the Bloor-Danforth subway line.

Motorists are just a few minutes from the Kennedy Road on-ramp to Highway 401, which provides commuters with access to most of Toronto's major highways.

HISTORY:

The history of Guildwood revolves around The Guild Inn, which was founded in 1932 by Rosa and Spencer Clark as a retreat for artists and craftsmen. "The Guild of All Arts," as it was then known, featured workshops and studios in a picturesque setting atop the Scarborough Bluffs.

During the Second World War, The Guild Inn was used as an official naval base called HMCS Bytown II, and then later as a specialized military hospital known as Scarborough Hall. After the war, The Guild Inn was returned to the Clarks and its popularity rose to new heights.

In the 1950s rising taxes forced the Clarks to sell 400 acres of their property to the developers who built the present-day Guildwood neighbourhood. In 1978 the Metropolitan Toronto and Region Conservation Authority purchased the remainder of the Guild Inn estate, thus preserving its beauty for future generations to explore and enjoy.

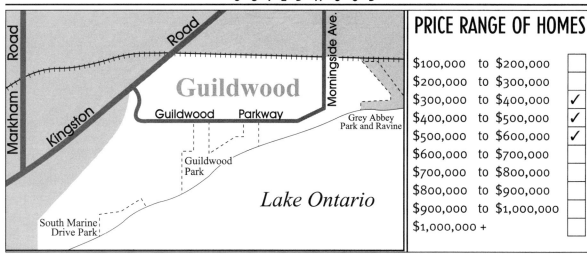

PRICE RANGE OF HOMES

$100,000 to $200,000		
$200,000 to $300,000		
$300,000 to $400,000	✓
$400,000 to $500,000	✓
$500,000 to $600,000	✓
$600,000 to $700,000	
$700,000 to $800,000	
$800,000 to $900,000	
$900,000 to $1,000,000	
$1,000,000 +	

OVERVIEW:

Guildwood is one of Toronto's most beautiful and exclusive neighbourhoods. The main entrance to the Guildwood neighbourhood is marked by a formal stone pillar and cast iron gateway, situated at Kingston Road and Guildwood Parkway.

The major landmark in this neighbourhood is the historic Guild Inn, located at 201 Guildwood Parkway. The Guild Inn is situated on 90 acres of property overlooking the Scarborough Bluffs. Tourists and local residents come to the Guild Inn to enjoy its historic architectural walking tour and rustic woodland nature trail.

Guildwood has an active community association that produces its own newsletter as well as sponsoring various neighbourhood events. One of these events is Guildwood Day, which is held in June and features a pancake breakfast, games, races, crafts, a parade along Guildwood Parkway and an evening barbecue.

HOMES:

Guildwood features an excellent mix of houses, including bungalows, split-level and detached two-storey homes built in the 1950s and 1960s, and newer, custom-designed homes . Many Guildwood houses feature front porches that look out onto the tree-lined streets and lush gardens that are trademarks of this neighbourhood. Also noteworthy are the many houses situated on the south side of Guildwood Parkway that command a spectacular view of Lake Ontario.

The stretch of Guildwood Parkway west of Livingston Road contains a mix of townhouses, multiplex dwellings, and low-rise apartment buildings. There is also a luxury condominium apartment building just south of Kingston Road, at the entrance gates to this neighbourhood.

SHOPPING:

The Guildwood Shopping Plaza, located at the southeast corner of Guildwood Parkway and Livingston Road, serves the immediate needs of the residents of this community. This shopping plaza has an upscale tone and friendly neighbourhood appeal. The mix of stores here includes a large supermarket, a pharmacy, a barber shop, a bakery, a bank, a beauty salon, a travel agency, a postal outlet, a veterinarian clinic, and professional and medical offices. The Guildwood Public Library is also located at this shopping plaza.

RECREATION:

The Guild Inn at Guildwood Park is a former artists' colony that now serves as an inn with a restaurant, and banquet and conference facilities. The picturesque Guild Inn gardens are decorated with sculptures and architectural remnants from Toronto's past. A promenade on these grounds leads to the Scarborough Bluffs, overlooking Lake Ontario. The Guildwood Park also features nature trails that wind their way through a majestic century old Carolinian forest.

SCHOOLS:

(P)   Guildwood, 225 Livingston Rd., (416) 396-6295
(P)   Jack Miner Sr., 405 Guildwood Pkwy., (416) 396-6375
(P)   Poplar Rd., Jr., 66 Dearham Wood., (416) 396-6525
(PH) Sir Wilfred Laurier C.I., 145 Guildwood Pkwy., (416) 396-6820

TRANSPORTATION:

Guildwood has its own Go Train station which is part of a Lakeshore service that links up with Union Station in downtown Toronto. Guildwood residents are also served by bus routes on Guildwood Parkway and on Kingston Road.

Motorists can get to downtown Toronto in approximately 25 minutes via Kingston Road.

HISTORY: In the 1850s, Highland Creek was the largest residential and business centre in the former Township of Scarborough. Richard Schofield, in *Scarborough Then and Now,* explains, "The combination of the Kingston Road, the Old Danforth Road and the Highland Creek coming together in one location encouraged the village's rapid growth in the early 19th century."

Highland Creek was officially recognized as a community in 1852, when it was granted its own post office. Highland Creek also had its own school, Presbyterian, Catholic, and Methodist churches, and a number of general stores, blacksmith shops and hotels that catered to the travellers along Kingston Road. Highland Creek remained a rural farming community right up until the 1950s, when the present-day neighbourhood was developed.

Highland Creek's historical landmarks include the W.J. Morrish General Store, circa 1891, situated on Old Kingston Road; the third Highland Creek Public School, circa 1918, located on Military Trail; and the Miller Lash/McLean Estate, circa 1914, which is situated on the University of Toronto's Scarborough College campus.

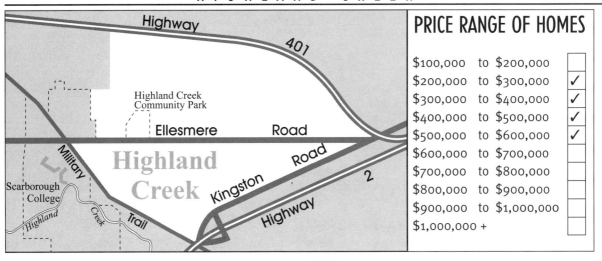

PRICE RANGE OF HOMES

$100,000 to $200,000	
$200,000 to $300,000	✓
$300,000 to $400,000	✓
$400,000 to $500,000	✓
$500,000 to $600,000	✓
$600,000 to $700,000	
$700,000 to $800,000	
$800,000 to $900,000	
$900,000 to $1,000,000	
$1,000,000 +	

OVERVIEW:

This neighbourhood has a small-town feel that emanates from its main street shopping district situated along Old Kingston Road. Here you will find a historic cemetery that dates back to around 1800, and colourful wall murals that depict life from Highland Creek's pioneer days.

Highland Creek residents celebrate the history of their neighbourhood every year on Highland Creek Heritage Day. This event is highlighted by a giant parade that takes place along Old Kingston Road. This parade features antique cars, marching bands, floats, children's rides, a merchants' fair and flea market, crafts, home baked goods and a dance at the local legion hall.

HOMES:

Highland Creek contains a large number of frame or brick bungalows built in the 1920s, 1930s, 1940s and 1950s. Many of these cosy, white, frame houses were originally summertime cottages.

Highland Creek's housing stock is currently in transition as many of the original homes are being replaced by a collection of new custom-designed houses that feature double garages, interlock driveways and luxury interior finishes.

SHOPPING:

Highland Creek residents do most of their shopping on Old Kingston Road, which has the character of a main street, in a small town. The focal point of this shopping district is the old fashioned Highland Creek Plaza which includes a food market, a hair salon, a florist, a bakery, a bookstore, a bank, a dry cleaners, a florist, a home decorating store and professional offices. The mix of shopping around this plaza includes neighbourhood restaurants, and a beer- and wine-making establishment.

RECREATION:

Highland Creek Community Park located off Ellesmere Road is a large park that features a baseball diamond and a children's playground. The Highland Creek Public Library is located east of the park at 3550 Ellesmere Road. This library offers storytime and reading club programs for children.

Colonel Danforth Park, which forms the southern boundary of this neighbourhood, is a deep ravine valley that is popular for family picnics, bike rides, casual strolls and hiking. This park can be accessed off Kingston Road and along Old Kingston Road.

SCHOOLS:

(P) Highland Creek, 1410 Military Trail, (416) 396-6330
(P) Meadowvale, 761 Meadowvale Rd. N., (416) 396-6470
(P) Morrish, 61 Canmore Blvd., (416) 396-6730
(PH) West Hill, 299 Morningside Ave., (416) 396-6630
(C) Cardinal Lèger, 600 Morrish Rd., (416) 393-5419

TRANSPORTATION:

The north-south Morningside Avenue and Meadowvale Road buses connect passengers to the Kennedy station on the Bloor-Danforth subway line. The Ellesmere Road bus connects passengers to the Scarborough Town Centre, which provides a connection to the Bloor-Danforth subway station and the Go Transit system.

Motorists can gain immediate access to Highway 401 on-ramps at Morningside Avenue and Meadowvale Road. Highway 401 links motorists to the Don Valley Parkway which ushers commuters to downtown Toronto in approximately 30 minutes. An alternative and more scenic route for those heading downtown is to take Kingston Road west to Lakeshore Boulevard.

HISTORY:
The Hillside neighbourhood is named after Hillside, a Gothic-style mansion built in 1872 by William A. Milne, on the hillside of the Rouge River Valley. Hillside is still standing today at the corner of Old Finch Avenue and Sewells Road.

The Hillside community has a long and proud farming tradition. The spiritual centre of this rural hamlet was the Hillside Church, built in 1877 at Finch Avenue and Reesor Road. This historic church is still standing at 361 Old Finch Avenue. The Hillside Schoolhouse, built in 1872, is located on Meadowvale Road where it now serves as an outdoor education centre for the City of Toronto.

Many of the old Hillside farms were expropriated in 1972 by the provincial government for the building of the proposed Pickering Airport, which was never developed. In 1995 both the government and privately owned Hillside properties were incorporated into the Rouge Park conservation area.

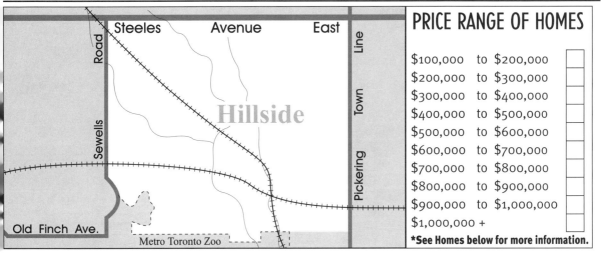

PRICE RANGE OF HOMES

$100,000 to $200,000	
$200,000 to $300,000	
$300,000 to $400,000	
$400,000 to $500,000	
$500,000 to $600,000	
$600,000 to $700,000	
$700,000 to $800,000	
$800,000 to $900,000	
$900,000 to $1,000,000	
$1,000,000 +	

*See Homes below for more information.

OVERVIEW:
Hillside is unique in that it is the only Toronto neighbourhood that is entirely incorporated as part of a public park. The Rouge Park is one of the largest urban parks in North America. This conservation park features woodlands and valleys, meadows and farmland. Hillside is a vital component of Rouge Park as it is the last place in Toronto where wide-scale farming takes place.

When you drive through Hillside you will pass through furrowed fields anchored by time-weathered barns, open meadows filled with frolicking birds and thickly treed woodlots brimming with rugged Manitoba maples and majestic pine trees. Here you begin to sense how the pioneers must have felt when much of Toronto was in this state.

As you keep on driving through this rolling countryside you will bypass creeks, streams and rivers, jockey over railway tracks and single-lane bridges and, if you're lucky, catch a fleeting glimpse of a red fox or a white tailed deer. Hillside truly is country in the city.

HOMES:
There are approximately 86 homes in the Hillside neighbourhood, of which about 20 are privately owned and the rest are owned by the provincial government. The Hillside properties owned by the government are managed by the Ontario Realty Corporation, which rents them out to qualified applicants. Many of these applicants are farmers who must undergo a selection process that also involves the Ministry of Agriculture and Food. Non-working-farm applicants are put on a waiting list, which currently includes about 300 applicants who want to enjoy the feeling of living in the country while at the same time being only a half-hour drive from downtown Toronto.

The typical Hillside property is on-half acre to five acres in size, however, the larger working farms are generally 50 to 200 acres in size. Most of the farm houses in Hillside are 60 to 90 years old. The rents here are lower than marketplace rents, due to the fact that these are older homes and utility costs are generally higher and, even more significantly, there are no city services available to this community. This means no water, sewers, sidewalks or street lights and plenty of bumpy roads. The Ontario Realty Corporation does provide a general maintenance of its properties.

There are a limited amount of private properties in Hillside that can be sold to the public. However if you are looking for raw land to build a subdivision on, you have come to the wrong place. The Rouge Park does not allow for any further residential development on these lands.

*No recent sales of Hillside homes were available at the time of printing of this publication.

SHOPPING:
Hillside residents get to their shopping destinations by car. The most popular places to shop are the Pickering Town Centre, and the Markville Mall at Highway 7 and McCowan Road.

RECREATION:
The Hillside neighbourhood is part of the Rouge Park mosaic that includes a unique combination of woodlands, valleys, meadows, rivers and farmland that all combine to form Canada's largest urban park. Rouge Park trails can be accessed at the Pearse House Interpretive Centre, located on Meadowvale Road, just opposite the Toronto Zoo. The Toronto Zoo, which forms the southern boundary of this neighbourhood, is situated on 710 acres of land and features over 5,000 animals. This zoo features different theme areas including South America, Eurasia Pavilion, North American pavilion, African Pavilion, Indo-Malayan Pavilion and Canadian Animal Domain.

SCHOOLS:
(P) John G. Diefenbaker, 70 Dean Park Rd., (416) 396-6390
(P) Chief Dan George, 185 Generation Blvd., (416) 396-6150
(P) Rouge Valley, 30 Durnford Rd., (416) 396-6433
(P) Highland Creek, 1410 Military Trail, (416) 396-6330
(P) West Hill, 299 Morningside Ave., (416) 396-6630
(PH) West Hill C.I., 350 Morningside Ave., (416) 396-6864

TRANSPORTATION:
The Hillside neighbourhood is not serviced by public transit. Motorists can take Old Finch Avenue or Steeles Avenue east to Markham Road which links up with Toronto's commuter highways. Downtown Toronto is approximately a half-hour drive from this neighbourhood.

SW

HISTORY:

L'Amoreaux's first settler was Josue L'Amoreaux, a loyalist of French Huguenot descent who arrived here with his wife, seven children and two nephews around 1816. The spiritual centres of this pioneer community were St. Paul's Church L'Amoreaux and Christie's Methodist Church, which were both established in the 1840s. While these churches are no longer standing, their cemeteries have endured. St. Paul's L'Amoreaux cemetery is tucked away at the southwest corner of Finch and Warden avenues, while Christie's Methodist Church cemetery is now part of a small park at the entranceway to the Bridlewood Mall.

In 1847, L'Amoreaux was given the designation as School Section 1, in the former Township of Scarborough. A few years later, in 1854, a post office was established here. L'Amoreaux's transition from a farming hamlet to a modern day subdivision took place in the 1950s, 1960s and 1970s. The Devonsleigh House, built in 1850, is a visual reminder of L'Amoreaux's past. This historic home is located at 4125 Steeles Avenue East where it is now a popular restaurant.

PRICE RANGE OF HOMES	
$100,000 to $200,000	
$200,000 to $300,000	✓
$300,000 to $400,000	✓
$400,000 to $500,000	✓
$500,000 to $600,000	✓
$600,000 to $700,000	✓
$700,000 to $800,000	✓
$800,000 to $900,000	
$900,000 to $1,000,000	
$1,000,000 +	

OVERVIEW:

L'Amoreaux is located at the north end of Toronto, which accounts for its distinctly suburban character. Here you will find winding, tree-lined streets, pedestrian-friendly sidewalks and well-maintained family homes. The planned subdivision communities of Bridlewood, Wishing Well, and Bamburgh, which are part of the greater L'Amoreaux neighbourhood, each contain their own school, shopping and parks.

L'Amoreaux neighbourhood landmarks include the Tam O'Shanter Golf course off Kennedy Road, Bridlewood Mall at Warden Avenue, the Ontario Hydro Fields south of McNicol Avenue, and L'Amoreaux Park and Scarborough Grace Hospital, which are both situated on Birchmount Avenue.

HOMES:

L'Amoreaux's houses were built during the 1950s, 1960s and 1970s. These houses are situated on lots that are typically 40 to 70 feet in width and feature attached or built-in garages.

The house styles here include ranch bungalows, split-level and two-storey homes. There are also pockets of townhouse communities and high-rise apartment buildings located along the peripheral streets of this neighbourhood.

The largest houses in L'Amoreaux are the two-storey, executive-style houses located near the Tam O'Shanter Golf Course. These homes are situated on expansive well-treed lots. Some of these houses back onto the golf course.

SHOPPING:

L'Amoreaux's largest shopping centre is the Bridlewood Mall, located at the northwest corner of Finch and Warden avenues. This indoor shopping mall features over 60 stores and is anchored by two department stores.

L'Amoreaux also contains a large number of smaller shopping plazas found along its main arterial streets. Most of these shopping plazas feature bilingual English and Asian signage, reflecting the diverse population in this neighbourhood. Asian food markets and restaurants, as well as herb and health food stores, are part of this shopping mix.

RECREATION:

 L'Amoreaux Park, located between Birchmount and Kennedy roads from Silver Springs Blvd to Burnt Park Drive, is one of Toronto's largest and most diverse recreational parks. Highlights of this park include Kidstown, an outdoor water playground for children, the L'Amoreaux Tennis Centre, which offers year-round tennis, and the

L'Amoreaux Community Recreation Centre. This park also includes a paved walkway, a pond, a stream, a bridge and nature habitats.

The Tam O'Shanter Golf Course, located off Birchmount Road just north of Sheppard, is a public course operated by the City of Toronto. This golf course is known for its variety of links holes and challenging water hazards.

St. Paul's L'Amoreaux Centre, located at 3333 Finch Avenue East, is a multi-purpose facility for adults 55 and over. Some of the programs offered here include bowling, dancing, yoga, art class, mini-tennis, men's and ladies' snooker, and field trips.

The L'Amoreaux neighbourhood has two public libraries. These include the Bridlewood Branch located inside the Bridlewood Mall, and the Steeles Branch located in the Bamburgh Gardens shopping plaza. Both these libraries offer a variety of community based programming.

SCHOOLS:

(P)	Bridlewood Jr., 60 Bridlewood Blvd., (416) 396-6080	
(P)	North Bridlewood Jr., (416) 50 Collingbrooke Blvd., (416) 396-6500	
(P)	Beverly Glen Jr., 85 Beverly Glen Blvd., (416) 396-6055	
(P)	David Lewis, 130 Fundy bay Blvd., (416) 396-5810	
(P)	Fairglen Jr., 2200 Pharmacy Ave., (416) 396-6325	
(P)	Lynngate Jr., 129 Cass Ave., (416) 396-6425	
(P)	Terry Fox, 185 Wintertime Blvd., (416) 396-6600	
(PH)	L'Amoreaux C.I., 2501 Bridletowne Circle, (416) 396-6745	
(PH)	Dr. Norman Bethune, 200 Fundy Bay Blvd., (416) 396-8200	
(PH)	Sir John A. Macdonald C.I., 2300 Pharmacy Ave., (416) 396-6793	
(PH)	Stephen Leacock C.I., 2450 Birchmount Rd., (416) 396-8000	
(C)	St. Aidan, 3521 Finch Ave. E., (416) 393-5350	
(C)	St. Cyprian, 3150 Pharmacy Ave., (416) 393-5378	
(C)	St. Henry, 100 Bamburgh Circ., (416) 393-5395	
(C)	St. John Fisher, 44 Kelvinway Dr., (416) 393-5352	
(C)	St. Maximillian Kolbe, 100 Fundy bay Blvd., (416) 393-5412	
(C)	St. Sylvester, 260 Silver Springs Blvd., (416) 393-5373	
(CH)	Mary Ward, 3200 Kennedy Rd., (416) 393-5544	

TRANSPORTATION:

The Sheppard, Finch and Steeles avenues buses connect passengers to their respective stations on the Yonge-University-Spadina subway line. The Victoria Park, Warden Avenue and Kennedy roads buses provide connecting routes to the Bloor-Danforth subway line.

Motorists are within five minutes of the Highway 401 on-ramps south of Sheppard Avenue. This commuter highway provides quick and easy access to the Don Valley Parkway, which ushers motorist to downtown Toronto's business and entertainment districts.

SW

HISTORY:

The history of Malvern began in 1856, when the Malvern Post Office was opened in David Brown's general store, which stood at the southeast corner of Finch Avenue and Markham Road. This post office was named after a resort town in England.

A year after the post office was opened, Senator David Reesor – formerly of Markham Village – began selling "Village Lots" in Malvern. Reesor trumpeted Malvern as the future "Capital of Scarborough," anticipating that the Grand Trunk Railway would extend a branch line through here. Unfortunately, when the Grand Trunk Railway began service to this area in 1871, it bypassed Malvern in favour of the neighbouring village of Agincourt.

While Malvern never did become a prosperous railway centre, it flourished as a farming community for over 100 years. In the late 1950s the Canada Mortgage and Housing Corporation expropriated Malvern's farms to build a "model community" of affordable homes. The first residents of this modern day Malvern community moved into their homes in 1972.

Ed. Note: The former Malvern Schoolhouse, built in 1872, is still standing today at 5810 Finch Avenue, and is now a private school.

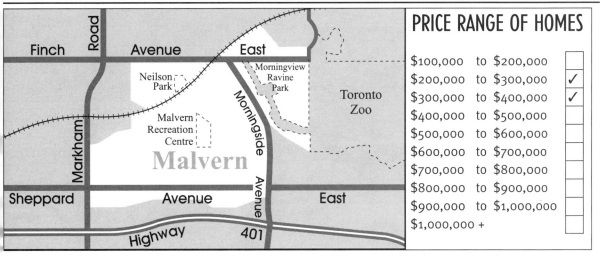

PRICE RANGE OF HOMES

$100,000 to $200,000		
$200,000 to $300,000		✓
$300,000 to $400,000		✓
$400,000 to $500,000		
$500,000 to $600,000		
$600,000 to $700,000		
$700,000 to $800,000		
$800,000 to $900,000		
$900,000 to $1,000,000		
$1,000,000 +		

OVERVIEW:

Malvern is located at the northeast end of the City of Toronto. This neighbourhood has retained its rural roots by preserving mature trees, ravine woodlots and parklands.

Malvern's affordable real estate has traditionally attracted many new Canadians to this neighbourhood. There are over 60 different cultures represented here, with the most dominant ethnic groups being people of Afro-Canadian, British, Chinese, and East Indian background.

HOMES:

Malvern's residential housing was built from the 1970s right through to the 1990s. The mix of houses here includes single-family detached homes, semi-detached homes, townhouses, low-rise garden apartments and high-rise apartment buildings. There are also a fair number of subsidized housing communities within the Malvern neighbourhood that offer rents geared towards income.

SHOPPING:

Malvern residents do most of their shopping at the Malvern Town Centre, which is conveniently located in the middle of this neighbourhood at Tapscott and Neilson roads. This modern, indoor shopping centre is anchored by a popular supermarket and a discount department store. The mix of stores here includes an equal number of retail chain stores and independently owned stores.

RECREATION:

The Malvern Recreation Centre, located at 30 Sewells Road, is a multi-use facility that features an indoor ice arena and sports fields. The Malvern Community Public Library is also part of this community centre. This library has an excellent selection of multilingual books and videos.

The Neilson Park Fieldhouse, located in Neilson Park off Neilson Road south of Finch Avenue, was built in the 1860s. This historic home has been beautifully restored and now serves as a community centre offering meeting rooms, workshops and craft programs. Neilson Park also has baseball diamonds, sports fields, and picnic areas.

The McLevin Park/Scott Westney House at 180 McLevin Avenue, offers a community centre with neighbourhood programming and tennis court facilities.

The Toronto Zoo forms the eastern boundary of this neighbourhood. This zoo offers 710 acres of parkland with over 5,000 animals in their natural habitats. Just to the east of the zoo is Rouge Park, which is one of the largest parks within an urban area in North America. This park contains over 700 varieties of wild plants, and its thick forest is home to a variety of wildlife including deer, coyotes, fox, raccoons, hawks, owls and a variety of bird species. Rouge Park can be accessed from the Pearse House Interpretive Centre, located off Meadowvale Road across from the Toronto Zoo.

SCHOOLS:

(P)	Malvern Jr., 70 Mammoth Hall Trail, (416) 396-6440	
(P)	Tom Longboat Jr., 37 Crow Trail, (416) 396-6610	
(P)	White Haven Jr., 105 Invergordon Ave., (416) 396-6645	
(P)	Alexander Sterling, 70 Fawcett Trail, (416) 396-6020	
(P)	Burrows Hall Jr., 151 Burrows Hall Blvd., (416) 396-6105	
(P)	Emily Carr, 90 John Tabor Trail, (416) 396-6230	
(P)	Fleming, 20 Littles Rd., (416) 396-6862	
(P)	Grey Owl Jr., 150 Wickson Trail, (416) 396-6290	
(P)	Lucy Maud Montgomerey, 95 Murison Blvd., (416) 396-6838	
(P)	Heritage Park, 80 Old Finch Ave., (416) 396-6207	
(P)	Mary Shadd, 135 Hupfield Trail, (416) 396-6450	
(P)	Dr. Marion Hilliard Sr., 280 Washburn Way, (416) 396-6195	
(PH)	Lester B. Pearson C.I., 150 Tapscott Rd., (416) 396-5892	
(C)	St. Barnabas, 30 Washburn Way, (416) 393-5351	
(C)	St. Bede, 521 Sewells Rd., (416) 393-5425	
(C)	St. Columba, 10 John Tabor Trail, (416) 393-5380	
(C)	Mother Teresa, 40 Sewells Rd., (416) 393-5538	
(PRI)	Whitefield Christian Academy, 5810 Finch Ave. East, (416) 297-1212	

TRANSPORTATION:

Malvern provides its residents with a myriad of public transit options. There is bus service on all the main streets and many of the interior streets in this neighbourhood. The Sheppard and Finch avenues buses connect passengers to stations on the Yonge-University-Spadina subway line. The north-south routes include Morningside Avenue, and Neilson and Markham roads. These bus lines provide connections to the Toronto and Scarborough rapid transit lines and the Go Transit bus and train lines.

Malvern is bordered by major arterial roadways including Finch, Sheppard and Morningside avenues and Markham Road, all of which provide good access to different parts of the city. Markham and Neilson roads and Morningside Avenue provide motorists with quick and easy access to Highway 401 on-ramps south of Sheppard Avenue.

HISTORY:
Maryvale was originally part of the former Village of Ellesmere, a thriving farming hamlet that was centred along today's Ellesmere Road. The Village of Ellesmere prospered during the 1800s, with its own school, post office and church. There were also blacksmith shops, a wagon-making shop and two sawmills.

In the early 1950s, Ellesmere's market gardens and dairy farms gave way to the present-day Maryvale subdivision. Maryvale is named after the former Maryvale farm, noted for the breeding and raising of race horses. This farm was situated on the site of the present day Maryvale Public School. A horse-shoe from the old Maryvale farm is mounted on a commemorative plaque in the foyer of the Maryvale Public School.

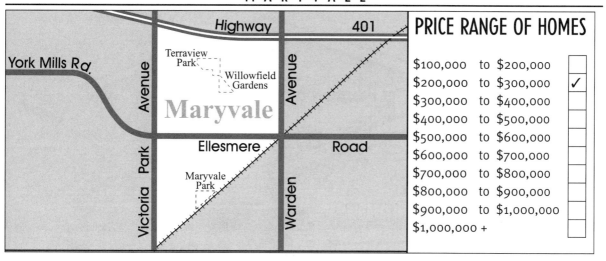

PRICE RANGE OF HOMES	
$100,000 to $200,000	
$200,000 to $300,000	✓
$300,000 to $400,000	
$400,000 to $500,000	
$500,000 to $600,000	
$600,000 to $700,000	
$700,000 to $800,000	
$800,000 to $900,000	
$900,000 to $1,000,000	
$1,000,000 +	

OVERVIEW:

Maryvale is bordered on the north by Highway 401, on the east by an industrial corridor, and on the south by the Canadian Pacific railway line.

This small, family-oriented neighbourhood revolves around the Maryvale Public School, located south of Ellesmere Road off Pharmacy Avenue. The Maryvale Junior YMCA is based at this school and Maryvale Park and Community Centre are adjacent to the school.

HOMES:

Maryvale's housing stock consists primarily of cosy brick bungalows and 1.5-storey houses built in the 1950s. These homes are well maintained and nicely landscaped. The lots are a good size and include a private driveway, usually with a garage.

SHOPPING:

Maryvale residents do most of their shopping at the Parkway Mall, a medium-sized indoor mall located at the southeast corner of Ellesmere Road and Victoria Park Avenue. This mall is anchored by a large department store and a supermarket. It has over 80 stores and restaurants. Included in this mix are a large number of men's and ladies' fashion shops, home decorating and improvement stores, and professional and medical offices.

Ellesmere Road offers a mix of small shopping plazas and larger retail stores, including a Home Depot, a video store, a beer store, and a golf centre. Medical and professional offices are also situated along this route.

RECREATION:

Maryvale Park, situated off Pharmacy Avenue, offers a myriad of recreational facilities including tennis courts, an outdoor pool, a wading pool, a baseball diamond, sports fields, and a children's playground.

SCHOOLS:

(P)   Maryvale, 1325 Pharmacy Ave., (416) 396-6455
(P)   Terraview-Willowfield, 95 Pachino Blvd.,
       (416) 396-6595
(PH) Wexford C.I., 1176 Pharmacy Ave., (416) 396-6874
(C)   Our Lady of Wisdom, 10 Japonica Rd., (416) 393-5273

TRANSPORTATION:

Bus services along Victoria Park, Pharmacy and Warden avenues connect passengers to stations on the Bloor-Danforth subway line, while the Ellesmere Road bus links up with the Yonge-University-Spadina subway line.

Motorists can get downtown in approximately 20 minutes via the Don Valley Parkway, which can be accessed off Lawrence Avenue, just west of Victoria Park Avenue. Highway 401 on-ramps at Victoria Park and Warden avenues are conveniently located at the north end of this neighbourhood.

HISTORY: This neighbourhood was originally called Milliken's

Corners. It was named after Norman Milliken, a United Empire Loyalist who settled here in 1807. Milliken established a lumbering business, a hotel and livery stables near the corner of Steeles Avenue and Kennedy Road.

The Milliken name is also associated with the Town of Markham, north of Steeles Avenue. In fact, the Milliken Post Office established in 1859 was situated on the north side of Steeles Avenue, which marks the border between Scarborough (now Toronto) and the Town of Markham.

Milliken remained a rural community up until the 1970s, when its furrowed farm fields gave way to the modern subdivisions that now define this neighbourhood.

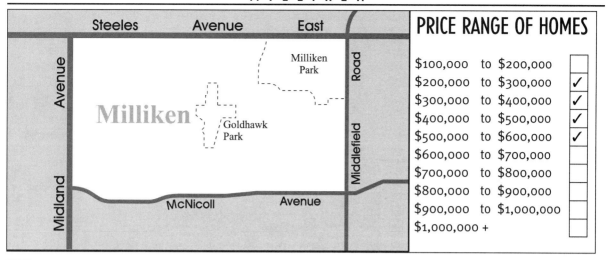

PRICE RANGE OF HOMES	
$100,000 to $200,000	
$200,000 to $300,000	✓
$300,000 to $400,000	✓
$400,000 to $500,000	✓
$500,000 to $600,000	✓
$600,000 to $700,000	
$700,000 to $800,000	
$800,000 to $900,000	
$900,000 to $1,000,000	
$1,000,000 +	

OVERVIEW:

Milliken is located at the very northeast end of Toronto. The rising tide of urbanization only reached this neighbourhood in the 1980s. In fact, the last large parcel of farmland in Milliken has only recently been developed along Steeles Avenue.

This neighbourhood has many outstanding features, including a modern public library and neighbourhood centre, the beautifully designed Milliken Park, and the Milliken Park Recreational Trail that winds its way through the neighbourhood.

HOMES:

Milliken's housing stock consists primarily of modern two-storey detached houses built in the 1980s and 1990s. These family-style houses are small to medium in size with attached garages and private drives. The houses here are fairly close together and typically feature 25- to 35-foot lots.

Milliken also contains a handful of townhouse complexes and condominium apartment buildings located in the McCowan Road and Alton Towers Drive section of this neighbourhood.

SHOPPING:

The largest shopping centre in this neighbourhood is the Milliken Wells Shopping Plaza located off McCowan Road at Alton Towers Circle. This plaza is anchored by a large supermarket and features mostly Chinese retailers including food shops, a video store, an herbal store and a variety of restaurants.

There are a number of smaller shopping plazas stretched along Steeles Avenue and on Middlefield Road at McNicoll Avenue. In addition to everyday convenience-type stores the mix of shopping here includes Chinese restaurants, herbal stores, vegetarian shops, and food markets.

RECREATION:

Milliken Park located at Steeles Avenue and McCowan Road is ideal for picnics or large social gatherings. This park has a small banquet hall, gazebos and a beautiful garden area that is centred around an elaborately designed man-made pond. Milliken Park also features a paved recreational trail and a modern children's playground.

The Goldhawk Park Public Library and Neighbourhood Centre, located at 295 Alton Towers Circle, is part of a multi-use recreational complex that includes a large outdoor playing area with baseball diamonds, basketball courts and a children's playground. This public library offers children's programming and the neighbourhood centre has a meeting room that is used for a variety of local functions.

SCHOOLS:

(P)   Agnes Macphail, 112 Goldhawk Trail, (416) 396-6015
(P)   Banting and Best, 380 Goldhawk Trail, 396-5800
(P)   Macklin, 136 Ingleton Blvd., (416) 396-6435
(P)   Milliken, 130 Port Royal Trail, (416) 396-6480
(P)   Port Royal, 408 Port Royal Trail, (416) 396-5595
(PH) Albert Campbell C.I., 1550 Sandhurst Circle, (416) 396-6684
(C)   Prince of Peace, 255 Alton Towers Circ, (416) 393-5416
(C)   St. Rene Goupil, 44 Port Royal Trail, (416) 393-5408
(C)   The Divine Infant, 30 Ingleton Blvd., (416) 393-5414

TRANSPORTATION:

Bus routes along Brimley, McCowan, and Middlefield roads provide connections to the Toronto Transit and Go Transit station at the Scarborough City Centre. The Steeles Avenue bus provides a connecting route to the Yonge-University-Spadina subway line

Motorists are approximately five minutes from Highway 401 on-ramps at McCowan and Brimley roads. This highway connects commuters to the Don Valley Parkway, which provides access to the downtown core.

HISTORY: The history of the Oakridge neighbourhood is centred

around the Oakridge Public School, which was built in 1913 on Danforth
Road, where Oakridge Park is now situated. This school was demolished in
1967 and replaced by a modern school on Byng Road. A date-stone memorial to the old Oakridge school stands at the Danforth Road entranceway to
Oakridge Park.

Oakridge's development was largely influenced by Danforth Road, one
of Toronto's oldest thoroughfares. Danforth Road had its own bus service
as early as 1918, which helped to attract many homeowners to this area.
Oakridge's growth was further enhanced in the 1950s, when the Bloor-
Danforth subway line was extended east to Warden Avenue.

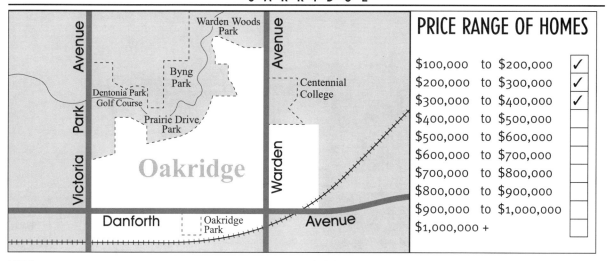

PRICE RANGE OF HOMES

$100,000 to $200,000	✓
$200,000 to $300,000	✓
$300,000 to $400,000	✓
$400,000 to $500,000	
$500,000 to $600,000	
$600,000 to $700,000	
$700,000 to $800,000	
$800,000 to $900,000	
$900,000 to $1,000,000	
$1,000,000 +	

OVERVIEW:

Oakridge is a mature neighbourhood that features an eclectic mix of older houses, a vibrant shopping district along Danforth Avenue and an abundance of recreational facilities and parkland.

Oakridge is bound on the north by ravine and park lands and on the south and east by the CN railway line and industry. A great deal of the social and recreational activity in this neighbourhood revolves around the Oakridge Community Recreation Centre on Pharmacy Avenue, and Oakridge Park on Danforth Avenue.

HOMES:

Oakridge houses come in a variety of sizes, shapes and styles. The original housing stock was built from the 1910s to the 1950s. Most of the older Oakridge houses were self-built and then added onto and improved over time. New home construction is currently taking place in this neighbourhood, as some of the older houses give way to custom-designed, modern homes.

SHOPPING:

Danforth Road is brimming with small, independently owned retail shops and restaurants that cater to the immediate needs of the surrounding neighbourhood.

A popular destination point for Oakridge residents is Shoppers World, located at the southwest corner of Danforth Road and Victoria Park Avenue. This large shopping plaza is known for its many discount stores.

RECREATION:

The Oakridge Community Recreation Centre, located at 63 Pharmacy Avenue, has a health club with cardio and weight equipment, a sauna and a whirlpool. This centre also contains meeting rooms that are used by local community groups. The City of Toronto offers year-round recreational programs in the evenings at the Oakridge Public School on Byng Avenue. The Oakridge Seniors Bocce Club at 6 Thora Road has two indoor bocce courts.

Oakridge Park, located in the centre of this neighbourhood off Danforth Road, is a pretty park with many excellent picnic spots. This neighbourhood park has a children's playground, a spray pool, a baseball diamond and a sports field.

SCHOOLS:

(P)   Oakridge Jr., 110 Byng Ave., (416) 396-6505
(P)   Warden Ave., Jr., 644 Warden Ave., (416) 396-6625
(PH) Birchmount Park C.I., 3663 Danforth Ave., (416) 396-6704
(C)   St. Dunstan, 14 Pharmacy Ave., (416) 393-5241

TRANSPORTATION:

Bus routes on Victoria Park and Warden avenues, and Danforth Road, connect passengers to stations on the Bloor-Danforth subway line. The Danforth Go Train station, on Main Street just south of the Danforth, ushers commuters to downtown Toronto's Union Station in approximately 15 minutes.

Danforth Road provides motorists with an east-west arterial roadway that leads right into the centre of Toronto. It is approximately a 20-minute drive to downtown Toronto along this route, through one of Toronto's most vibrant and colourful shopping districts.

HISTORY:
In the 1800s, Port Union was a booming waterfront village with thriving ship-building and commercial fishing industries, two hotels, a commercial wharf, and a variety of small businesses. In 1856, the Grand Trunk Railway opened a station in Port Union, which added to the importance of this waterfront village.

By 1865, Port Union's population had reached 100 people and it was granted its own post office. The two hotels that operated in Port Union during these boom times were said to have served "knock-em stiff" whiskey and "40 Rod Whiskey."

By the late 1800s Port Union's shipping industry had lost most of its business to the railway, and subsequently shut down. Port Union then went into a period of decline that lasted until the late 1940s, when the return of industry to this area sparked a residential housing boom. In the 1990s, Port Union reclaimed its waterfront with new housing that has helped connect this neighbourhood to its illustrious past.

Ed. Note: Port Union, north of Lawrence Avenue, is also referred to as Centennial, which makes reference to the north-south street that runs through the centre of this community. Centennial Street is named after Centennial Church, circa 1891, which still stands at the north end of Centennial Road off Kingston Road.

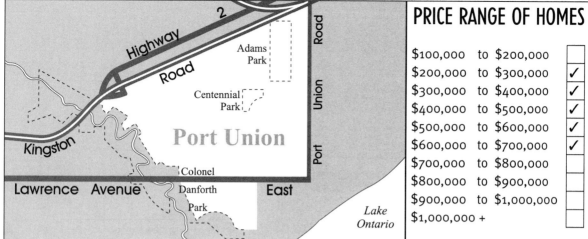

PRICE RANGE OF HOMES

$100,000	to	$200,000	
$200,000	to	$300,000	✓
$300,000	to	$400,000	✓
$400,000	to	$500,000	✓
$500,000	to	$600,000	✓
$600,000	to	$700,000	✓
$700,000	to	$800,000	
$800,000	to	$900,000	
$900,000	to	$1,000,000	
$1,000,000 +			

OVERVIEW:

Port Union is bounded on the south by the railway and to the west by Colonel Danforth Park — a well wooded ravine valley that ushers the Highland Creek on the last leg of its journey into Lake Ontario.

This is a very lush area with a combination of linear and sweeping streets, lined with beautiful, mature trees. In particular, the Port Union neighbourhood has some of the finest stands of pine trees in the City of Toronto.

HOMES:

This neighbourhood features a playful mix of architectural styles with elements of English, Spanish and Swiss designs woven into the tapestry of the houses found here. Many of the houses date from the 1940s and 1950s, and include frame cottages, ranch-style bungalows, split-level homes, and two-storey houses. There are also a fair number of new, custom-designed houses here.

Port Union Village, a new home subdivision located south of Lawrence Avenue, features a waterfront-inspired collection of semi-detached and detached houses as well as townhomes. These houses feature decorative architectural accents such as sweeping front porches, second-storey front decks and whimsical turrets that are designed to take advantage of Port Union Village's prime location overlooking Lake Ontario.

SHOPPING:

Centennial Plaza, located on the northwest corner of Port Union Road and Lawrence Avenue, features a deli and bakery, a hardware store, a video store, a flower store, a hair salon, a travel agency, professional offices, a pet store and animal clinic, a coffee shop, beer and liquor stores, restaurants, convenience stores, a medical centre, professional offices, and fast food restaurants.

The Lawson Road Plaza is a small shopping plaza serving the daily household needs of the residents located at the north end of this neighbourhood. This plaza includes a food market, a restaurant, banks, a hair salon, a dry cleaner and a gas station.

RECREATION:

The Port Union Recreation Centre and Public Library, located at 5450 Lawrence Avenue East, is a multi-use facility that includes a fitness centre, a seniors' centre, two activity rooms, and a large banquet hall. A public library is situated in the west wing of this centre.

Colonel Danforth Park, located along the western boundary of this neighbourhood, is a deep and heavily wooded ravine valley that is popular for family picnics, bike rides, casual strolls and hikes. Access to this park is available of Beechgrove Drive just south of Lawrence Avenue, and off Old Kingston Road just to the west of Meadowvale Road.

Adams Park, situated just west of Port Union Road on Lawson Road, is a popular neighbourhood landmark for families. This park contains a wading pool, a children's playground, sports fields, baseball diamonds, flower gardens and many excellent picnic spots.

SCHOOLS:

(P)   Centennial Road Jr., 271 Centennial Rd., (416) 396-6125
(P)   Charlottetown Jr., 85 Charlottetown Blvd., (416) 396-6135
(PH) Sir Oliver Mowat C.I., 5400 Lawrence Ave. E., (416) 396-6802
(C) St. Brendan, 186 Centennial Rd., (416) 393-5359

TRANSPORTATION:

Bus services along Lawrence Avenue, Lawson Road and Port Union Road connect passengers to the Rouge Hill Go Train station situated on Lawrence Avenue, west of Port Union Road. The Go Train provides a connecting route to downtown Toronto's Union Station and the Yonge-University-Spadina subway line.

Motorists can quickly access the Highway 401 on-ramp off Port Union Road or Highway 2 at Kingston Road. These commuter highways usher motorists to Toronto's business and entertainment districts.

HISTORY:
The history of the Rouge neighbourhood is typical of most neighbourhoods located at the north end of the city. This was primarily a rural farming community up until the 1950s, when Highway 401 was built across the southern perimeter of the Rouge neighbourhood.

The opening of Highway 401 led to the building of the first homes in this neighbourhood, along Sheppard Avenue in the early 1960s. However, the bulk of this neighbourhood was not developed until the 1970s and 1980s. The urbanization of the Rouge neighbourhood continues to evolve, with the addition of new residential subdivisions, a shopping centre, schools, parks and a recreation centre.

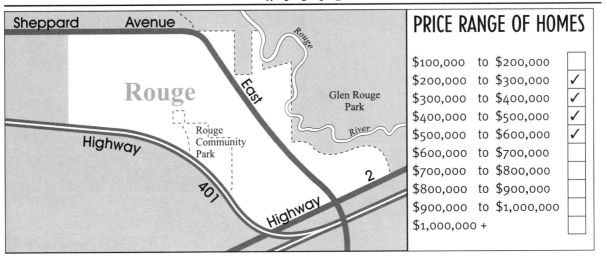

PRICE RANGE OF HOMES

$100,000 to $200,000	
$200,000 to $300,000	✓
$300,000 to $400,000	✓
$400,000 to $500,000	✓
$500,000 to $600,000	✓
$600,000 to $700,000	
$700,000 to $800,000	
$800,000 to $900,000	
$900,000 to $1,000,000	
$1,000,000 +	

OVERVIEW:

The Rouge neighbourhood is nestled between the Toronto Zoo on the north, the Rouge River Valley on the east and Highway 401 to the south. The natural beauty of this area quickly comes into focus along Sheppard Avenue, which provides a spectacular view of the Rouge River Valley.

This neighbourhood features a good mix of affordable housing. It has its own shopping, schools, parks and community centre, is well served by public transit, and is close to commuter highways.

HOMES:

The ranch-style bungalows and two-storey homes along Sheppard Avenue were built in the 1960s. These houses are situated on extra-wide and deep lots. Some of these lots stretch back 400 feet. Many of the houses on the east side of Sheppard Avenue command a spectacular view of the Rouge River Valley.

The majority of the two-storey detached and semi-detached homes were built in the 1970s, 1980s, and 1990s. There are also some townhouse communities and a handful of condominium apartment buildings located within this neighbourhood.

SHOPPING:

The Abbey Lane Shopping Centre, located off Rylander Boulevard, features a large supermarket, a Canadian Tire store, a pharmacy, banks, restaurants, a cleaners, a pet store, a hair salon, a post office, and an indoor children's playground.

RECREATION:

The Tall Pines Park and Neighbourhood Centre is located at 64 Rylander Boulevard, across from the Abbey Lane Shopping Centre. This is a modern facility with community meeting rooms. The park itself features two tennis courts and a children's playground.

The Rouge Community Park, conveniently situated in the middle of this neighbourhood, is ideal for a short nature hike or picnic and also features a baseball diamond. Further west of the Rouge Community Park is Dean Park, another naturalized park that features tennis courts.

Rouge Park, which forms the eastern boundary of this neighbourhood, is popular with nature enthusiasts, hikers, joggers and cross-country skiers. It is also the site of the Glen Rouge campground, which has over 100 camp sites. Access to this park is located east of Sheppard Avenue off Kingston Road.

SCHOOLS:

(P) Chief Dan George, 185 Generation Blvd., (416) 396-6150
(P) John G. Diefenbaker, 70 Dean Park Rd., (416) 396-6390
(P) Rouge Valley, 30 Durnford Rd., (416) 396-6433
(PH) Sir Oliver Mowat C.I., 5400 Lawrence Ave. E., (416) 396-6802

TRANSPORTATION:

Bus service along Sheppard Avenue East connects passengers to the Sheppard Station on the Yonge-University-Spadina subway line.

Motorists enjoy convenient access to Highway 401 from Sheppard Avenue and Highway 2, off Port Union Road. These two highways provide commuters with a variety of options, with connecting routes leading into and out of the city.

HISTORY: Scarborough Junction was first recognized as a community in 1873, when a post office using this name was opened in the Bell General Store, which stood on the southwest corner of Kennedy Road and St. Clair Avenue. The Junction part of this name referred to the two railways – the Grand Trunk and the Toronto-Nippising – that crossed paths at the south end of this neighbourhood.

By 1896, Scarborough Junction was the most heavily populated village in the former Township of Scarborough. It had its own school, general store, and the Bethel Methodist Church. The historic Bethel Church Cemetery is quietly tucked away off Kennedy Road, south of Eglinton Avenue.

The urbanization of Scarborough Junction took place in the late 1940s and the 1950s, when farm fields were replaced with rows of war veterans' housing and cosy little bungalows. These houses sold very quickly to young families that were looking for affordable houses in what was then the outskirts of Toronto.

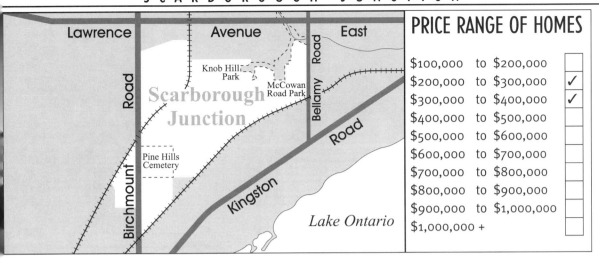

PRICE RANGE OF HOMES	
$100,000 to $200,000	
$200,000 to $300,000	✓
$300,000 to $400,000	✓
$400,000 to $500,000	
$500,000 to $600,000	
$600,000 to $700,000	
$700,000 to $800,000	
$800,000 to $900,000	
$900,000 to $1,000,000	
$1,000,000 +	

OVERVIEW:
Scarborough Junction is a culturally diverse, family-oriented neighbourhood. Scarborough Junction has many fine attributes including affordable homes, a vibrant shopping district along Eglinton Avenue, and convenient access to TTC and Go Transit stations.

HOMES:
The residential pocket south of Eglinton Avenue contains small bungalows, 1.5-storey houses and semi-detached homes built in the 1940s and 1950s.

North of Eglinton, subdivisions such as Treverton Park, located on the east side of Kennedy Road, contain somewhat larger bungalows, split-level houses and detached, two-storey homes. These houses were built in the 1950s and 1960s.

Scarborough Junction also contains a large number of high- and mid-rise rental apartment buildings, located on the peripheral streets of this neighbourhood. Many of these buildings are owned by the Toronto Community Housing Authority and offer rents geared towards income.

SHOPPING:
The main retail shopping corridor serving this neighbourhood is located along Eglinton Avenue. Here you will find a great variety of shopping including large supermarkets, a discount department store, home improvement stores, bargain and discount stores, a flea market, new car dealerships, auto service centres, restaurants, a sports bar, video stores, and professional and medical offices.

The Kennedy Park Plaza on Kennedy Road, and the Greystone Plaza at Danforth and Midland, are two smaller shopping plazas that cater to the everyday household needs of the residents of this neighbourhood.

RECREATION:
The Mid Scarborough Community Centre, located at 2467 Eglinton Avenue East, offers a variety of fitness, craft, dance and social programs for children, adults and seniors. This community centre also operates outdoor tennis courts.

Scarborough Junction has a large number of smaller parks with various amenities including baseball diamonds and children's playgrounds.

SCHOOLS:
(P)   Ionview, 90 Ionview Rd., (416) 396-6350
(P)   John McCrae Sr., 431 McCowan Rd., (416) 396-6395
(P)   McCowan Rd., Jr., (416) 425 McCowan Rd., (416) 396-6465
(P)   John A. Leslie., (416) 459 Midland Ave., (416) 396-6380
(PH)   R.H. King Academy, 3800 St. Clair Ave., E. (416) 396-5550
(C)   St. Maria Goretti, 21 Kenmark Blvd., (416) 393-5260
(CH)   Jean Vanier, 959 Midland Ave., (416) 393-5554

TRANSPORTATION:
Scarborough Junction residents have convenient access to the Eglinton Go Train station located just west of Bellamy Road. This train service connects commuters to downtown Toronto's Union Station in approximately 20 minutes.

Toronto Transit bus routes along Kennedy, Midland, McCowan and Bellamy roads and Eglinton Avenue connect passengers to stations on the Scarborough Rapid Transit and the Bloor-Danforth subway lines.

HISTORY:

Scarborough Village began in the 1830s as a crossroads village, centred around Markham and Kingston roads and Eglinton Avenue. In 1832 it became the first community in the former Township of Scarborough to have its own post office.

Robert R. Bonis, in *A History of Scarborough,* describes Scarborough Village in 1896 as "consisting only of a brick schoolhouse, a general store, a blacksmith shop, a building for the sale of farm implements, the Methodist parsonage, less than a dozen dwellings, and a large railway hotel converted to other uses."

Historical Scarborough Village landmarks include the Washington Manse, circa 1875, which is located at 14 Centre Street, and the Fred S. Cornell House, circa 1850, which was relocated to Thompson Memorial Park in 1962, when the present-day neighbourhood was being developed.

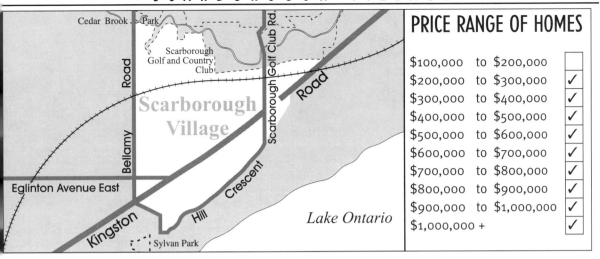

PRICE RANGE OF HOMES	
$100,000 to $200,000	
$200,000 to $300,000	✓
$300,000 to $400,000	✓
$400,000 to $500,000	✓
$500,000 to $600,000	✓
$600,000 to $700,000	✓
$700,000 to $800,000	✓
$800,000 to $900,000	✓
$900,000 to $1,000,000	✓
$1,000,000 +	✓

OVERVIEW:

Scarborough Village is a quiet neighbourhood that features affordable homes in the Eglinton Avenue area and executive homes south of Kingston Road, overlooking Lake Ontario. The Scarborough Bluffs and Toronto's east-end waterfront parks are just minutes away.

A revitalization is underway in this neighbourhood; construction has begun on a brand-new Scarborough Village Public School, situated just north of the former school on Centre Street.

HOMES:

The most expensive real estate in Scarborough Village is located south of Kingston Road. This residential pocket has a varied topography with winding streets, lush landscapes and many mature trees. Here you will find large estate homes mixed in with ranch-style bungalows and Tudor cottages. Many of the houses on the south side of Hill Crescent are especially sought after for their panoramic views of Lake Ontario.

The residential pocket north of Kingston Road includes cosy, cottage-style bungalows around Scarborough Village Park and modest brick bungalows, 1.5-storey houses and two-storey homes west of Markham Road.

SHOPPING:

Eglinton Avenue provides Scarborough Village residents with a myriad of shopping options. The many small shopping plazas located along this stretch feature a bevy of restaurants, as well as convenience stores, food markets, and new and used car dealerships. Markham Road is known for its selection of East and West Indian restaurants.

The Cederbrae Shopping Plaza is located nearby at the southwest corner of Lawrence Avenue and Markham Road. This shopping centre has recently been renovated and includes over 70 stores.

The Marklington Square Shopping Centre, located at the southeast corner of Markham Road and Eglinton Avenue, is a mid-sized shopping centre anchored by a large supermarket and a department store. Also included in this mix are a pharmacy, a camera shop, a bargain centre, a beer store and a video store.

RECREATION:

The Scarborough Village Recreation Centre, located at 3600 Kingston Road, is the home of the Scarborough Village Theatre. Three local award-winning theatre groups perform at this centre. This recreation centre also has an active seniors' program that offers ballroom, country, Latin and line dancing.

Scarborough Village Park, located off Scarborough Golf Club Road, features a baseball diamond with lighting for evening games.

SCHOOLS:

(P) Cedarbrook Jr., 56 Nelson St., (416) 396-6115
(P) Cedar Drive Jr., 21 Gatesview Ave., (416) 396-6120
(P) Mason Road Jr., 78 Mason Road, (416) 396-6460
(P) Scarborough Village, 3170 Eglinton Ave. E., (416) 396-6560
(PH) Cederbrae C.I., 550 Markham Rd., (416) 396-4400
(C) St. Boniface, 20 Markana Dr., (416) 393-5277

TRANSPORTATION:

The Eglinton Go Train station, located just west of Bellamy Road, provides commuters with train service to downtown Toronto's Union Station. This trip takes approximately 20 minutes.

The TTC also services this neighbourhood, with bus routes located along Bellamy, Markham, and Scarborough Golf Club roads as well as Eglinton Avenue.

Motorists are approximately 10 minutes from the Highway 401 on-ramp off Markham Road and approximately 25 minutes to downtown Toronto via Kingston Road.

HISTORY:
West Hill's history began in 1879, when it was granted a post office by the federal government. Prior to the opening of the post office, West Hill was considered part of the neighbouring Highland Creek community.

West Hill's earliest settlers were Irish immigrants from the County of Cork, who arrived here in the 1840s seeking refuge from the potato famine in their homeland. They settled mostly in two-room shacks in the Morningside and Lawrence Avenue area, which for a time was called Corktown. Many of these new Canadians found work in the building of the Grand Trunk Railway along Toronto's waterfront in 1856.

In 1906, the radial streetcar line connected West Hill to the rest of Toronto. The streetcar attracted many families to this area, which culminated in the opening of the West Hill Public School in 1921. The present-day neighbourhood was developed largely between the 1940s and 1960s.

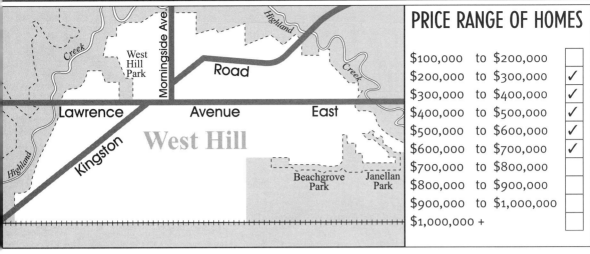

PRICE RANGE OF HOMES	
$100,000 to $200,000	
$200,000 to $300,000	✓
$300,000 to $400,000	✓
$400,000 to $500,000	✓
$500,000 to $600,000	✓
$600,000 to $700,000	✓
$700,000 to $800,000	
$800,000 to $900,000	
$900,000 to $1,000,000	
$1,000,000 +	

OVERVIEW:
West Hill is a culturally diverse, family-oriented neighbourhood located in the southeast part of Toronto. West Hill's natural beauty is derived from Morningside Park and Colonel Danforth Park. These two large ravine parks form the boundaries of this neighbourhood.

West Hill has many fine attributes, including a community centre, a public library, an abundance of parkland, a vibrant shopping district and affordable homes. Neighbourhood landmarks include the C.N. railway tracks that skirt the south end of this neighbourhood, and the University of Toronto's Scarborough campus, located off Morningside Avenue.

HOMES:
West Hill contains a large number of bungalow and 1.5-storey houses from the 1940s, 1950s and 1960s, mixed in with newer townhomes and recently built, custom-designed houses. The property sizes here are above average and the lots are well treed with many old pine and maple trees.

SHOPPING:
Kingston Road is lined with new- and used-car dealerships, motels, and small shopping plazas that contain food shops, restaurants and everyday convenience-type shopping. The West Hill shopping centre, located at the northeast corner of Lawrence and Kingston Road, includes a pharmacy, an electronics store, a bank, a family restaurant and a post office.

The Morningside Mall, located at Morningside and Lawrence avenues, features two floors of shopping and a third floor of professional offices. This mall contains a mix of approximately 60 corporate and independently owned stores.

Kingston Square, located across the street from the Morningside Mall, is anchored by a large supermarket and a discount department store. There are also fast food restaurants, a beer store, a video store, telephone and auto centres, and a restaurant that specializes in roti and curry dishes as well as tropical juices.

The small neighbourhood shopping plaza at Bennett Road and Lawrence Avenue is anchored by a Highland Farms supermarket. The retail mix here includes a flower shop, a pizza place, a travel agency, a hairstylist and a dry cleaners.

RECREATION:
The Heron Park Community Centre, located at 4285 Lawrence Avenue, is a multi-purpose recreational centre with an indoor ice arena, a swimming pool, a wading pool, a playground and a baseball diamond.

Colonel Danforth Park, located on the east side of this neighbourhood, is situated in a deep ravine valley and is popular with cyclists, walkers and joggers. Access to this park is available at both Kingston Road and Old Kingston Road.

Morningside Park, located along the western boundary of this neighbourhood, offers a mix of hardwood forests, large open meadows and the remnants of an old apple orchard. Paved trails pass through this park which is popular with cyclists and pedestrians. Cross-country skiing is popular here in the wintertime. You can access this park at Morningside Avenue south of Ellesmere Road.

SCHOOLS:
(P)   Eastview Jr., 20 Waldock St., (416) 396-6210
(P)   Galloway Road, 192 Galloway Rd., (416) 396-6245
(P)   Heron Park Jr., 280 Manse Rd., (416) 396-6320
(P)   Joseph Brant Sr., 270 Manse Rd., (416) 396-6400
(P)   Peter Secor Jr., 255 Coronation Dr., (416) 396-6520
(P)   St. Margaret's, 235 Galloway Rd., (416) 396-6550
(P)   W.M.G. Miller Jr., 60 Bennett Rd., (416) 396-6655
(PH) Maplewood H.S., 120 Galloway Rd., (416) 396-6765
(PH) Sir Robert Borden, 200 Poplar Rd., (416) 396-6810
(PH) West Hill C.I., 350 Morningside Ave., (416) 396-6864
(C)   St. Barbara, 25 Janray Dr., (416) 393-5274

TRANSPORTATION:
The Lawrence Avenue bus connects passengers to the Lawrence East subway station on the Bloor-Danforth subway line. The Kingston Road bus provides service to the Guildwood Go Train station. The train ride from this station to downtown Toronto's Union Station is approximately 25 minutes.

Motorists are approximately five minutes from the Morningside Avenue on-ramp to Highway 401. Kingston Road provides motorists with an alternate and more scenic route into the city.

HISTORY:
West Rouge was primarily farmland in 1926, when real estate developer Cecil White created the Rouge Hills subdivision. This development was intended to be a unique summer playground, with grand country estates spread out along the Rouge River. There were even plans for an elaborate canal system and private boathouses to service these estates.

Rouge Hills was never completed, however, a few of the cottages on Rouge Hills Drive and Riderwood Road are legacies of this subdivision. Year-round residential development of the West Rouge neighbourhood began in the 1940s, with individual lots being purchased by homeowners. Large parcels of land were subsequently developed by builders through the 1950s, 1960s and 1970s. More housing was added in the 1980s when the former Rouge Hills Golf and Country Club located in the Rouge Valley was sold to developers.

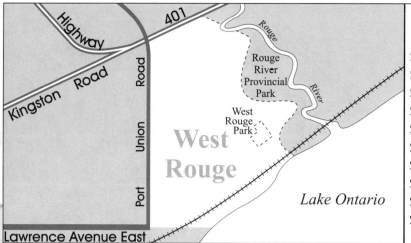

PRICE RANGE OF HOMES

$100,000 to $200,000	
$200,000 to $300,000	✓
$300,000 to $400,000	✓
$400,000 to $500,000	✓
$500,000 to $600,000	✓
$600,000 to $700,000	✓
$700,000 to $800,000	✓
$800,000 to $900,000	✓
$900,000 to $1,000,000	
$1,000,000 +	

OVERVIEW:

Nestled between the Rouge River Valley and Lake Ontario, the West Rouge is one of Toronto's most scenic neighbourhoods. West Rouge's gently sloping hillside is carved with winding roads and lined with towering trees, so that it resembles a cottage-country atmosphere.

West Rouge is a family-oriented neighbourhood with a very active community association. This association, in affiliation with the West Rouge sports and recreation association, runs a popular Family Day each September, and hosts New Years and Valentines Day dances, all of which are held at the West Rouge Community Centre.

HOMES:

West Rouge contains many former stone and frame summer cottages, built in the 1920s. These houses, now winterized, are situated mostly along Rouge Hills Drive. West Rouge also features many ranch-style bungalows, split-level homes and Tudor-style, two-storey homes from the 1950s, 1960s and 1970s, as well as pockets of new home subdivisions built in the 1980s and 1990s.

The West Rouge area around Lawrence Avenue has recently been converted into a "waterfront village" community that includes semi-detached houses as well as townhomes. The garages for these homes have been positioned off rear laneways, which makes for a more pleasing streetscape and emphasizes the architectural detail of these homes.

SHOPPING:

The West Rouge Plaza, at Port Union Road, is a convenient little plaza that contains a video store, a furniture store, a bakery, a hair salon, bowling, billiards, a sports bar and professional offices.

Centennial Plaza, located on the northwest corner of Port Union Road and Lawrence Avenue, features a deli and bakery, a hardware store, video store, flower shop, hair salon, travel agency, coffee shop, restaurants, convenience stores, a beer store, a liqour store, a pet shop, an animal clinic, professional offices and a medical centre.

The Ravine Park Plaza, located off Port Union Road at Fanfare Avenue, is a small local shopping plaza that caters to the everyday household needs of the West Rouge residents. The mix of stores here includes a large supermarket, a pharmacy, a video store, a hair salon, a bank, a bakery, a pet store, a collectables store and a hockey equipment shop.

RECREATION:

The West Rouge Community Centre, located on Rouge Hills Drive, boasts a banquet hall which can accommodate up to 350 people. This centre offers a variety of recreational programs for children and adults. The West Rouge Tennis Club is situated next to the community centre.

The West Rouge Sports and Recreation Association organizes a variety of community events including a winterfest and an Earth Day festival. A new program being offered by this association is "mature adult days." This program is held every Tuesday and includes lectures, nature walks, woodcarving and field trips.

The West Rouge Canoe Club has been a part of this community for over 40 years. This club operates at the Rouge Beach and offers canoe instruction for all ages and levels of ability. The West Rouge Canoe Club also operates a summer camp and hosts a two day international Dragon Boat festival in June. The West Rouge Canoe Club produced four Canadian paddlers at the 2000 Olympics. The West Rouge Soccer Club is one of the largest soccer clubs in the City of Toronto. This club operates year-round house leagues and rep teams at the local schools and parks. West Rouge also has an established baseball league program.

SCHOOLS:

(P)   West Rouge Jr., 401 Friendship Ave., (416) 396-6635
(P)   Joseph Howe Sr., 20 Winter Garden Trail, (416) 396-6405
(P)   William G. Davis Jr., 128 East Avenue, (416) 396-6650
(PH) Sir Oliver Mowat C.I., 5400 Lawrence Ave. E., (416) 396-6802

TRANSPORTATION:

West Rouge residents are within walking distance of the Rouge Hill Go Train station, located on Lawrence Avenue East. The train ride to downtown Toronto's Union Station is approximately 35 minutes.

Motorists are only a couple of minutes from the Port Union Road on-ramp to Highway 401. This commuter highway connects to all of Toronto's major highways leading into and out of the city.

SW

HISTORY: Wexford began in the 1840s as a crossroads community centred around The Rising Sun Inn, which was situated on the southwest corner of what is now the Lawrence and Pharmacy avenues intersection. This popular Inn was owned by Richard Sylvester, who hailed from Wexford County, Ireland.

In 1865, a post office was opened in Sylvester's Rising Sun Inn. Sylvester named this post office Wexford, which from that time onward, also became the official name of this community.

An historical landmark held over from Wexford's pioneer days is St. Jude's Church, situated on the east side of Victoria Park Avenue south of Lawrence Avenue. This church was built in 1848 by local farmers. St. Jude's is one of the oldest standing churches in Toronto.

Wexford endured as a quiet farming hamlet until the 1950s, when the present-day neighbourhood was developed.

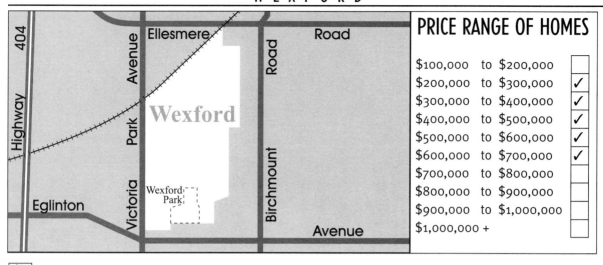

PRICE RANGE OF HOMES

$100,000 to $200,000		
$200,000 to $300,000	✓
$300,000 to $400,000	✓
$400,000 to $500,000	✓
$500,000 to $600,000	✓
$600,000 to $700,000	✓
$700,000 to $800,000	
$800,000 to $900,000	
$900,000 to $1,000,000	
$1,000,000 +	

OVERVIEW:
Wexford is a multi-cultural neighbourhood. Its diversity is celebrated on Lawrence Avenue, where an international array of food shops and restaurants can be found. This mix includes East and West Indian, Caribbean, African, Mediterranean, Greek and Italian businesses.

HOMES:
Wexford contains mostly bungalows and 1.5-storey houses built in the 1950s. These homes are situated on good-sized lots that feature private driveways and a garage.

Wexford has a large number of low- and high-rise apartment buildings, located on the peripheral streets of this neighbourhood.

SHOPPING:
Lawrence Avenue is brimming with small shopping plazas that contain a multicultural mix of restaurants and food shops. The shopping along Victoria Park Avenue is similar to Lawrence Avenue, although on a much smaller scale.

Eglinton Avenue offers a mix of big box stores, family-style restaurants, car dealerships, factory outlets, and shopping centres. The Golden Mile shopping mall, on the north side of Eglinton Avenue east of Victoria Park Avenue, was the largest shopping mall in Canada when it opened in 1954. Today this mall is anchored by a large department store and a supermarket, and also includes a handful of smaller retailers and a dental centre.

Eglinton Square, located across the street from the Golden Mile mall, is a community-oriented mall that runs a regular "Family Night Club" for kids, a "walk-a-mall" program, as well as seasonal events and promotions. Eglinton Square is anchored by the Bay department store and a Dominion supermarket.

The Wexford Heights Business Improvement Area, on Lawrence Avenue between Birchmount and Victoria Park avenues, hosts the annual Taste of Lawrence Festival the second week of July. This family-oriented event includes games, food, drinks, live entertainment and midway rides.

RECREATION:
The largest park in this neighbourhood is Wexford Park, which has a baseball diamond, sports fields, a children's playground and plenty of recreational greenspace.

Wexford Collegiate Institute, located at 1176 Pharmacy Avenue, has a gymnasium and indoor pool which host various Toronto Parks and Recreation programs.

SCHOOLS:
(P) Buchanan, 4 Buccanan Rd., (416) 396-6100
(P) George Peck, 1 Wayne Ave., (416) 396-6270
(P) Wexford, 1050 Pharmacy Ave., (416) 396-6640
(PH) Wexford C.I., 1176 Pharmacy Ave., (416) 396-6874

TRANSPORTATION:
Bus services along Eglinton, Lawrence, Warden, Pharmacy, and Victoria Park avenues connect passengers to stations on the Bloor-Danforth and Yonge-University-Spadina subway lines.

Motorists are just a few minutes from the Eglinton and the Lawrence Avenue on-ramps to the Don Valley Parkway and approximately a five-minute drive from Highway 401.

HISTORY: Woburn was originally named Elderslie. This name was changed in 1856, when a post office was opened in the Woburn Inn. The proprietor of the Woburn Inn was Thomas Dowswell, who hailed from a small town in England named Woburn.

The Woburn Inn was historically significant in that it was the original meeting place for the Scarborough Municipal Council. The former Township of Scarborough continued to conduct their meetings at the Woburn Inn until 1921, when council chambers were moved to Kingston Road.

When the urbanization of this neighbourhood took place in the 1950s, the historic Woburn Inn was demolished to make room for the Painted Post Plaza. A large stone marker with a historical plaque stands adjacent to the shopping plaza in tribute to the Woburn Inn.

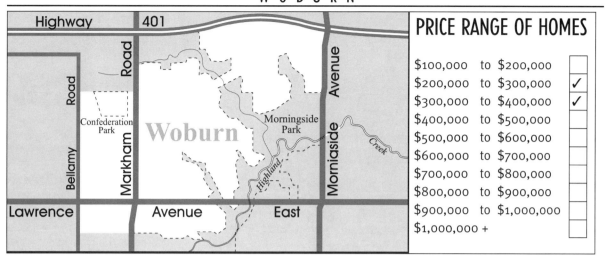

PRICE RANGE OF HOMES	
$100,000 to $200,000	
$200,000 to $300,000	✓
$300,000 to $400,000	✓
$400,000 to $500,000	
$500,000 to $600,000	
$600,000 to $700,000	
$700,000 to $800,000	
$800,000 to $900,000	
$900,000 to $1,000,000	
$1,000,000 +	

OVERVIEW:
Woburn is a quiet, family-oriented neighbourhood comprising winding, tree-lined streets that contain a good selection of moderately priced homes. This neighbourhood is bordered on the north by light industry and Highway 401. There is an abundance of parkland along the east and south perimeter of Woburn. Local landmarks include Centennial College (Progress Campus), the Scarborough Centennial Recreational Centre, Cedarbrae Mall and the Scarborough Golf and Country Club.

HOMES:
Woburn houses were built in the 1950s and 1960s. The style of houses found here include detached two-storey homes, split-level houses, bungalows and townhouses. There are also a large number of rental apartment buildings situated along Lawrence Avenue East. Masaryktown is a non-profit housing complex located at the south end of this neighbourhood, off Scarborough Golf Club Road.

SHOPPING:
Woburn's main shopping corridor is situated at the intersection of Lawrence Avenue and Markham Road. On the southwest corner is Cedarbrae Mall, which is anchored by a Zellers, a Canadian Tire, and a Loblaws supermarket. There are over 70 retailers at this mall.

The Cedar Heights Plaza, located on the northeast corner of Markham Road and Lawrence Avenue, features a large Chinese supermarket, a pharmacy, a discount department store, a hardware store, a sports store, bargain stores, professional and medical offices, a family restaurant and an East and West Indian food shop.

Ellesmere Road is lined with small shopping plazas, discount warehouses and factory outlets that are open to the public. There is also a large garden centre and a bingo emporium situated along this shopping corridor.

The Painted Post Plaza, located at the corner of Painted Post Drive and Markham Road, contains a small collection of neighbourhood-oriented stores including a bank, a hairstylist, a beauty salon, a dry cleaner, a convenience store, a fish-and-chips restaurant and an East Indian restaurant.

RECREATION:
The Scarborough Centennial Recreation Centre, located at 1967 Ellesmere Road, has two indoor ice arenas. The main arena is used for hockey leagues and programs, while the Ice Galaxy arena is used for figure skating and pleasure skating. This centre also contains a large auditorium with a 200-person seating capacity, and a children's "tots' room." The large park next to the community centre has tennis courts, a baseball diamond and basketball courts.

The Cedarbrook Community Centre and Park, off Daphne Road, is set in a lush ravine setting. The modern community centre has a second-floor ballroom and sundeck that offers scenic views of the adjacent parkland. The Cedar Ridge Creative Centre, located at 225 Confederation Drive, is a visual arts centre offering gallery space for artists as well as various art courses and workshops.

SCHOOLS:
(P)	Bellmere Jr., 470 Brimorton Dr.,	(416) 396-6040
(P)	Brooks Rd., 85 Keeler Blvd.,	(416) 396-6095
(P)	Cedarbrae C.I., 550 Markham Rd.,	(416) 396-4400
(P)	Cornell Jr., 61 Holmfirth Terrace,	(416) 396-6175
(P)	Heather Heights Jr., 80 Slan Ave.,	(416) 396-6305
(P)	Henry Hudson Sr., 350 Orton Park Rd.,	(416) 396-6310
(P)	Woburn Jr., 40 Dormington Dr.,	(416) 396-6670
(PH)	Cedarbrae C.I., 550 Markham Rd.,	(416) 396-4400
(PH)	Woburn C.I., 2222 Ellesmere Rd.,	(416) 396-4575
(C)	St. Barbara, 25 Janray Dr.,	(416) 393-5274
(C)	St. Thomas More, 2300 Ellemere Rd.,	(416) 393-5322

TRANSPORTATION:
Woburn residents are served by bus services on Bellamy, Markham and Ellesmere roads. These routes connect with the Scarborough Rapid Transit and Go Transit lines.

Motorists can take Markham Road north to Highway 401, which provides commuters with connecting routes to most parts of the city. Motorists travelling south on Markham Road can quickly link up with Kingston Road, which offers a scenic route into downtown Toronto.

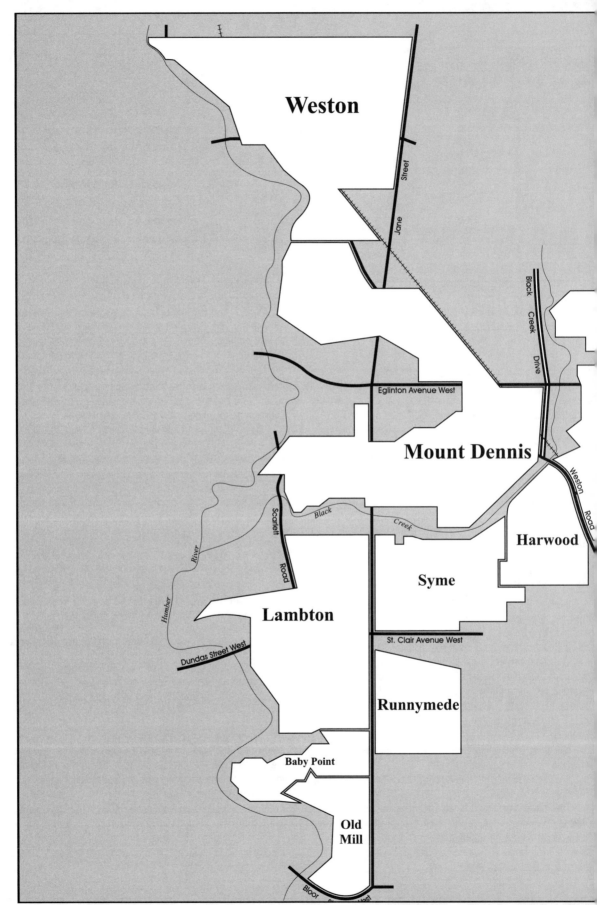

Weston

Jane Street

Black Creek Drive

Eglinton Avenue West

Mount Dennis

Weston Road

Harwood

Scarlett Road

Black Creek

Syme

Humber River

Lambton

St. Clair Avenue West

Dundas Street West

Runnymede

Baby Point

Old Mill

Bloor Street West

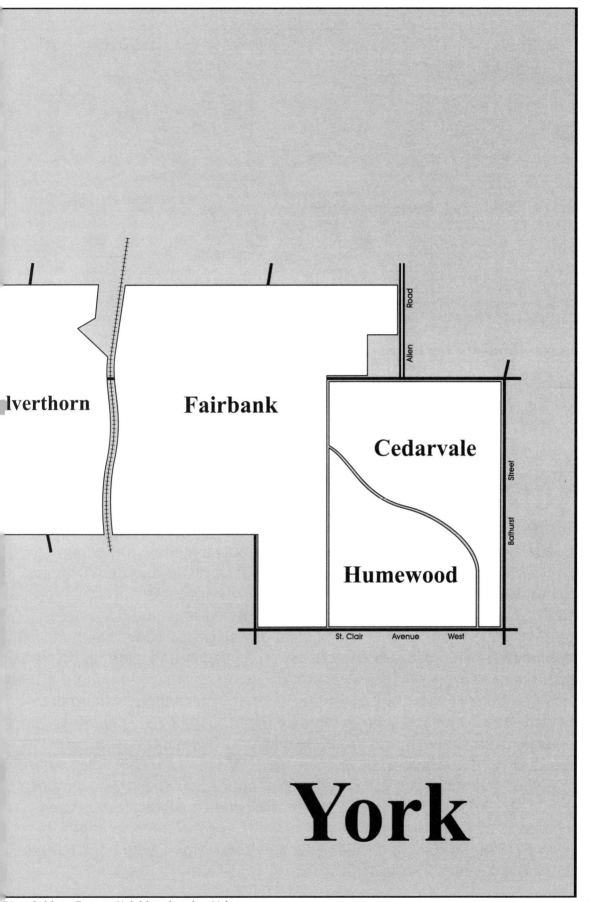

lverthorn

Fairbank

Allen Road

Cedarvale

Bathurst Street

Humewood

St. Clair   Avenue   West

York

R CATAPAN 85

HISTORY:

Baby Point's rich history dates back to the 1600s, when it was a prosperous Seneca Nation village known as Teiaiagon. The Seneca people found Teiaiagon to be the perfect location for conducting their fur-trading activities, as this high peninsula of land located in a bend of the Humber River, was easily defended from attack.

The Seneca village had long since been abandoned when the Honourable James Baby settled here in 1816. The present-day neighbourhood is named after Baby, a member of a prominent Quebec fur trading family and a former politician in Upper Canada.

Baby's settlement was a virtual Garden of Eden. A lush apple orchard occupied much of the land, and salmon swam in the Humber River. There was even a spring of fresh water that flowed from the hillsides. This water was bottled and shipped around the world.

Baby's heirs continued to live in Baby Point until 1910, when the government acquired Baby Point with the intention of establishing a military fortress and army barracks on this site. As fate would have it the government changed its plans and sold Baby Point to developer Robert Home Smith, who began developing the Baby Point subdivision in 1912.

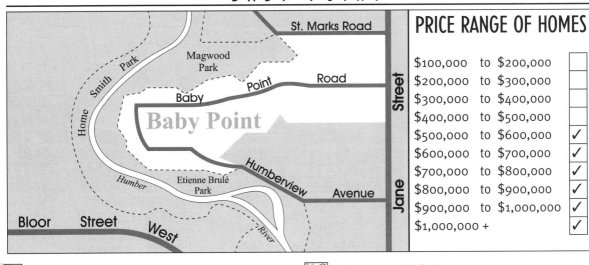

PRICE RANGE OF HOMES	
$100,000 to $200,000	
$200,000 to $300,000	
$300,000 to $400,000	
$400,000 to $500,000	
$500,000 to $600,000	✓
$600,000 to $700,000	✓
$700,000 to $800,000	✓
$800,000 to $900,000	✓
$900,000 to $1,000,000	✓
$1,000,000 +	✓

OVERVIEW:
The historic stone gates at the corner of Jane Street and Baby Point Road mark the entrance to this exclusive west-end neighbourhood.

Baby Point is situated on a peninsula of land overlooking the Humber River. It is surrounded by ravine and parkland and is one of the prettiest settings in Toronto.

Ed. Note: Long-time Baby Point residents pronounce the name of this neighbourhood "Bobby Point," using the French pronunciation for Baby, after whom this neighbourhood is named.

HOMES:
The signature streets in this neighbourhood are Baby Point Road and Baby Point Crescent, both of which feature large English-manor houses shaded by towering oak trees. Many of these houses back onto the Humber valley ravine, with some commanding a magnificent view of the Humber River.

There are also more modest two-storey detached houses located near the Jane Street and Baby Point Road entrance to this neighbourhood. These houses contain rich oak trim and oak doors as well as fireplaces. The majority of Baby Point houses were built in the 1920s and 1930s.

SHOPPING:
Baby Point residents enjoy the convenience of being able to walk to the Baby Point Village shopping district at Annette and Jane streets. This shopping district includes a floral design store, a home decorating store, a sporting goods store, a neighbourhood pub, a European deli and bakery, a coffee shop, an art gallery, an antique shop, and a grocery market.

RECREATION:
The social and recreational centre of this neighbourhood is the Baby Point Club, located off Baby Point Road. This private neighbourhood club features two tennis courts, lawn bowling and a log cabin clubhouse that hosts various social events throughout the year.

Baby Point is also an excellent place for exercise walks, jogging and cycling. Its picturesque, winding streets and hilly terrain provide a good challenge for fitness enthusiasts.

Baby Point residents can walk to Etienne Brûlé Park which has a paved trail that follows the course of the Humber River. This multi-purpose trail is ideal for walking, jogging, cycling and cross-country skiing. This park is also popular for fishing and picnics. Across the street from the park is the Old Mill Tennis Club, which includes four public tennis courts.

The Humber Theatre, located on the south side of Bloor Street west of Jane Street, is a popular venue for moviegoers, as this theatre screens current Hollywood releases.

SCHOOLS:
(P)   Humbercrest Public, 14 St. Marks Rd., (416) 394-2370
(PH)   Runnymede C.I., 569 Jane St., (416) 394-3200
(C)   St. James, Humbercrest Blvd., (416) 393-5275

TRANSPORTATION:
Baby Point residents can take the Jane Street bus to the Jane station on the Bloor-Danforth subway line, or may walk to the station which is about 15 minutes from the Baby Point gates.

Motorists enjoy quick and easy access to Lake Shore Boulevard and the Gardiner Expressway via the South Kingsway. Lake Shore Boulevard whisks motorists to Toronto's Harbourfront and financial district, and provides links to all of the major highways leading in and out of the city.

HISTORY: Cedarvale's residential development began in 1912, when Sir Henry Mill Pellatt, the builder of Toronto's famous Casa Loma, registered a plan of subdivision for the south end of this neighbourhood. The beaux-arts street gates on Claxton Boulevard set the tone for this high-class residential neighbourhood.

The original subdivision plan was registered under the name Cedar Vale. "Vale" denoted the ravine that runs through the centre of this neighbourhood and "Cedar" makes reference to the many cedars that grew in the wet lowlands of the ravine.

The Cedarvale Ravine, which has long been the foundation of this neighbourhood, was threatened in 1966, when the proposed Spadina Expressway was slated to run straight through the ravine on its way downtown. Some Cedarvale houses were expropriated and the floor of the ravine was clearcut to make room for the expressway.

Fortunately, strong opposition to the expressway was voiced throughout the city, and in 1974 the decision was made to stop the Spadina Expressway (officially called the W.R. Allen Road) at Eglinton Avenue, thus preserving the centrepiece of this popular Toronto neighbourhood.

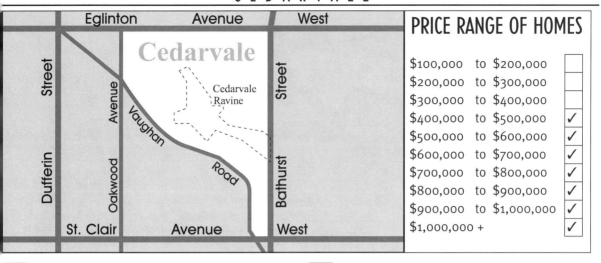

PRICE RANGE OF HOMES	
$100,000 to $200,000	
$200,000 to $300,000	
$300,000 to $400,000	
$400,000 to $500,000	✓
$500,000 to $600,000	✓
$600,000 to $700,000	✓
$700,000 to $800,000	✓
$800,000 to $900,000	✓
$900,000 to $1,000,000	✓
$1,000,000 +	✓

OVERVIEW:

The defining feature of this neighbourhood is the Cedarvale Ravine, which cuts a wide diagonal swath through the middle of Cedarvale. This ravine provides numerous recreational opportunities.

Cedarvale has an established Jewish community that has grown up around the Holy Blossom Temple and Beth Tzedec Synagogue, which are both situated on Bathurst Street.

HOMES:

Cedarvale's Tudor- and Georgian-style houses were built mostly between 1920 and 1950. The bigger and more expensive Cedarvale homes are on premium lots overlooking the ravine.

Cedarvale's interior streets contain a mix of good-sized family homes and sturdy little starter homes. There are also a number of multiplex houses and walk-up apartment buildings located on the periphery of this neighbourhood.

SHOPPING:

Eglinton Avenue West is one of Toronto's most glamorous and ritzy shopping districts. Included in the mix are high-end fashion stores, gift and home improvement stores, specialty food shops, professional services and an excellent variety of restaurants.

The shopping district further west along Eglinton Avenue and on Vaughan Road between Oakwood Avenue and Dufferin Street features the largest concentration of Caribbean shops, restaurants, and services in Toronto.

RECREATION:

The Cedarvale Ravine can be accessed through Cedarvale Park at Ava and Everden roads. This ravine is enjoyed by walkers, cyclists, joggers, bird watchers and in the wintertime cross country skiers. Cedarvale Ravine is part of the historic Belt Line Railway path – an old commuter railway right of way – that dates back to the 1880s.

Cedarvale Park, located at the north end of the ravine, provides local residents with a multi-use recreational space that includes tennis courts, playing fields and the Phil White indoor ice arena.

SCHOOLS:

(P)   Arlington Middle, 501 Arlington Ave., (416) 394-2200
(P)   Cedarvale Community, 145 Ava Rd., (416) 394-2244
(P)   J.R. Wilcox Community, 231 Ava Rd., (416) 394-2388
(PH) Vaughan Road C.I. 529 Vaughan Rd., (416) 394-3222
(PH) Forest Hill C.I., 730 Eglinton Ave., W., (416) 393-1860
(C)   St. Alphonsus, 60 Atlas Ave., (416) 393-5326
(PJ) Leo Baeck Day School, 1950 Bathurst St., (905) 709-3636
(PJ) United Synagogue, 1700 Bathurst St., (416) 781-5658

TRANSPORTATION:

Bus service on Bathurst Street and Vaughan Road connects passengers to the Bathurst station on the Bloor-Danforth subway line. The Eglinton Avenue Road West bus connects passengers to the Eglinton station on the Yonge-University-Spadina subway line.

Motorists are just minutes from the Allen Road Expressway at Eglinton Avenue. This expressway feeds into Highway 401 and its network of commuter highways. Bathurst Street is a main arterial road that provides quick and convenient access into the core of the city.

HISTORY: Fairbank is named after the former Fairbank Farm, which had been owned by a pioneer settler named Matthew Parsons. The Fairbank Farm was situated just north of Eglinton Avenue between Dufferin and Keele streets.

Fairbank's early development centred around the intersection of Dufferin Street and Eglinton Avenue. This neighbourhood began with a one-room school house, which was built in the 1860s and was followed by a hotel, a post office, a church and a handful of stores.

A stone marker from the original Fairbank school house has been preserved on the south wall of the present-day Briar Hill School. The only other vestiges of the old Fairbank community are the Fairbank United Church, circa 1889, located at 2750 Dufferin Street, and a Georgian-style house located at 108 Stayner Avenue. This red brick house was built in 1852 by Jacob P. Ross, a Fairbank farmer.

Fairbank's growth from a rural hamlet to a big-city neighbourhood began to take shape in 1892 when the short-lived Belt Line Railway opened a station here. Fairbank's development was further enhanced in 1924 when the Toronto streetcar railway began service to this area.

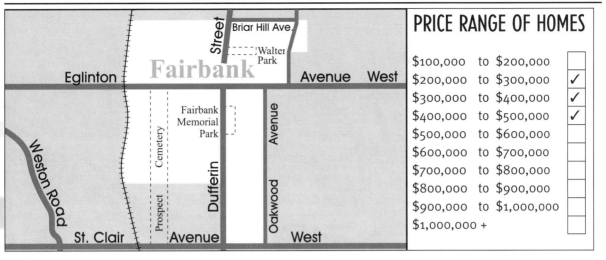

PRICE RANGE OF HOMES

$100,000 to $200,000	
$200,000 to $300,000	✓
$300,000 to $400,000	✓
$400,000 to $500,000	✓
$500,000 to $600,000	
$600,000 to $700,000	
$700,000 to $800,000	
$800,000 to $900,000	
$900,000 to $1,000,000	
$1,000,000 +	

OVERVIEW:

The defining feature of the Fairbank neighbourhood is its topography, which features a series of rolling hills that climb their way northward from Rogers Road to the northern tip of Fairbank at Briar Hill Avenue. Many of these hills are bisected by curvilinear one-way streets that add an old-world charm to the neighbourhood.

The Fairbank neighbourhood offers modest house prices and convenient access to transit and highways. Fairbank's demographics include a large number of people of Italian, Portuguese, and West Indian heritage.

HOMES:

Fairbank contains an interesting mix of early 1900s working-class houses, postwar brick and stucco bungalows, and new home developments. There are also a fair number of apartment buildings located on the periphery of the neighbourhood.

The charming homes perched on the hills in the centre of Fairbank are located in a setting that is reminiscent of an old-world village. Many of these homes feature pretty decks that take advantage of the hilltop vistas of many Fairbank homes.

SHOPPING:

Eglinton Avenue West is a multi-cultural shopping strip that has been dubbed "the avenue to the world." Shoppers in this area can choose from hundreds of stores including bargain shops, fashion boutiques, jewellery stores, and West Indian and Jamaican restaurants.

Dufferin Street offers a mix of local shops as well as chain stores that attract shoppers from all over the city. Included in this mix are a number of new- and used-car dealerships, shopping plazas, and restaurants.

The Castlefield Design and Decor district along Castlefield Road at Caledonia is marked by distinctive street banners and features some of Toronto's top home design and decor retailers.

RECREATION:

The Fairbank Memorial Community Centre at 2213 Dufferin Street offers a myriad of programs for children and adults. This centre also operates a non-profit seniors' club which offers a variety of clinics, workshops and special events for adults 55 years of age and over. To the north of the community centre is the Fairbank Memorial Park. This park has two baseball diamonds, a children's playground, a basketball court and a swimming pool.

Fairbank is also home to the Art Starts Neighbourhood Cultural Centre at 1672 Eglinton Avenue West. Art Starts offers classes in theatre, music, visual arts and crafts. There are also innovative workshops, performances, and rehearsal and studio space for artists.

SCHOOLS:

(P)	Brial Hill Junior, 100 Briar Hill Ave., (416) 394-2226
(P)	Fairbank Memorial Community, 555 Harvie Ave., (416) 394-2333
(P)	Fairbank Middle, 2335 Dufferin St., (416) 394-2323
(P)	F.H. Miller Junior, 300 Caledonia Rd., (416) 394-2336
(PH)	George Harvey C.I., 1700 Keele St., (416) 394-3180
(PH)	York Memorial C.I., 2690 Eglinton Ave., W., (416) 394-3000
(C)	D'Arcy McGee, 20 Bansley Ave., (416) 393-5318
(C)	St. John Bosco, 75 Holmesdale Rd., (416) 393-5305
(C)	St. Nicolas of Bari, 363 Rogers Rd., (416) 393-5355
(C)	St. Thomas Aquinas, 636 Glenholme Ave., (416) 393-5236

TRANSPORTATION:

Fairbank residents are well served by bus routes that criss-cross this neighbourhood. The Rogers Road and Eglinton Avenue buses connect to stations on the Yonge-University-Spadina subway line, while the bus lines serving Oakwood Avenue, Dufferin Street and Caledonia Road connect to stations on the Bloor-Danforth subway line.

Motorists can gain quick access to the city core via Dufferin Street, which extends all the way down to the Toronto Harbourfront. For those commuting outside the city, the Allen Expressway, off Eglinton Avenue, is approximately a five-minute drive from this neighbourhood. This expressway offers quick access to Highway 401.

SW

HISTORY: The Harwood neighbourhood emerged in the 1920s with
the opening of the Harwood Presbyterian Church on Weston Road. This
church and the surrounding neighbourhood are named after a Ms. Harwood,
who donated the land on which Harwood Church was built. The former
Harwood Church, situated at 274 Weston Road, is now in use by another
church of Christian denomination.

Harwood has traditionally been a working-class community. Many of this
neighbourhood's earliest residents were employed at the Hinds Brothers brick-
yard or at the Overland car factory, which were both situated on Weston Road.

Harwood's second phase of residential development took place after the
Second World War. New home development along St. Clair Avenue West has
helped revitalize this old Toronto neighbourhood.

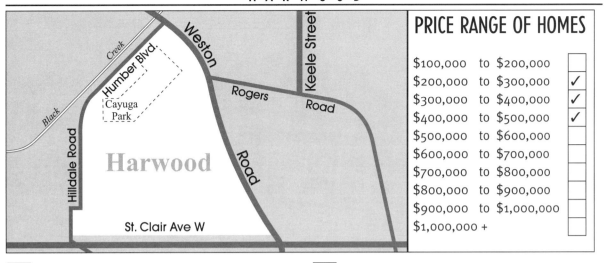

PRICE RANGE OF HOMES

$100,000 to $200,000	
$200,000 to $300,000	✓
$300,000 to $400,000	✓
$400,000 to $500,000	✓
$500,000 to $600,000	
$600,000 to $700,000	
$700,000 to $800,000	
$800,000 to $900,000	
$900,000 to $1,000,000	
$1,000,000 +	

OVERVIEW:

Harwood is a working-class neighbourhood that is located on the top of an escarpment overlooking the Black Creek Valley. Harwood is bordered by the Black Creek to the north, and Lavender Creek to the south and west. These natural barriers limit access to this quiet and unassuming neighbourhood.

HOMES:

The houses in the Harwood neighbourhood were built over a very long period of time, beginning in the early 1900s and progressing until the 1960s. These houses include many different styles of bungalows and semi-detached homes.

Many of the houses on the peripheral streets bordering this neighbourhood are situated on a high plateau of land that offers excellent views of the Black Creek Valley.

SHOPPING:

Harwood residents can walk to the shopping district along Weston Road. This retail corridor features small variety stores, home improvement stores and restaurants. There are also large leather and shoe factory outlets along this route.

The St. Clair Avenue West retail corridor is brimming with convenience -ype stores and restaurants. Big Box retailers, including Canadian Tire and Home Depot, have recently opened in this shopping district.

RECREATION:

Harwood is one of the few Toronto neighbourhoods to have its own designated community town hall. The Harwood Hall, located at 85 Cayuga Avenue, is used extensively by the Harwood Seniors' Group and the York Lions Steel Band. It is also used for community meetings.

Harwood Park is located across the street from the Harwood Public School. This park features a baseball diamond, a children's playground, a walking path and little hills that are used for tobogganing. Cayuga Park, located off Cayuga Avenue, has a modern children's playground and a walking path that leads down into the Black Creek Valley.

SCHOOLS:

(P) Harwood Junior, 50 Leigh St., (416) 394-2350
(P) Rockcliffe Middle, 400 Rockcliffe Blvd.,
     (416) 394-3100
(PH) Frank Oke S.S., 500 Alliance Ave., (416) 394-3158
(CH) Archbishop Romero, 99 Humber Blvd.,
     (416) 393-5555

TRANSPORTATION:

The Rockcliffe Avenue bus and the Weston Road bus connect passengers to the Runnymede and the Keele stations respectively, on the Bloor-Danforth subway line. The St. Clair Avenue West bus connects to the St. Clair West station on the Yonge-University-Spadina subway line.

St. Clair Avenue West is a major arterial roadway that guides passengers into the downtown core. From Black Creek Drive, motorists are approximately 10 minutes to highway 400 and 401.

HISTORY: The Humewood neighbourhood is named after Humewood,
the country estate of William Hume Blake, who was a prominent lawyer and
politician in early Toronto. Blake built Humewood in the 1850s and named it
after his ancestral home in Ireland.

The former 25-acre Humewood estate was carved into various plans of
subdivision in the late 1800s and early 1900s. Humewood Park was part of
the old estate grounds and Humewood Drive was originally a private
laneway to the estate.

The Humewood house was sold by the Blake family in the 1870s. Shortly
thereafter it burned down, but was replaced by a similar house built on the
foundation of the original home.

In 1912 the Humewood house was purchased by the Anglican Diocese as
a refuge for young women in distress. It has undergone many renovations
and additions since this time, however, it remains a local landmark, standing proudly at 40 Humewood Drive.

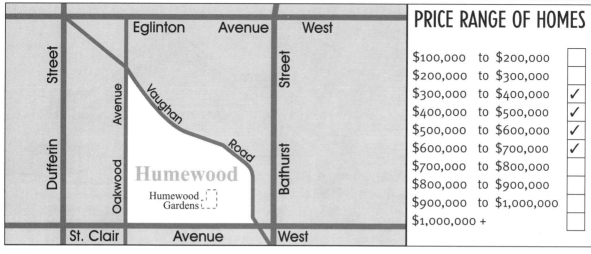

PRICE RANGE OF HOMES	
$100,000 to $200,000	
$200,000 to $300,000	
$300,000 to $400,000	✓
$400,000 to $500,000	✓
$500,000 to $600,000	✓
$600,000 to $700,000	✓
$700,000 to $800,000	
$800,000 to $900,000	
$900,000 to $1,000,000	
$1,000,000 +	

OVERVIEW:

Humewood is an established, family-oriented neighbourhood conveniently located approximately 15 minutes from Toronto's financial and entertainment districts. There are many amenities such as parks and schools located in the interior of this neighbourhood while shopping and public transit are easily accessed from St. Clair Avenue.

Humewood's intimate streetscape is enhanced by the many tree-lined streets and culs-de-sac found throughout the neighbourhood. Many of these streets are one-way, with very few through streets, which helps to minimize the traffic flow in this quiet tucked-away neighbourhood.

HOMES:

Humewood's detached and semi-detached houses come in a variety of shapes and sizes. These houses were built mostly between 1910 and 1925 and feature a wide variety of architectural styles including Tudor-, English-cottage-, and Edwardian-style homes. Front porches and expansive dormer windows are characteristic of many of the houses in this neighbourhood.

Humewood Court, a cul-de-sac which runs off of Humewood Drive just north of St. Clair, is noteworthy for containing some of the finest art deco walk-up apartment buildings in Toronto.

SHOPPING:

Humewood residents enjoy the luxury of being able to walk to a tremendous variety of shops and restaurants along St. Clair Avenue West. Included in this shopping mix are fruit and vegetable markets, discount stores, banks, drug stores, fast food restaurants and a bingo hall.

The shopping district on Eglinton Avenue West and on Vaughan Road between Oakwood Avenue and Dufferin Street features Toronto's largest concentration of Caribbean shops and restaurants.

RECREATION:

A variety of recreational programs for preschoolers, children, youths, adults and seniors are offered at the Humewood Community School at 15 Cherrywood Avenue. Some of these programs include Ballet Bunnies (preschoolers), co-ed fitness (adults), and the Humewood Senior Citizens' Club. This school also has a sports field, baseball diamonds and a children's playground. Vaughan Road Collegiate Institute at 529 Vaughan Road has an indoor pool that is used for children's and adult's aquatics.

Humewood Park, located between Humewood Drive and Pinewood Avenue, is one of Toronto's prettier strolling gardens. It features gently sloping lawns, a forest of maple trees, park benches and a paved walkway that winds its way through this quaint park. Graham Park, on Atlas Avenue just north of St. Clair, is a small park with a children's playground and a basketball court.

The newly built Oakwood Village Library and Arts Centre at 341 Oakwood Avenue includes a new state-of-the-art theatre. Dance classes, film nights, and yoga are just some of the programs offered at the centre.

SCHOOLS:

(P)   Humewood Community School, 15 Cherrywood Avenue, (416) 394-2383
(PH) Vaughan Road C.I., 529 Vaughan Rd., (416) 394-3222
(PH) Oakwood C.I., 991 St. Clair Ave., W., (416) 393-1780
(C)   St. Alphonsus, 60 Atlas Ave., (416) 393-5326
(PC) St. Michaels College, 1515 Bathurst St., (416) 653-3180

TRANSPORTATION:

The St. Clair West streetcar connects passengers to the St. Clair station on the Yonge-University-Spadina subway line while the Vaughan Road bus connects passengers to the St. Clair West station also on the Yonge-University-Spadina-Subway line. The Bathurst Street bus connects passengers to the Bathurst station on the Bloor-Danforth subway line.

Motorists are five to 10 minutes from the Allen Expressway which links commuters to Highway 401.

HISTORY:
Lampton is named after the Lampton Mill, built in 1845 on the east bank of the Humber River. At its peak the Lampton Mill produced 150 barrels of flour a day. This profitable mill was owned by William Pearce Howlan, who was a father of Confederation. Howland named his mill after John J. Lampton, who visited this area when he was Governor General of Canada. *Ed. Note: The high-rise apartment building located at 4075 Old Dundas Street is situated on the former site of the Lampton Mill.*

Across the road from the Lampton Mill on Old Dundas Street stood the Howland general store and post office, and next to that was The Lampton Mills Hotel. The mill, the general store and the post office were destroyed by fire in 1915, however, the Lampton Hotel survived. This historic building, located at 4066 Old Dundas Street, has recently been restored and now serves as a community and heritage centre.

While many of Lampton's first residents were employed at the Lampton Mill, many other residents found employment at the Canadian Pacific Railway yards north of Dundas Street. Lampton was also known for its market gardens, which were situated on the fertile plain of the Humber River Valley. These market gardens were still operating up until the 1950s when the Warren Park area was subdivided for residential development.

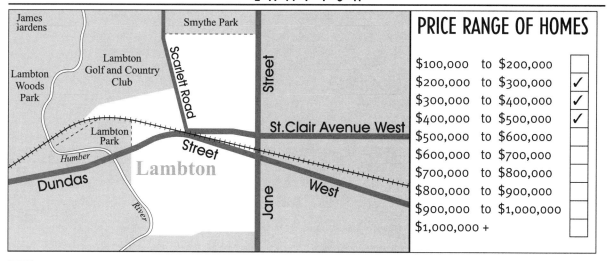

PRICE RANGE OF HOMES

$100,000	to	$200,000	
$200,000	to	$300,000	✓
$300,000	to	$400,000	✓
$400,000	to	$500,000	✓
$500,000	to	$600,000	
$600,000	to	$700,000	
$700,000	to	$800,000	
$800,000	to	$900,000	
$900,000	to	$1,000,000	
$1,000,000 +			

OVERVIEW:

The natural beauty of the Lampton area, with its hills and dales and old oak trees, is shaped by the picturesque Humber River Valley that forms the south and west boundaries of this neighbourhood.

Lampton is divided into three distinct pockets. The oldest part of Lampton is centred around Old Dundas Street and is still referred to by its historic name, Lampton Mills. The area north of Dundas Street is known as Lampton Park, while the community in the valley, south of Dundas Street, is known as Warren Park, or simply "the Valley."

Ed. Note: Historically, the Lampton Mills community extended over to the west bank of the Humber River in the Government Road area. However, this residential pocket is now generally considered to be part of the larger Kingsway Park neighbourhood.

HOMES:

Lampton contains some charming workmens' cottages near Dundas Street that date back to the mid- to late 1800s. These tiny houses were built for the mill workers and their families. The apartment building at 4075 Old Dundas Street was built on the footplate of the old Lampton Grist Mill.

The Valley in the Warren Park school area still contains a small number of workmens' cottages and a few of the old market-gardener homesteads. However, the bulk of the housing stock in the Valley consists of semi-detached brick houses built in the 1950s and 1960s. Many of these homes back onto parkland and command excellent vistas of the Humber River.

The Lampton Park houses north of Dundas Street and south of Foxwell Avenue were built largely in the early 1900s by employees of the railroad. The houses in the Foxwell Avenue area east of the Lampton Golf and Country Club were built after the Second World War and feature some of the prettier brick and stone Tudor bungalows in the city.

SHOPPING:

The shopping in this neighbourhood is spread out along Dundas Street, Scarlett Road and Jane Street. There is a small shopping plaza named Coopers Mills located at 4020 Dundas Street. The Coopers Mills name is historic in that it makes reference to William Cooper, the first settler and mill owner in the Lampton community. (Cooper sold his Lampton holdings to the aforementioned William Howland.)

Jane Park Plaza at Black Creek Drive is the largest shopping plaza in the neighbourhood. It features a large grocer, a pharmacy, a video store, a beer store, a bank, a post office and a medical clinic.

RECREATION:

Lampton Park is located off Howland Avenue north of Dundas Street. This picturesque park features a large stand of black oak trees and is situated on a high topographical plain overlooking the Humber River Valley. In the middle of Lampton Park is the Lampton Arena which is the home of the Warren Park Hockey Association and the York Figure Skating Club.

Lampton Park is part of a network of city parks that follow a 10-kilometre trail along the Humber River. This paved trail passes through James Gardens, an English garden that features spring-fed ponds, rustic bridges and colourful floral displays. This trail links cyclists to the Martin Goodman Trail on the Toronto waterfront.

Smythe Park located off Scarlett Road is designated as a wildlife protection area. The Black Creek winds its way through the centre of this park, whose many marshes and ponds are frequented by mallard ducks and Canada geese. Smythe Park also has plenty of recreation with two outdoor swimming pools, two tennis courts, two baseball diamonds and a modern children's playground.

The Lampton Golf and Country Club off Scarlett Road has been a neighbourhood landmark since it first opened in 1902. This scenic golf course is traversed by both the Black Creek and the Humber River, making it one of the prettier golf courses in Toronto.

SCHOOLS:

(P)   Lampton Park Community, 50 Bernice Cres., (416) 394-3070
(P)   Warren Park Junior, 135 Varsity Rd., (416) (416) 394-3140
(P)   Humbercrest Public, 14 St. Marks Rd., (416) 394-2370
(C)   St, James, 230 Humbercrest, (416) 393-5275
(C)   Archbishop Romero Secondary School, 99 Humber Blvd., (416) 393-5555

TRANSPORTATION:

Lampton residents are well served by public transit. Regular bus service on Jane and Dundas Streets connect passengers to stations on the Bloor-Danforth subway line. The Dundas Street West bus also provides a connecting route to the Kipling subway and Go Train stations. There is also rush-hour bus service from Warren Park in the valley to the Jane subway station. Scarlett Road has limited bus service to the Jane subway station.

Lampton is conveniently situated for those commuting by car. Bloor Street will take motorists downtown in about 20 minutes and the Lester B. Pearson International Airport is approximately a 15-minute drive from Lampton.

SW

HISTORY:
Mount Dennis is named after John Dennis, a Loyalist ship-builder from Philadelphia who settled on a farm here in the early 1800s. The Dennis family operated a saw mill and a woollen factory on their property, which took in all of the present day Mount Dennis neighbourhood.

During the late 1800s, Mount Dennis was known for its brick yards, the Conn Smythe Sand and Gravel Pit, and a handful of market gardens that operated on the fertile plain of what is now Eglinton Flats.

In 1893 Mount Dennis built its first school, which was followed by a post office and some general stores along Weston Road. In 1916 the Kodak Company moved into Mount Dennis and became the areas largest employer.

By the 1920s, Mount Dennis had grown to the point where a plebiscite was held regarding its incorporation as a town. The "No" vote won and Mount Dennis remained part of what was then York Township.

During the 1950s the large open fields and bush in this area gave way to new subdivisions, as Mount Dennis grew from a rural outpost to an urban neighbourhood.

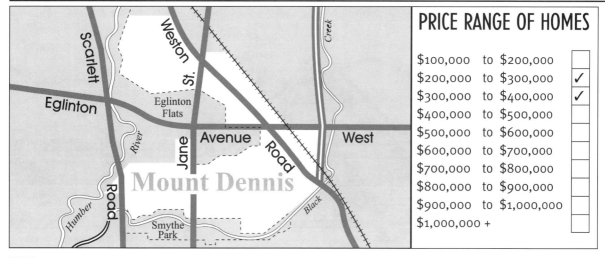

PRICE RANGE OF HOMES

$100,000 to $200,000	
$200,000 to $300,000	✓
$300,000 to $400,000	✓
$400,000 to $500,000	
$500,000 to $600,000	
$600,000 to $700,000	
$700,000 to $800,000	
$800,000 to $900,000	
$900,000 to $1,000,000	
$1,000,000 +	

OVERVIEW:

Mount Dennis is a surprising mix of hills and dales located on one of the highest topographical plains in the City of Toronto. It is surrounded by ravine and parkland and is bordered on the west by the Humber River and on the east by the Black Creek.

This is a culturally diverse neighbourhood; there are over 30 different ethnic groups represented at the local public school.

HOMES:

Mount Dennis houses were built in stages in every decade from the late 1800s all the way up to the 1960s. This is why there are so many different styles of homes present here. Ironically now that this neighbourhood has finally filled-in, some of the original houses are now being replaced by newer custom designed houses.

A large number of Mount Dennis homes look out onto the Humber River Valley or onto one of the many parks situated within the Mount Dennis neighbourhood.

SHOPPING:

The primary Mount Dennis shopping district is located on Weston Road. This stretch of stores has recently been designated as a business improvement area. Plans are underway to develop special events and festivals for this shopping area with an emphasis on celebrating the various multicultural communities within the Mount Dennis neighbourhood.

Mount Dennis residents are also served by a handful of small shopping plazas located along Jane Street that contain a good mix of stores catering to the everyday household needs of the residents of this neighbourhood. Lambton Avenue also has a limited amount of shopping including variety stores, a grocery store and a dry cleaner.

RECREATION:

Mount Dennis is rich in parkland. Jasper Park and Noble Park, located in the interior of the neighbourhood, are medium-sized parks geared towards children. Westlake Memorial Park, located off Jaspar Avenue, is named after the Westlake brothers, Thomas, Albert and George who died in action during the Second World War. This park contains a children's playground, a baseball diamond and some of the steepest tobogganing hills in Toronto.

Eglinton Flats is a scenic greenspace of wide open parkland divided into four areas by Jane Street and Eglinton Avenue. It has paved trails, a large pond, picnic benches, sports fields and 12 tennis courts. The Eglinton Flats Winter Tennis Club puts a bubble on six of the courts during the wintertime, which are then made available to the public either on a pay-as-you-play basis or by membership. Seasonal permits for the sports fields are available to organized leagues and individual groups. Year round washroom/changerooms are available on site.

The Scarlett Woods Golf Course, located in the southwest pocket of Eglinton Flats, is an executive-length par-62 course suitable for both beginners and experts. This course features many challenging par-three holes and is rated as moderately difficult.

The newly renovated Mount Dennis Community Hall on Holly Street offers year round programs to Mount Dennis residents as well as serving as an administrative centre for many recreational programs within this district. The Mount Dennis Public Library at 1123 Weston Road offers programs for children and seniors.

SCHOOLS:

(P)	Bala Avenue Community, 6 Bala Avenue, (416) 394-2210
(P)	Cordella Junior, 175 Cordella Ave., (416) 394-2258
(P)	Dennis Avenue Community, 17 Dennis Avenue (416) 394-2311
(P)	Roseland Junior, 990 Jane St., (416) 394-3110
(PH)	Frank Oke Secondary School, 500 Alliance Ave., (416) 394-3158
(PH)	York Humber, 100 Emmett Ave., (416) 394-3280
(C)	Our Lady of Victory, 92 Lambton Ave., (416) 393-5247
(CH)	Archbishop Romero, 99 Humber Blvd., (416) 393-5555

TRANSPORTATION:

Mount Dennis residents have excellent access to public transit. The Jane Street and Weston Road buses connect to the Bloor-Danforth subway line, while the Trethewey Drive and Eglinton Avenue buses connect to the Eglinton station on the Yonge-University-Spadina subway line.

Motorists are approximately a 10-minute drive from Highway 401, which connects to all the major highways leading into and out of the city. For those travelling downtown by car, take Jane Street south to Bloor across to Windermere Avenue. From there, head south to Lake Shore Boulevard which will usher you into Toronto's financial and entertainment districts.

HISTORY:
The historic Old Mill neighbourhood, located on the banks of the Humber River, was a favourite fishing and hunting spot for people of the First Nations tribes long before the first European pioneers settled here in the 1790s.

In 1793 the Kings Mill – the forerunner to today's Old Mill – was built in order to process lumber for the first homes in Toronto, which was then known as the Town of York. A series of fires forced the Mill to be re-built three times. Today the skeletal ruins of the last grist mill, also destroyed by fire in 1881, provide the backdrop for the Old Mill hotel, spa and restaurant.

The Old Mill restaurant and tea garden was opened in 1914, at the outbreak of the First World War. The Old Mill attracted a clientele from all over the city and doubled as a sales office for Home Smith and Company, which developed this neighbourhood in the 1920s and 1930s.

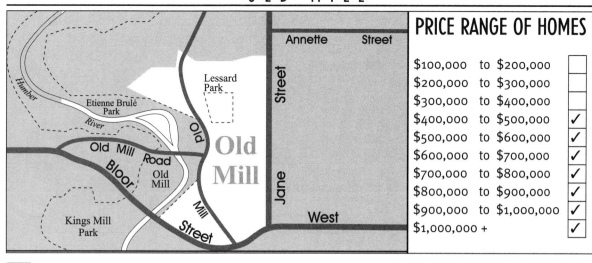

PRICE RANGE OF HOMES	
$100,000 to $200,000	
$200,000 to $300,000	
$300,000 to $400,000	
$400,000 to $500,000	✓
$500,000 to $600,000	✓
$600,000 to $700,000	✓
$700,000 to $800,000	✓
$800,000 to $900,000	✓
$900,000 to $1,000,000	✓
$1,000,000 +	✓

OVERVIEW:

The Old Mill neighbourhood is nestled along the thickly wooded slopes of the Humber River Valley. This is an ideal neighbourhood for families, as it offers miles of parkland with a myriad of recreational opportunities.

This neighbourhood has many unique and special landmarks including the Old Mill Inn and Spa, the Old Mill bridge that spans the Humber River, and of course the Humber River itself, which has recently been designated as a Canadian Heritage River.

HOMES:

The houses in this neighbourhood were built between 1920 and 1940. These distinctly Tudor-style homes range in size from cosy two-bedroom bungalows to four-bedroom two-storey houses. All of the houses are detached and contain many decorative features, like leaded glass windows, rich wood trim and hardwood floors. Many of the houses back onto the ravine or overlook the Old Mill and the Humber River.

The most diverse street in this neighbourhood is Old Mill Road. This street contains a mix of houses, a co-op apartment building, a rental apartment building, and a few luxury condominiums. Many of these homes command a spectacular view of the Humber River Valley.

SHOPPING:

The Bloor West Village shopping district is a five- to 10-minute walk from most of the homes in this neighbourhood. This shopping district is known for its European food shops, gift shops and specialty stores. Residents of this neighbourhood are also within close proximity of the Kingsway Village shopping district located just west of the Bloor Street bridge at Royal York and Bloor.

RECREATION:

Etienne Brûlé Park, situated across the street from the Old Mill Restaurant, features a paved trail that follows the route of the Humber River and is perfect for walking, jogging, cycling and, in the winter, cross-country skiing. Etienne Brûlé Park is also a popular spot for picnics and for fishing in the Humber River. Across the street from the park is the Old Mill Tennis Club which contains four courts that are open to the public at designated times.

Movie goers can catch all of the latest Hollywood films at the Humber Theatre at Bloor and Jane streets.

SCHOOLS:

(P)   Humbercrest, 14 St. Marks Rd., (416) 394-2370
(PH) Runnymede C.I., 569 Jane St., (416) 394-3200
(C)   St. Pius X, 71 Jane St., (416) 393-5237

TRANSPORTATION:

This neighbourhood is well served by public transit. The Old Mill subway station on Riverside Drive at Bloor Street and the Jane subway station at Jane and Bloor streets both connect passengers to the Bloor-Danforth subway line.

Motorists are 20 minutes away from both downtown Toronto and the Pearson International Airport.

SW

HISTORY:

The Runnymede neighbourhood was developed on the former estate of John Scarlett, who settled in this area in 1808. Scarlett quickly rose to prominence as proprietor of a number of mills along the banks of the Humber River.

In 1838 Scarlett built a rough-cast English-cottage-style house named Runnymede, which was situated at the present-day intersection of Dundas and Runnymede roads. While the Runnymede house is no longer standing, Runnymede High School, Runnymede Hospital, Runnymede Road and many of the local churches are named after this landmark.

The Charles Goad Atlas map of 1893 shows all the streets in this neighbourhood laid out and named, however, very few houses were actually built in Runnymede until the early 1900s.

Ed. Note: Wilbert G. Thomas, author of The Legacy of York*, provides us with an interesting bit of Runnymede trivia, noting that the Runnymede district held the distinction of having a Canadian naval warship named after it during the Second World War.*

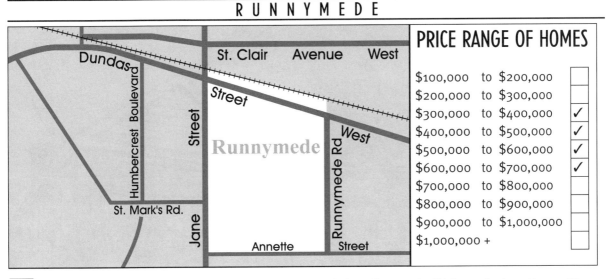

PRICE RANGE OF HOMES

$100,000	to	$200,000	
$200,000	to	$300,000	
$300,000	to	$400,000	✓
$400,000	to	$500,000	✓
$500,000	to	$600,000	✓
$600,000	to	$700,000	✓
$700,000	to	$800,000	
$800,000	to	$900,000	
$900,000	to	$1,000,000	
$1,000,000 +			

OVERVIEW:

Runnymede is a quiet, family-oriented neighbourhood with affordable houses, a good selection of schools, and convenient access to shopping and transportation. Runnymede is nestled between some of Toronto's more affluent neighbourhoods including Baby Point, Bloor West Village and High Park.

The residential tone of this neighbourhood is interrupted only on its northern boundary along the Dundas Street West commercial corridor. To the north of Dundas Street are light industry and the Canadian Pacific Railway tracks.

HOMES:

Runnymede's tree-lined streets are lined with an eclectic mix of houses including grand Victorian mansions on Windermere Avenue at St.Johns Road, English-cottage- and Tudor-style houses on Humbercrest Boulevard, pre- and post-war bungalows, duplex and triplex dwellings, and a vast array of detached and semi-detached homes.

The reason why there is no discernable building pattern to these houses is due to the fact that they were built in stages from approximately 1890 to 1950. Runnymede houses feature many different types of exteriors including wood, insulbrick, frame siding, stucco, brick and stone. Many Runnymede houses feature gambrel roofs that have a distinctive barn-like appearance. This type of roof was popular in the early 1900s. New townhomes have recently been added to the mix of houses in this neighbourhood.

SHOPPING:

Runnymede residents have many shopping options available to them. Jane Street features a good mix of stores including a pharmacy, a local grocer, antique stores, and variety stores. Annette Street has a quaint collection of stores and restaurants grouped together near Jane Street, including a popular florist, gift shop, tennis store, sports store, neighbourhood diners and a European deli.

Dundas Street, east of Jane Street attracts local as well as regional shoppers. This commercial strip includes two shopping plazas, fast food outlets, bars and restaurants, gas stations and car repair shops, fitness and self-defence schools, and beer and liquor stores. A Loblaws superstore, with a vast selection of groceries, take-out prepared foods, dry cleaning and photo finishing, is prominently positioned on Dundas Street, a few blocks west of Jane Street.

RECREATION:

Runnymede residents are within walking distance of Etienne Brûlé and Home Smith parks, situated alongside the Humber River. These scenic parks include walking, jogging, cycling and cross-country trails as well as fishing and family picnic spots.

Runnymede Park, a medium-sized park just north of the railway tracks off of Cobalt Avenue, is a multi-faceted park that features a children's playground, a wading pool, and sports fields. Runnymede Park is also the home of the George Bell Arena, which is used extensively by local ice hockey leagues.

The Jane-Dundas Library at 620 Jane Street offers many resources including books, CDs, videos, and various library programs.

SCHOOLS:

(P)	Humbercrest Public, 14 St. Marks Rd.,	(416) 394-2370
(P)	King George Junior, 25 Rexford Rd.,	(416) 394-3060
(PH)	Runnymede C. I., 569 Jane Street,	(416) 394-3200
(C)	James Culnan, 605 Willard Ave.,	(416) 393-5325
(P)	St. James, 230 Humbercrest Blvd.,	(416) 393-5275

TRANSPORTATION:

Runnymede residents are well served by public transit. Bus routes on Jane, Annette and Dundas streets connect to stations on the Bloor-Danforth subway line. The Jane station at Bloor Street is a 15- to 20-minute walk from most of the houses in this neighbourhood.

Dundas and Bloor Streets are both major east-west arterial roadways that provide motorists with direct access to downtown Toronto in 20 to 25 minutes. For those travelling outside the city, Black Creek Drive is just five minutes north and links motorists to Toronto's commuter highways.

HISTORY:
The Silverthorn neighbourhood is named after Aaron Silverthorn, who settled here with his wife and three sons in 1825. The old Silverthorn homestead was located high on a hill near the present-day Silverthorn and Eglinton avenues.

Aaron's son, Francis, inherited his father's property and turned it into a successful cattle farm. Francis was also a pioneer in dietetics and healthy living. He made honey and salt-free biscuits and sold these products under the banner of the "Silverthorn Honey and Hardtack Company." Francis Silverthorn died in 1894 at the age of 79.

The former Silverthorn farm was opened up for residential development in 1914 under the name Silverthorn Heights. Sales were brisk and the subdivision filled in very quickly. However, it wasn't until the late 1920s that Silverthorn residents would receive the basic city services such as water, sewers and paved roads that they enjoy today.

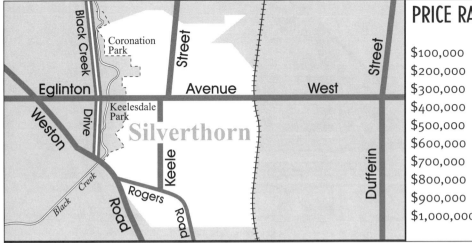

PRICE RANGE OF HOMES

$100,000	to	$200,000	
$200,000	to	$300,000	✓
$300,000	to	$400,000	✓
$400,000	to	$500,000	
$500,000	to	$600,000	
$600,000	to	$700,000	
$700,000	to	$800,000	
$800,000	to	$900,000	
$900,000	to	$1,000,000	
$1,000,000 +			

OVERVIEW:
Silverthorn is a working-class neighbourhood filled with affordable homes within a reasonable commuting distance of downtown Toronto. Silverthorn has an established Italian community, as well as being home to many new Canadians from a myriad of different backgrounds.

Silverthorn's hilly terrain is the distinguishing feature of this neighbourhood. The predominantly one-way streets that twist and wind through Silverthorn's gently rolling hills are a refreshing change from the grid-like street pattern common in so many Toronto neighbourhoods.

HOMES:
The majority of Silverthorn houses were built between 1914 and 1930. These modest brick and frame houses include two-storey detached and semi-detached houses as well as 1.5-storey and bungalow detached houses.

Silverthorn houses have an old-world charm as they sit perched upon gently rolling hills in a village-like setting.

SHOPPING:
The main shopping thoroughfare in Silverthorn is situated along Eglinton Avenue. Here you will find local convenience stores mixed in with professional and medical offices. The Westside Mall, on Eglinton Avenue at Caledonia Road, is anchored by national department and grocery stores.

Rogers Road also has a fairly busy retail strip that includes the Black Creek Super Value Shopping Centre just west of Keele Street.

RECREATION:
A cluster of recreational activities are available in the Black Creek Drive and Eglinton Avenue area. The Centennial building at 2694 Eglinton Avenue East has an indoor swimming pool as well as being the home of a local historical museum.

There are four large public parks located along Black Creek Drive near Eglinton Avenue. Starting at the north end, Trethewey Park is a nature revitalization area on the banks of the Black Creek. This is an ideal spot for picnickers and nature enthusiasts. Coronation Park is a mix of sports and leisure. This park has a T-ball and softball leagues, as well as two tennis courts, a children's playground and a woodland trail. North and South Keelesdale Park feature large sports fields and baseball diamonds. The Chris Tonks Ice Arena is also situated in South Keelesdale Park.

The Silverthorn Public Library, at 1748 St. Clair Avenue West, is famous for appearing on the opening sequence of the syndicated *Book Mice* television show. Children from all over Canada and as far away as the United States have stopped in to visit the home of the book mice. The staff at this library even conduct a Book Mice tour, much to the delight of the children who visit here.

SCHOOLS:
(P)   Silverthorn Junior School, 55 Ypres Rd., (416) 394-3124
(P)   Kane Middle, 300 Kane Avenue, (416) 394-3033
(C)   St. Matthew, 18 Lavender Rd., (416) 393-5240
(PH) George Harvey C.I., 1700 Keele St., (416) 394-3180
(PH) York Memorial C. I., 2690 Eglinton Ave. W., (416) 394-3000

TRANSPORTATION:
The Keele Street and Rogers Road buses connect to the Keele and Ossington stations on the Bloor-Danforth subway line. The Eglinton Avenue bus connects to the Eglinton station on the Yonge-University-Spadina subway line.

Motorists can get to downtown Toronto's financial and entertainment districts in approximately 20 minutes using Keele Street, which is the main north-south street running through Silverthorn. For motorists travelling out of the city, the Allen Expressway, off Eglinton Avenue, is approximately 15 minutes from Silverthorn.

HISTORY:
This neighbourhood is named after George Syme, a Scotsman who immigrated to Canada with his family in 1862. Syme settled in this district in the 1870s, when he purchased 25 acres of fine gardening land in the Black Creek Valley.

Syme cultivated plants, fruits and vegetables on his farm. He quickly became wealthy, providing produce for the Toronto food markets. In 1898 Syme left farming to embark on what would be a very successful political career. Syme was elected to the York Township Community Council. He then went on to become one of the longest-serving school trustees in Ontario.

In the early 1900s Syme decided to sell his Black Creek Valley property. In an act of great generosity Syme donated part of his land to York Township. When the local school was built in 1909, on land donated by George Syme, it was fittingly named George Syme School in memory of its benefactor.

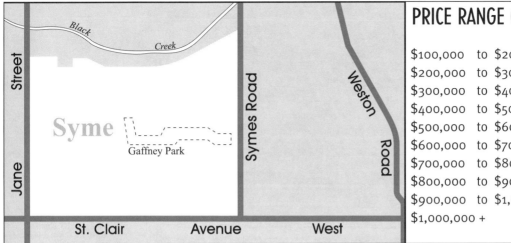

PRICE RANGE OF HOMES	
$100,000 to $200,000	
$200,000 to $300,000	✓
$300,000 to $400,000	✓
$400,000 to $500,000	
$500,000 to $600,000	
$600,000 to $700,000	
$700,000 to $800,000	
$800,000 to $900,000	
$900,000 to $1,000,000	
$1,000,000 +	

OVERVIEW:

The Syme neighbourhood is surrounded by the natural beauty and rolling topography of the Black Creek Valley. It has an abundance of parkland and also features its own community centre.

Rockcliffe Middle School provides a microcosm of the ethnic make-up of this neighbourhood. In the main foyer of this school are a sea of flags that represent the more than 40 cultural backgrounds of the student population here.

HOMES:

This neighbourhood contains a small number of former market-garden cottages that date back to the late 1800s. These houses pre-date the subdivision of this neighbourhood and, as such, are set back further from the road than the rest of the houses. Most of George Syme's houses were built in the early 1900s. House styles range from Victorian semi-detached houses, to detached houses with gambrel roofs that resemble the look of a country barn. There are also many variations of bungalows as well as some larger recently built homes.

SHOPPING:

There are scattered amounts of small shops, variety stores, and restaurants located along St. Clair Avenue West. Further north along Jane Street, there are a handful of neighbourhood shopping plazas.

RECREATION:

Black Creek Park is a large open green space located off Rockcliffe Boulevard. The Black Creek flows through the centre of this park guided by a concrete channel that has been designed for flood control measures. The Toronto Region Conservation Authority began tree planting in this park in 1991 as part of their Black Creek Rehabilitation Project. The Toronto parks and recreation department has recently put a paved walkway in Black Creek Park making it more pedestrian friendly.

Caffney Park is a narrow greenbelt that begins at Castleton Avenue and ends at Blakely Avenue. This park includes a paved trail, a children's playground and panoramic views of the Black Creek Valley.

The George Syme Community School located at 69 Pritchard Avenue offers a variety of recreational programs to residents of this community.

The Dave Appleton Community Centre situated at 33 Pritchard Avenue serves as the home of the George S. Syme Seniors' Centre of York. This centre hosts a variety of clinics, workshops and special events. Bingo and dancing are popular activities at this centre which includes its own Syme Café.

SCHOOLS:

(P)   George Syme Community, 69 Pritchard Ave., (416) 394-2340
(P)   Rockcliffe Middle School, 400 Rockcliffe Blvd., (416) 394-3100
(PH) Frank Oke S.S., 500 Alliance Ave., (416) 394-3158
(CH) Archbishop Romero, 99 Humber Blvd., (416) 393-5555

TRANSPORTATION:

The Rockcliffe Boulevard and the Jane Street buses connect passengers to the Runnymede and Jane stations on the Bloor-Danforth subway line. The St. Clair bus travels to the St. Clair West station on the Yonge-University-Spadina subway line.

Motorist can access Highway 401 in approximately 10 minutes via Black Creek Drive. St. Clair Avenue West is a major arterial roadway that provides a direct route into the core of the city.

R CATAPAN

HISTORY:
Weston's history dates back to the 1790s, when it was a tiny hamlet known simply as "The Humber." Weston's first settlers were mill owners who were attracted to this area by its rich timber resources and the water-power potential of the Humber River.

The Weston name is attributed to the Wadsworth brothers, who came to this area in 1828 and purchased a local flour mill and general store. They renamed this community Weston after their ancestral home in Weston-super-Mare, Somerset, England.

Weston's early development took place on both sides of the Humber River. However, in 1850 a disastrous flood destroyed the west-bank settlement. Weston's fortunes would take a turn for the better when first the Grand Trunk Railway (1856) and then the Toronto Grey and Bruce Railway (1869) began service to this area. The railway and associated industry brought great prosperity to Weston.

Weston was first incorporated as a village in 1881 and then as a town in 1915. Weston remained an independent town until 1967 when it amalgamated with the former Borough of York, which in 1998 amalgamated with the City of Toronto.

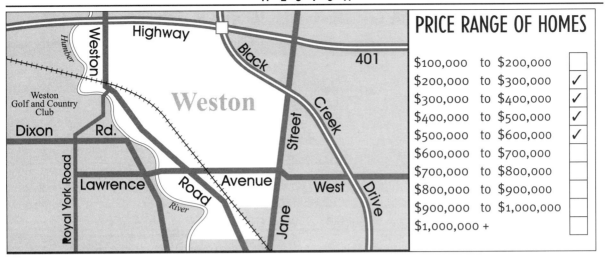

PRICE RANGE OF HOMES	
$100,000 to $200,000	
$200,000 to $300,000	✓
$300,000 to $400,000	✓
$400,000 to $500,000	✓
$500,000 to $600,000	✓
$600,000 to $700,000	
$700,000 to $800,000	
$800,000 to $900,000	
$900,000 to $1,000,000	
$1,000,000 +	

OVERVIEW:

Weston still looks and feels more like a small Ontario town than a big-city neighbourhood. This is not surprising considering the two dominant features in Weston's history, the Humber River and the Railway, are still important landmarks in this community.

Weston's abundant civic pride is evident along Weston Road, which serves as the main street in the neighbourhood. Large green and gold road signs on Weston Road welcome visitors to this community. Weston Road also serves as the parade route for the annual Weston Santa Clause Parade, held every December.

HOMES:

Weston has a large collection of Victorian-style houses dating back to its days as a village in the mid to late 1800s. These Victorian gems as well as some early 1900 Edwardian-style houses are located south of Church Street and the Humber Memorial Church Hospital.

The north pockets of Weston, around Pelmo Park and Fairglen Crescent, were not part of Old Weston. These subdivisions were built up between the late 1940s and the early 1960s and consist mostly of Tudor- and ranch-style bungalows mixed in with back and side-split houses.

The apartment towers that line Weston Road were built in the late 1950s and early 1960s. Most of these rental apartment buildings are on the west side of Weston Road and command excellent views of the Humber River Valley.

Weston's renewed popularity has also led to the recent addition of many new housing developments within this neighbourhood.

SHOPPING:

Weston Road serves as the main street in this neighbourhood, especially where shopping is concerned. This business improvement area features cast iron street lamps and special blue and white street signs that proudly let passers-by know they are in the Town of Weston. This street is brimming with everything from car dealerships to fast food restaurants and small retail shops.

The Crossroads Centre on Weston Road just south of Highway 401 is a big-box retail centre that features a good mix of high-profile national chain stores.

RECREATION:

Like most Ontario towns Weston has its own motto visible on all of its street signs. This motto, "Home of the Bicycle," refers to the Canada Cycle and Motor Company, which was based in Weston until 1970 and was reputed to have been at one time the largest bicycle manufacturer in the world. Weston no longer manufactures bicycles, but it does have an excellent bike path that follows the Humber River all the way south to the Martin Goodman Trail on the Toronto waterfront.

Lions Park, off Hickory Tree Road overlooking the Humber River, is the largest park in Weston. This park has four tennis courts, two baseball diamonds, two swimming pools, a snack bar, and a children's playground. Lions Park is also the home of the Weston Lions Recreation Arena that offers ice rentals and banquet hall facilities. National Hockey League All Star Paul Coffey played in the Weston Minor Hockey League that operates out of this arena.

The Weston Golf and Country Club, located off St. Phillips Road, hosted the 1955 Canadian Open where the illustrious Arnold Palmer won his first professional tournament.

SCHOOLS:

(P)   C.R. Marchant Middle, 1 Ralph St., (416) 394-2268
(P)   H.J. Alexander Community, 30 King St., (416) 394-2359
(P)   Weston Memorial Jr., 200 John St., (416) 394-3150
(PH) Weston C.I., 100 Pine St., (416) 394-3250
(C)   St. John the Evangelist, 23 George St., (416) 393-5244

TRANSPORTATION:

The buses on Weston Road and Jane Street connect directly to stations on the Bloor-Danforth subway line. Bus service on Lawrence Avenue connects passengers to the Lawrence subway station on the Yonge-University-Spadina subway line. Weston also has its own Go Train station located on Lawrence Avenue West at Weston Road.

Weston Road and Jane Street provide motorists with direct access to highways 400 and 401.

INDEX OF NEIGHBOURHOODS

BIBLIOGRAPHY

Ali, Yvette and Suttle, Aine. Riverdale 2000: *Vision for a Healthier Community*. Toronto, 1994.

Anthony, Karen. *For the love of nature, a case for survival*, The Cedarvale Ravine. Toronto, 1978.

Arthur, Eric, revised by Otto, Stephen A. *Toronto No Mean City* Toronto: University of Toronto Press, 1986.

Baker, Donna. *The Rosedale Walk 1827-1973*. Toronto: Central YMCA, 1974

Baker, Donna. *Moore Park: an introductory history*. Toronto: Moore Park Residents Association, 1984.

Benn, Carl. *The King's Mill On The Humber 1793-1803*. Etobicoke: Etobicoke Historical Society, 1979.

Bernard, J. *Riverview Walk*. Toronto: North Toronto Walking Tours, 1992.

Bathurst Davenport Community Association. *A Brief History of Our Neighbourhood*. Toronto: Bathurst Davenport Community Association, 1995.

Bonis R. Robert. *A History Of The Village Of Agincourt*. Scarborough, 1965.

Bonis R. Robert. *A History of Scarborough*. Scarborough: Scarborough Public Library, 1968.

Bull, William Perkins. *Spadunk*. Toronto, 1935.

Beasley, David. *North Toronto A Study of Suburban Development*. Toronto: University of Toronto, 1965.

Bluemenson, John. *Ontario Architecture: A Guide to Styles and Building Terms 1784 to the Present*. Markham, Ontario: Fitzhenry and Whiteside, 1990.

Boylen, J.C., *York Township: An Historical Summary*. Toronto: The Municipal Corporation of the Township of York and The Board of education of the Township of York, 1954.

Cabbagetown Preservation Association. *Touring Old Cabbagetown*. Toronto, 1992.

Campbell, Mary and Myrvold, Barbara. *The Beach In Pictures 1793 - 1932. Toronto*: Toronto Public Library Board, 1988.

Campbell, Mary and Myrvold, Barbara. *Historical Walking Tour of Kew Beach*. Toronto: Toronto Public Library Board, 1995.

Charlesworth, Heather. *A CYCLOPAEDIA OF CANADIAN BIOGRAPHY, NATIONAL BIOGRAPHICAL SERIES THREE*. Toronto: The Hunter-Rose Company Ltd, 1919.

Carleton's Century 1889-1989. Toronto: Carleton Village Public School, 1989.

City of North York. *Directory to The Inventory of Heritage Properties*. North York: City of North York Parks and Recreation Department, Culture Branch, 1996.

City of Toronto Archives. *TORONTO ISLAND The City Years*. Toronto: City of Toronto Archives, 1980.

City of Toronto Planning and Development Department. Toronto *Walking Tours: Bloor-Yorkville, St. Lawrence, Chinatown and the Grange, Central Waterfront*. Toronto: City of Toronto Planning and Development Department, 1997.

City of Toronto Planning and Development Department. *Cityplan '91 Proposals Report*. Toronto: City of Toronto Planning and Development Department, June, 1991.

City of Toronto Planning and Development Department. *CONSULTANT'S STUDY The Open Spaces of Toronto: A Classification Final Report*. Toronto: City of Toronto Planning and Development Department. July, 1991.

City of Toronto Planning and Development Department. *King-Parliament Official Plan Part Two*. Toronto: City of Toronto Planning and Development Department. January, 1996.

City of Toronto Planning and Development Department. *THE McGILL/GRANBY STUDY ISSUES AND PROPOSALS*. Toronto: City of Toronto Planning and Development Department. May, 1980.

City of Toronto Planning and Development Department. *Preserving Neighbourhood Streetscapes*. Toronto: City of Toronto Planning and Development Department. May, 1996.

City of Toronto Planning and Development Department. *SOUTH PARKDALE Part Two Official Plan*. Toronto: City of Toronto Planning and Development Department. November, 1990.

City of Toronto Planning & Development Department. *ST. JAMES TOWN Revitalization Social Analysis*. Toronto: City of Toronto Planning and Development Department. May, 1988.

City of Toronto Planning and Development Department. *Toronto Neighbourhoods the Next Ten Years*. Toronto: City of Toronto Planning and Development Department. June, 1985.

City of Toronto Planning and Development Department. *Trefann Court Final Recommendations*. Toronto: City of Toronto Planning and Development Department. April, 1982.

City of Toronto Planning and Development Department. *Wallace Emerson. Part Two Official plan proposals*. Toronto: City of Toronto Planning and Development Department. 1977.

City of Toronto Planning and Development. *Garrison Common North Part two Official Plan Proposals*. Toronto: City of Toronto Planning and Development Department. March, 1994.

City of Toronto Planning Board. *Part Two Official Plan Proposals Dovercourt Park*. Toronto: City of Toronto Planning and Development Department. May, 1977.

City of Toronto Planning Board. *NEIGHBOURHOOD PLAN PROPOSALS Junction Triangle*. Toronto: City of Toronto Planning and Development Department. 1979.

City of Toronto Planning Board. *Final Recommendations Niagara*. Toronto: City of Toronto Planning Board. October, 1978.

Community History Project. *CITY PLAN 91' Brief with Recommendations*. Toronto: Spadina Road Library. 1991.

Community History Project. 1995. *The Davenport Trail*. Toronto: Spadina Road Library. 1995.

Cruikshank, Frederick. *History of Weston*. Weston Ontario: Weston Historical Society, 1983

Cundiff Brad. *The Hike Ontario Guide To Walks Around Toronto*, Toronto: A Boston Mills Press Book. 1994.

Currell, Harvey. *The Mimico Story*. Mimico, Ontario: Town of Mimico and Library Board, 1967.

Degan M. *Leslie Ville of Yesteryear*. Toronto: Leslie Street Public School, 1957.

Dendy, William & Kilbourn, William. *Toronto Observed Its Architecture Patrons and History*. Toronto: Oxford University Press, 1986.

Dendy, William *Lost Toronto*. Toronto: Oxford University Press, 1978.

Eadie R.H. *A Short History of the Community of Old Malvern Village*. Scarborough: Malvern Committee, 1973.

Eadie R.H. *History of the Community of Woburn*. Wexford, Scarborough, 1973

East York Planning Department. *Borough of East York Official Plan*. East York, 1994.

East York Public Library. *Fascinating Facts about East York*. East York: East York Public Library, 1996.

Ellis, John Jr. *WINDERMERE*. Toronto: Swansea Historical Society, 1992.

Etobicoke Historical Board/Local Architectural Conservation Advisory Committee. *Villages of Etobicoke*. Weston, Ontario: 1983.

Fancher, Diana. *Carleton & Davenport REVISITED*. Toronto: West Toronto Junction Historical Society Toronto, 1992.

Firth, Edith G. *The Town of York. 1793-1815* Toronto: University of Toronto Press, 1962.

Freeman, E. B. *Toronto's Geological Past – an introduction*. Toronto: Ontario Division of Mines, 1975.

Fulford, Robert. *Accidental City*. Toronto: Macfarlane Walter & Ross, 1995.

Gage, S. R., and Whiteson, Leon. *The Liveable City The Architecture and Neighbourhoods of Toronto*. Oakville: Mosaic Press, 1982.

Garner, Hugh. *Cabbagetown*. Toronto: McGraw-Hill Ryerson, 1968.

Givin A. Robert. *The Story of Etobicoke*. Toronto: Etobicoke Historical Society, 1977.

Goad, Charles, E. 1880,1884,1890,1893,1899,1903,1910,1923. *Goad Insurance Plan Atlas*. Toronto: Charles E. Goad, 1923.

Guildwood Village Community Association. *Guildwood Village Welcome Home*. Report on the select committee on the Guild Inn development plan. Scarborough, 1991.

Guthrie, Ann. Don Valley Legacy, *A Pioneer History*. Erin Ontario. The Boston Mills Press, 1986

Hall, Harry and Blanche. *Memories of a place called Humber Bay*. Humber Bay, 1993.

Hanson. K. J. March. *The Village of Brockton: A Century of History*. Toronto: Brockton High School, 1981.

Harney, F. Robert. *Gathering Place*: Peoples and Neighbourhoods of Toronto, 1834-1945. Toronto: Multicultural History Society of Ontario, 1985.

Harris, Marjorie. Toronto: *The City of Neighbourhoods*. Toronto: Key Porter Books, 1984.

Hart W. Patricia. *Pioneering in North York*. A History of the Borough. Toronto: General Publishing, 1968.

Heyes, Esther. *Etobicoke From Furrow to Borough*. Etobicoke, Ontario: Borough of Etobicoke Civic Centre, 1974.

Historical Atlas of the County of York. Toronto, 1878.

History of Toronto and County of York, Ontario 2 vols. Toronto: Blackett Robinson, 1885.

History of the McMurrich Public School District. Toronto: McMurrich Jr. School and Winona Senior School, 1968.

Munroe, Elva. *History of the community of Ellesmere*. Scarborough Township, 1958.

Myrvold, Barbara. *The People of Scarborough, A History*. Toronto: The Scarborough Public Library Board, 1997.

Holyrod, Violet. *Alderwood*: Where the Alders Grew. 1993.

Hopkins, Jeanne. *North York Communities*. North York: Heritage Section. Property and Economic Development Department, 1994.

Humphreys A. Barbara, and Sykes, Meredith. *The Buildings of Canada*. Toronto: The Readers Digest Association (Canada) Ltd., 1980.

Hutcheson, Stephanie. *Yorkville in Pictures 1853 to 1883*, Toronto: Toronto Public Library Board, 1978.

Information and Communication Services Division, Department of the City Clerk. *TOURIFIC T.O. SESQUICENTENNIAL CELEBRITY WALKING TOURS: ROSEDALE, FOREST HILL, KENSINGTON & LITTLE ITALY, LESLIE STREET SPIT, THE GRANGE & CHINATOWN, TORONTO ISLANDS BIKE TOUR, WEST TORONTO JUNCTION, CABBAGETOWN, THE DANFORTH, THE ANNEX & SEATON VILLAGE, DOWN WENDIGO WAY A WALKING TOUR OF SWANSEA, MOORE PARK RAVINE, THE PORT DISTRICT BICYCLE TOUR, SUNNYSIDE, YORKVILLE, NORTH TORONTO BIKE TOUR*. Toronto: City of Toronto Planning and Development Department

Ingolfsrud, Elizabeth and Keefer, Alec. *Kingsway Park Triumph in Design*: An Architectural Study of a Planned Community in Etobicoke, 1924 - 1947. Etobicoke: Toronto Region Architectural Conservancy, 1994.

Ivy, Bill. *A Little Wildernesss*. The Natural History of Toronto. Toronto: Oxford University Press, 1983.

Jackes, Lyman B. *Tales of North Toronto*. Toronto: North Toronto Business Men's Association, 1948.

Kasher, Robert J. *Passport's Guide to Ethnic Toronto*. Illinois: NTC Publishing Group, 1997.

Kelly, Colleen. *CABBAGETOWN IN PICTURES*. Toronto: Toronto Public Library Board, 1984.

Kinsella, Joan C. *A Walking Tour Of The Old Deer Park Farm Area*. Toronto: Toronto Public Library, 1984.

Kinsella, Joan C. *Historical Walking Tour of Deer Park*. Toronto: Toronto Public Library Board, 1996.

Kluckner, Michael. Toronto: *The Way It Was*. Toronto: Whitecap Books (Toronto) Ltd., 1988.

Lamont, Graham. *Toronto and York County, A Sample Study*. Don Mills, Ontario: J. M. Dent & Sons (Canada) Ltd., 1970.

Laycock, Margaret, and Myrvold Barbara. *PARKDALE IN PICTURES: ITS DEVELOPMENT TO 1889*. Toronto: Toronto Public Library Board, 1991.

Lennon, M.J. *Memories of Toronto Island*. Cheltenham: The Boston Mills Press, 1980.

Lewis, V. *Earlscourt*. Toronto: University of Toronto Press, 1920.

Lilliman, Kevin and Parsons, Jennifer. *Toronto 1837: A Model City*. Toronto: Toronto's First Post Office, 1995.

Lister, Jim. *East York an Illustrated History*. East York, 1983.

Loverseed, V. Helga. *North York: Realizing the Dream*. Burlington, Ontario: Windsor Publications, 1988.

Mackay, Claire and Wales, Johnny. *The Toronto Story*. Toronto: Annick Press Ltd, 1990.

Martyn, Lucy Booth. *Toronto, 100 Years of Grandeur*. Toronto: Pagurian Press, 1978.

Martyn, Lucy Booth. Aristocratic *Toronto: 19th Century Grandeur*. Toronto: Gage Publishers, 1980.

Mays, John Bentley. *Emerald City*. Toronto: Penguin Books Canada Ltd., 1994.

McClaskey, Marilyn. *Don Mills From Farmland To A Community*. Toronto: 1997.

McLeod, Norman. *WALKING TOUR OF SWANSEA*. Toronto: The Swansea Historical Society, 1996.

McHugh, Patricia. *Toronto Architecture: a city guide*. Toronto: McClelland & Stewart Inc., 1989.

Middleton, Jesse Edgar. *The Municipality of Toronto: A History 3 vols*. Toronto: Dominion Publishing Company, 1923.

Moon, Lynda, and Myrvold, Barbara, and Ridler, Elizabeth. *Historical Walking Tour of Lawrence Park*. Toronto: Toronto Public Library Board, 1995.

Myrvold, Barbara. *Historical Walking Tour of the Danforth*. Toronto: Toronto Public Library Board, 1992.

Myrvold, Barbara. *Historical Walking Tour of Kensington Market & College Street*. Toronto: Toronto Public Library Board, 1993.

North Toronto Historical Society. *Village of Bedford Park Walk*. Toronto: North Toronto Historical Society, 1996.

North Toronto Historical Society. *Eglinton-Pears Park Walk*. Toronto: North Toronto Historical Society.

North Toronto Historical Society. *Davisville Village Walk*. Toronto: North Toronto Historical Society.

North Toronto Historical Society. *Glen Grove Park Walk*. Toronto: North Toronto Historical Society.

North Toronto Historical Society. *Blythwood-Sherwood Park Walk*. Toronto: North Toronto Historical Society.

North York Parks and Recreation Department, Culture Branch. Blazing a Road to Grandeur, North York's Yonge Street communities. North York, 1996.

Parkdale – A Centennial History. Toronto: Toronto Public Library, 1978.

Patterson, Cynthia, Mcdougall, Carol, and Levin, George. *Bloor-Dufferin in Pictures*. Toronto: Toronto Public Library Board, 1986.

Patterson Ross, *The Development of Kingsway Park*, Etobicoke. Toronto: Urban History Review, 1985.

Rempel, j.i. *The Town Of Leaside, a brief history*. Toronto: East York Historical Society, 1982

Rice, A. B., edited by Joan Miles. *West Toronto Junction Revisited*. Toronto: West Toronto Junction Historical Society, 1992.

Ritchie, Don. *North Toronto*. Erin, Ontario: Boston Mills Press, 1992.

Robertson, John Ross. 1894-1914 *Landmarks of Toronto 6 vols* Toronto: J. Ross Robertson, 1914.

Royal Commision on the Future of the Toronto Waterfront. Toronto: Minister of Supply and Services Canada, 1992.

Rust - D' Eye. George H. *CABBAGETOWN REMEMBERED*. Toronto: Stoddart Publishing Co., 1993.

Scadding, Henry (Edited By Frederick H. Armstrong). *Toronto Of Old*. Toronto: Toronto & Oxford Dundurn Press, 1987.

Sewell John. *The Shape of the City*. Toronto: University of Toronto Press Incorporated, 1993.

Schofield, Richard and Meredyth, and Whynot, Karen. *Scarborough Then and Now*. Scarborough: Scarborough Board of Education and Scarborough Historical Society, 1996.

Schofield, Richard. *Home Sweet Home*. Scarborough: Scarborough Local Architectural Conservation and Advisory Committee, 1996.

Scott, Ian. *Discover Your Neighbourhood Heritage*. Toronto: Learnxs Press, 1976.

Shiels, Judy and Appleby, Mary. *Sidelights of History. A Guide to Etobicoke's Century Buildings*. Etobicoke: Etobicoke Historical Board, 1975.

Slaight, Annabel. *Exploring Toronto*. Toronto: Greey de Pencier, 1977.

Smith, Ken. *No Mean Business*. Don Mills: Toronto Real Estate Board, 1989.

Spilsbury, R. John. *Fact and Folk Lore. Highland Creek, Hillside, Port Union, West Hill. Cobourg*, Ontario: Haynes Print Company, 1974

Tancock, A. Elizabeth. *This Beautiful Valley, The Story of York Mills*. Toronto: The York Pioneer, 1983.

Thomas G. Wilbert. *The Legacy of York*. Toronto: Historical Committee of the City of York, 1992.

Toronto Chapter of Architects. *Exploring Toronto*. Toronto: Architectural Canada, 1977.

Toronto Sussex-Ulster Residents Association. Sussex-Ulster's *First Century Walking Tour of the Area*. Toronto: Toronto Sussex-Ulster Residents Association, 1979.

The Toronto 200 Committee. *Community History: Italian Community, Portuguese Community*. Toronto: City of Toronto, 1993.

Third Annual Report of the City Planning Board. Toronto: City of Toronto Planning Board, 1941.

Toronto Historical Board. *Inventory of Heritage Properties*. Toronto: The Toronto Historical Board, 1991.

Toronto Public Library Board. *NORTH TORONTO IN PICTURES 1889-1912*. Toronto: Toronto Public Library, 1974.

Yundt, S.E, and Augaitis, D.B. *FROM PITS TO PLAYGROUNDS* Toronto: Ministry Of Natural Resources Ontario, 1992.

BIOGRAPHY

AUTHOR

David Dunkelman was born and raised in Toronto. He attended the University of Western Ontario where he studied journalism and earned a Bachelor of Arts degree. Upon graduation, David returned home to Toronto where he spent the early years of his professional career managing and publishing several of Toronto's community newspapers. It was in the community newspaper field that David's keen interest in Toronto neighbourhoods was first developed.

In 1990, David embarked on a real estate career which has allowed him to study and explore Toronto's neighbourhoods from an entirely different perspective. David is currently a Broker at Royal LePage Johnston & Daniel Division.

ILLUSTRATORS

Roark Andrade is a graduate of the Ontario College of Art and Design who works in both natural and digital media. Roark works as a video producer for Autodesk Canada as well as a studio instructor at the Art Gallery of Ontario. Roark also runs www.FineArtHomes.com, through which he and a network of artists provide fine art commissions.

Katherine S. Brown's first job was illustrating for Walt Disney Productions while attending The Art College of Design in Los Angeles. Since continuing her illustrative career with Holt, Rinehart & Winston Publishing Co. in Toronto, she branched off into advertising for 25 years as an art director and illustrator for O & M, V & B, Bates and Baker/Lovick with 32 National and International awards. Katie now free-lances out of her Kingsway stone cottage with her marketing executive husband Brad, and their dog-with-attitude, Sootie.

Lisa Butler is a graduate of Ryerson University. Lisa is a freelance designer who provides a myriad of design services to both small and large companies. Lisa resides in Toronto's west end.

Riccardo Cattapan is a graduate of the University of Toronto, where he earned the degree of Bachelor of Fine Arts and the degree of Bachelor of Architecture. Riccardo began his professional career at Zeidler Roberts Partnership Architects. During his six years at Zeidler Roberts, Riccardo worked as a senior designer on many national and international projects. Riccardo has recently been hired by Cornoyer Hedrick, one of the leading architectural firms in the United States.

William Atenn Chong grew up in the City of Toronto. He first gained an appreciation for houses while working in the home renovation business. William's interest in houses led to his studying architecture at Ryerson Polytechnic University, and interior decorating at George Brown College. William now runs his own company, Custom Home Portraits in Watercolours by William Atenn Chong. He has been commissioned to do home portraits for clients from across Canada. William currently resides in Scarborough with his wife and two children.

Stephen Wilson A.O.C.A. is a graduate of the Ontario College of Art and Design where he completed a program in environmental design. Stephen has worked as an illustrator for various Toronto based companies. He has also overseen residential and commercial design and renovation projects here in the city. Stephen currently lives in The Beach neighbourhood.

There's more to a house than meets the eye.

Is the home structurally sound? Are there any hidden repair costs?
Is the electrical system adequate and safe?
Is the heating/cooling system in good working order?

Before you buy, talk to the professionals at
National Home Inspection Ltd.

NATIONAL HOME INSPECTION

416-467-7809 or **416-INSPECT**
Proudly serving our clients since 1983!

Denise Wilson, RBC Branch Manager
MaRS Centre, 101 College Street, Toronto
denise.wilson@rbc.com
Tel 416 542 1237
www.rbc.com

Being prepared to buy a home will set you up for success!

It is important to have your financing pre-arranged so that you will be in the best negotiating position possible.

I work closely with you and your real estate agent so that your home buying experience is simple while recognizing the importance of competitive rates and delivering a tailor-made solution based on your needs.

The key to choosing a mortgage is to know your options.

The more you know, the more likely you'll save money now and in the future. That's why we are dedicated to helping you find the right mortgage based on your budget, circumstances, needs and goals.

Our clients prosper and benefit from their relationship with RBC, and we are the gateway to resources of RBC Financial Group, Canada's leading financial institution. In my position as branch manager, I am privileged to be working with a diverse, international client base including some of the world's most dynamic individuals and their families.

I look forward to introducing you to RBC's expertise and capability, and helping you with your home financing and other financial needs.

NOTES

NOTES

NOTES

NOTES

NOTES